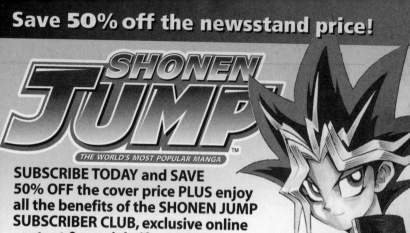
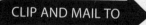

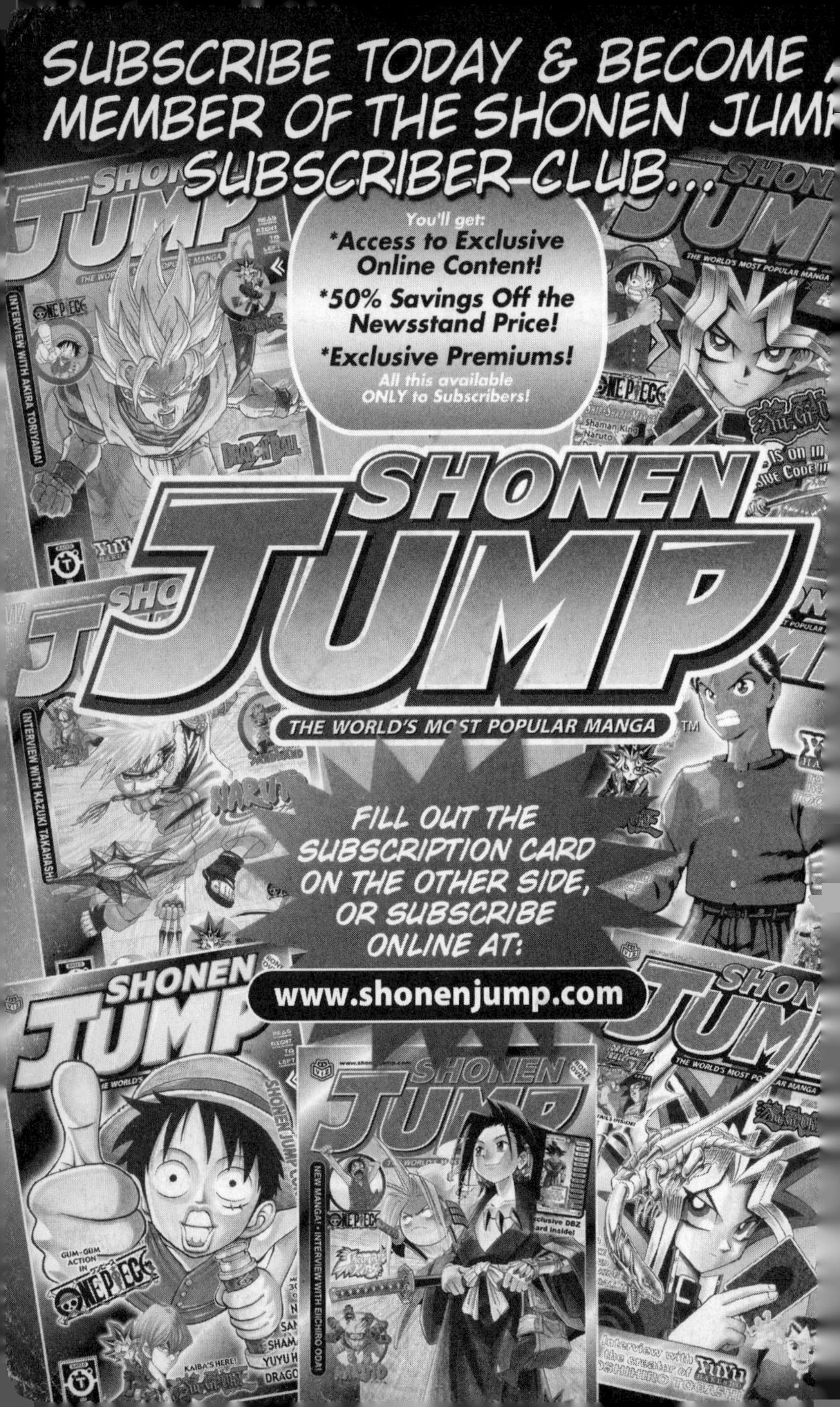

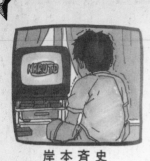

岸本斉史

Thanks to everyone's support, *Naruto* has finally become an animated series!

I wrote in the first manga volume, "The first time I won an award...I was so happy." And when my first comic book was published, I was 10 times happier still.

But the anime makes me 100 times happier! So please watch the *Naruto* anime *and* keep reading the manga.

Oh! But I guess I'm happiest knowing that people are still enjoying *Naruto*. Yup, that's it!

—*Masashi Kishimoto, 2002*

Author/artist Masashi Kishimoto was born in 1974 in rural Okayama Prefecture, Japan. After spending time in art college, he won the Hop Step Award for new manga artists with his manga **Karakuri** (Mechanism). Kishimoto decided to base his next story on traditional Japanese culture. His first version of **Naruto**, drawn in 1997, was a one-shot story about fox spirits; his final version, which debuted in **Weekly Shonen Jump** in 1999, quickly became the most popular ninja manga in Japan.

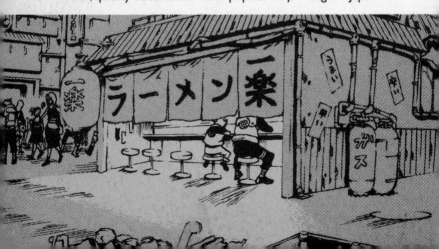

NARUTO VOL. 14
The SHONEN JUMP Manga Edition

This graphic novel contains material that was originally published in English in **SHONEN JUMP** #51-53.

STORY AND ART BY MASASHI KISHIMOTO

Translation & English Adaptation/Mari Morimoto
Touch-up Art & Lettering/Inori Fukuda Trant
Additional Touch-up/Josh Simpson
Design/Sean Lee
Editor//Joel Enos

Managing Editor/Frances E. Wall
Editorial Director/Elizabeth Kawasaki
Editor in Chief, Books/Alvin Lu
Editor in Chief, Magazines/Marc Weidenbaum
Sr. Director of Acquisitions/Rika Inouye
Sr. VP of Marketing/Liza Coppola
Exec. VP of Sales & Marketing/John Easum
Publisher/Hyoe Narita

Printed in the U.S.A.

Published by VIZ Media, LLC
P.O. Box 77010
San Francisco, CA 94107

SHONEN JUMP Manga Edition
10 9 8 7 6 5 4 3 2 1
First printing, May 2007

THE WORLD'S
MOST POPULAR MANGA

www.viz.com

www.shonenjump.com

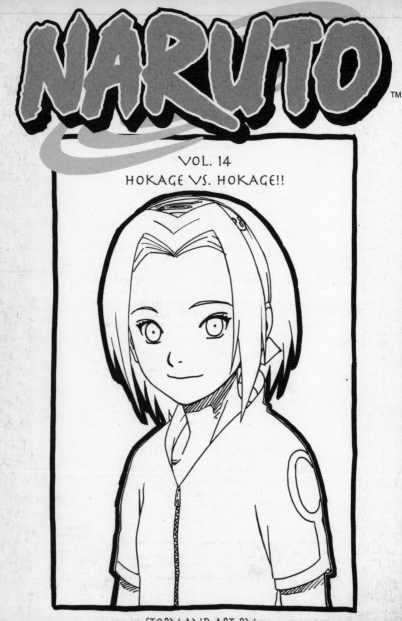

NARUTO™

VOL. 14
HOKAGE VS. HOKAGE!!

STORY AND ART BY
MASASHI KISHIMOTO

SAKURA サクラ

Smart and studious, Sakura is the brightest of Naruto's classmates, but she's constantly distracted by her crush on Sasuke. Her goal: to win Sasuke's heart!

NARUTO ナルト

When Naruto was born, a destructive fox spirit was imprisoned inside his body. Spurned by the older villagers, he's grown into an attention-seeking trouble-maker. His goal: to become the village's next *Hokage*.

SASUKE サスケ

The top student in Naruto's class, Sasuke comes from the prestigious Uchiha clan. His goal: to get revenge on a mysterious person who wronged him in the past.

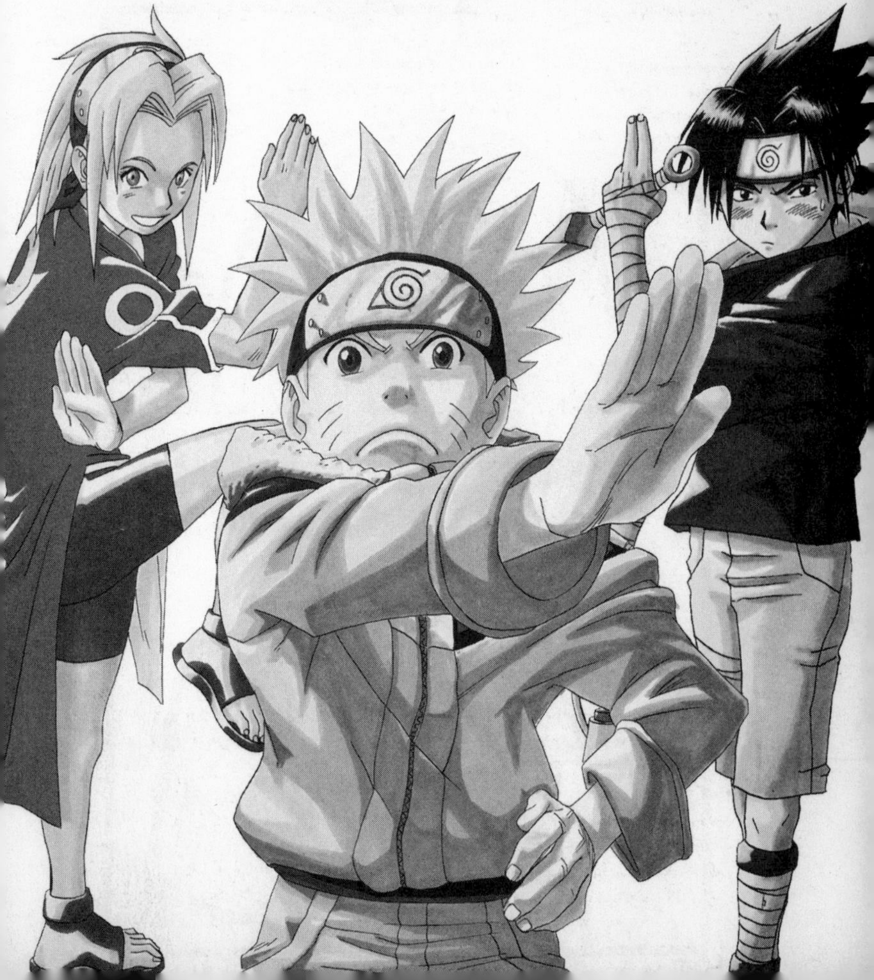

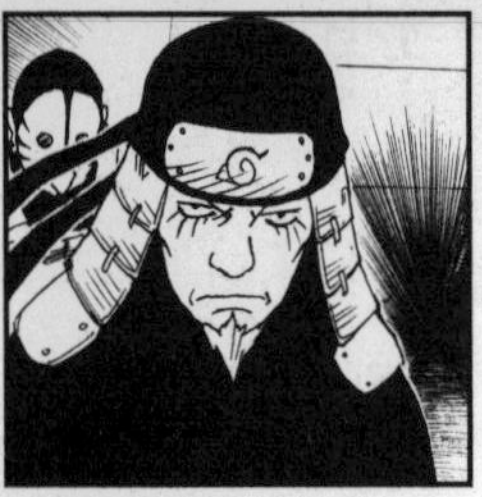

The Third Hokage 三代目火影

The leader of Konohagakure. He was retired, but stepped back into the position when the fourth Hokage was killed by the Nine-Tailed Fox.

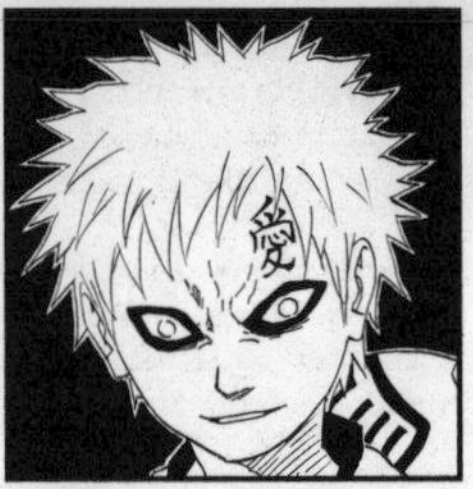
愛

Gaara 我愛羅

Mysterious, bloodthirsty Gaara is one of the scariest – and strangely familiar – ninja Naruto has ever encountered.

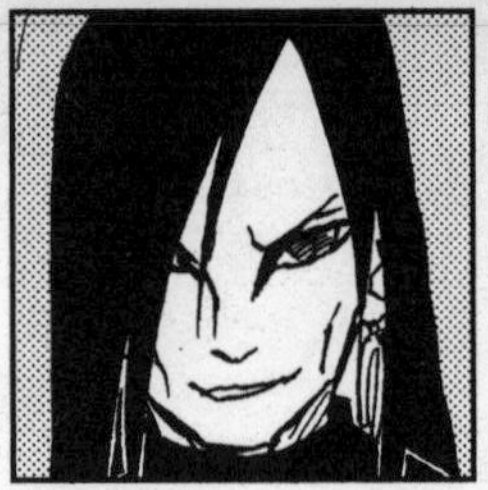

Orochimaru 大蛇丸

A nefarious master of disguise with a master plan of total revenge against the Third Hokage – for what exactly we have yet to learn.

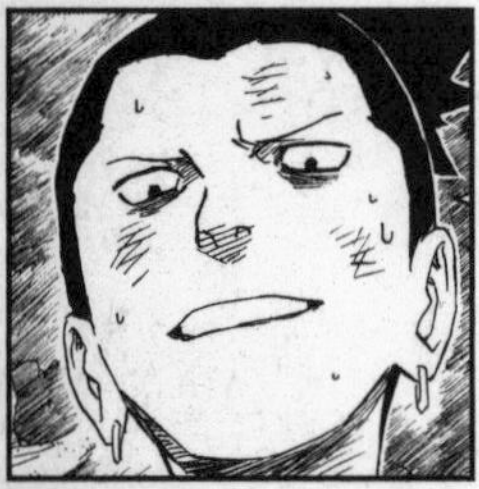

Shikamaru シカマル

One of Naruto's classmates. He specializes in the Shadow Possession technique, and is a skilled ninja despite his lazy demeanor.

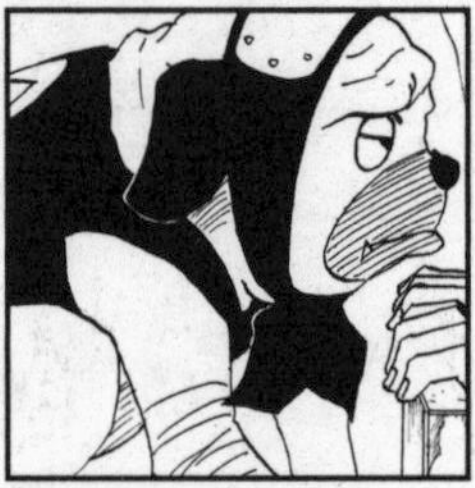

Pakkun パックン

A talking dog and excellent tracker who's also a loyal companion to Naruto's teacher Kakashi. Pakkun watches over his students whenever Kakashi can't.

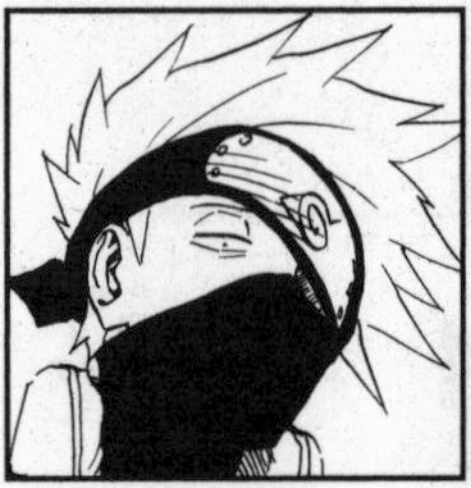

Kakashi カカシ

Although he doesn't have an especially warm personality, Kakashi is protective of his students.

THE STORY SO FAR...

Twelve years ago, a destructive nine-tailed fox spirit attacked the ninja village of Konohagakure. The *Hokage*, or village champion, defeated the fox by sealing its soul into the body of a baby boy. Now that boy, Uzumaki Naruto, has grown up to become a ninja-in-training, learning the art of *ninjutsu* with his teammates Sakura and Sasuke.

The Chunin Exams come to a shocking conclusion! As Sasuke and Gaara face off, an invasion commences, halting the exams for good. Sasuke takes off after the fleeing Gaara, and Kakashi sends Naruto, Sakura and Shikamaru after him. As Chaos Spreads, Orochimaru, disguised as Kazekage, takes the Third Hokage hostage. Orochimaru's "Operation Destroy Konoha" is under way, complete with a dastardly – and forbidden – secret weapon...

NARUTO

VOL. 14
HOKAGE VS. HOKAGE!!

CONTENTS

Number 118: Detainment...!!

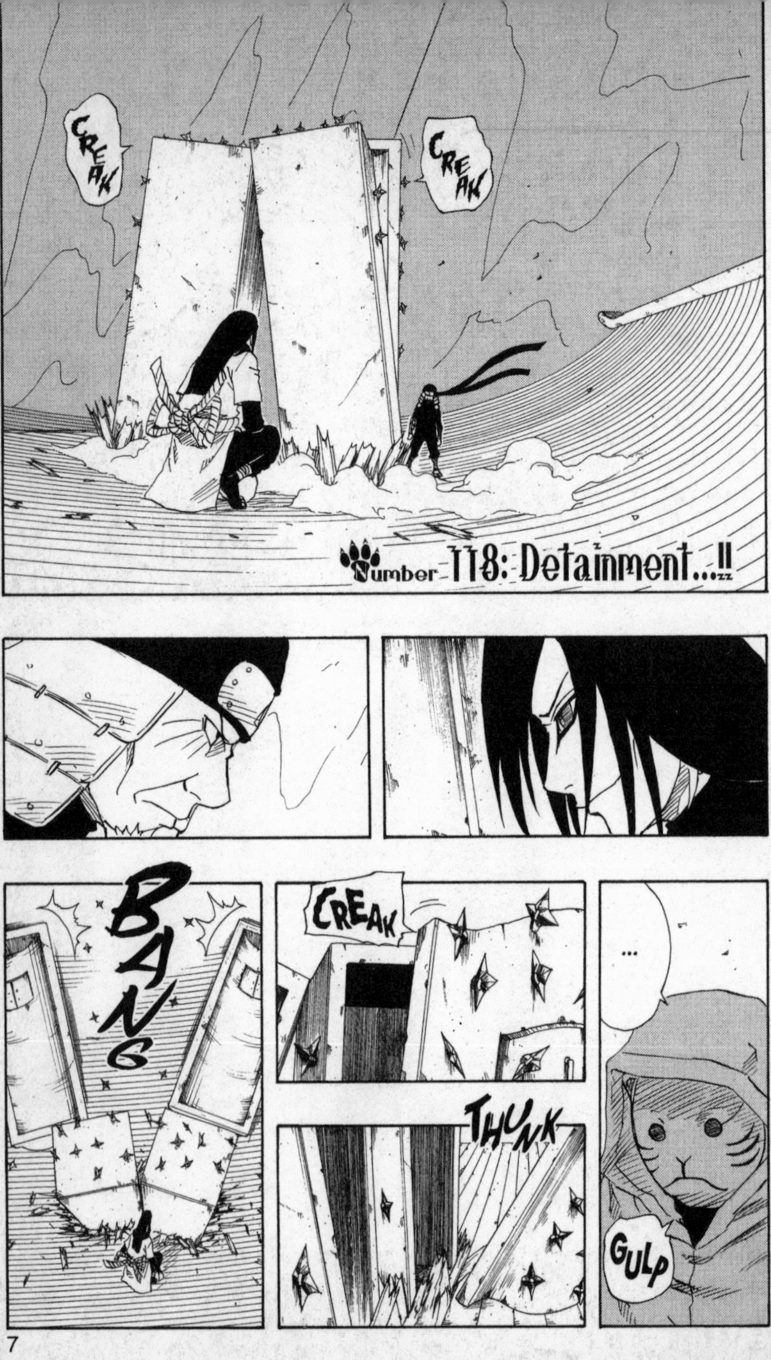
CREAK
CREAK
...
GULP
CREAK
THUNK
BANG

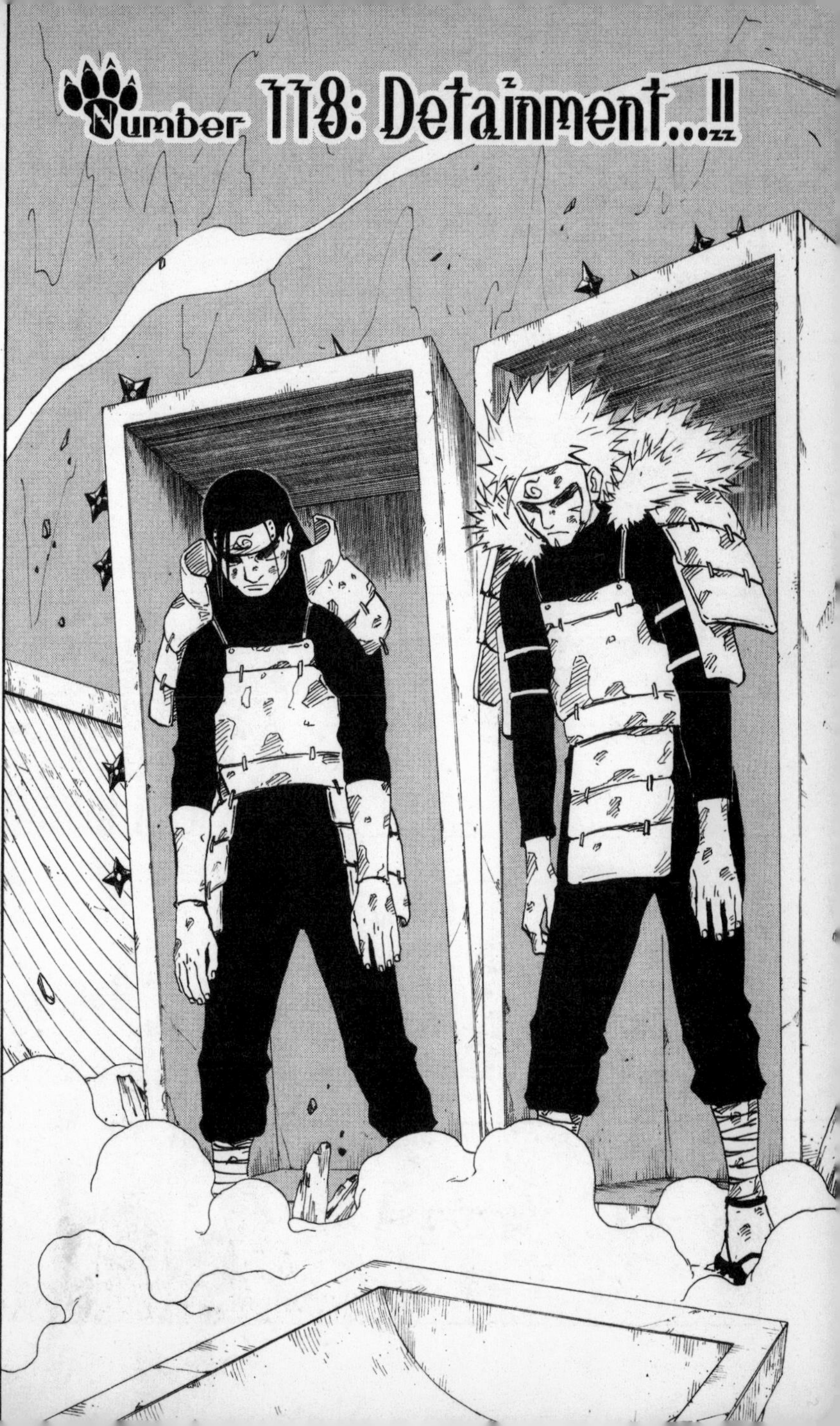
Number 118: Detainment...!!

READ THIS WAY

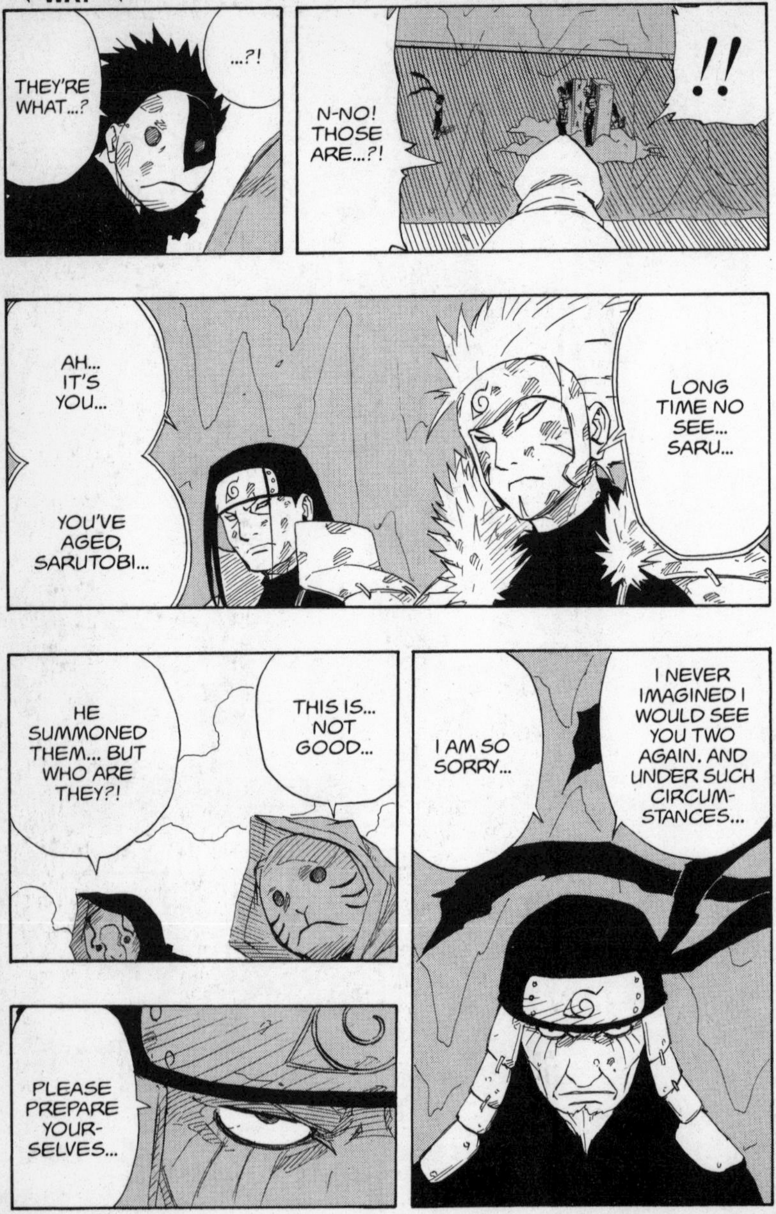
!!
N-NO! THOSE ARE...?!
...?!
THEY'RE WHAT...?
LONG TIME NO SEE... SARU...
AH... IT'S YOU...
YOU'VE AGED, SARUTOBI...
I NEVER IMAGINED I WOULD SEE YOU TWO AGAIN. AND UNDER SUCH CIRCUM-STANCES...
I AM SO SORRY...
THIS IS... NOT GOOD...
HE SUMMONED THEM... BUT WHO ARE THEY?!
PLEASE PREPARE YOUR-SELVES...

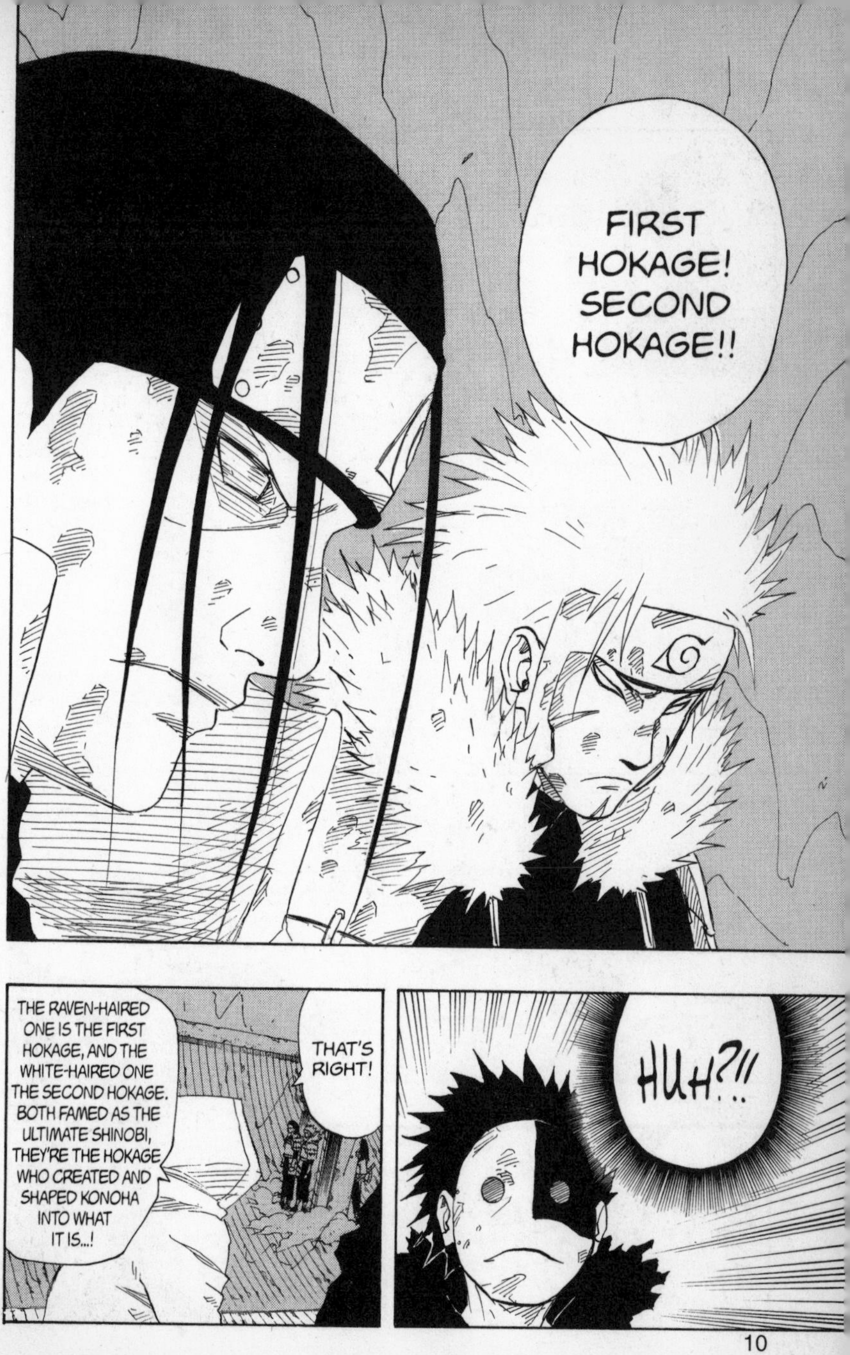
FIRST HOKAGE! SECOND HOKAGE!!
HUH?!!
THAT'S RIGHT!
THE RAVEN-HAIRED ONE IS THE FIRST HOKAGE, AND THE WHITE-HAIRED ONE THE SECOND HOKAGE. BOTH FAMED AS THE ULTIMATE SHINOBI, THEY'RE THE HOKAGE WHO CREATED AND SHAPED KONOHA INTO WHAT IT IS...!

READ THIS WAY

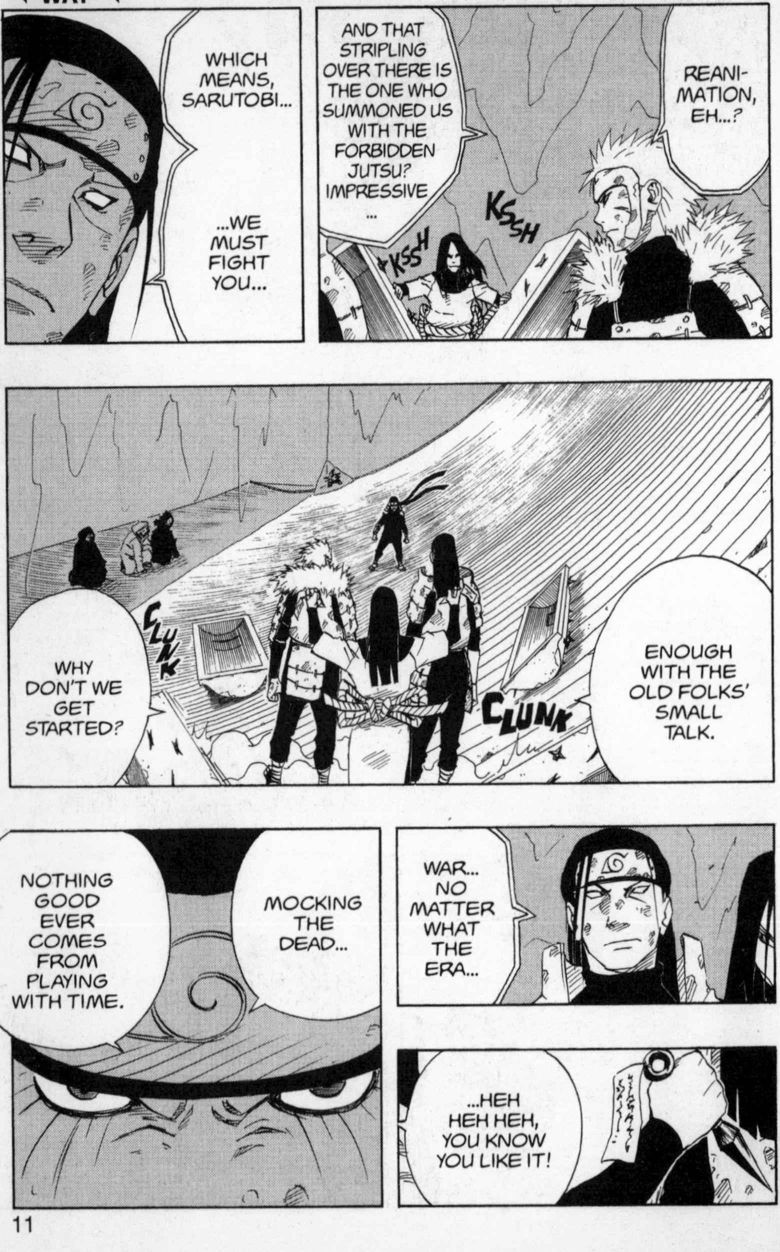
REANIMATION, EH...?
AND THAT STRIPLING OVER THERE IS THE ONE WHO SUMMONED US WITH THE FORBIDDEN JUTSU? IMPRESSIVE...
KSSH
KSSH
WHICH MEANS, SARUTOBI...
...WE MUST FIGHT YOU...
ENOUGH WITH THE OLD FOLKS' SMALL TALK.
CLUNK
CLUNK
WHY DON'T WE GET STARTED?
WAR... NO MATTER WHAT THE ERA...
...HEH HEH HEH, YOU KNOW YOU LIKE IT!
MOCKING THE DEAD...
NOTHING GOOD EVER COMES FROM PLAYING WITH TIME.

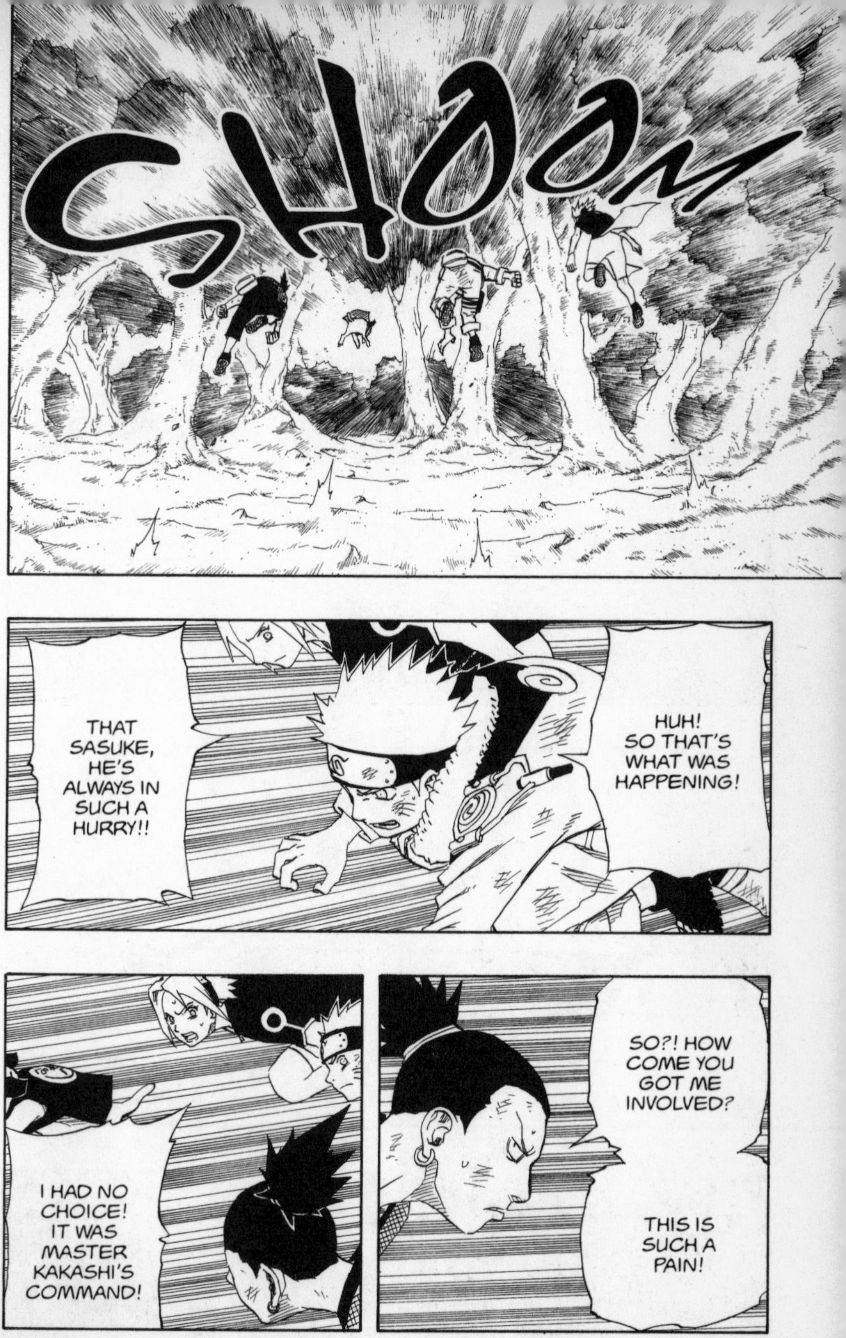
SHOOM
HUH! SO THAT'S WHAT WAS HAPPENING!
THAT SASUKE, HE'S ALWAYS IN SUCH A HURRY!!
SO?! HOW COME YOU GOT ME INVOLVED?
THIS IS SUCH A PAIN!
I HAD NO CHOICE! IT WAS MASTER KAKASHI'S COMMAND!

READ THIS WAY

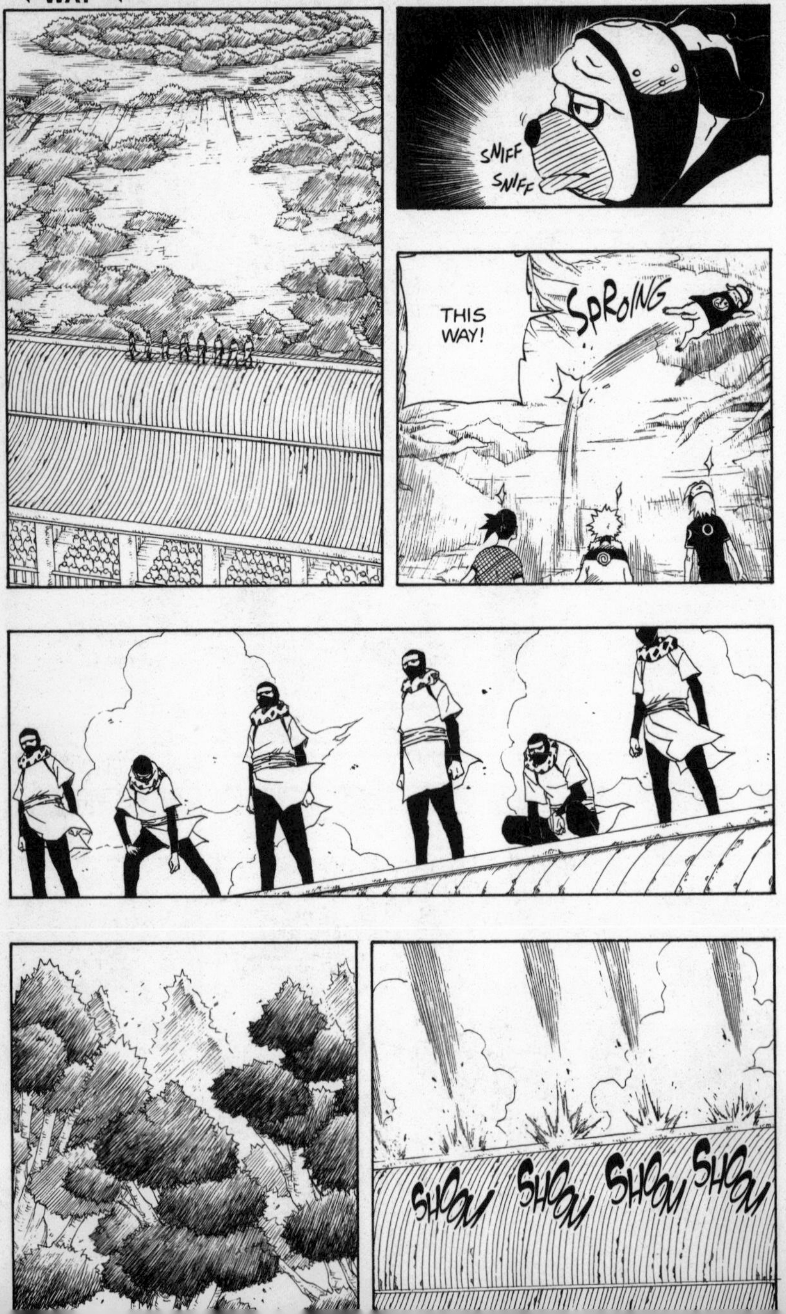
SNIFF
SNIFF
SPROING
THIS WAY!
SHOOM
SHOOM
SHOOM
SHOOM

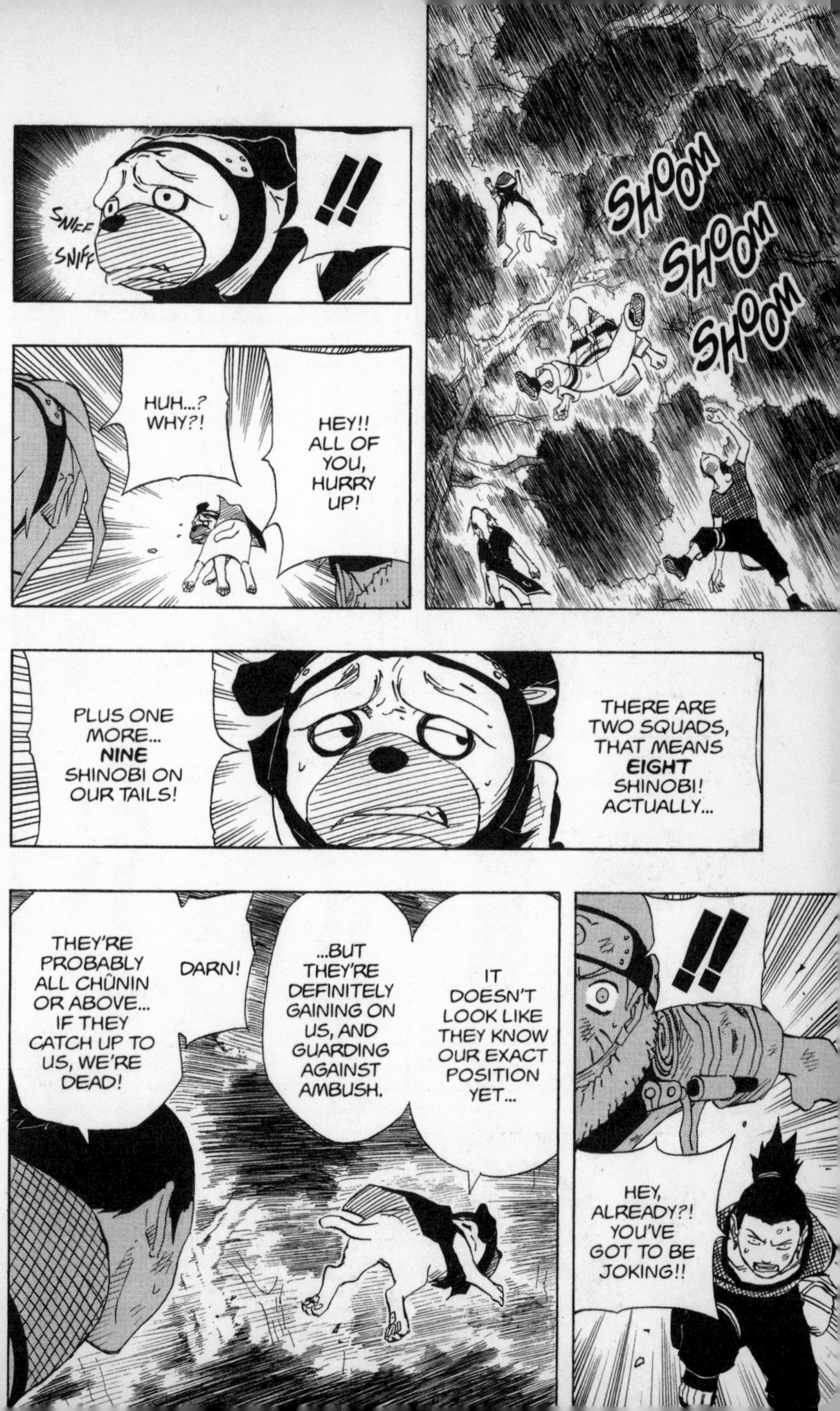
SHOOM
SHOOM
SHOOM
!!
SNIFF
SNIFF
HEY!! ALL OF YOU, HURRY UP!
HUH...? WHY?!
THERE ARE TWO SQUADS, THAT MEANS **EIGHT** SHINOBI! ACTUALLY...
PLUS ONE MORE... **NINE** SHINOBI ON OUR TAILS!
!!
HEY, ALREADY?! YOU'VE GOT TO BE JOKING!!
IT DOESN'T LOOK LIKE THEY KNOW OUR EXACT POSITION YET...
...BUT THEY'RE DEFINITELY GAINING ON US, AND GUARDING AGAINST AMBUSH.
DARN!
THEY'RE PROBABLY ALL CHÛNIN OR ABOVE... IF THEY CATCH UP TO US, WE'RE DEAD!

READ THIS WAY

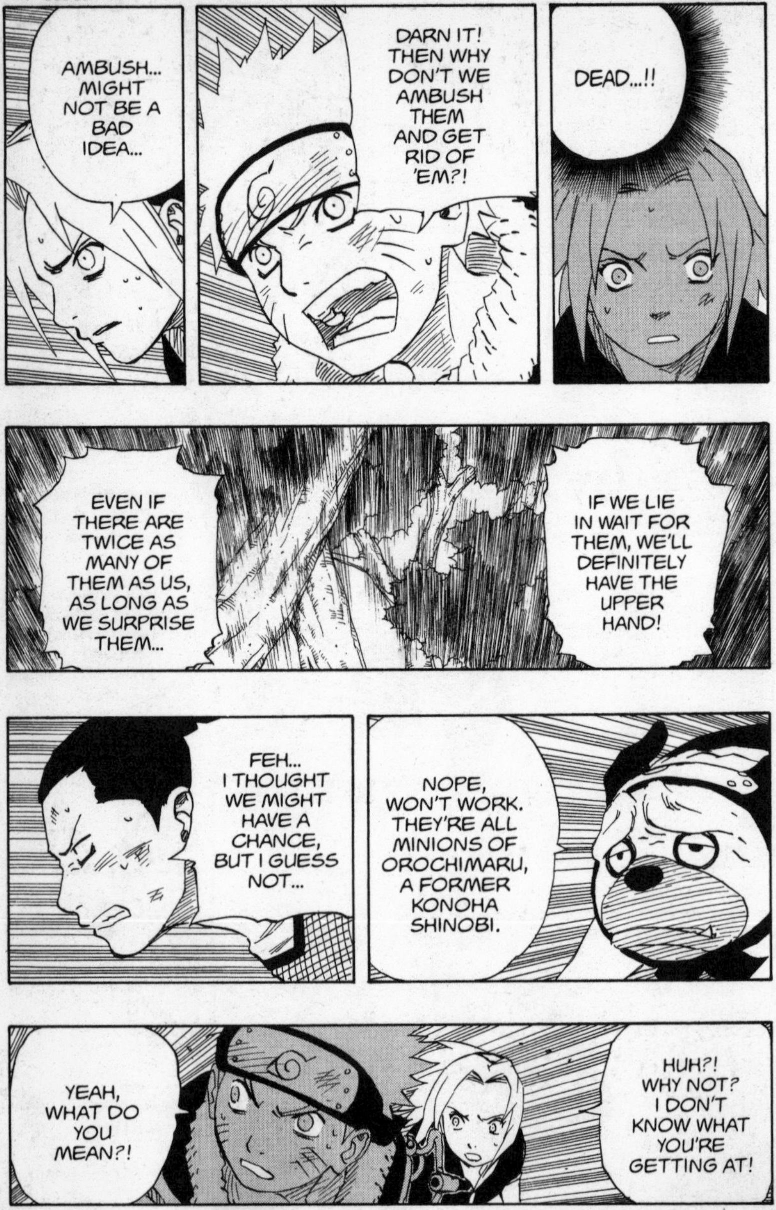
DEAD...!!
DARN IT! THEN WHY DON'T WE AMBUSH THEM AND GET RID OF 'EM?!
AMBUSH... MIGHT NOT BE A BAD IDEA...
IF WE LIE IN WAIT FOR THEM, WE'LL DEFINITELY HAVE THE UPPER HAND!
EVEN IF THERE ARE TWICE AS MANY OF THEM AS US, AS LONG AS WE SURPRISE THEM...
NOPE, WON'T WORK. THEY'RE ALL MINIONS OF OROCHIMARU, A FORMER KONOHA SHINOBI.
FEH... I THOUGHT WE MIGHT HAVE A CHANCE, BUT I GUESS NOT...
HUH?! WHY NOT? I DON'T KNOW WHAT YOU'RE GETTING AT!
YEAH, WHAT DO YOU MEAN?!

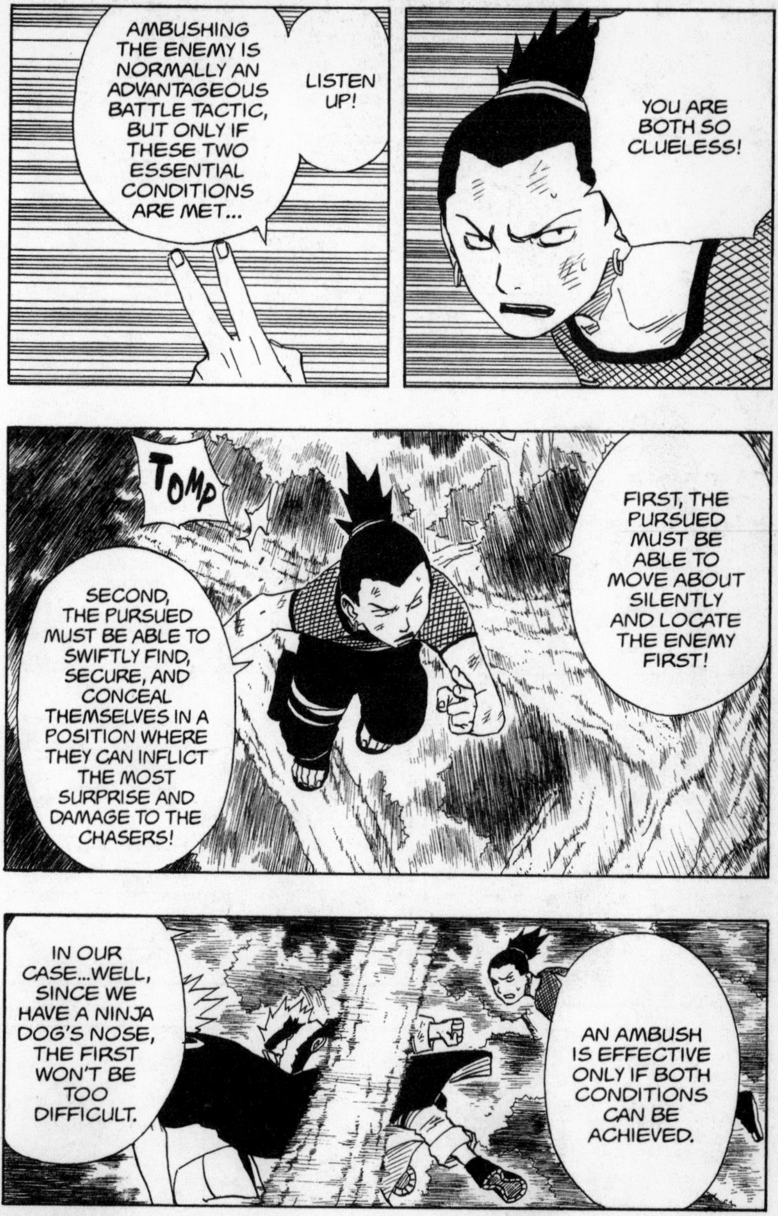
YOU ARE BOTH SO CLUELESS!
LISTEN UP!
AMBUSHING THE ENEMY IS NORMALLY AN ADVANTAGEOUS BATTLE TACTIC, BUT ONLY IF THESE TWO ESSENTIAL CONDITIONS ARE MET...
FIRST, THE PURSUED MUST BE ABLE TO MOVE ABOUT SILENTLY AND LOCATE THE ENEMY FIRST!
TOMP
SECOND, THE PURSUED MUST BE ABLE TO SWIFTLY FIND, SECURE, AND CONCEAL THEMSELVES IN A POSITION WHERE THEY CAN INFLICT THE MOST SURPRISE AND DAMAGE TO THE CHASERS!
AN AMBUSH IS EFFECTIVE ONLY IF BOTH CONDITIONS CAN BE ACHIEVED.
IN OUR CASE...WELL, SINCE WE HAVE A NINJA DOG'S NOSE, THE FIRST WON'T BE TOO DIFFICULT.

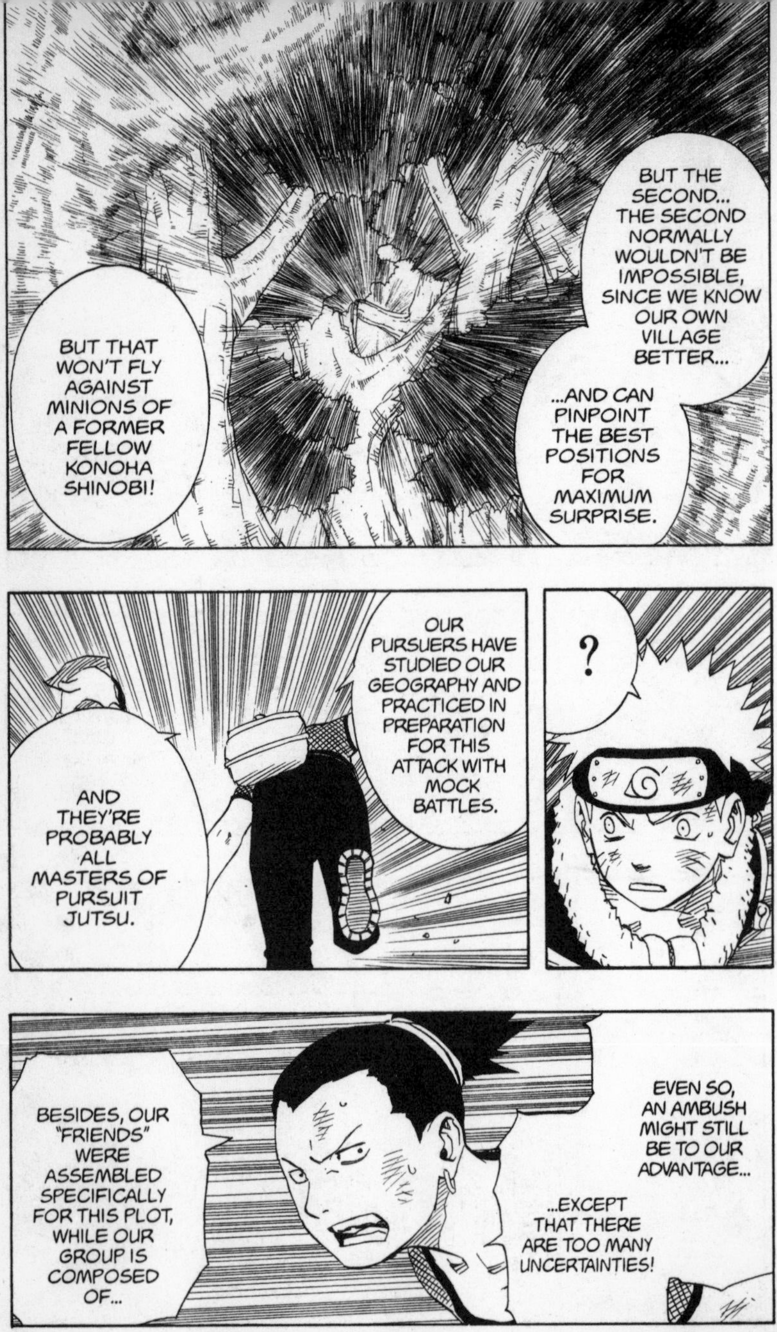
BUT THE SECOND... THE SECOND NORMALLY WOULDN'T BE IMPOSSIBLE, SINCE WE KNOW OUR OWN VILLAGE BETTER...
...AND CAN PINPOINT THE BEST POSITIONS FOR MAXIMUM SURPRISE.
BUT THAT WON'T FLY AGAINST MINIONS OF A FORMER FELLOW KONOHA SHINOBI!
?
OUR PURSUERS HAVE STUDIED OUR GEOGRAPHY AND PRACTICED IN PREPARATION FOR THIS ATTACK WITH MOCK BATTLES.
AND THEY'RE PROBABLY ALL MASTERS OF PURSUIT JUTSU.
EVEN SO, AN AMBUSH MIGHT STILL BE TO OUR ADVANTAGE...
...EXCEPT THAT THERE ARE TOO MANY UNCERTAINTIES!
BESIDES, OUR "FRIENDS" WERE ASSEMBLED SPECIFICALLY FOR THIS PLOT, WHILE OUR GROUP IS COMPOSED OF...

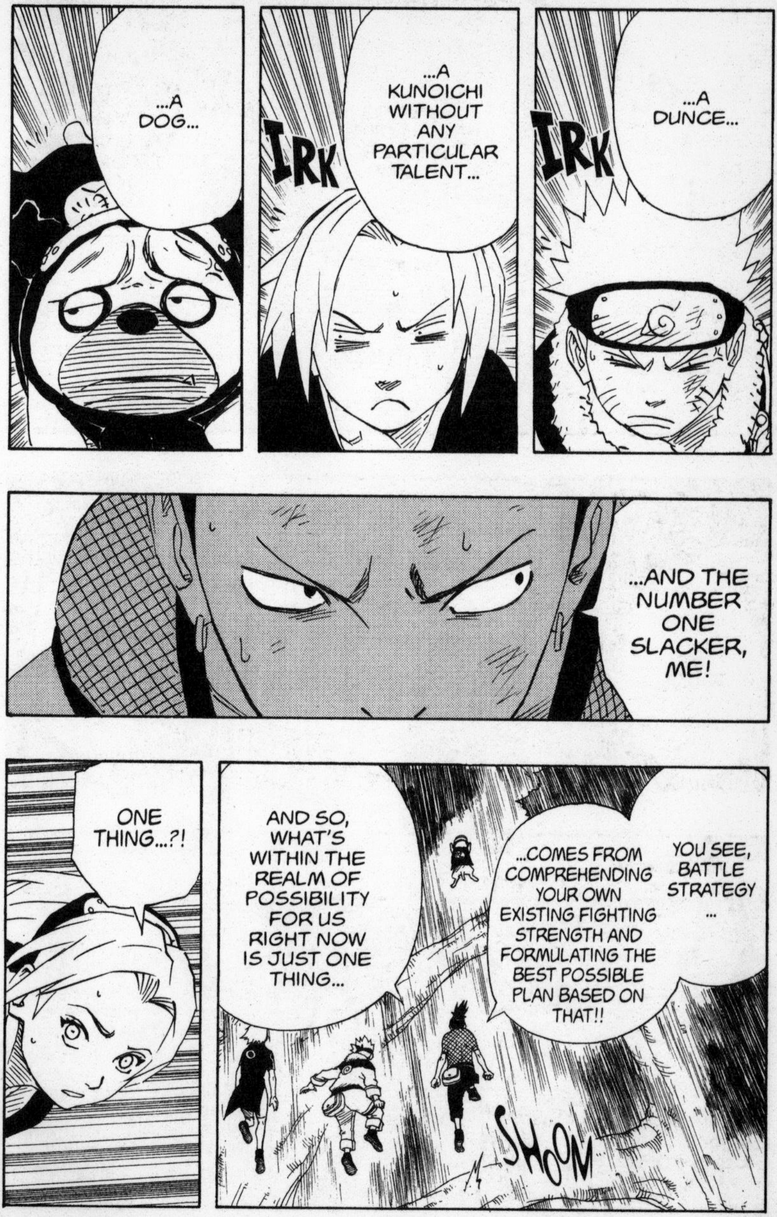
IRK
...A DUNCE...
IRK
...A KUNOICHI WITHOUT ANY PARTICULAR TALENT...
...A DOG...
...AND THE NUMBER ONE SLACKER, ME!
YOU SEE, BATTLE STRATEGY ...
...COMES FROM COMPREHENDING YOUR OWN EXISTING FIGHTING STRENGTH AND FORMULATING THE BEST POSSIBLE PLAN BASED ON THAT!!
AND SO, WHAT'S WITHIN THE REALM OF POSSIBILITY FOR US RIGHT NOW IS JUST ONE THING...
SHOOM
ONE THING...?!

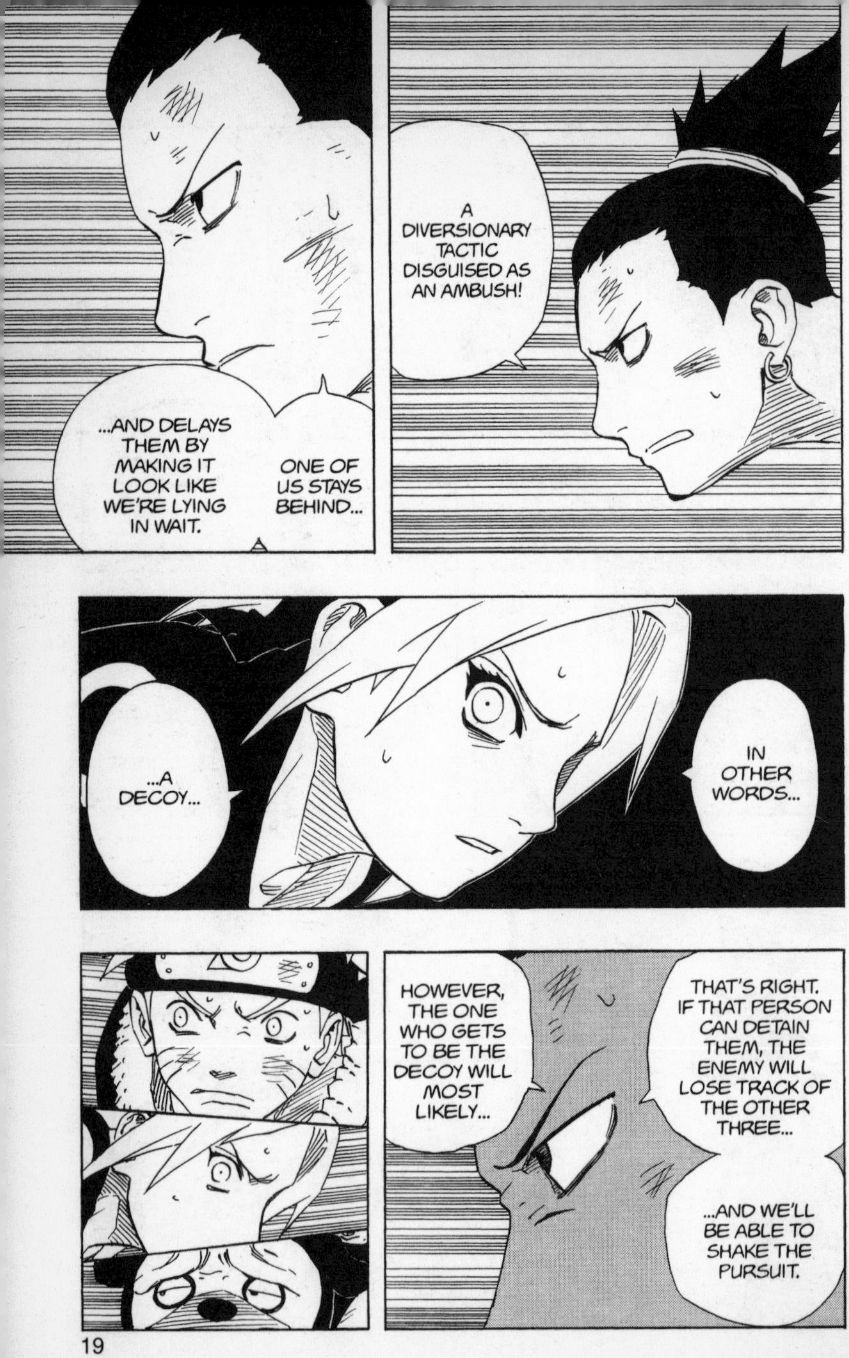
A DIVERSIONARY TACTIC DISGUISED AS AN AMBUSH!
ONE OF US STAYS BEHIND...
...AND DELAYS THEM BY MAKING IT LOOK LIKE WE'RE LYING IN WAIT.
IN OTHER WORDS...
...A DECOY...
THAT'S RIGHT. IF THAT PERSON CAN DETAIN THEM, THE ENEMY WILL LOSE TRACK OF THE OTHER THREE...
...AND WE'LL BE ABLE TO SHAKE THE PURSUIT.
HOWEVER, THE ONE WHO GETS TO BE THE DECOY WILL MOST LIKELY...

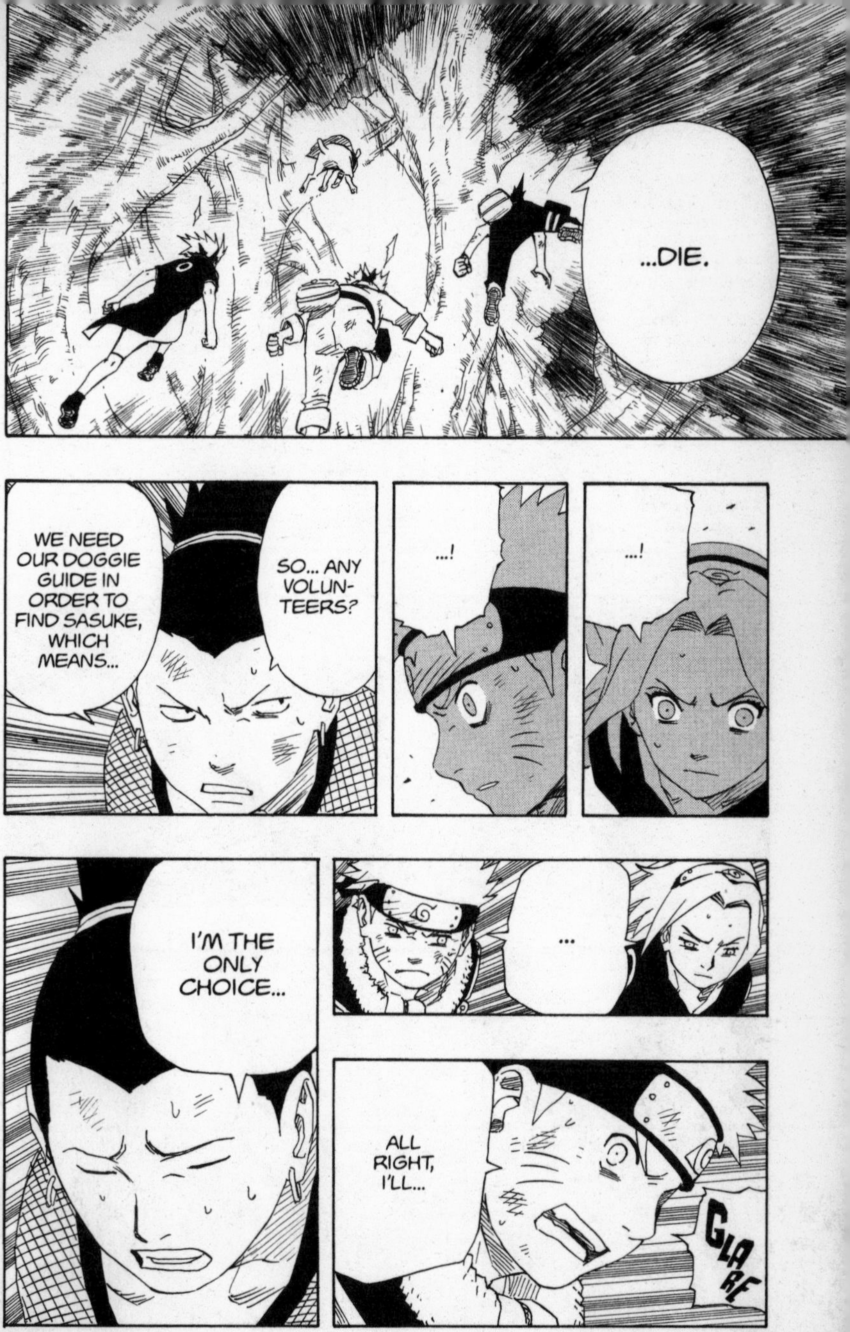

...DIE.
...!
...!
SO... ANY VOLUNTEERS?
WE NEED OUR DOGGIE GUIDE IN ORDER TO FIND SASUKE, WHICH MEANS...
...
ALL RIGHT, I'LL...
GLARE
I'M THE ONLY CHOICE...

READ THIS WAY

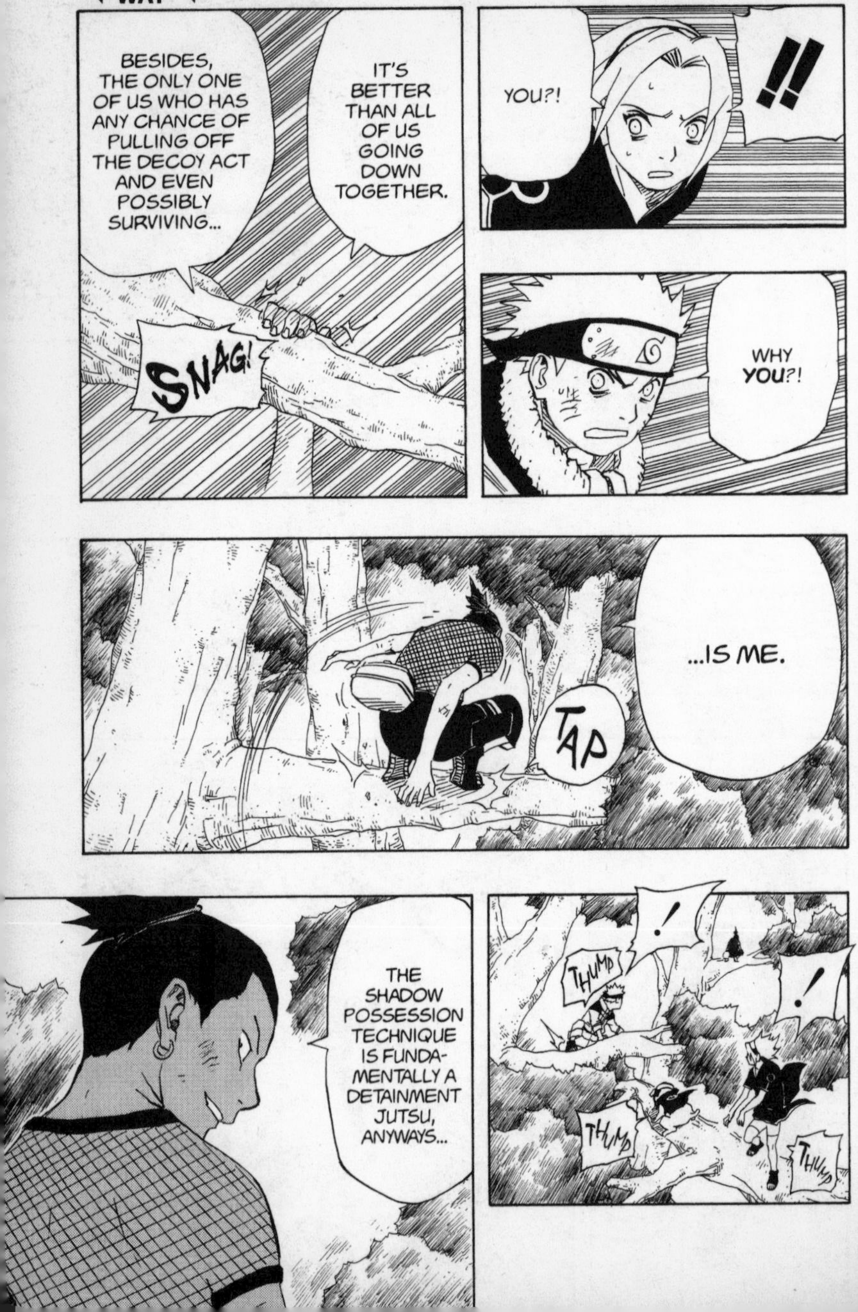
YOU?!
!!
WHY YOU?!
IT'S BETTER THAN ALL OF US GOING DOWN TOGETHER.
BESIDES, THE ONLY ONE OF US WHO HAS ANY CHANCE OF PULLING OFF THE DECOY ACT AND EVEN POSSIBLY SURVIVING...
SNAG!
...IS ME.
TAP
!
THUMP
!
THUMP
THUMP
THE SHADOW POSSESSION TECHNIQUE IS FUNDAMENTALLY A DETAINMENT JUTSU, ANYWAYS...

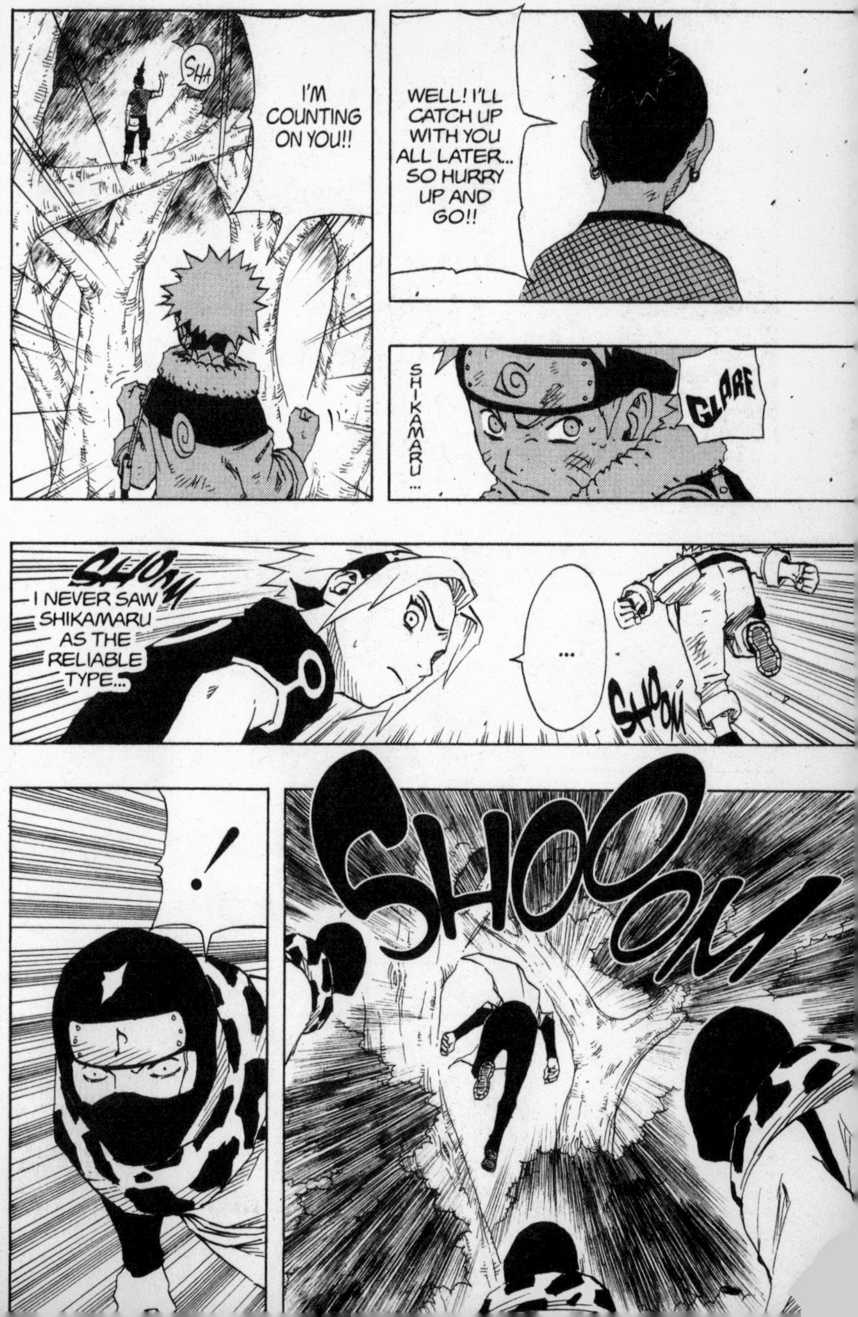
WELL! I'LL CATCH UP WITH YOU ALL LATER... SO HURRY UP AND GO!!
SHA
I'M COUNTING ON YOU!!
GLARE
SHIKAMARU...
SHOOM
...
SHOOM
I NEVER SAW SHIKAMARU AS THE RELIABLE TYPE...
SHOOOOM
!

READ THIS WAY

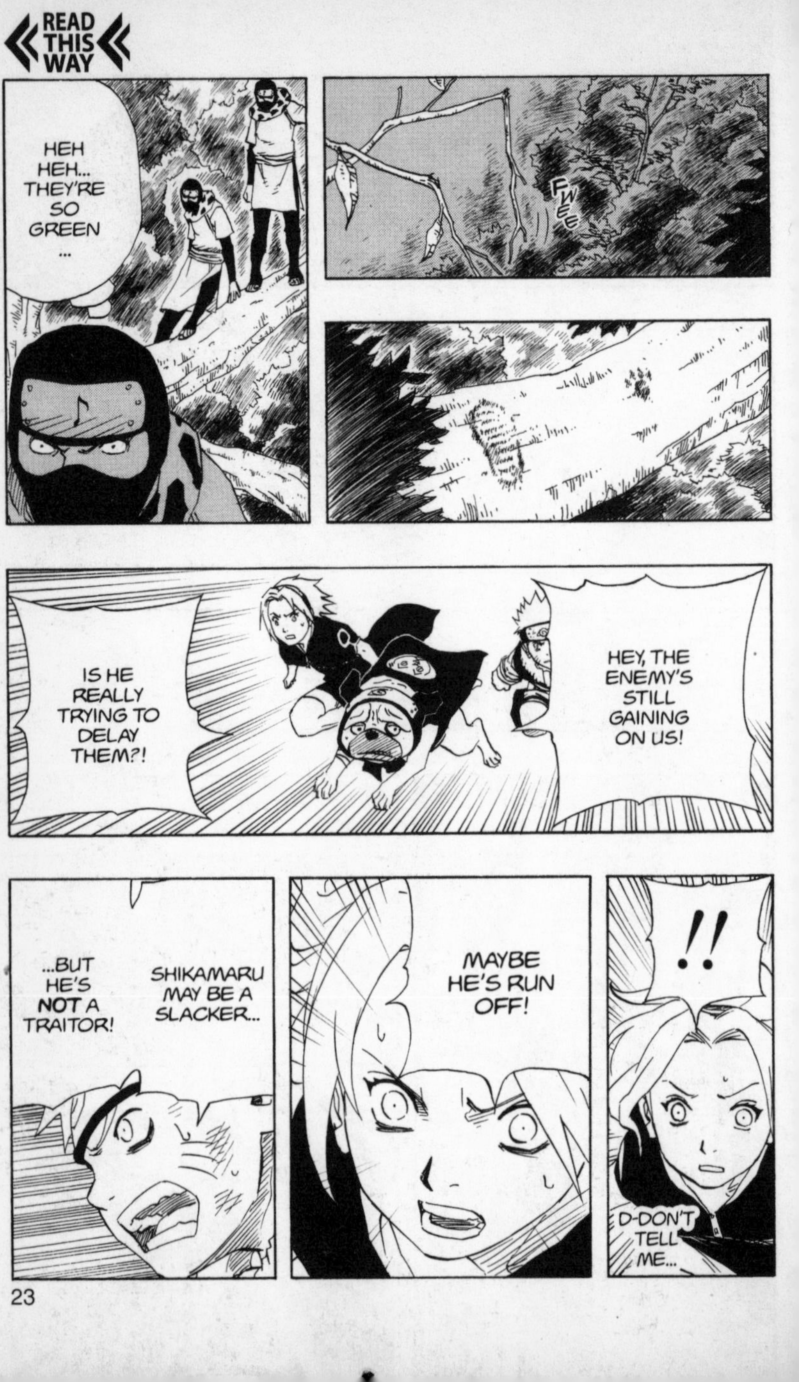
FWEE
HEH HEH... THEY'RE SO GREEN ...
HEY, THE ENEMY'S STILL GAINING ON US!
IS HE REALLY TRYING TO DELAY THEM?!
!!
D-DON'T TELL ME...
MAYBE HE'S RUN OFF!
SHIKAMARU MAY BE A SLACKER...
...BUT HE'S NOT A TRAITOR!

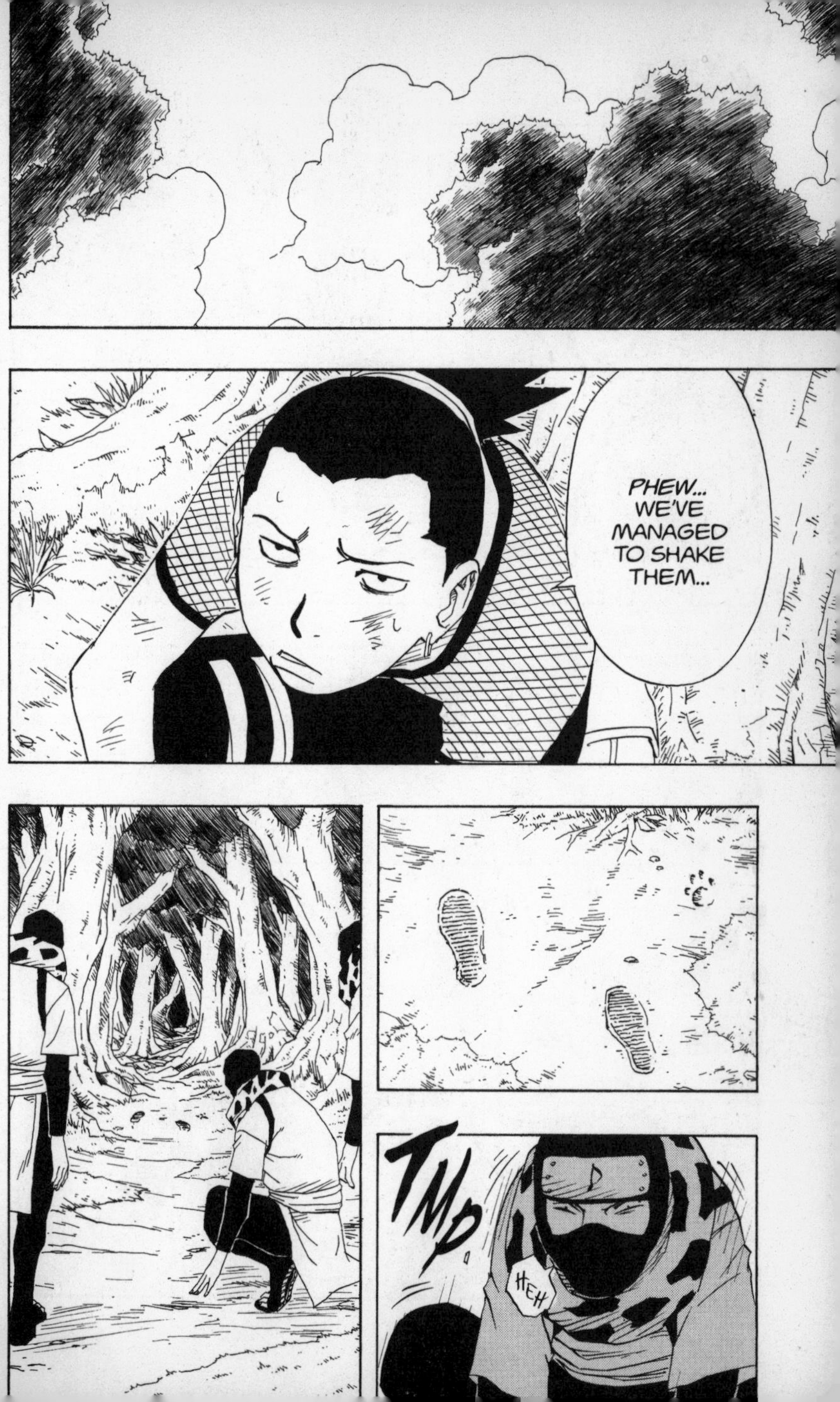
PHEW... WE'VE MANAGED TO SHAKE THEM...
TMP
HEH

READ THIS WAY

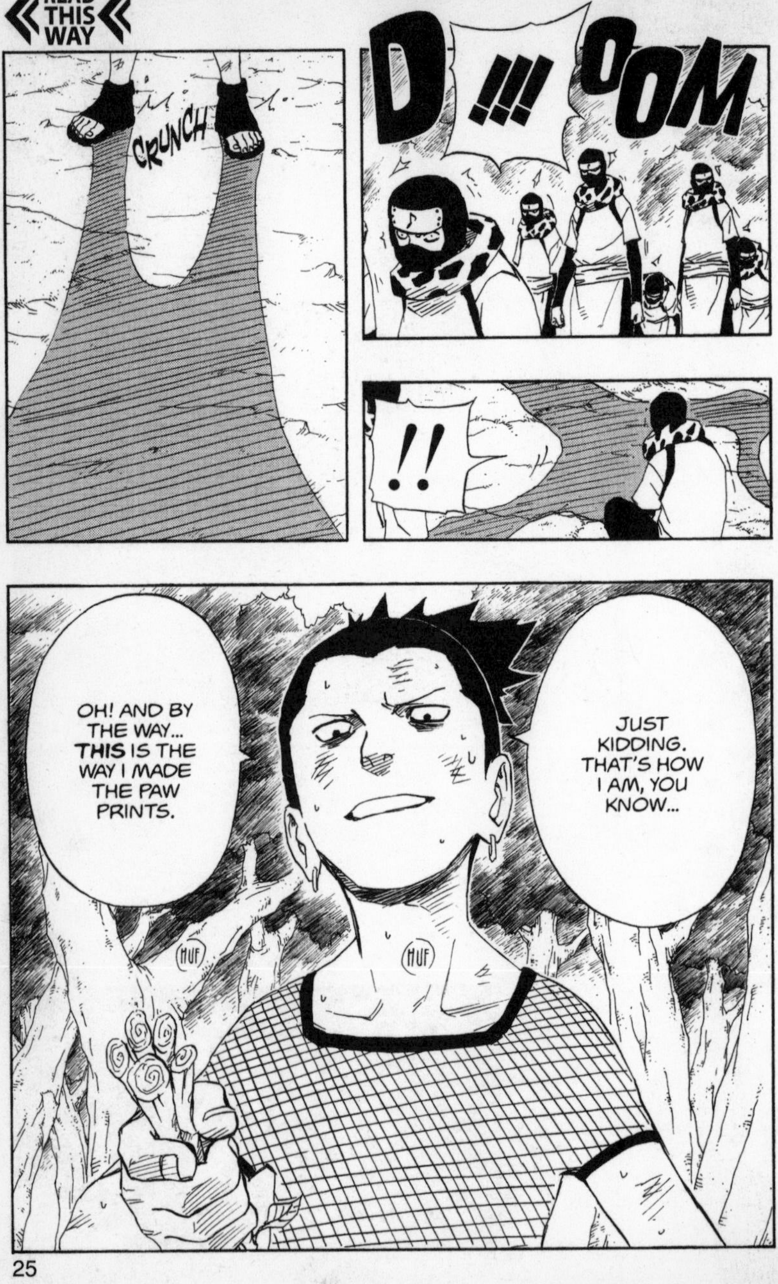

D!!!OOM
!!
CRUNCH
JUST KIDDING. THAT'S HOW I AM, YOU KNOW...
HUF
OH! AND BY THE WAY... **THIS** IS THE WAY I MADE THE PAW PRINTS.
HUF

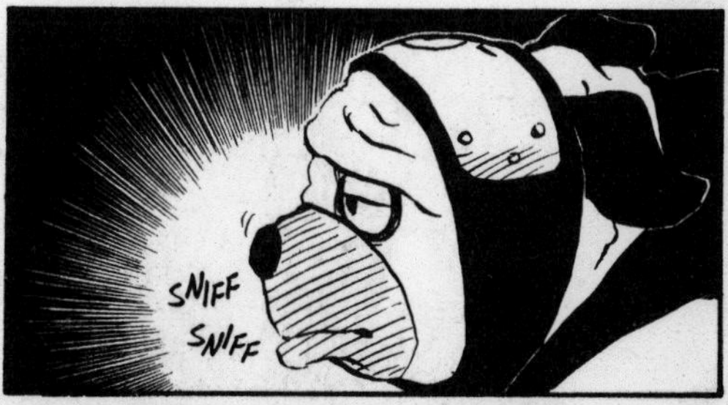
SNIFF
SNIFF

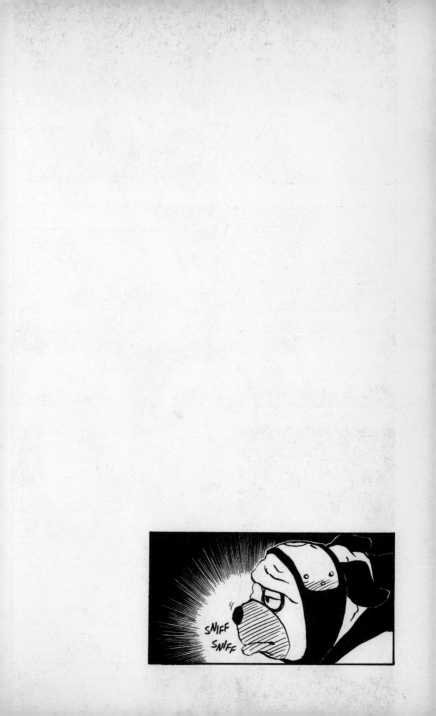

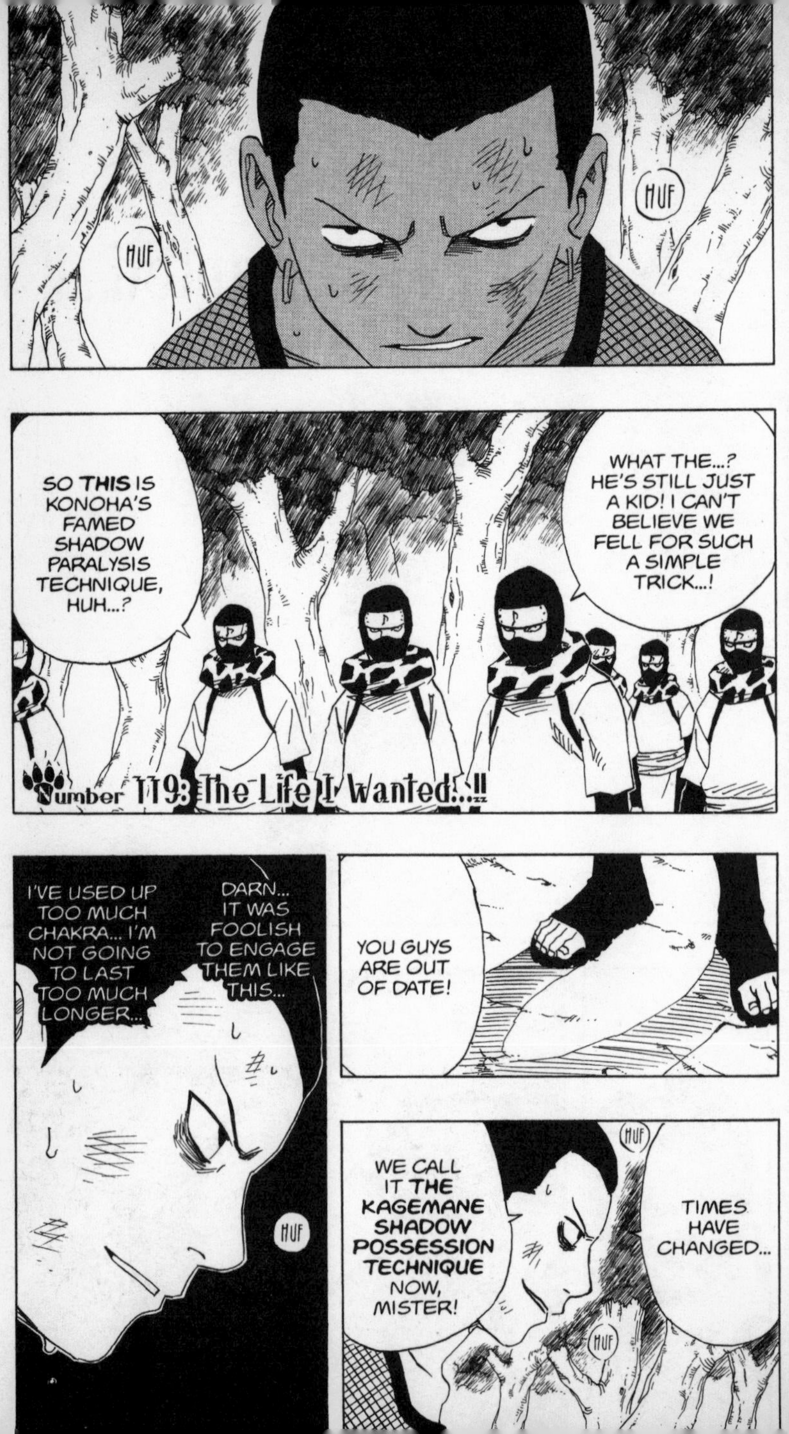
HUF
HUF
WHAT THE...? HE'S STILL JUST A KID! I CAN'T BELIEVE WE FELL FOR SUCH A SIMPLE TRICK...!
SO THIS IS KONOHA'S FAMED SHADOW PARALYSIS TECHNIQUE, HUH...?
Number 119: The Life I Wanted...!!
YOU GUYS ARE OUT OF DATE!
HUF
TIMES HAVE CHANGED...
WE CALL IT THE KAGEMANE SHADOW POSSESSION TECHNIQUE NOW, MISTER!
HUF
DARN... IT WAS FOOLISH TO ENGAGE THEM LIKE THIS...
I'VE USED UP TOO MUCH CHAKRA... I'M NOT GOING TO LAST TOO MUCH LONGER...
HUF

Number 119: The Life I Wanted...!!

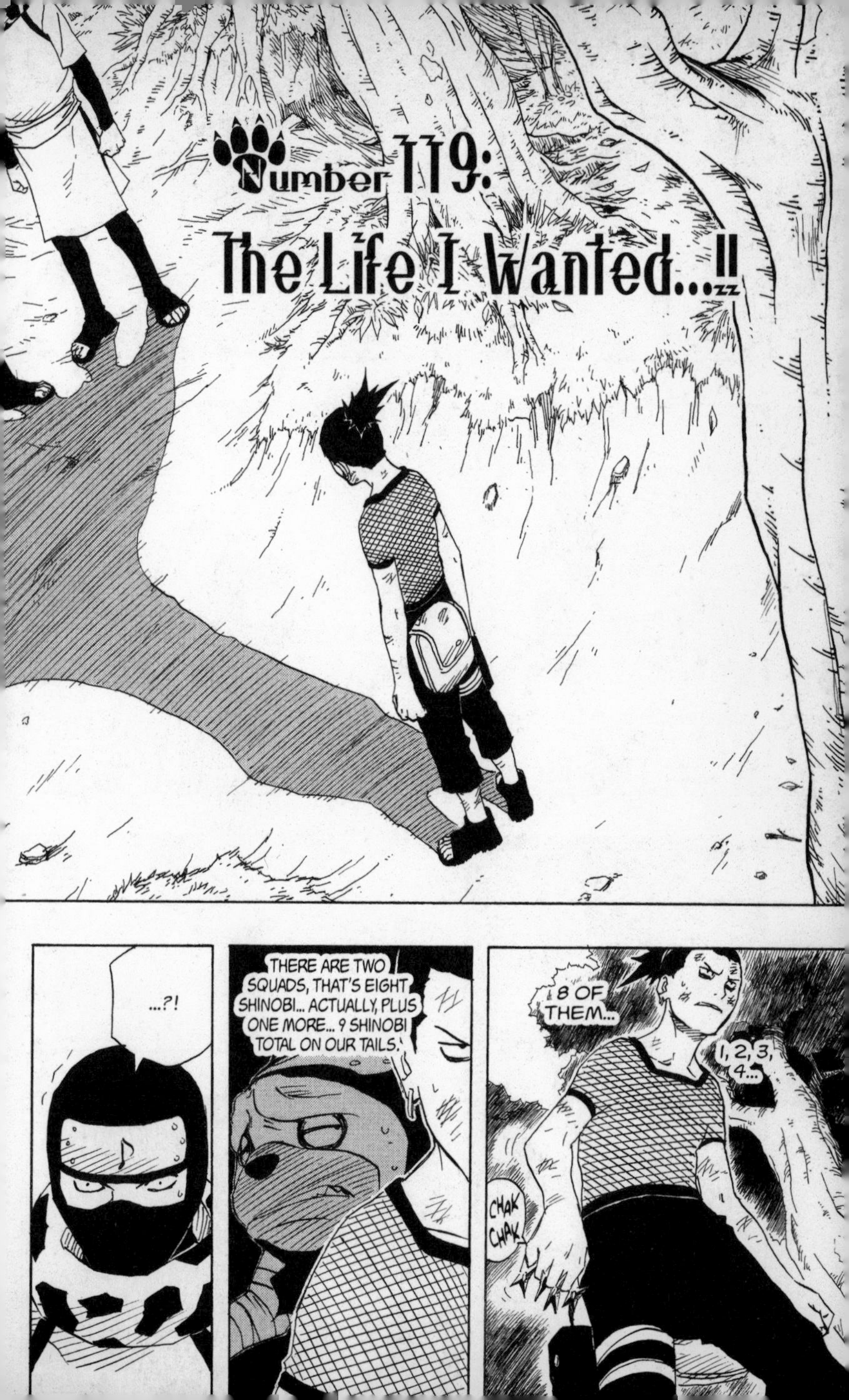
8 OF THEM...
1, 2, 3, 4...
CHAK CHAK
THERE ARE TWO SQUADS, THAT'S EIGHT SHINOBI... ACTUALLY, PLUS ONE MORE... 9 SHINOBI TOTAL ON OUR TAILS.
...?!

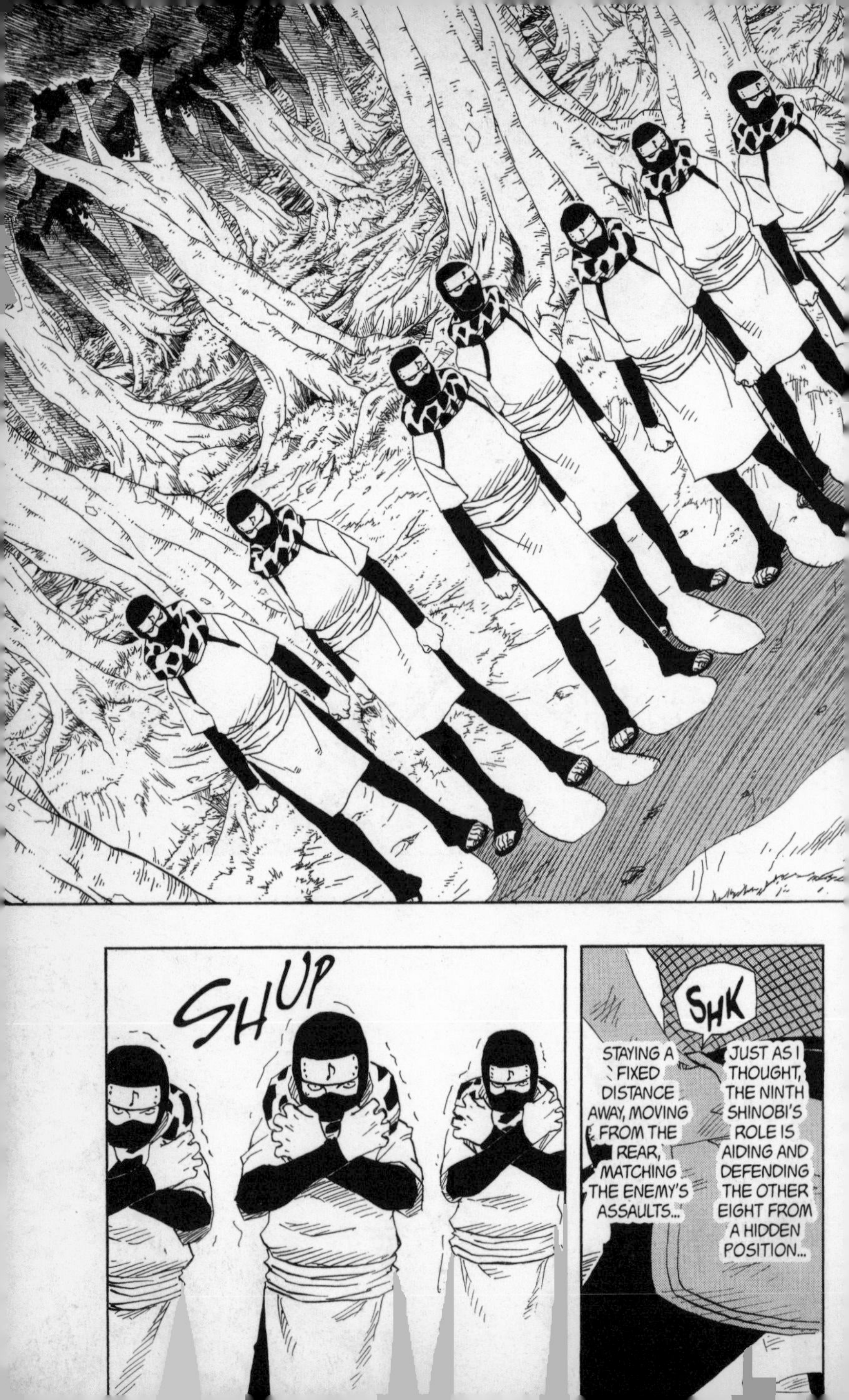
SHK
JUST AS I THOUGHT, THE NINTH SHINOBI'S ROLE IS AIDING AND DEFENDING THE OTHER EIGHT FROM A HIDDEN POSITION...
STAYING A FIXED DISTANCE AWAY, MOVING FROM THE REAR, MATCHING THE ENEMY'S ASSAULTS...
SHUP

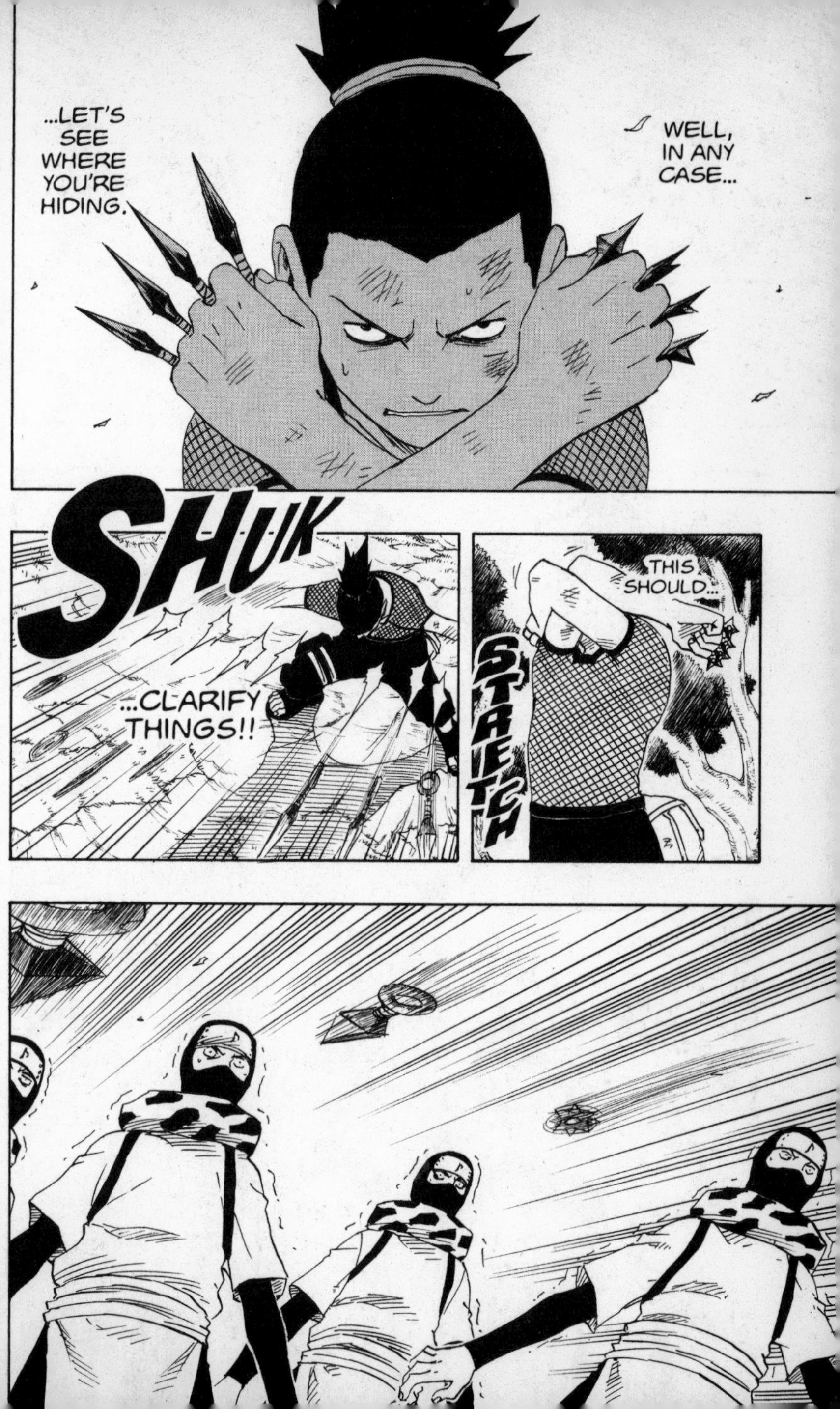
WELL, IN ANY CASE...
...LET'S SEE WHERE YOU'RE HIDING.
THIS SHOULD...
STRETCH
SHUK
...CLARIFY THINGS!!

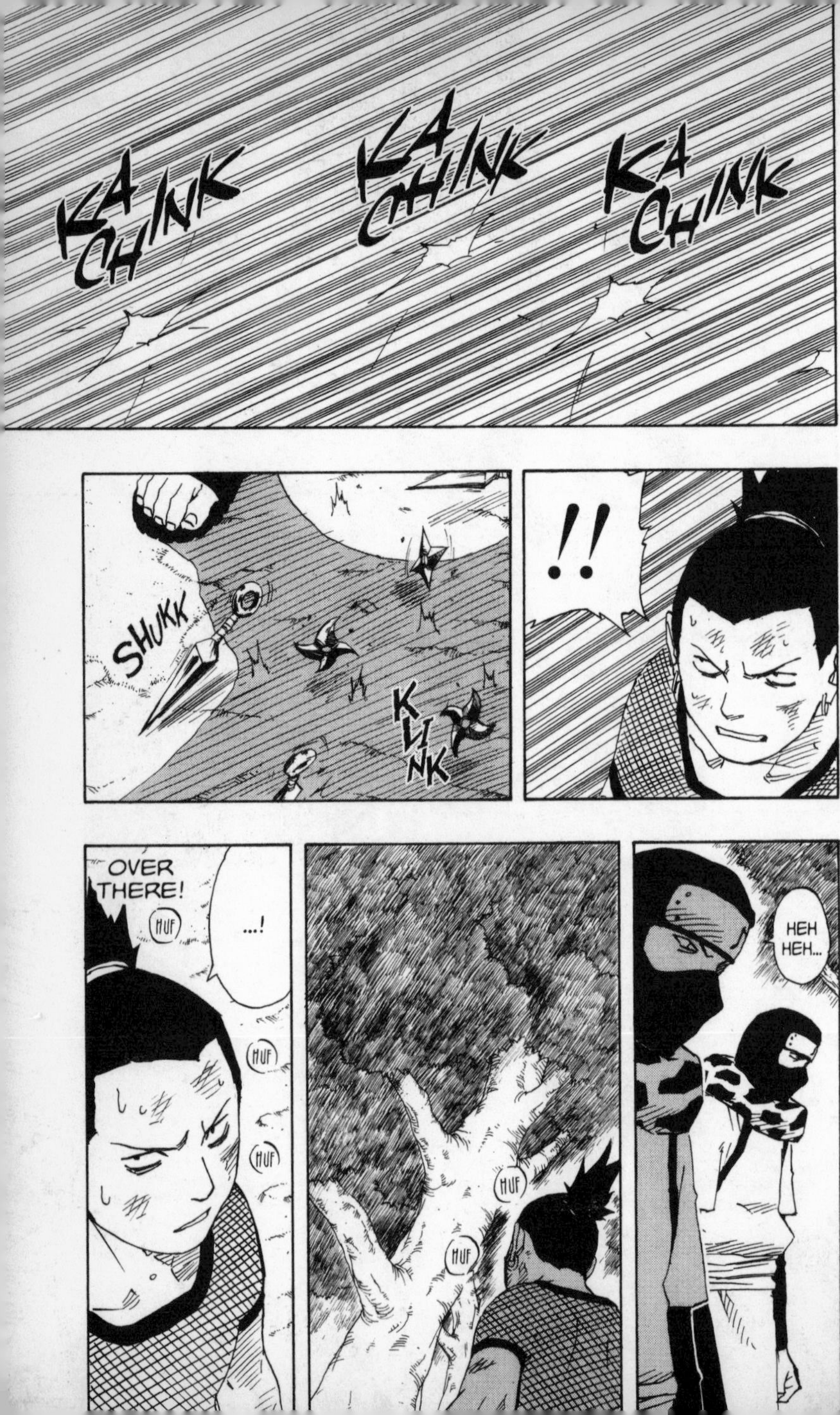
KA CHINK
KA CHINK
KA CHINK
!!
SHUKK
KLINK
HEH HEH...
HUF
HUF
...!
OVER THERE!
HUF
HUF
HUF

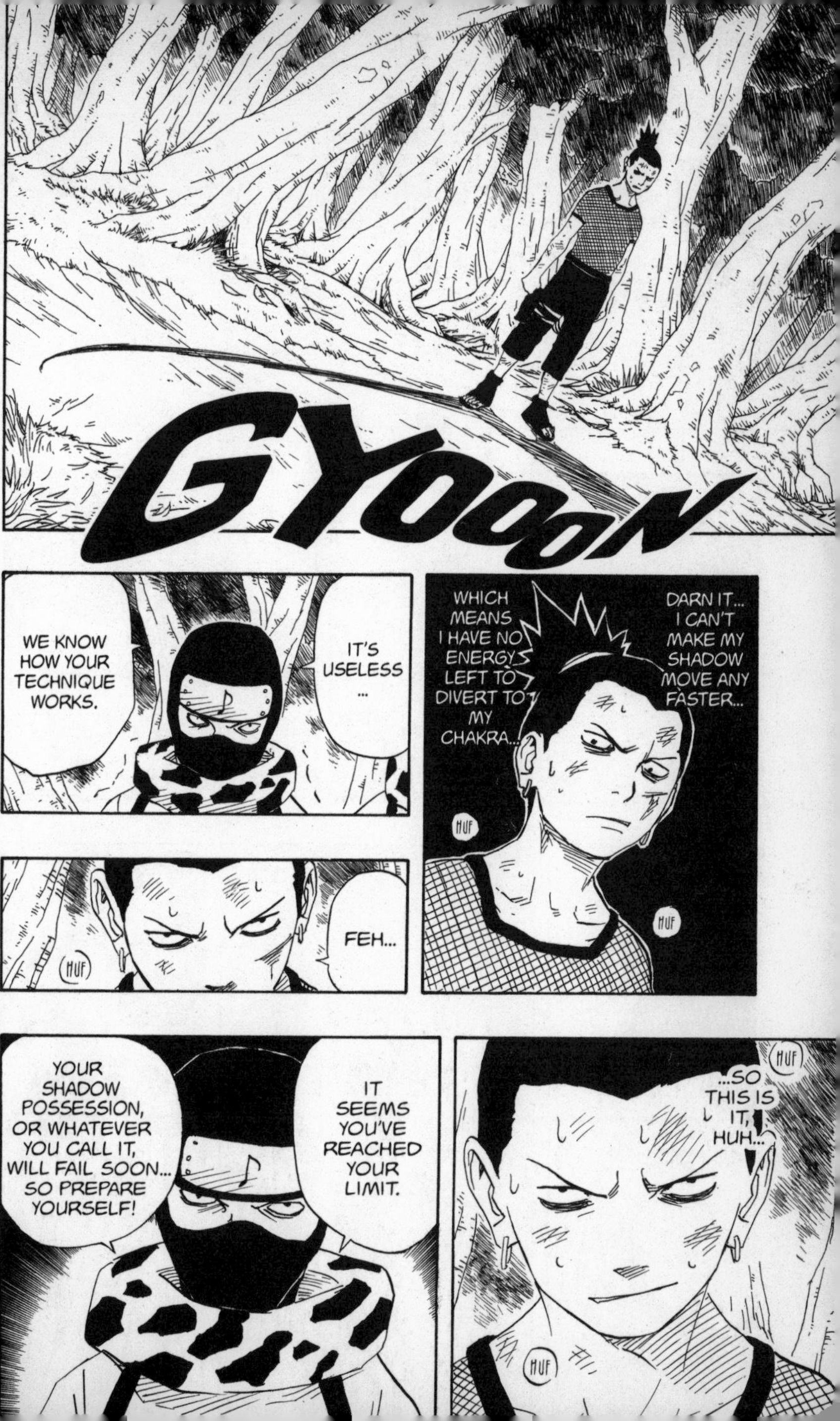
GYOOON
DARN IT... I CAN'T MAKE MY SHADOW MOVE ANY FASTER...
WHICH MEANS I HAVE NO ENERGY LEFT TO DIVERT TO MY CHAKRA...
HUF
HUF
IT'S USELESS...
WE KNOW HOW YOUR TECHNIQUE WORKS.
FEH...
HUF
HUF
...SO THIS IS IT, HUH...
HUF
IT SEEMS YOU'VE REACHED YOUR LIMIT.
YOUR SHADOW POSSESSION, OR WHATEVER YOU CALL IT, WILL FAIL SOON... SO PREPARE YOURSELF!

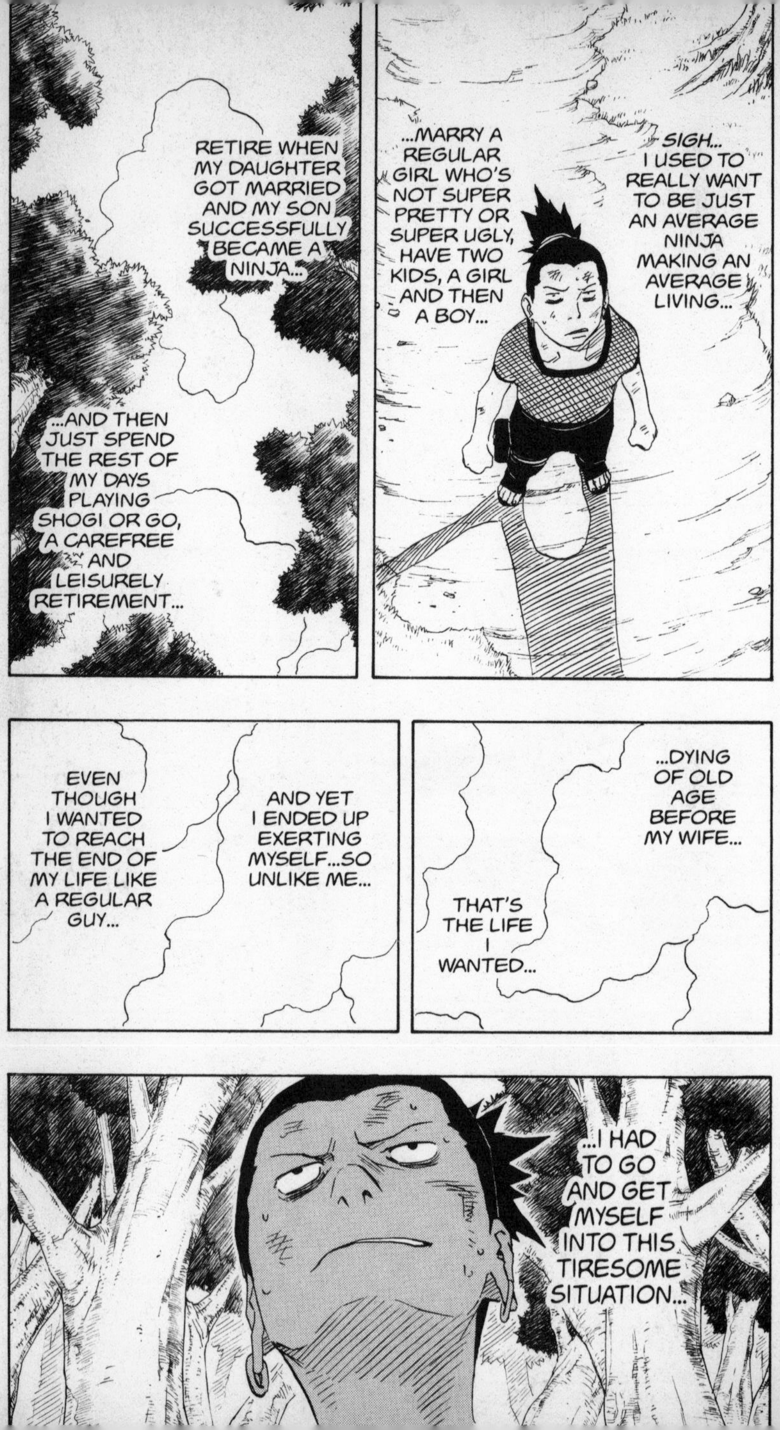
SIGH... I USED TO REALLY WANT TO BE JUST AN AVERAGE NINJA MAKING AN AVERAGE LIVING...
...MARRY A REGULAR GIRL WHO'S NOT SUPER PRETTY OR SUPER UGLY, HAVE TWO KIDS, A GIRL AND THEN A BOY...
RETIRE WHEN MY DAUGHTER GOT MARRIED AND MY SON SUCCESSFULLY BECAME A NINJA...
...AND THEN JUST SPEND THE REST OF MY DAYS PLAYING SHOGI OR GO, A CAREFREE AND LEISURELY RETIREMENT...
...DYING OF OLD AGE BEFORE MY WIFE...
THAT'S THE LIFE I WANTED...
EVEN THOUGH I WANTED TO REACH THE END OF MY LIFE LIKE A REGULAR GUY...
AND YET I ENDED UP EXERTING MYSELF...SO UNLIKE ME...
...I HAD TO GO AND GET MYSELF INTO THIS TIRESOME SITUATION...

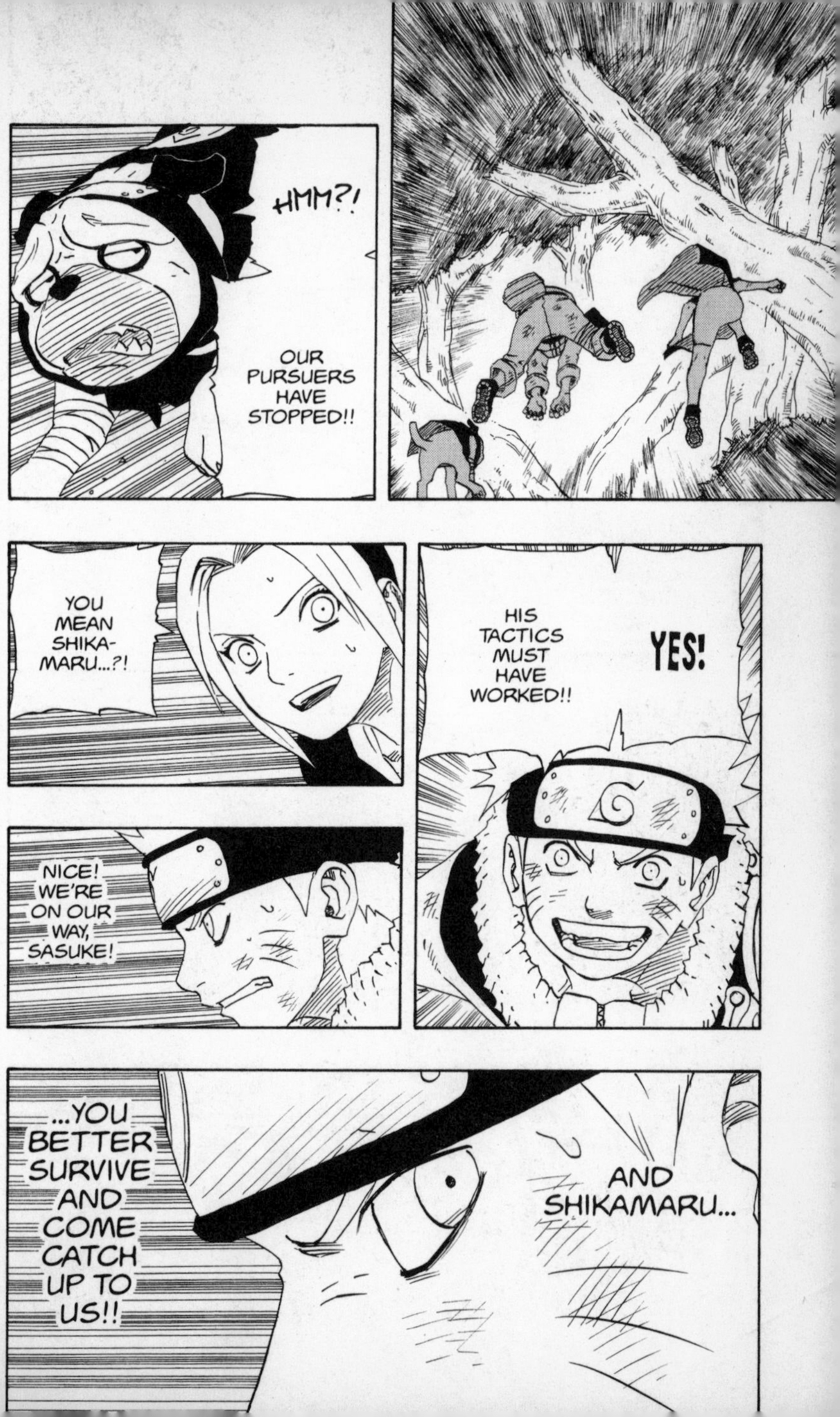
HMM?!
OUR PURSUERS HAVE STOPPED!!
YES!
HIS TACTICS MUST HAVE WORKED!!
YOU MEAN SHIKA-MARU...?!
NICE! WE'RE ON OUR WAY, SASUKE!
AND SHIKAMARU...
...YOU BETTER SURVIVE AND COME CATCH UP TO US!!

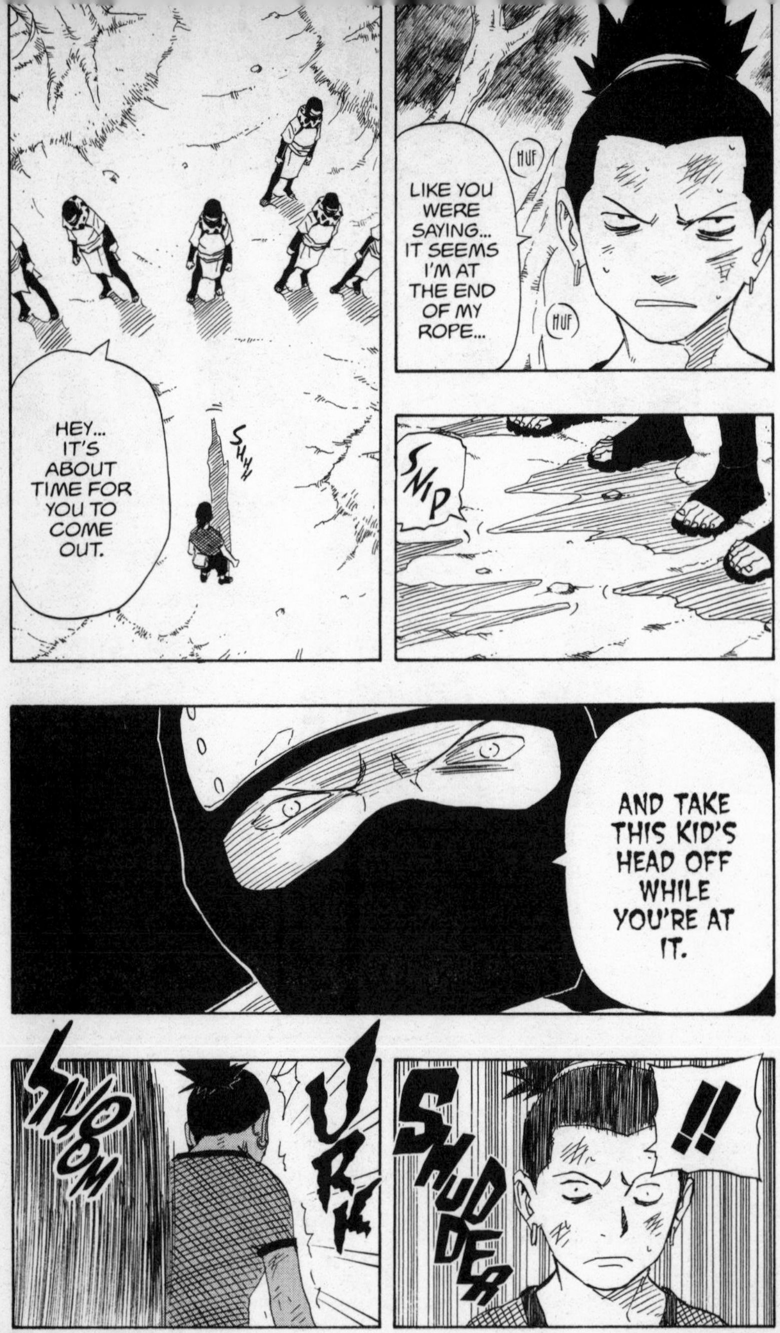
HUF
LIKE YOU WERE SAYING... IT SEEMS I'M AT THE END OF MY ROPE...
HUF
SNIP
HEY... IT'S ABOUT TIME FOR YOU TO COME OUT.
SHHH
AND TAKE THIS KID'S HEAD OFF WHILE YOU'RE AT IT.
!!
SHUDDER
URK
SHOOM

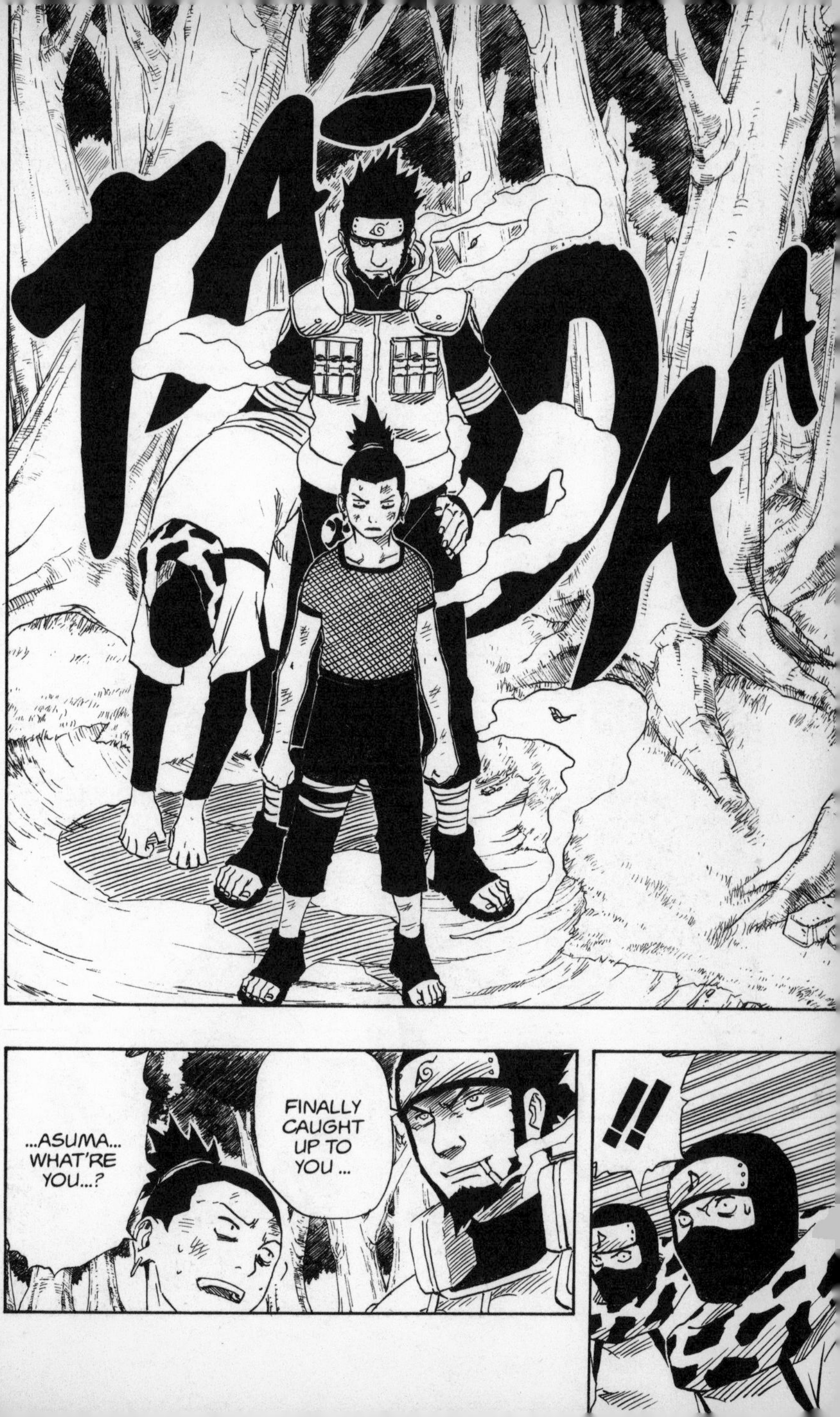
TA DA
!!
FINALLY CAUGHT UP TO YOU ...
...ASUMA... WHAT'RE YOU...?

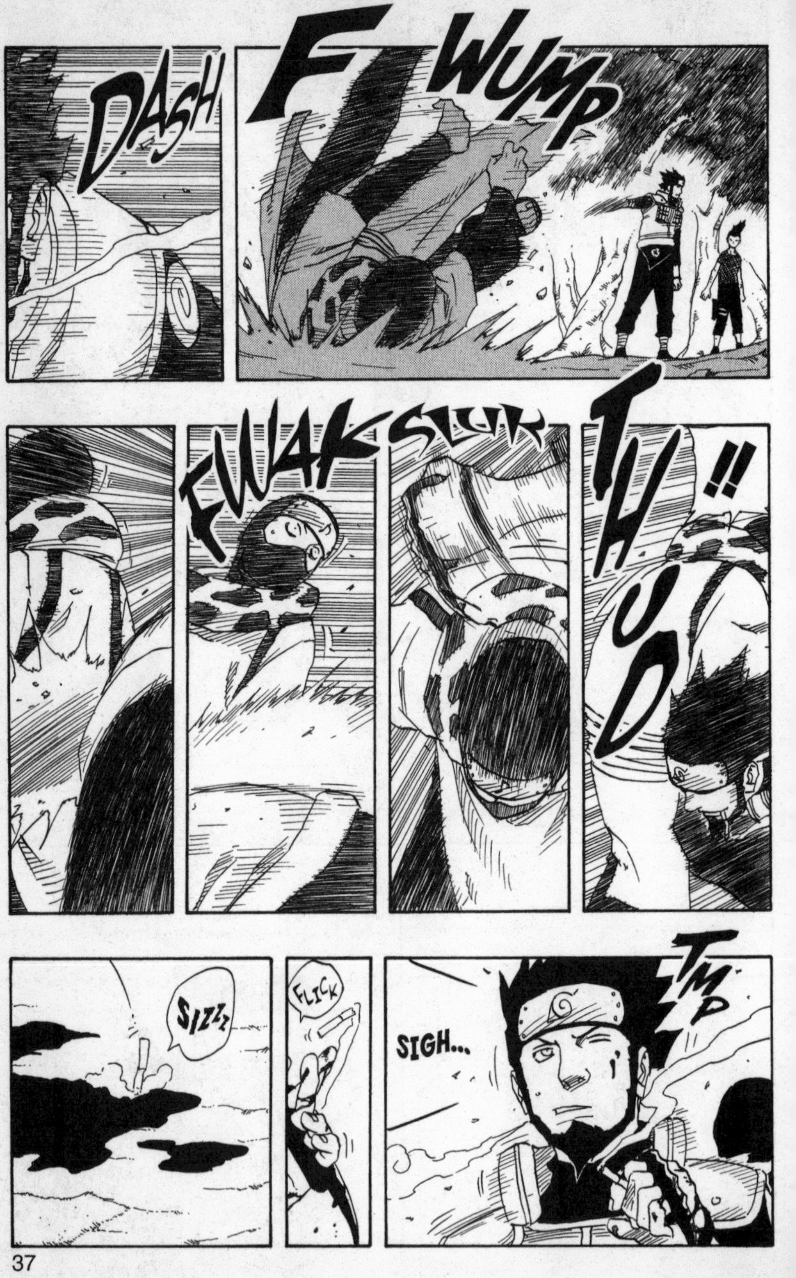
FWUMP
DASH
THUD!!
SLURK
FWAK
TMP
SIGH...
FLICK
SIZZZ

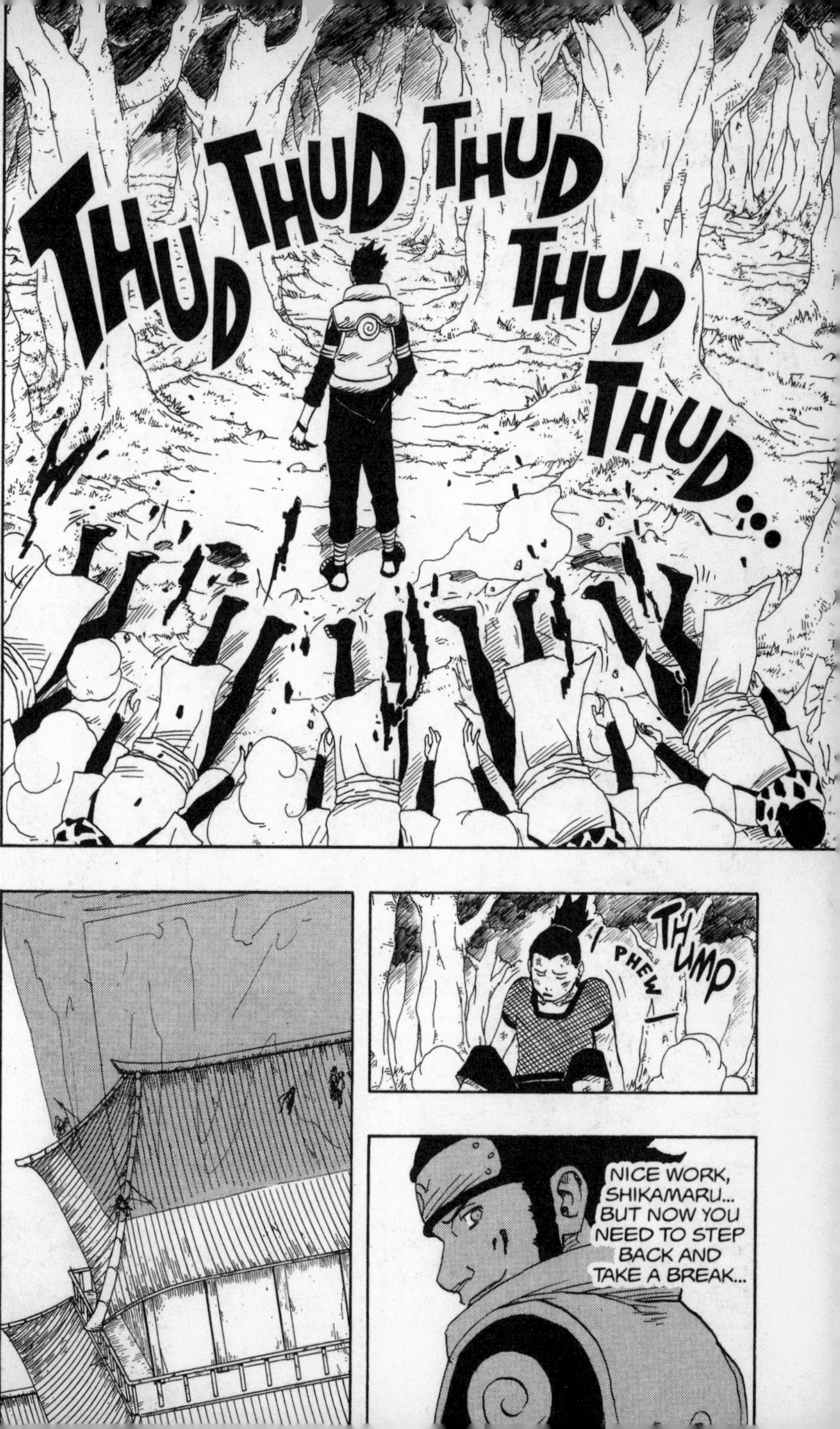
THUD THUD THUD THUD THUD THUD...
PHEW
THUMP
NICE WORK, SHIKAMARU... BUT NOW YOU NEED TO STEP BACK AND TAKE A BREAK...

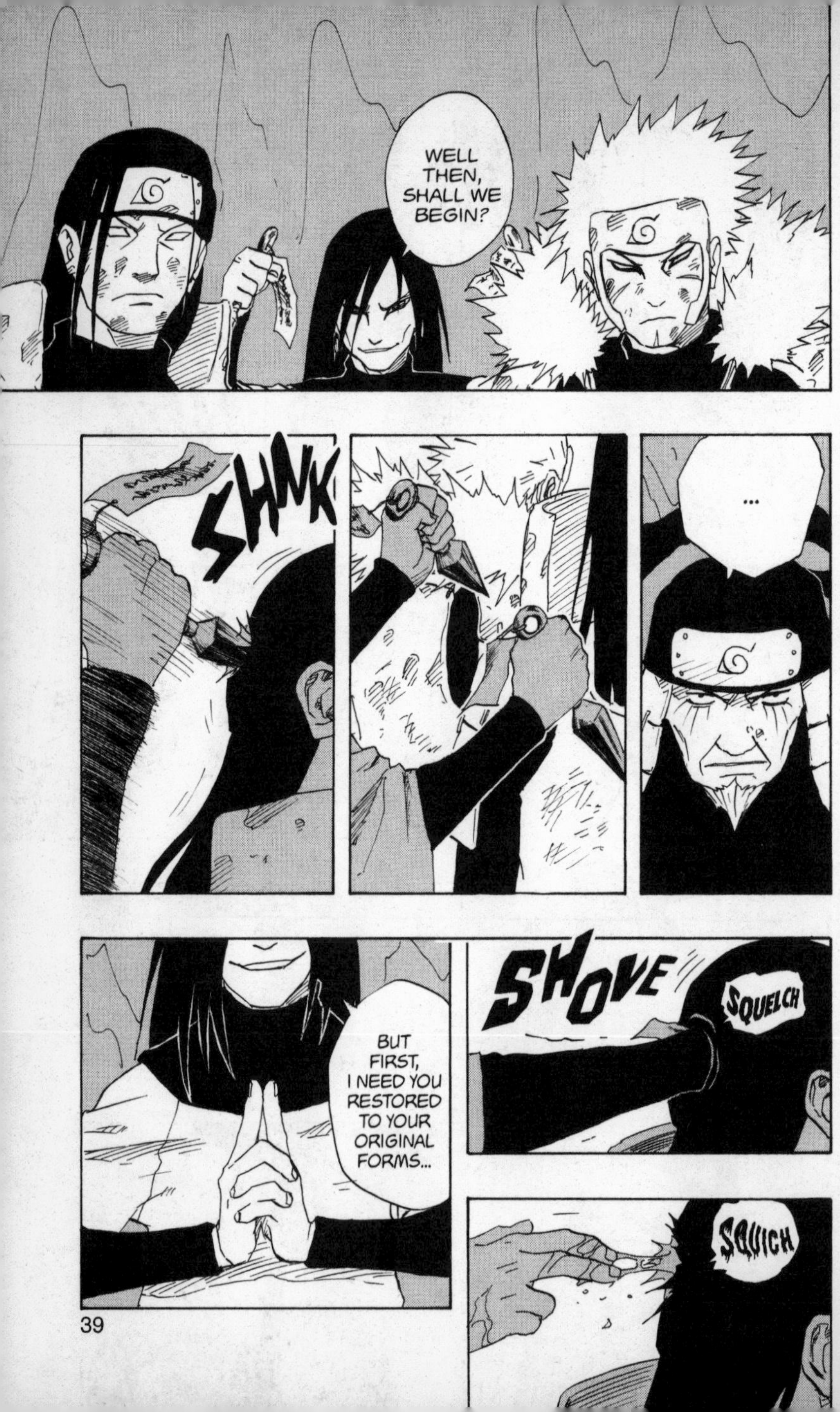
WELL THEN, SHALL WE BEGIN?
...
SHNK
SHOVE
SQUELCH
SQUICH
BUT FIRST, I NEED YOU RESTORED TO YOUR ORIGINAL FORMS...

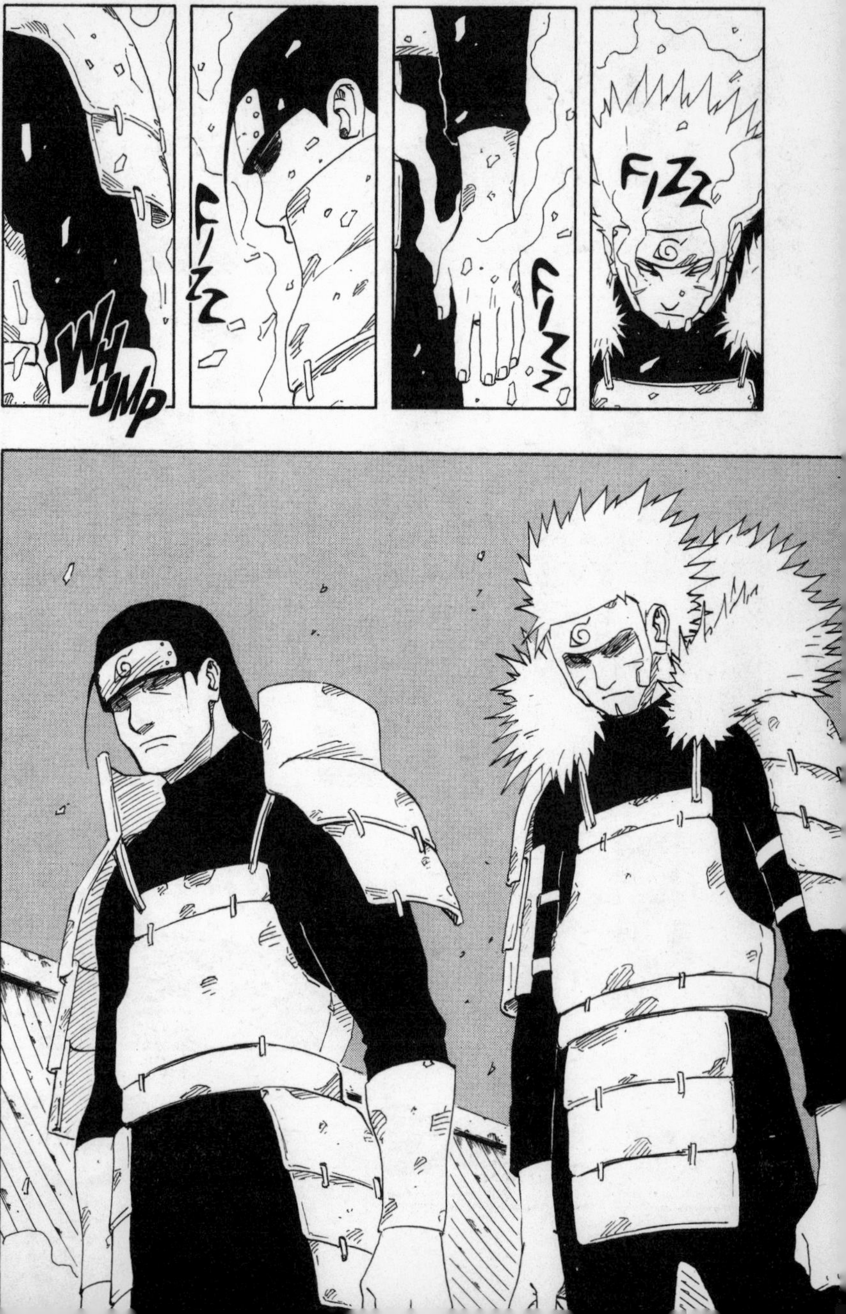
FIZZ
FIZZ
FIZZ
WHUMP

READ THIS WAY

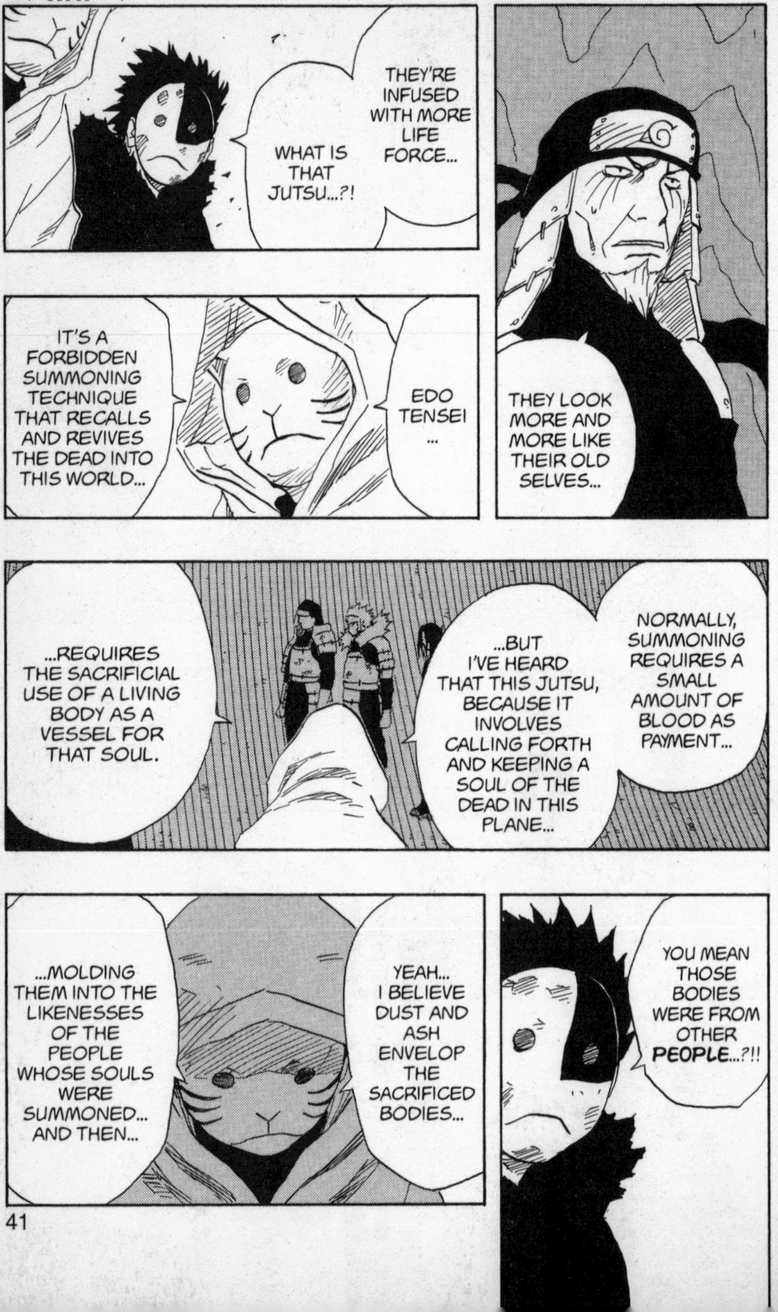

THEY LOOK MORE AND MORE LIKE THEIR OLD SELVES...
THEY'RE INFUSED WITH MORE LIFE FORCE...
WHAT IS THAT JUTSU...?!
EDO TENSEI ...
IT'S A FORBIDDEN SUMMONING TECHNIQUE THAT RECALLS AND REVIVES THE DEAD INTO THIS WORLD...
NORMALLY, SUMMONING REQUIRES A SMALL AMOUNT OF BLOOD AS PAYMENT...
...BUT I'VE HEARD THAT THIS JUTSU, BECAUSE IT INVOLVES CALLING FORTH AND KEEPING A SOUL OF THE DEAD IN THIS PLANE...
...REQUIRES THE SACRIFICIAL USE OF A LIVING BODY AS A VESSEL FOR THAT SOUL.
YOU MEAN THOSE BODIES WERE FROM OTHER **PEOPLE**...?!!
YEAH... I BELIEVE DUST AND ASH ENVELOP THE SACRIFICED BODIES...
...MOLDING THEM INTO THE LIKENESSES OF THE PEOPLE WHOSE SOULS WERE SUMMONED... AND THEN...

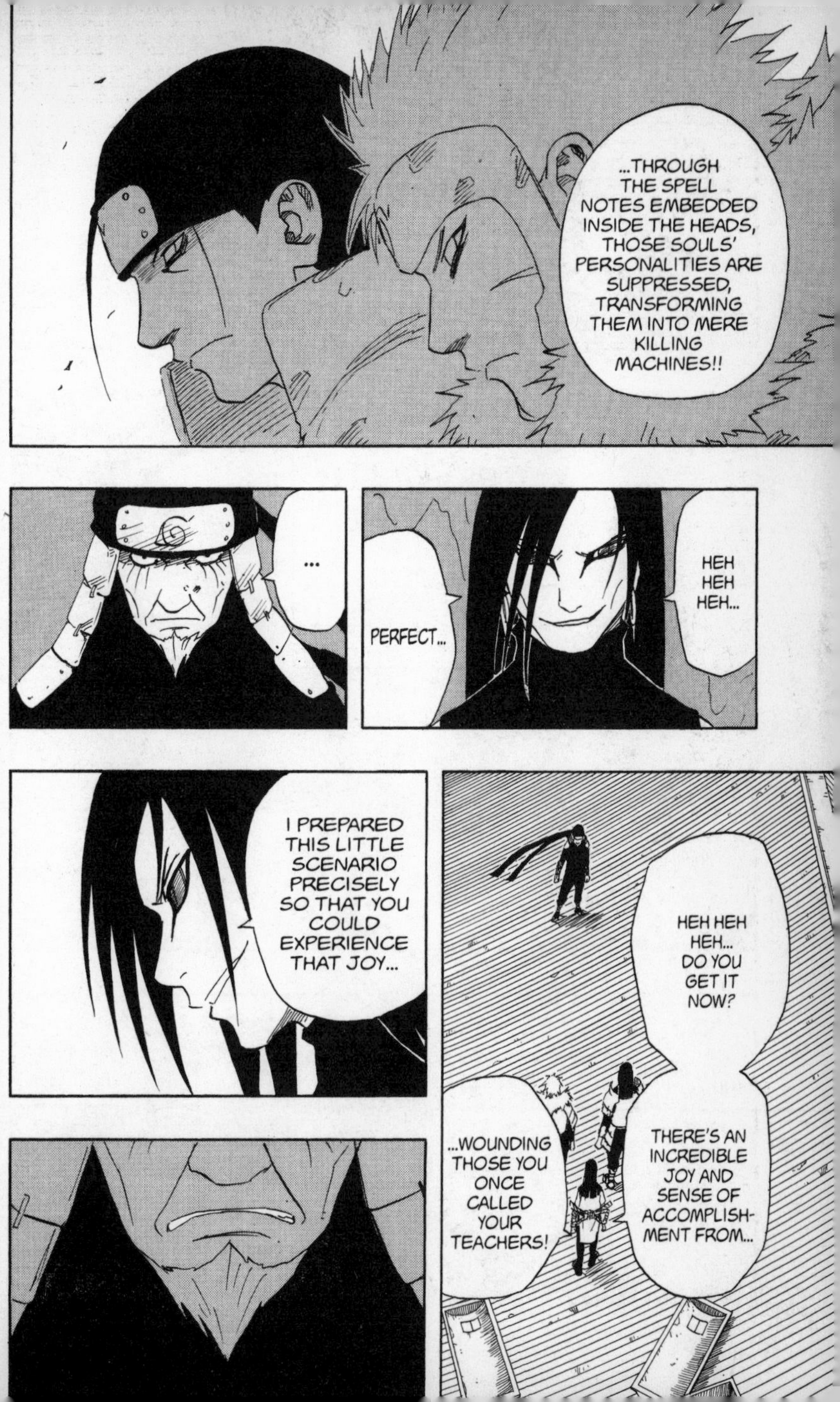
...THROUGH THE SPELL NOTES EMBEDDED INSIDE THE HEADS, THOSE SOULS' PERSONALITIES ARE SUPPRESSED, TRANSFORMING THEM INTO MERE KILLING MACHINES!!
HEH HEH HEH...
PERFECT...
...
HEH HEH HEH... DO YOU GET IT NOW?
THERE'S AN INCREDIBLE JOY AND SENSE OF ACCOMPLISHMENT FROM...
...WOUNDING THOSE YOU ONCE CALLED YOUR TEACHERS!
I PREPARED THIS LITTLE SCENARIO PRECISELY SO THAT YOU COULD EXPERIENCE THAT JOY...

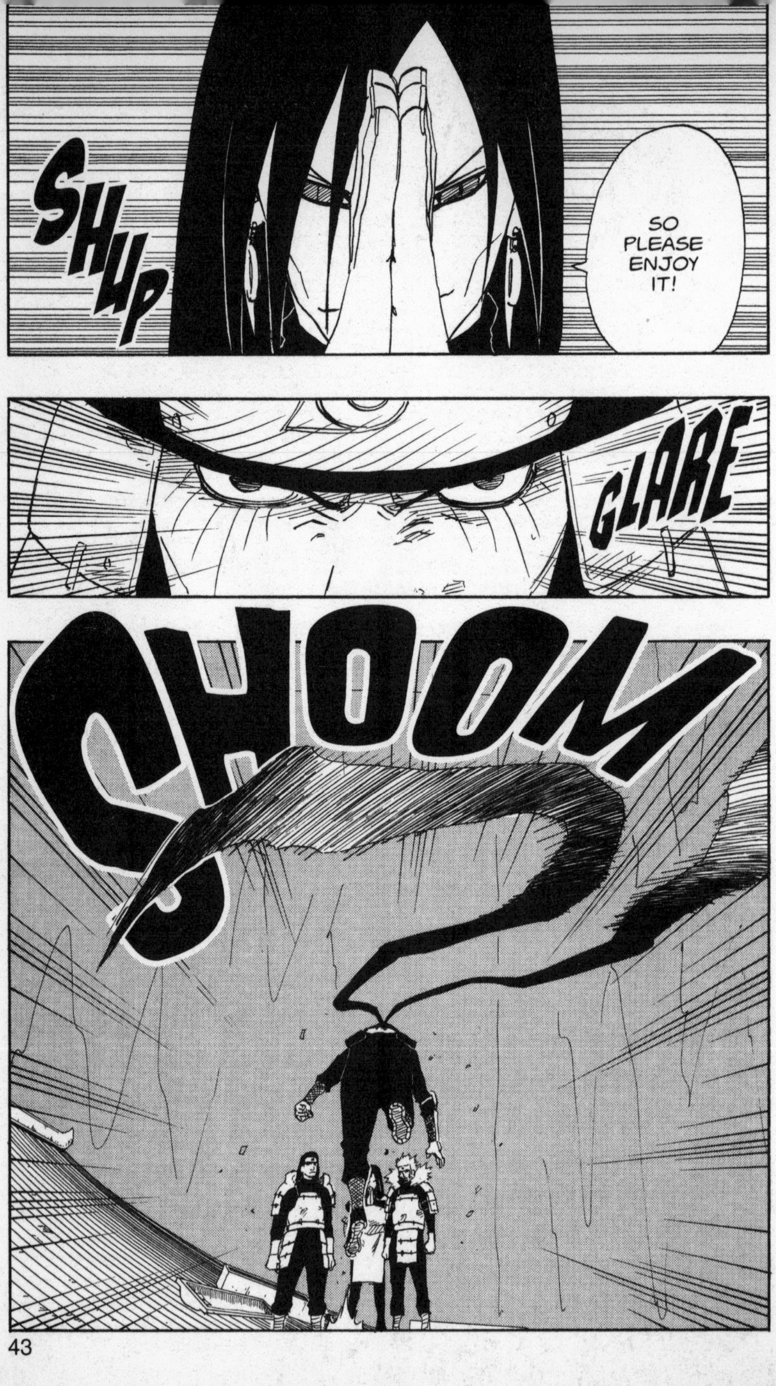
SO PLEASE ENJOY IT!
SHUP
GLARE
SHOOM

THE WORLD OF KISHIMOTO MASASHI
MY PERSONAL HISTORY, PART 19

EVEN AS I WAS COMPLETING MY SECOND YEAR OF COLLEGE, I STILL COULDN'T DRAW AN ADEQUATE MANGA. THAT'S WHEN I SUDDENLY ASKED MYSELF, "WHAT IS MANGA?" REALIZING THAT I HAD TO UNDERSTAND MANGA MORE THOROUGHLY, I DECIDED THAT I NEEDED TO TAKE IT APART AND ANALYZE IT. SO I CAME TO KNOW THAT THE BASIC ELEMENTS OF MANGA ARE CHARACTERS, MOTIF, STORY, THEME, DIRECTION IN THE FORM OF PICTURE COMPOSITION (WIDE ANGLE, ZOOM IF USING CAMERA ANGLES AS AN ANALOGY), SOUND (SOUND EFFECTS), ACTION, EFFECTS, ONE-, TWO- AND THREE-POINT LINEAR PERSPECTIVE FOR THE BACKGROUND, AND THEN TIMING, SENSE, AND MANY OTHER FACTORS. AND WHILE MY COMPREHENSION WAS GREAT, AS I CONTINUED MY ANALYSIS I STARTED SEEING MORE AND MORE THINGS THAT I WASN'T GOOD AT OR SKILLS THAT I LACKED. FEELING OVERWHELMED BY THE AMOUNT OF LEARNING AND HONING I STILL HAD TO DO, I FELL INTO A SMALL PANIC. I BEGAN TO UNDERSTAND THAT UNLESS I COMPREHENDED AND MASTERED ALL THOSE FACTORS MYSELF, I COULDN'T EVEN BEGIN TO DRAW EVEN A SIMPLE "WELL, IT'S KINDA INTERESTING" LIGHT-READ TYPE OF MANGA.

SOMEHOW, I SUDDENLY BECAME TERRIFIED OF MANGA, THINKING OF THEM AS MONSTERS, AND BECAME AFRAID OF DRAWING MANGA. THAT PAINFUL PERIOD LASTED FOR SEVERAL MONTHS; AND JUST AS I WAS SLIDING INTO AN EMOTIONALLY DRAINED STATE, A FRIEND OF MINE BOUGHT AN ISSUE OF JUMP AND STARTED READING *SLAM DUNK* IN MY ROOM... WHEN I LOOKED AT HIS FACE, I NOTICED THAT HE HAD AN AVID AND HAPPY EXPRESSION. AND THEN, WHEN HE FINISHED THE CHAPTER, HE EXCLAIMED, "WOW! *SLAM DUNK* IS SO COOL!!"

SUDDENLY, I HAD AN URGE TO ASK HIM A QUESTION. THIS QUESTION WAS A REALLY SCARY QUESTION FOR ME TO ASK. FOR THAT FRIEND WAS ONE WHO WOULD NEVER LIE TO ME, AND HE ALSO KNEW MANGA WELL. SO THIS IS WHAT I ASKED:

"WHAT'S THE DIFFERENCE BETWEEN *SLAM DUNK* AND MY MANGA? WHY IS *SLAM DUNK* SO COOL AND INTERESTING?"

OF COURSE, I MYSELF ALSO LOVED *SLAM DUNK*, AND WOULD BE THE FIRST TO ADMIT THAT IT WAS VERY INTERESTING! I JUST WANTED TO GET AN OUTSIDE, OBJECTIVE VIEW OF THE DIFFERENCES BETWEEN *SLAM DUNK* AND MY MANGA.
MY FRIEND REPLIED THUS:

"YOU CAN TELL FROM READING IT HOW MUCH MR. INOUE TAKEHIKO REALLY LOVES BASKETBALL. AND YOU CAN FEEL HOW MUCH FUN HE HAS DRAWING *SLAM DUNK*, AND IT'S LIKE MR. INOUE'S DRAWING IT WITH THE MESSAGE 'PLEASE READ IT, BASKETBALL IS LOTS OF FUN' TO THE READERS. WITH YOUR MANGA, I'M SURE YOU'RE DRAWING BECAUSE YOU REALLY LOVE IT TOO, BUT IT'S JUST NOT COMING THROUGH AS FUN... IT'S LIKE, YOU'RE HAVING ALL THE FUN BY YOURSELF AND WE'RE BEING LEFT OUT OR LEFT BEHIND. THERE'S NO SENSE OF 'PLEASE READ IT'..."

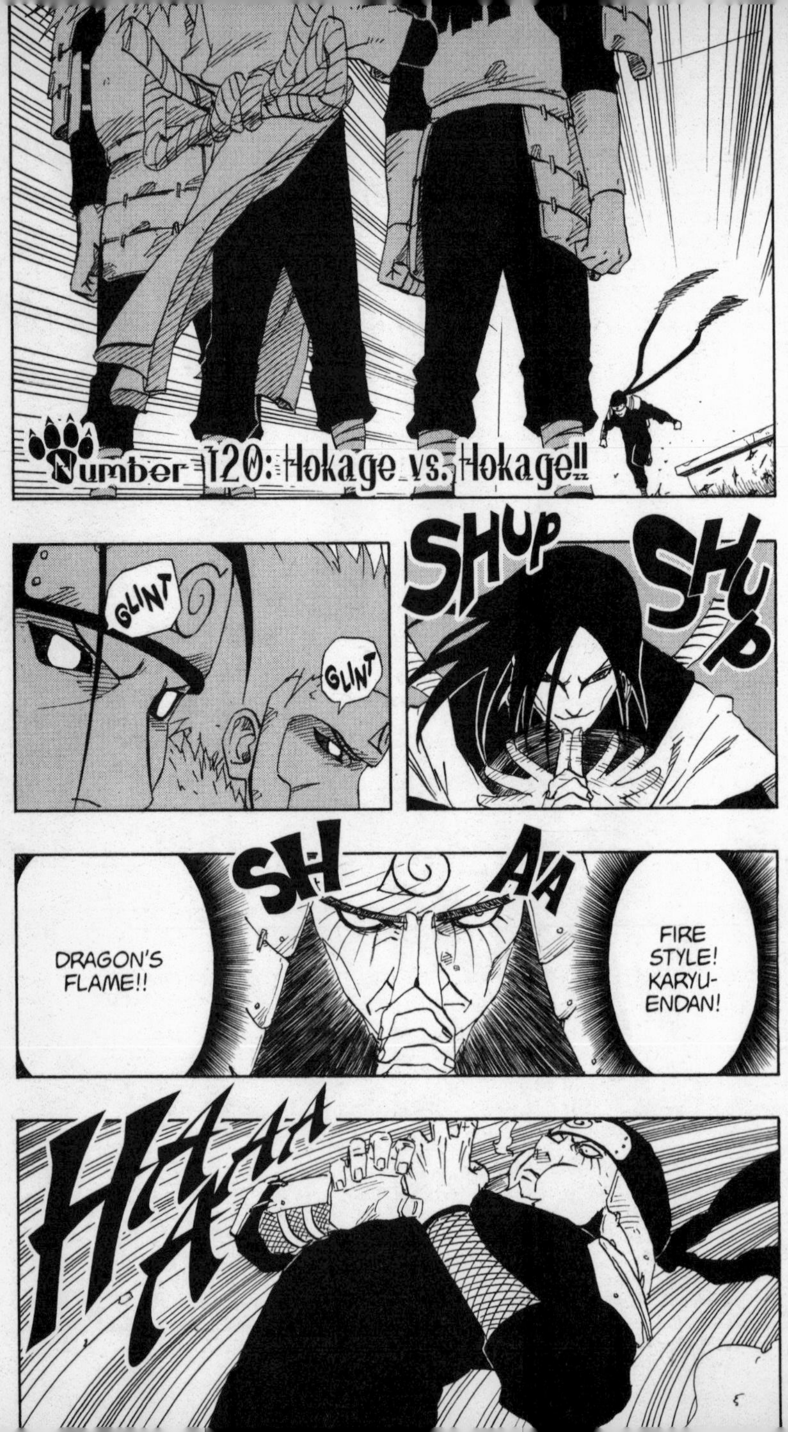
Number 120: Hokage vs. Hokage!!
SHUP SHUP
GLINT
GLINT
SH AA
FIRE STYLE! KARYU-ENDAN!
DRAGON'S FLAME!!
HYAAA

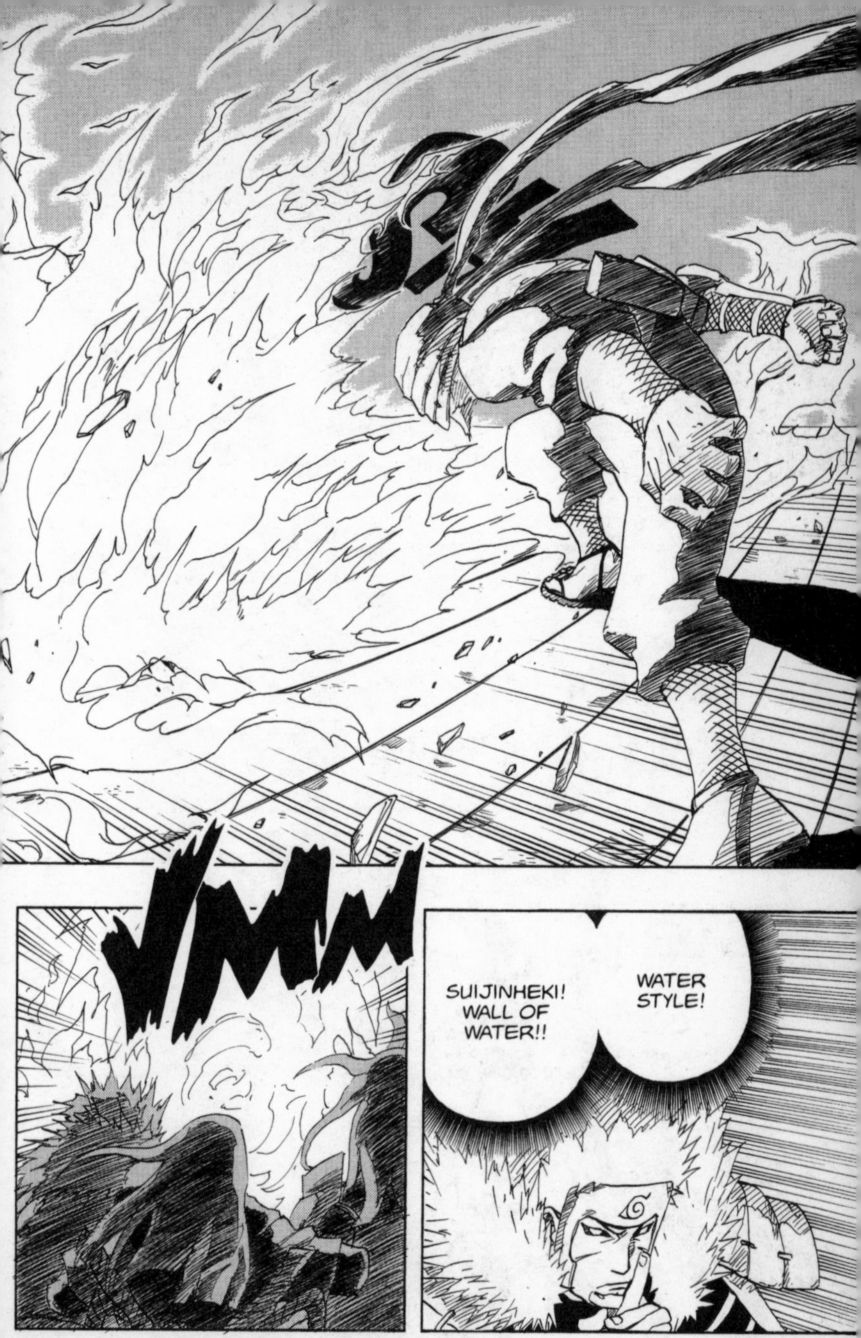
WATER STYLE!
SUIJINHEKI! WALL OF WATER!!
VMM

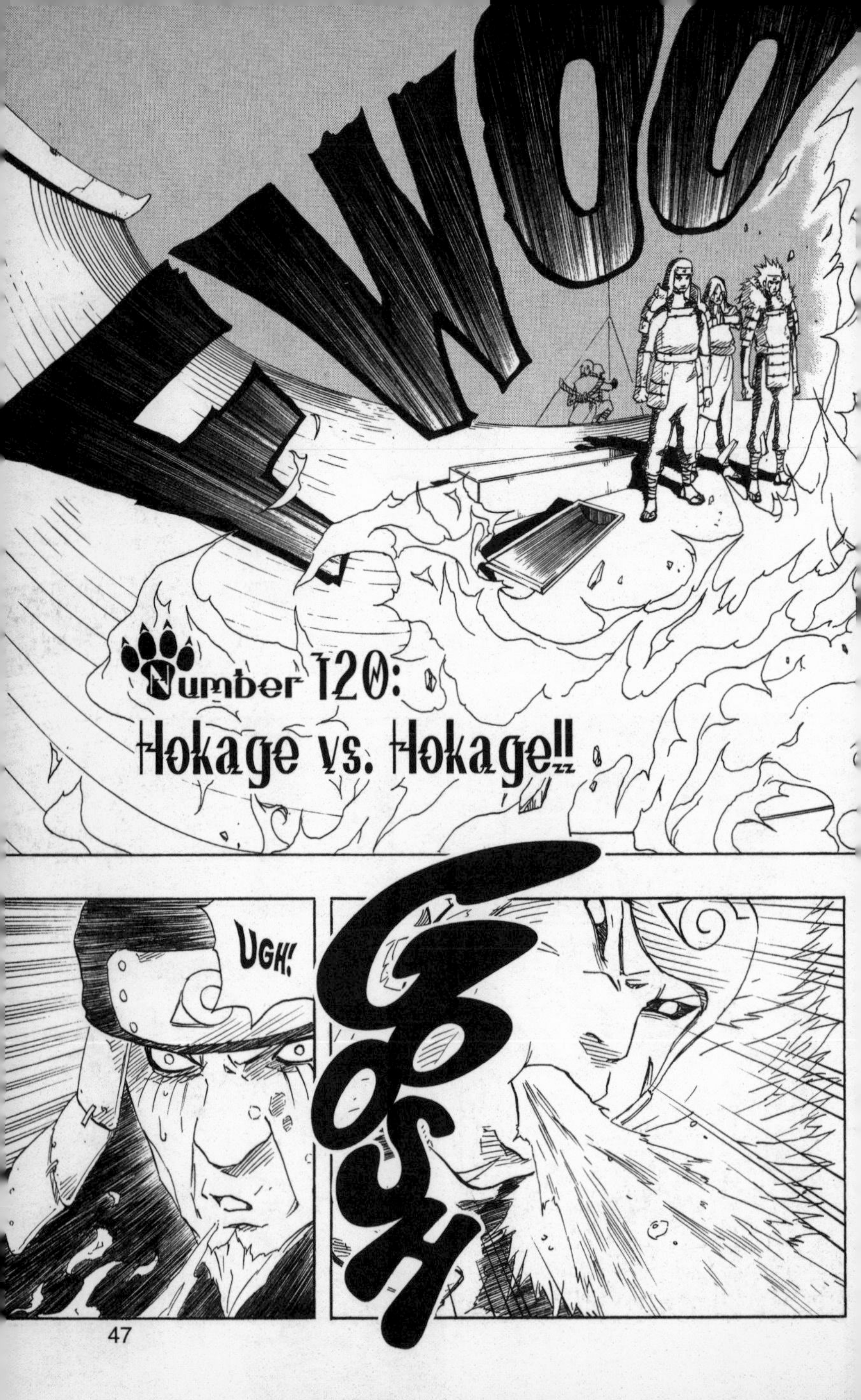
FWOO
Number 120:
Hokage vs. Hokage!!
GOOSH
UGH!

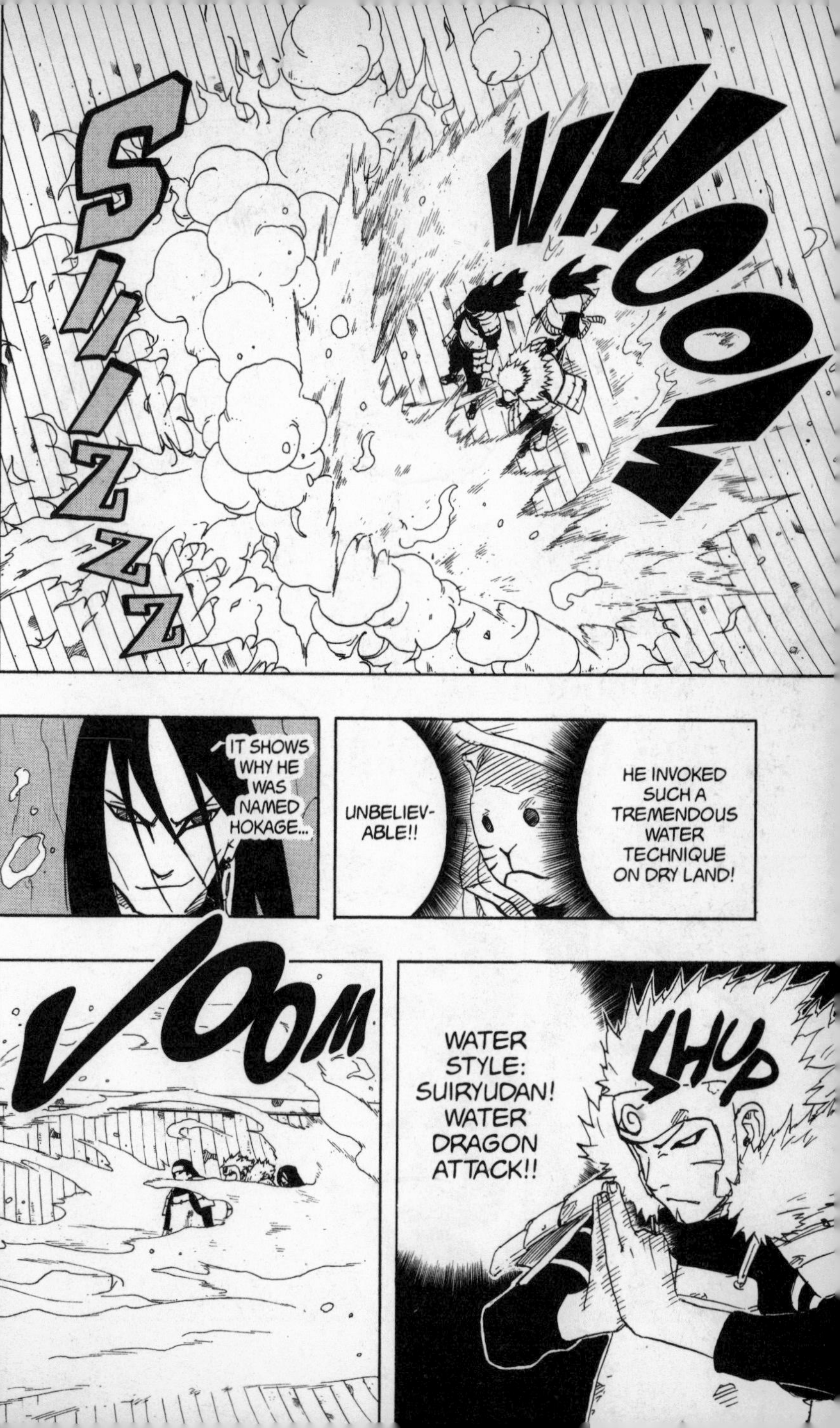
WHOOM
SIIIZZZ
HE INVOKED SUCH A TREMENDOUS WATER TECHNIQUE ON DRY LAND!
UNBELIEV-ABLE!!
IT SHOWS WHY HE WAS NAMED HOKAGE...
SHUP
WATER STYLE: SUIRYUDAN! WATER DRAGON ATTACK!!
VOOM

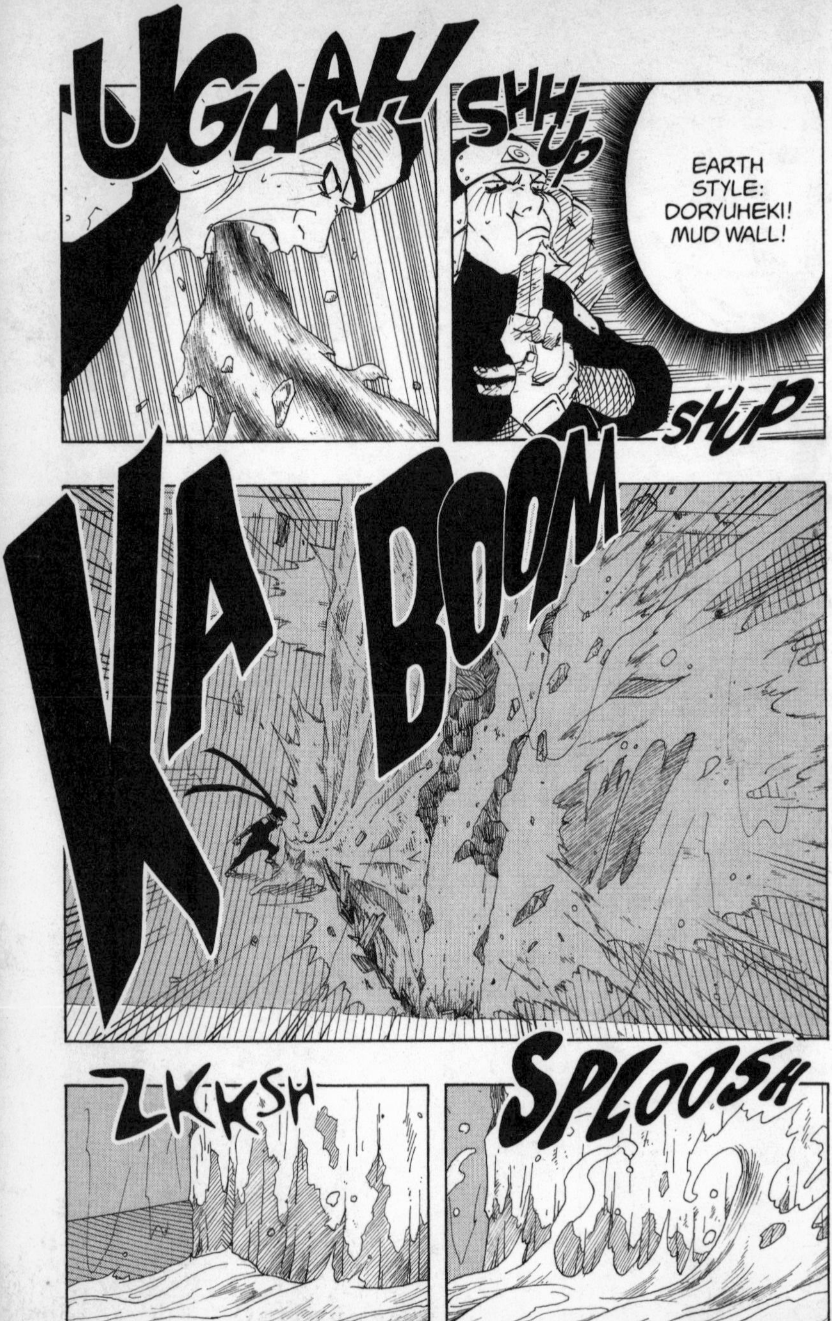
SHHUP
EARTH STYLE: DORYUHEKI! MUD WALL!
SHUP
UGAAH
KA BOOM
SPLOOSH
ZKKSH

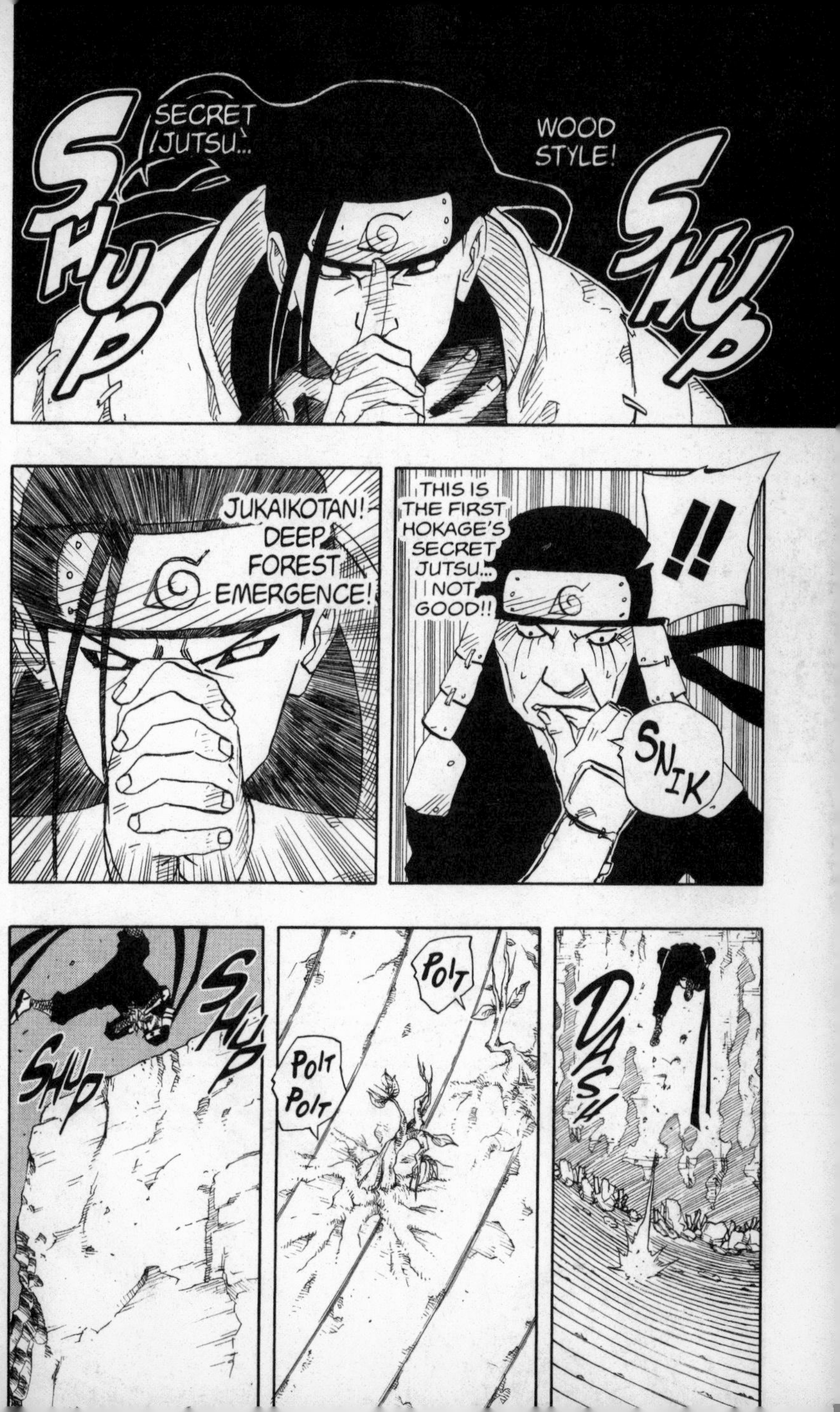
SHUP
WOOD STYLE!
SECRET JUTSU...
SHUP
!!
THIS IS THE FIRST HOKAGE'S SECRET JUTSU... NOT GOOD!!
SNIK
JUKAIKOTAN! DEEP FOREST EMERGENCE!
DASH
POIT
POIT POIT
SHUP
SHUD

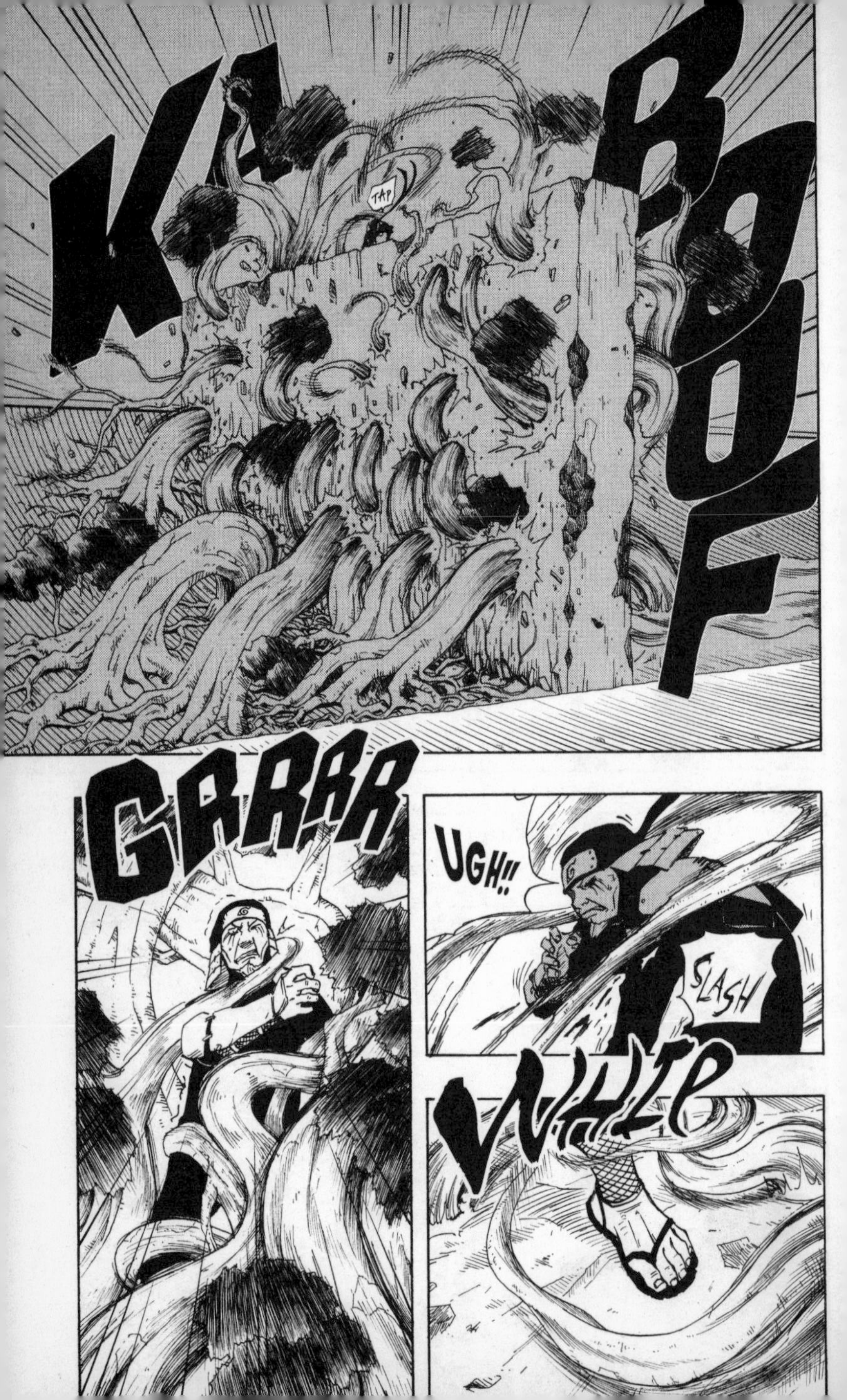
KABOOF
TAP
UGH!!
SLASH
WHIP
GRRRR

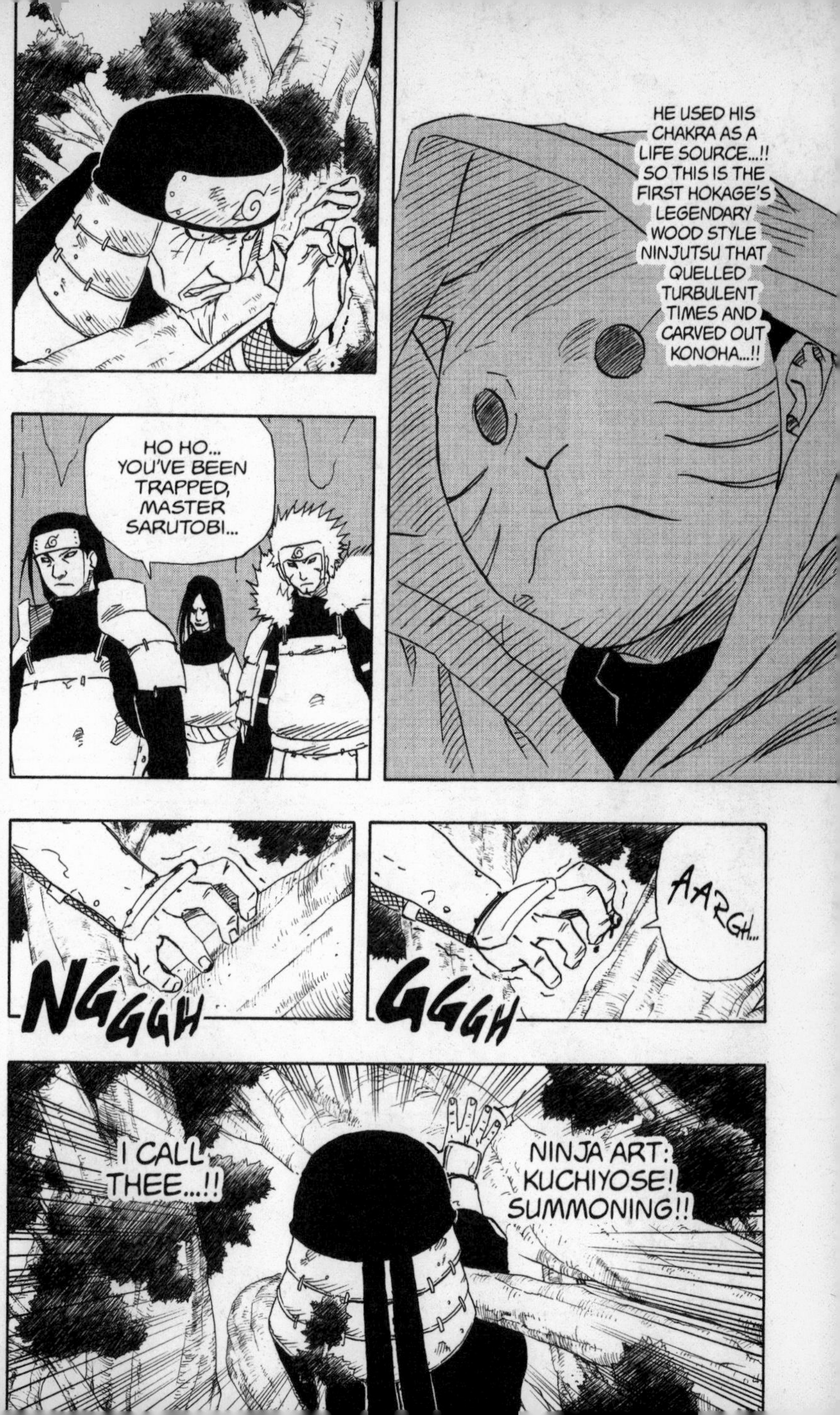
HE USED HIS CHAKRA AS A LIFE SOURCE...!! SO THIS IS THE FIRST HOKAGE'S LEGENDARY WOOD STYLE NINJUTSU THAT QUELLED TURBULENT TIMES AND CARVED OUT KONOHA...!!
HO HO... YOU'VE BEEN TRAPPED, MASTER SARUTOBI...
AARGH...
GGGH
NGGGH
NINJA ART: KUCHIYOSE! SUMMONING!!
I CALL THEE...!!

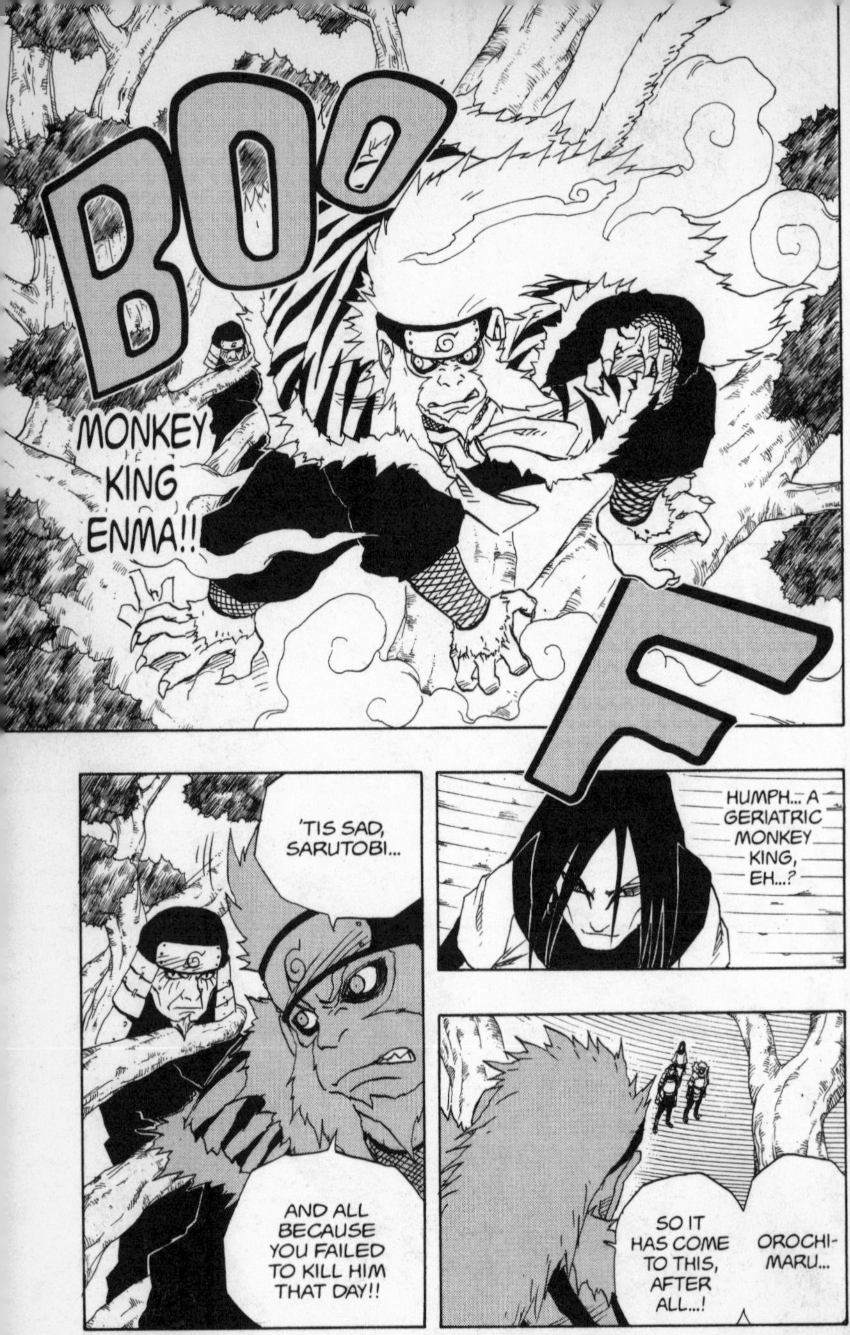
BOOF
MONKEY KING ENMA!!
HUMPH... A GERIATRIC MONKEY KING, EH...?
OROCHI-MARU...
SO IT HAS COME TO THIS, AFTER ALL...!
'TIS SAD, SARUTOBI...
AND ALL BECAUSE YOU FAILED TO KILL HIM THAT DAY!!

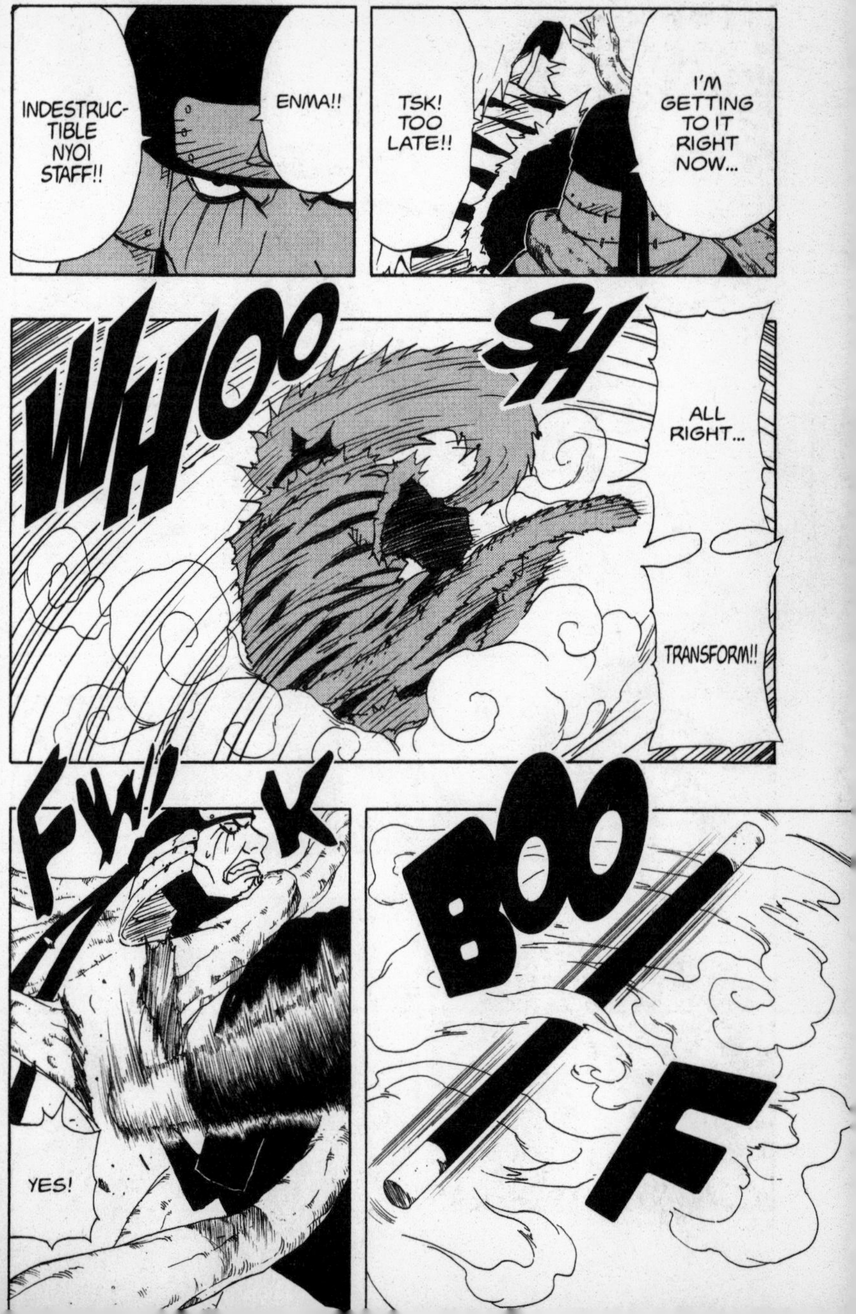
I'M GETTING TO IT RIGHT NOW...
TSK! TOO LATE!!
ENMA!!
INDESTRUCTIBLE NYOI STAFF!!
ALL RIGHT...
TRANSFORM!!
WHOOSH
BOOF
FWIK
YES!

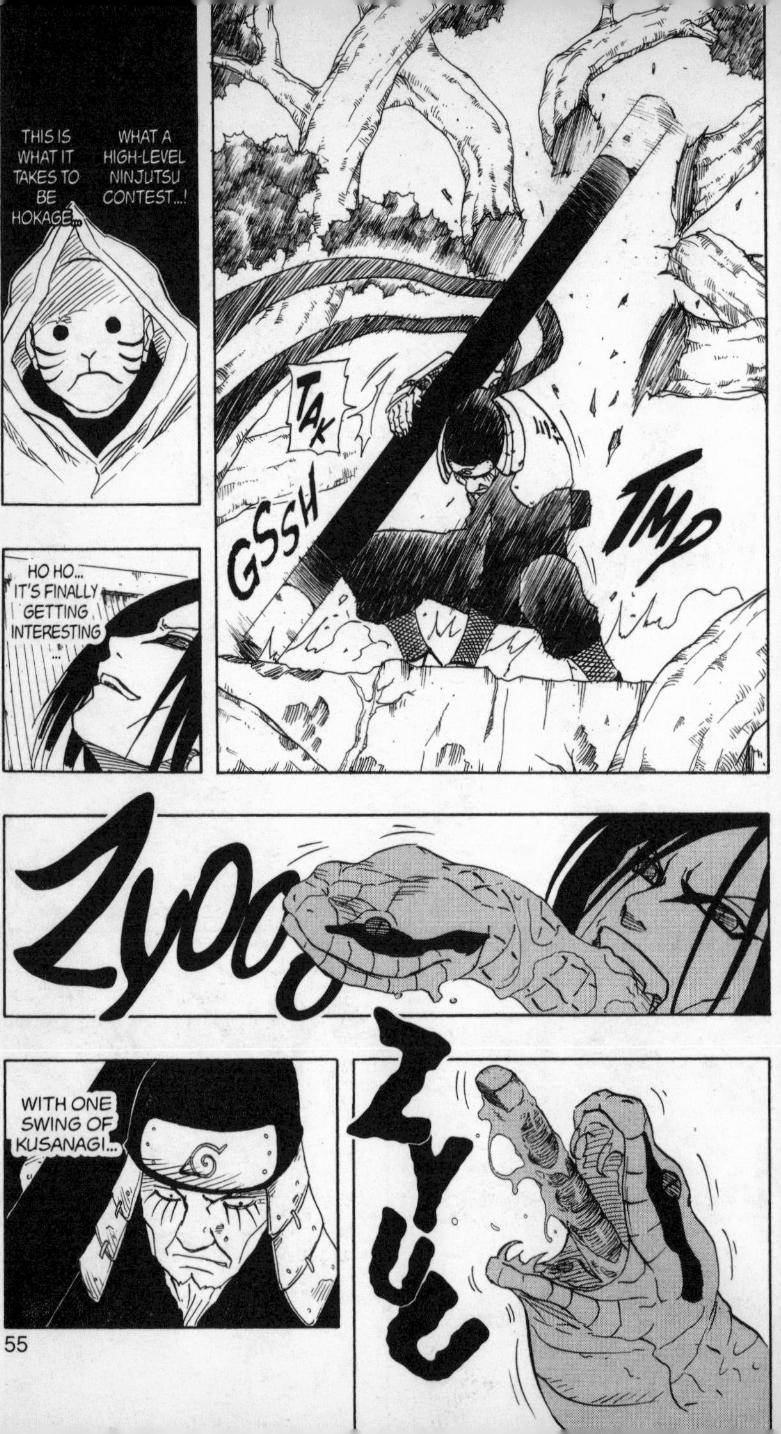
TAK
GSSH
TMP
WHAT A HIGH-LEVEL NINJUTSU CONTEST...!
THIS IS WHAT IT TAKES TO BE HOKAGE...
HO HO... IT'S FINALLY GETTING INTERESTING...
ZYUU
WITH ONE SWING OF KUSANAGI...

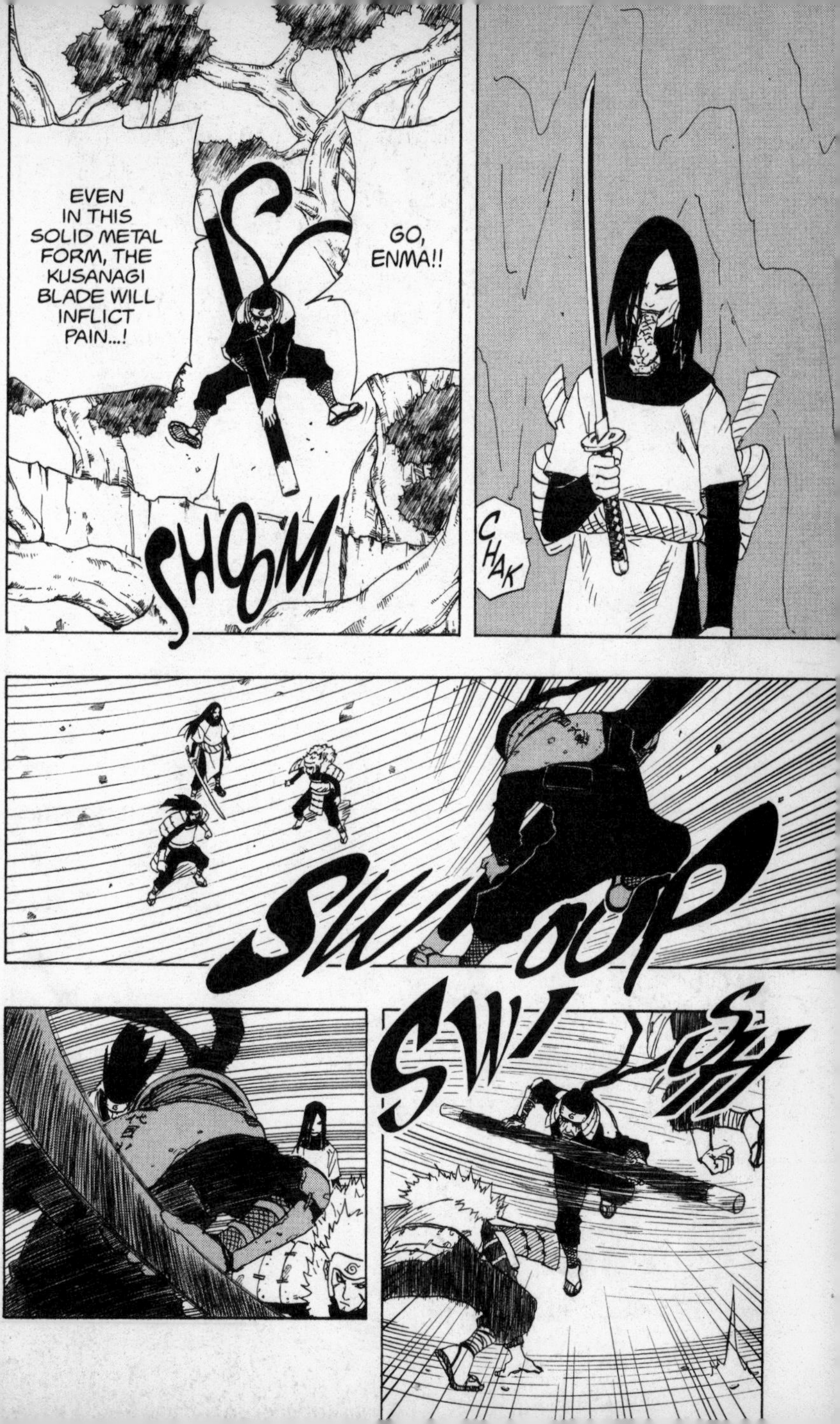
CHAK
GO, ENMA!!
EVEN IN THIS SOLID METAL FORM, THE KUSANAGI BLADE WILL INFLICT PAIN...!
SHOOM
SW OOP
SW SH

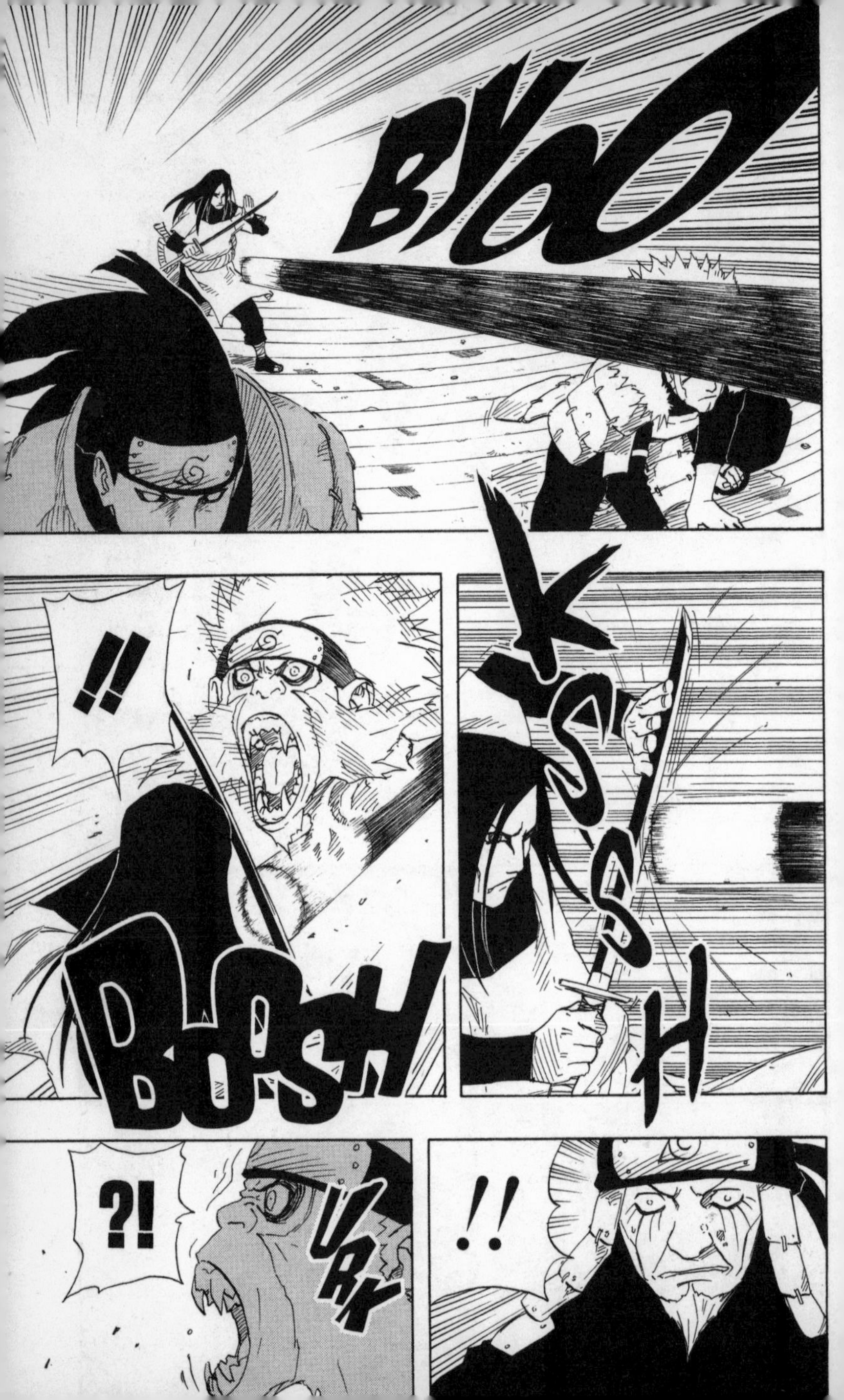
BYOO
KSSH
!!
BOPSH
!!
?!
URK

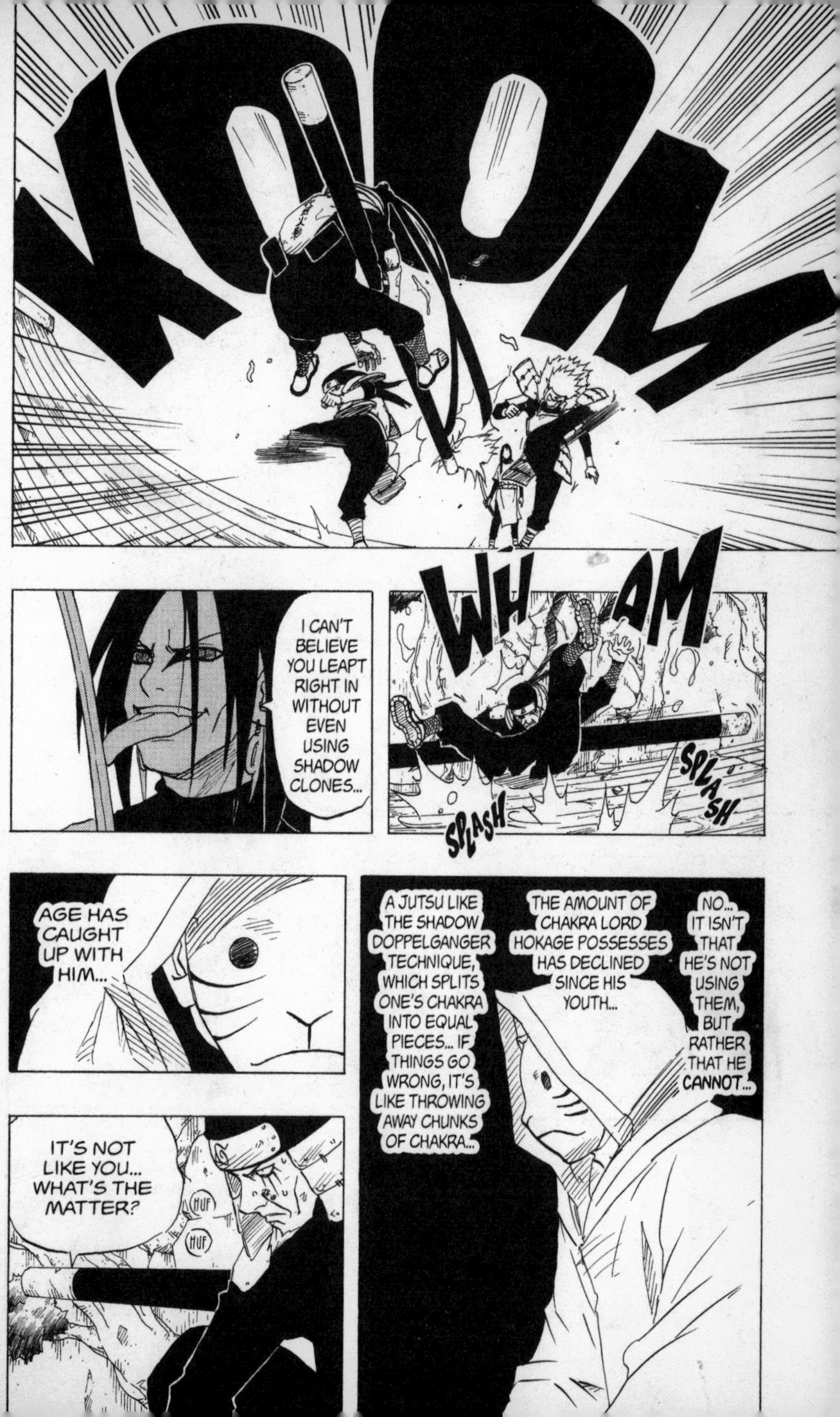
VOOM
WHAM
SPLASH
SPLASH
I CAN'T BELIEVE YOU LEAPT RIGHT IN WITHOUT EVEN USING SHADOW CLONES...
NO... IT ISN'T THAT HE'S NOT USING THEM, BUT RATHER THAT HE **CANNOT**...
THE AMOUNT OF CHAKRA LORD HOKAGE POSSESSES HAS DECLINED SINCE HIS YOUTH...
A JUTSU LIKE THE SHADOW DOPPELGANGER TECHNIQUE, WHICH SPLITS ONE'S CHAKRA INTO EQUAL PIECES... IF THINGS GO WRONG, IT'S LIKE THROWING AWAY CHUNKS OF CHAKRA...
AGE HAS CAUGHT UP WITH HIM...
IT'S NOT LIKE YOU... WHAT'S THE MATTER?
HUF
HUF

READ THIS WAY

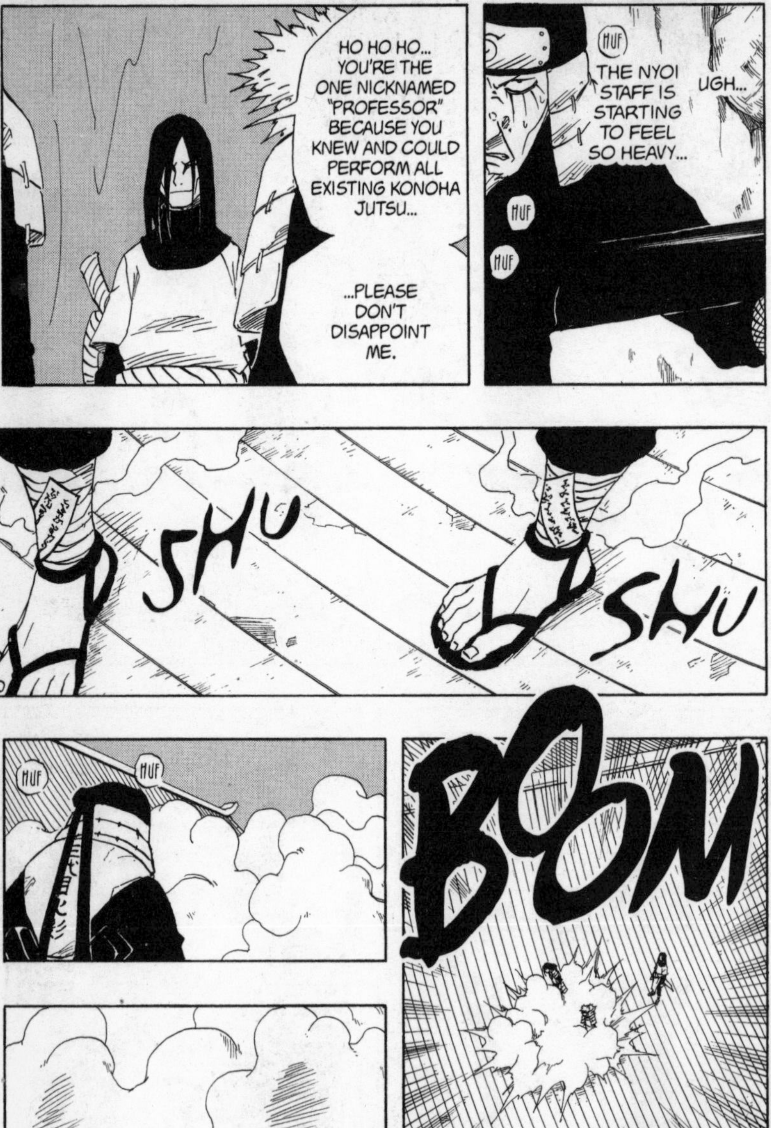
HUF
THE NYOI STAFF IS STARTING TO FEEL SO HEAVY...
UGH...
HUF
HUF
HO HO HO... YOU'RE THE ONE NICKNAMED "PROFESSOR" BECAUSE YOU KNEW AND COULD PERFORM ALL EXISTING KONOHA JUTSU...
...PLEASE DON'T DISAPPOINT ME.
SHU
SHU
BOOM
HUF
HUF

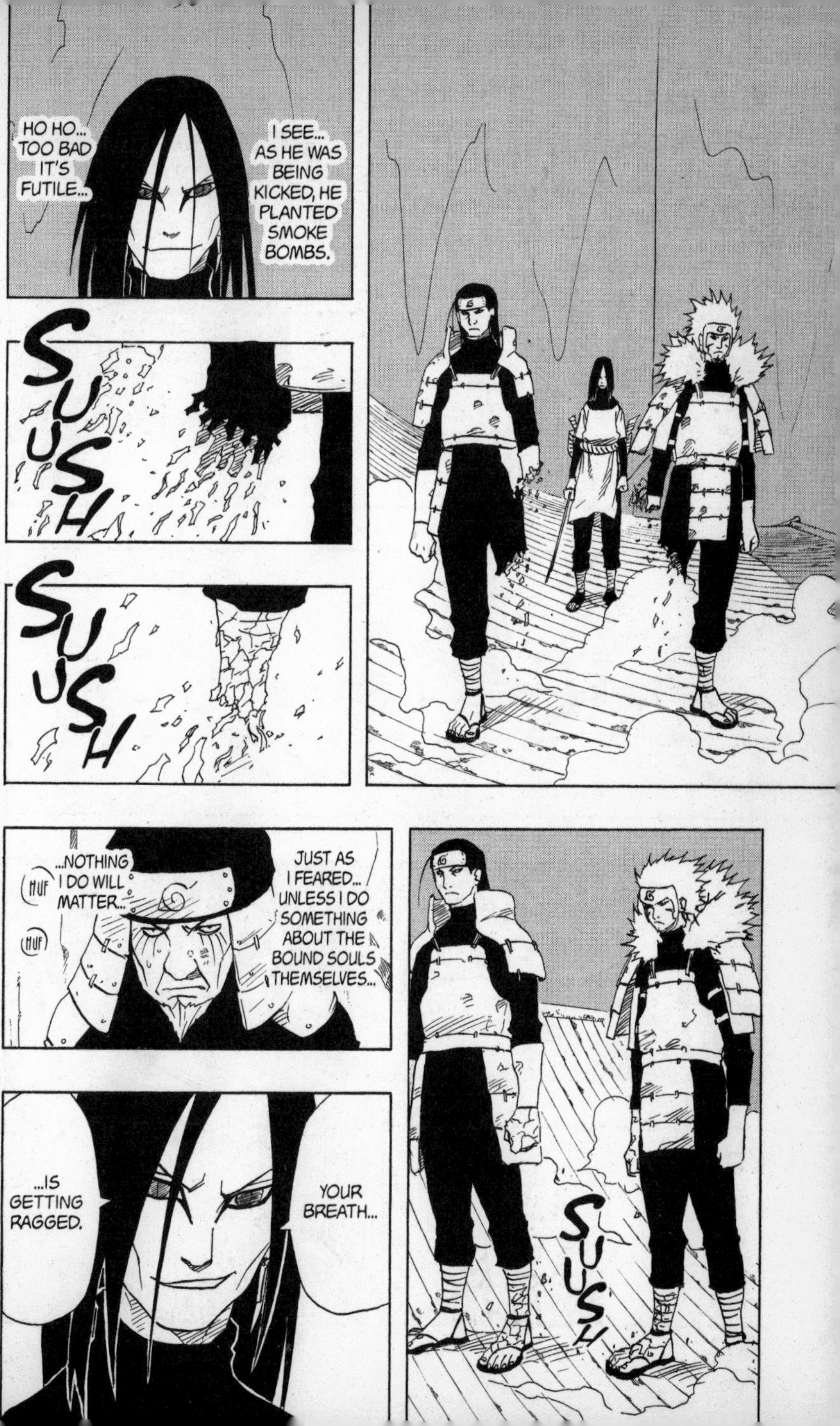
I SEE... AS HE WAS BEING KICKED, HE PLANTED SMOKE BOMBS.
HO HO... TOO BAD IT'S FUTILE...
SUUSH
SUUSH
SUUSH
JUST AS I FEARED... UNLESS I DO SOMETHING ABOUT THE BOUND SOULS THEMSELVES...
...NOTHING I DO WILL MATTER...
HUF
HUF
YOUR BREATH...
...IS GETTING RAGGED.

READ THIS WAY

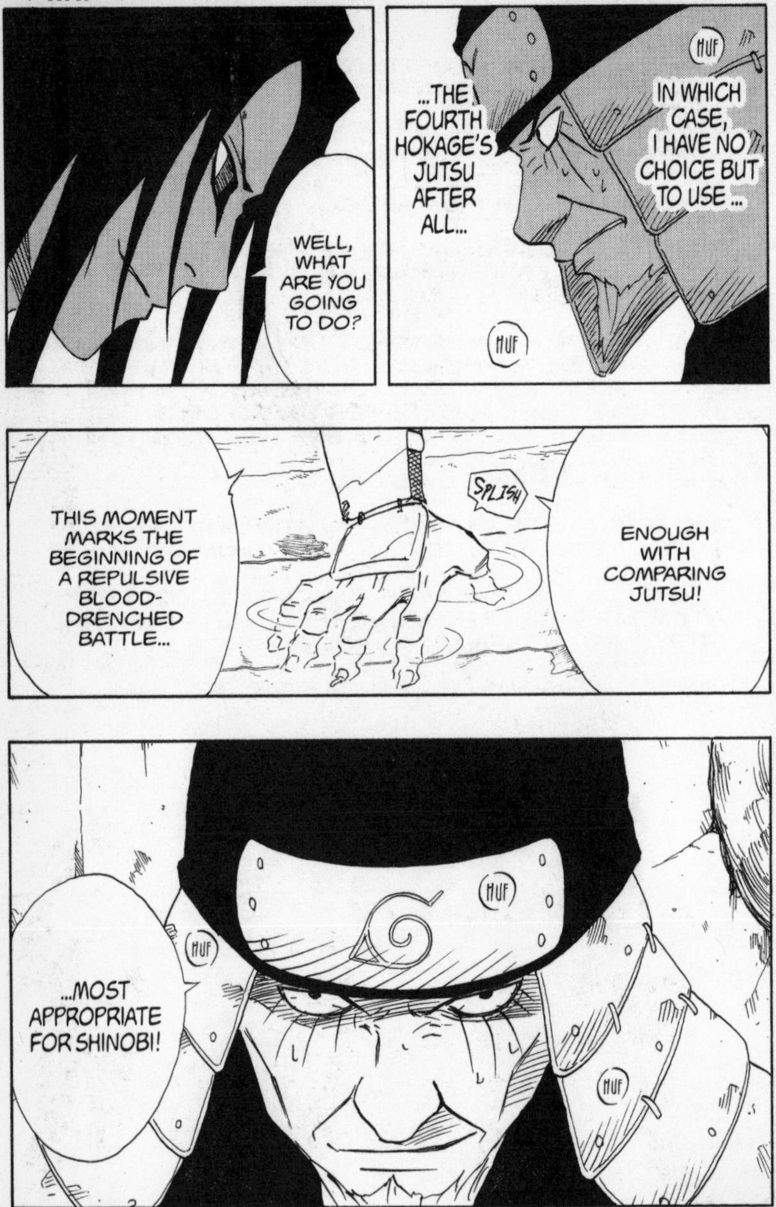
HUF
IN WHICH CASE, I HAVE NO CHOICE BUT TO USE ...
...THE FOURTH HOKAGE'S JUTSU AFTER ALL...
HUF
WELL, WHAT ARE YOU GOING TO DO?
ENOUGH WITH COMPARING JUTSU!
SPLISH
THIS MOMENT MARKS THE BEGINNING OF A REPULSIVE BLOOD-DRENCHED BATTLE...
HUF
HUF
HUF
...MOST APPROPRIATE FOR SHINOBI!

THE WORLD OF KISHIMOTO MASASHI
MY PERSONAL HISTORY, PART 19 (CONTINUED)

WHEN I HEARD THE TRUTH, IT DID DEFLATE ME, BUT I CONTINUED TO POSE THE SAME QUESTION TO OTHER FRIENDS OF MINE. AND YET I KEPT GETTING SIMILAR RESPONSES FROM THEM AS WELL.

AND THEN, IT CAME TO ME. THERE ARE MANY DIFFERENT ELEMENTS TO DRAWING MANGA, BUT THE MOST IMPORTANT PRINCIPLE IS...

"ONE MUST HAVE FUN DRAWING ONE'S OWN MANGA. AND THEN, WHAT'S EVEN MORE CRITICAL IS TO BE AWARE OF ONE'S AUDIENCE AND DRAW FOR THE READERS' ENJOYMENT. EVERYTHING MUST BE FOR THE READERS. ONE MUST BE ABLE TO CHANGE THE EXPRESSIONS ON THEIR FACES AND MAKE THEM SAY 'WOW! THAT IS SO COOL!' WHEN THEY'VE FINISHED READING IT!!"

AND AFTER A LITTLE WHILE, I REALIZED THAT THIS IS WHAT IS MEANT BY "ENTERTAINMENT." IT'S IMPORTANT TO GRASP THE PRACTICAL ASPECTS OF DRAWING MANGA, BUT AS LONG AS ONE DRAWS THINKING "I'M GOING TO BE AN ENTERTAINER!!" I FEEL THAT THE OTHER THINGS WILL QUIETLY AND NATURALLY FALL INTO PLACE.

I AM STILL LEARNING NEW THINGS EVERY DAY.

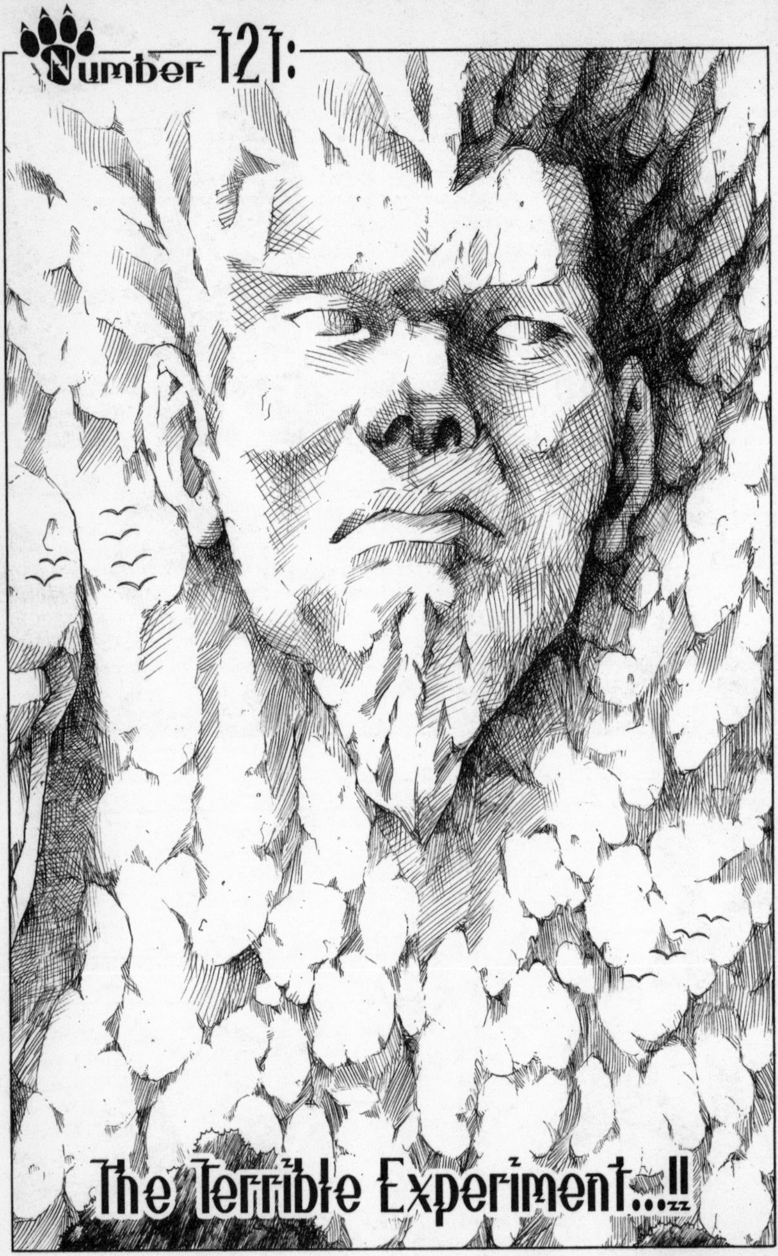
Number 121:
The Terrible Experiment...!!

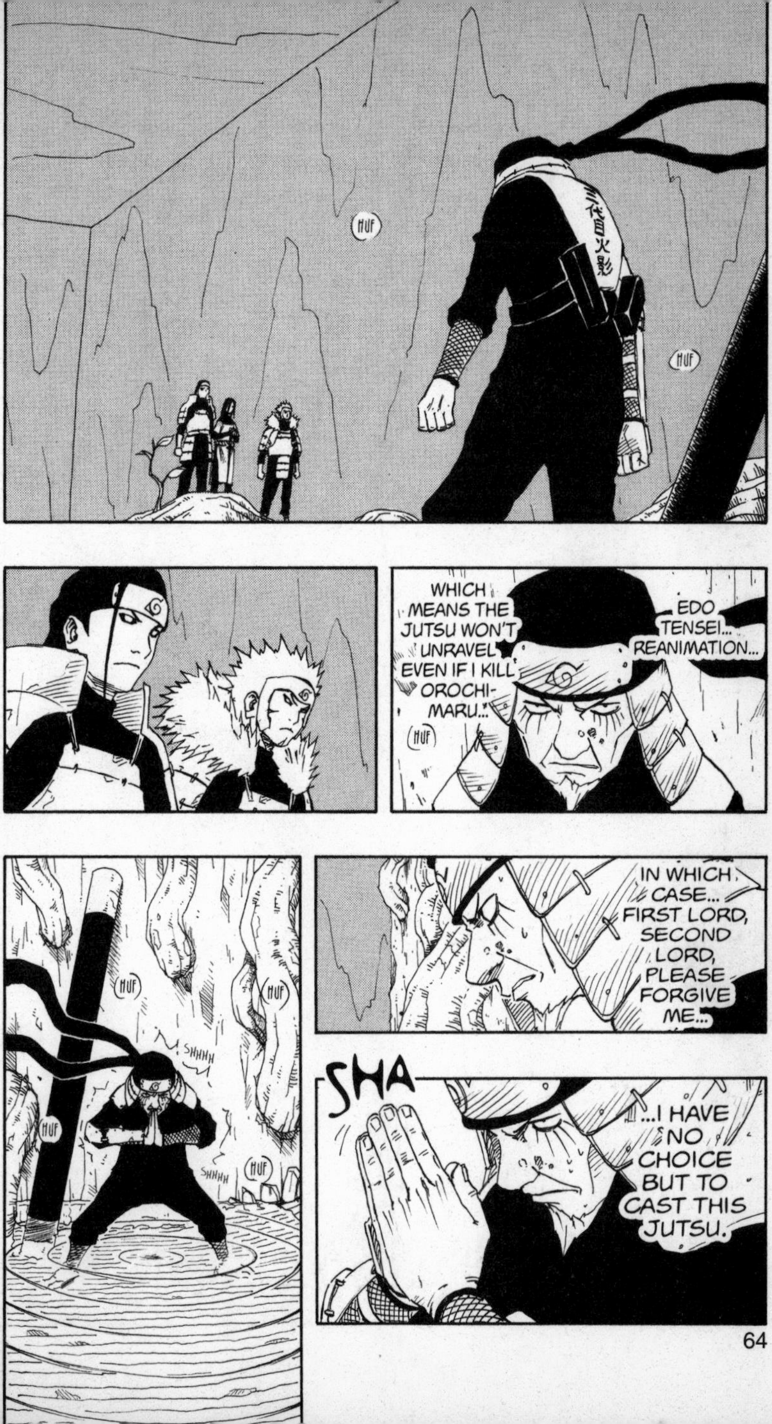

HUF
三代目火影
HUF
EDO TENSEI... REANIMATION...
WHICH MEANS THE JUTSU WON'T UNRAVEL EVEN IF I KILL OROCHIMARU...
HUF
IN WHICH CASE... FIRST LORD, SECOND LORD, PLEASE FORGIVE ME...
SHA
...I HAVE NO CHOICE BUT TO CAST THIS JUTSU.
HUF
HUF
SHHHH
HUF
SHHHH
HUF

READ THIS WAY

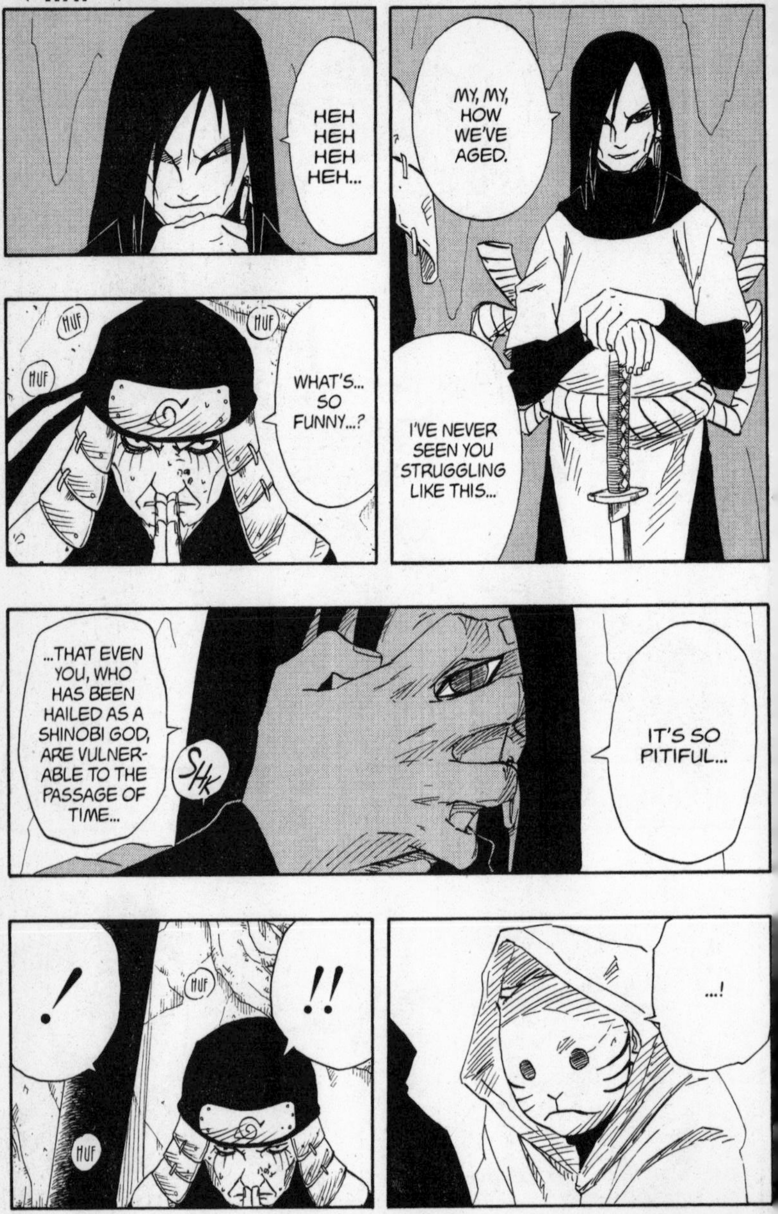

MY, MY, HOW WE'VE AGED.
I'VE NEVER SEEN YOU STRUGGLING LIKE THIS...
HEH HEH HEH HEH...
HUF
HUF
HUF
WHAT'S... SO FUNNY...?
IT'S SO PITIFUL...
...THAT EVEN YOU, WHO HAS BEEN HAILED AS A SHINOBI GOD, ARE VULNERABLE TO THE PASSAGE OF TIME...
SHK
...!
!!
HUF
!
HUF

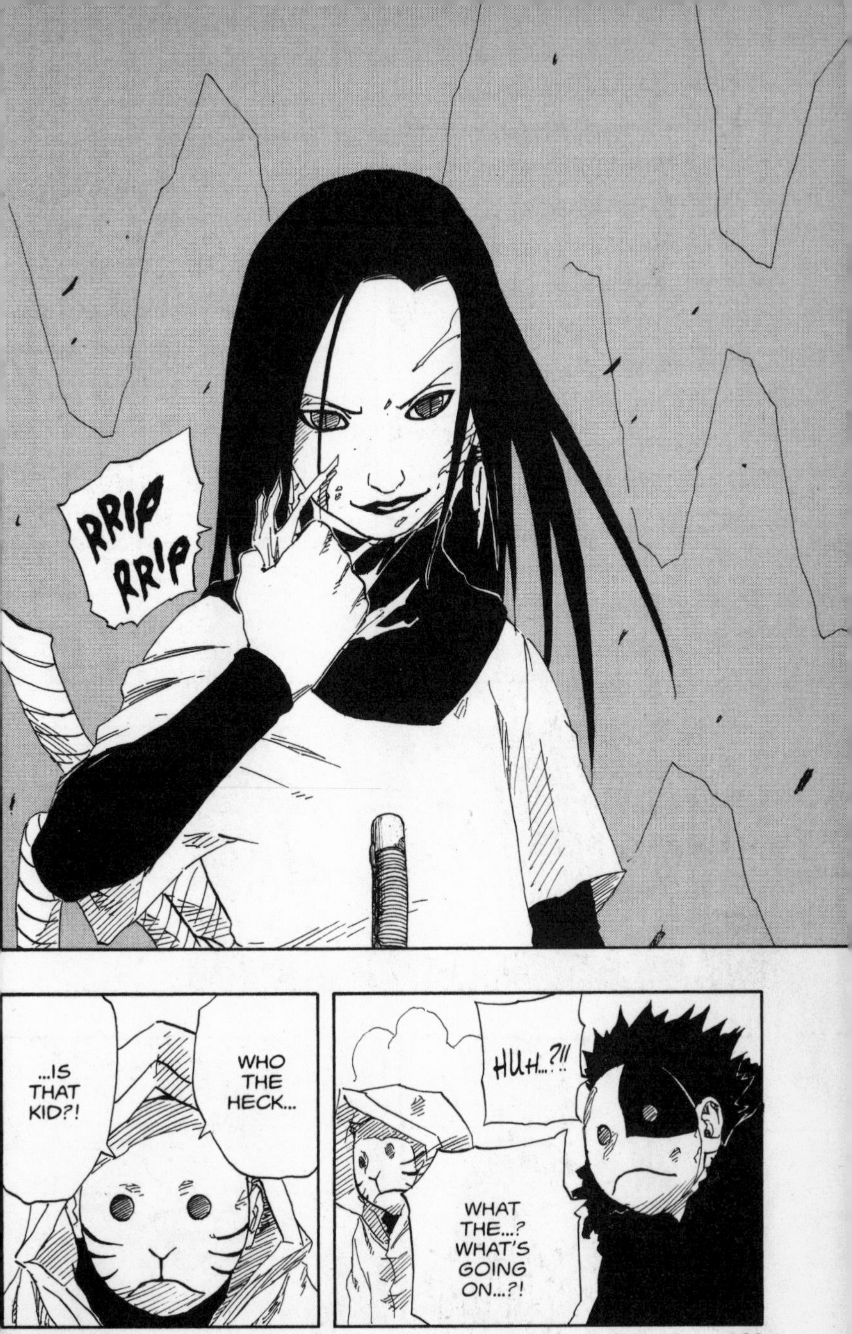
RRIP RRIP
HUH...?!!
WHAT THE...? WHAT'S GOING ON...?!
WHO THE HECK...
...IS THAT KID?!

READ THIS WAY

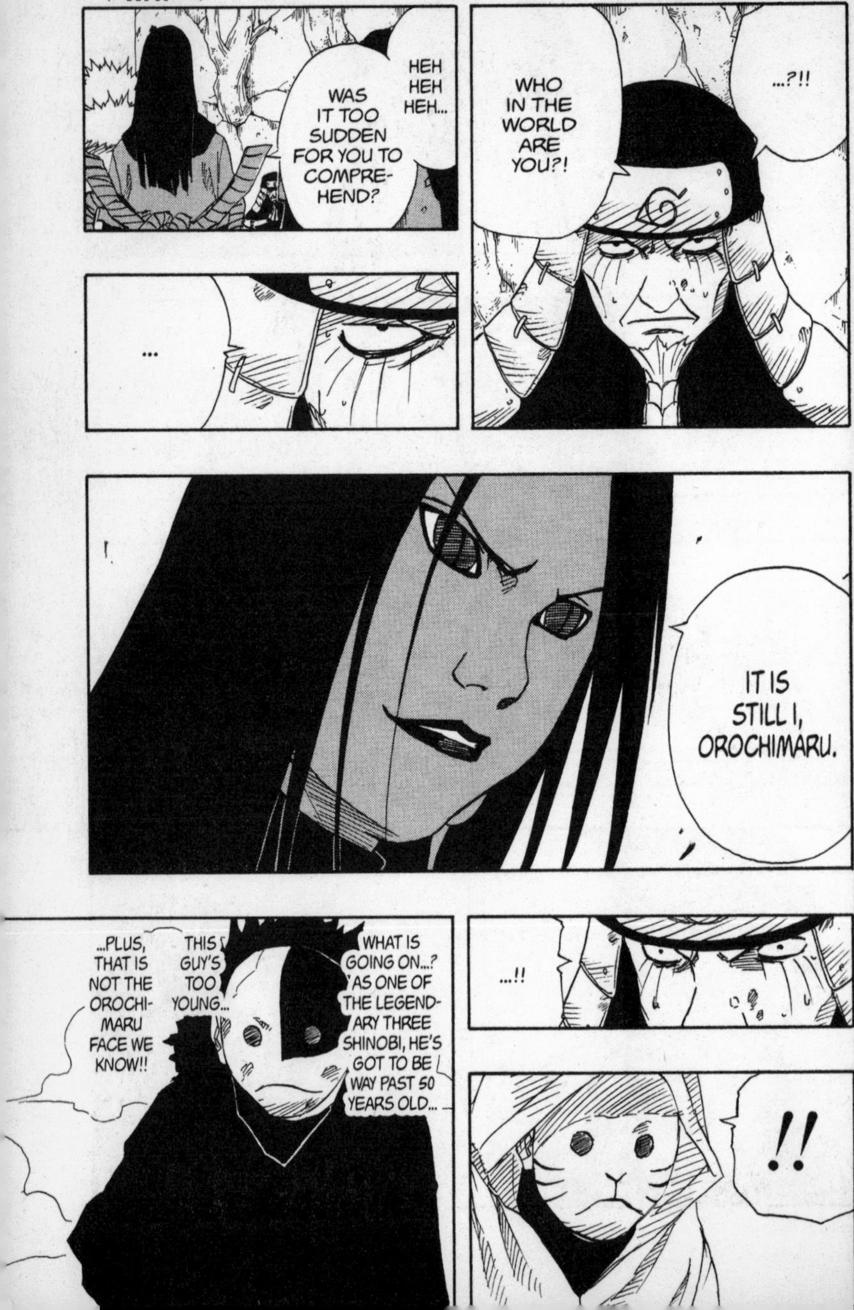

...?!!
WHO IN THE WORLD ARE YOU?!
HEH HEH HEH...
WAS IT TOO SUDDEN FOR YOU TO COMPRE-HEND?
...
IT IS STILL I, OROCHIMARU.
...!!
!!
WHAT IS GOING ON...? AS ONE OF THE LEGEND-ARY THREE SHINOBI, HE'S GOT TO BE WAY PAST 50 YEARS OLD...
THIS GUY'S TOO YOUNG...
...PLUS, THAT IS NOT THE OROCHI-MARU FACE WE KNOW!!

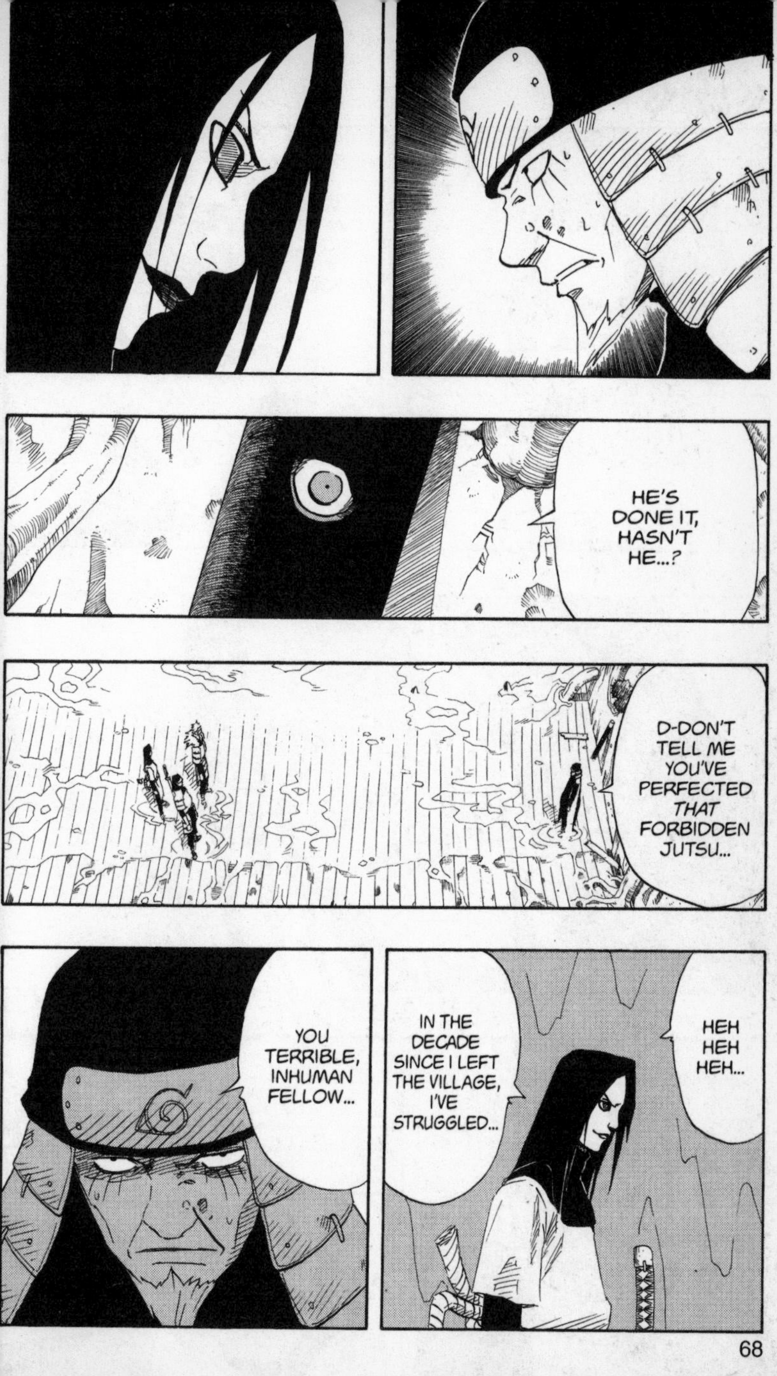
HE'S DONE IT, HASN'T HE...?
D-DON'T TELL ME YOU'VE PERFECTED *THAT* FORBIDDEN JUTSU...
HEH HEH HEH...
IN THE DECADE SINCE I LEFT THE VILLAGE, I'VE STRUGGLED...
YOU TERRIBLE, INHUMAN FELLOW...

READ THIS WAY

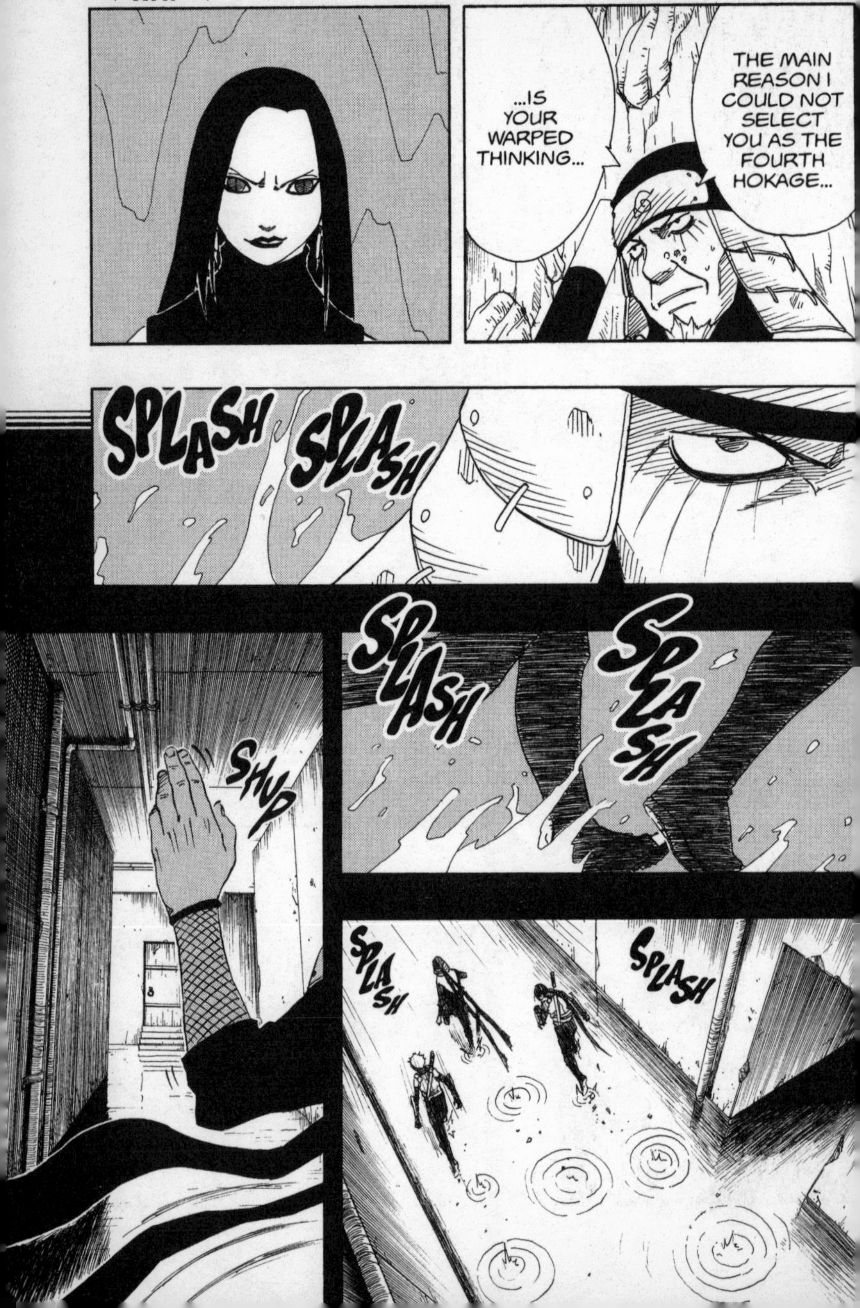
THE MAIN REASON I COULD NOT SELECT YOU AS THE FOURTH HOKAGE...
...IS YOUR WARPED THINKING...
SPLASH
SPLASH
SPLASH
SPLASH
SPLASH
SPLASH
SHUP

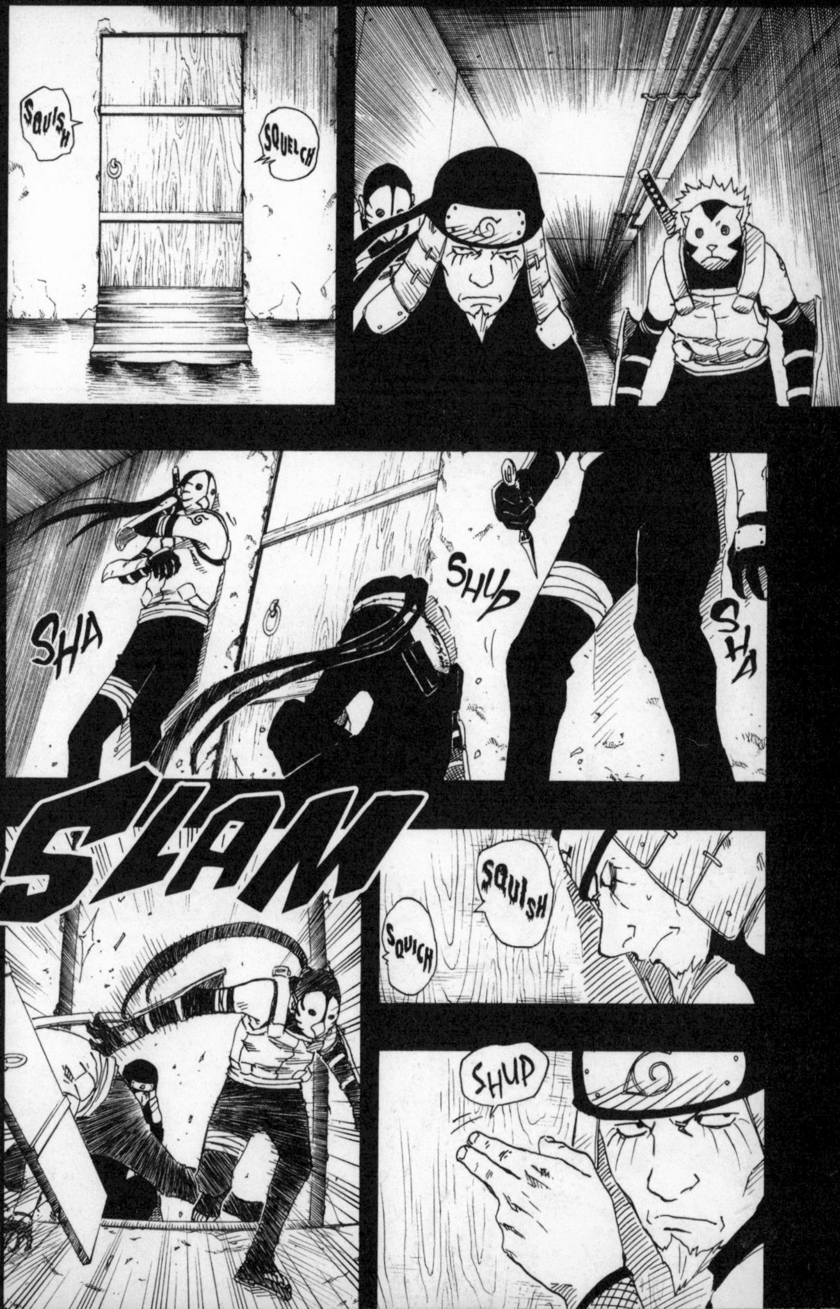
SQUISH
SQUELCH
SHA
SHUP
SHA
SQUISH
SQUICH
SHUP
SLAM

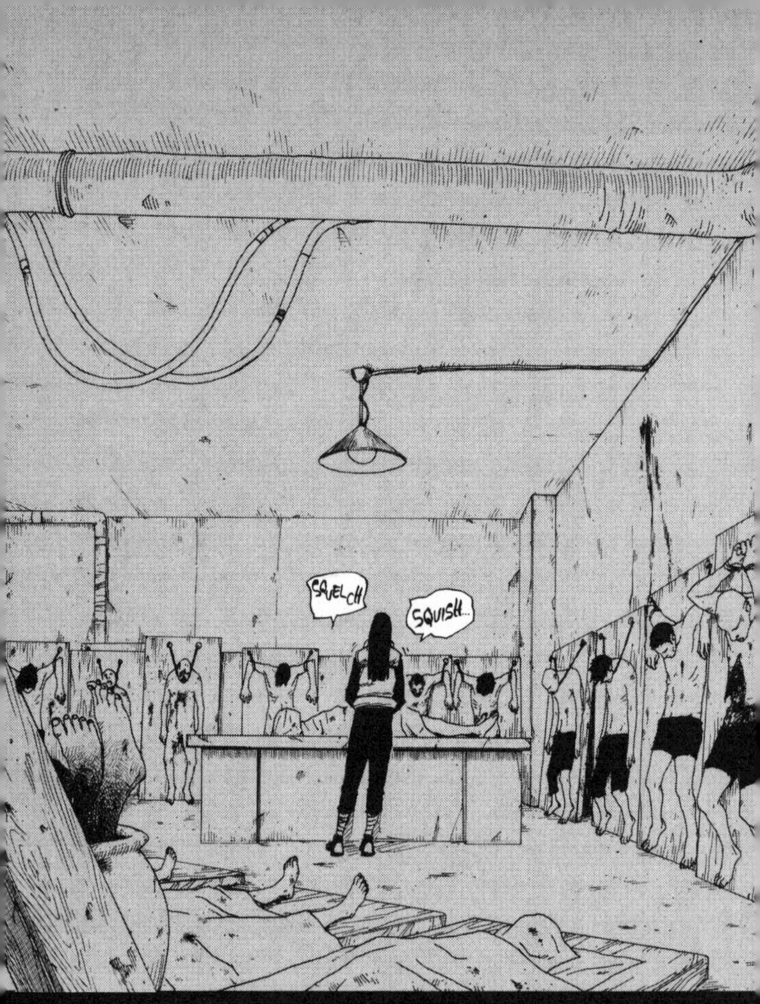
SQUELCH
SQUISH...
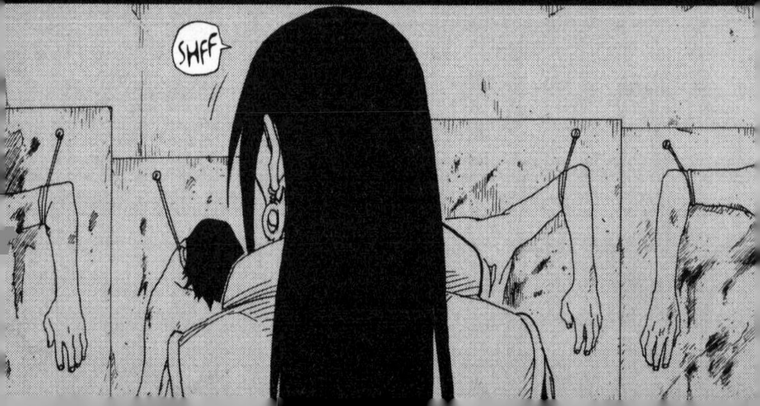
SHFF

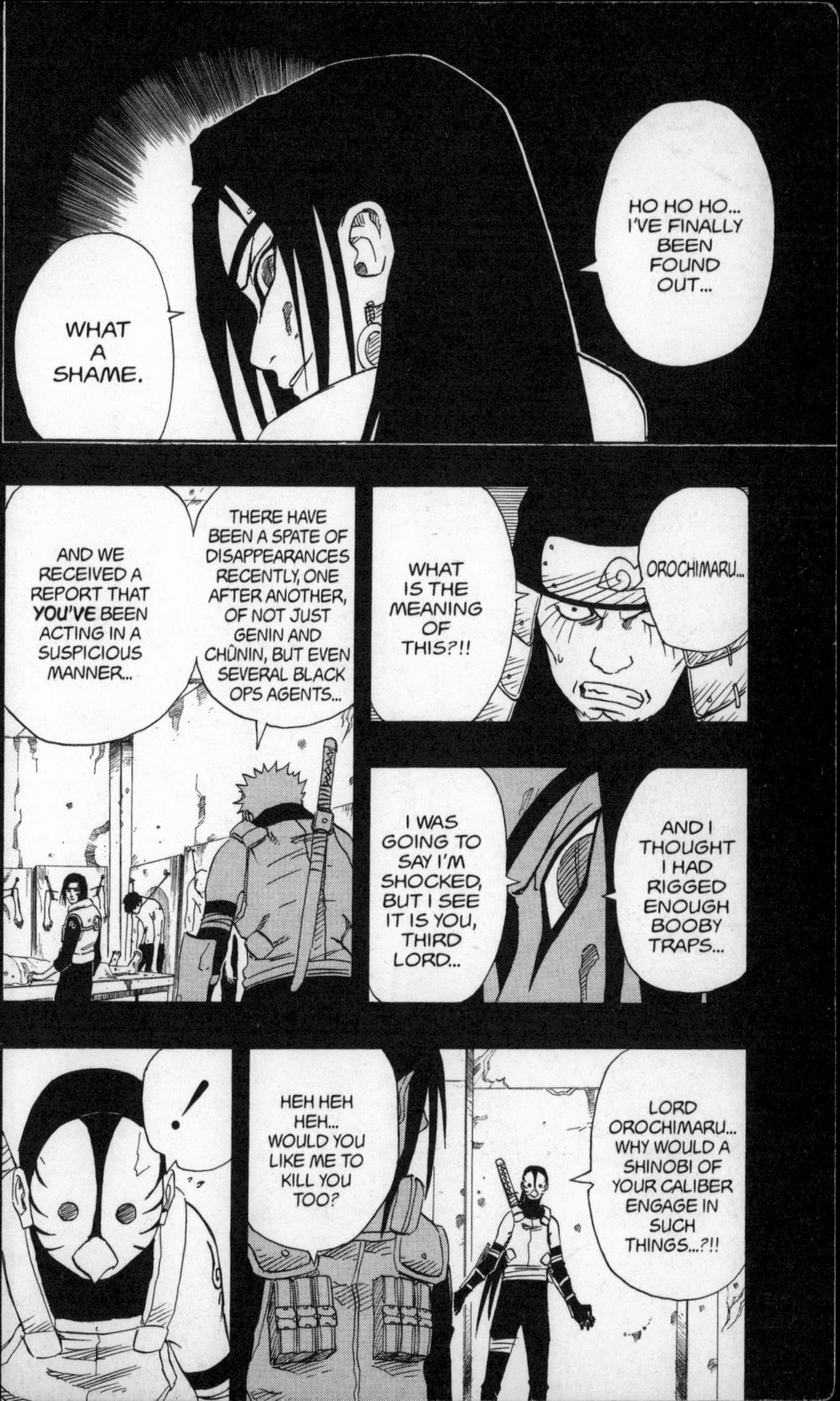

HO HO HO... I'VE FINALLY BEEN FOUND OUT...
WHAT A SHAME.
OROCHIMARU...
WHAT IS THE MEANING OF THIS?!!
AND I THOUGHT I HAD RIGGED ENOUGH BOOBY TRAPS...
I WAS GOING TO SAY I'M SHOCKED, BUT I SEE IT IS YOU, THIRD LORD...
THERE HAVE BEEN A SPATE OF DISAPPEARANCES RECENTLY, ONE AFTER ANOTHER, OF NOT JUST GENIN AND CHŪNIN, BUT EVEN SEVERAL BLACK OPS AGENTS...
AND WE RECEIVED A REPORT THAT **YOU'VE** BEEN ACTING IN A SUSPICIOUS MANNER...
LORD OROCHIMARU... WHY WOULD A SHINOBI OF YOUR CALIBER ENGAGE IN SUCH THINGS...?!!
HEH HEH HEH... WOULD YOU LIKE ME TO KILL YOU TOO?
!

READ THIS WAY

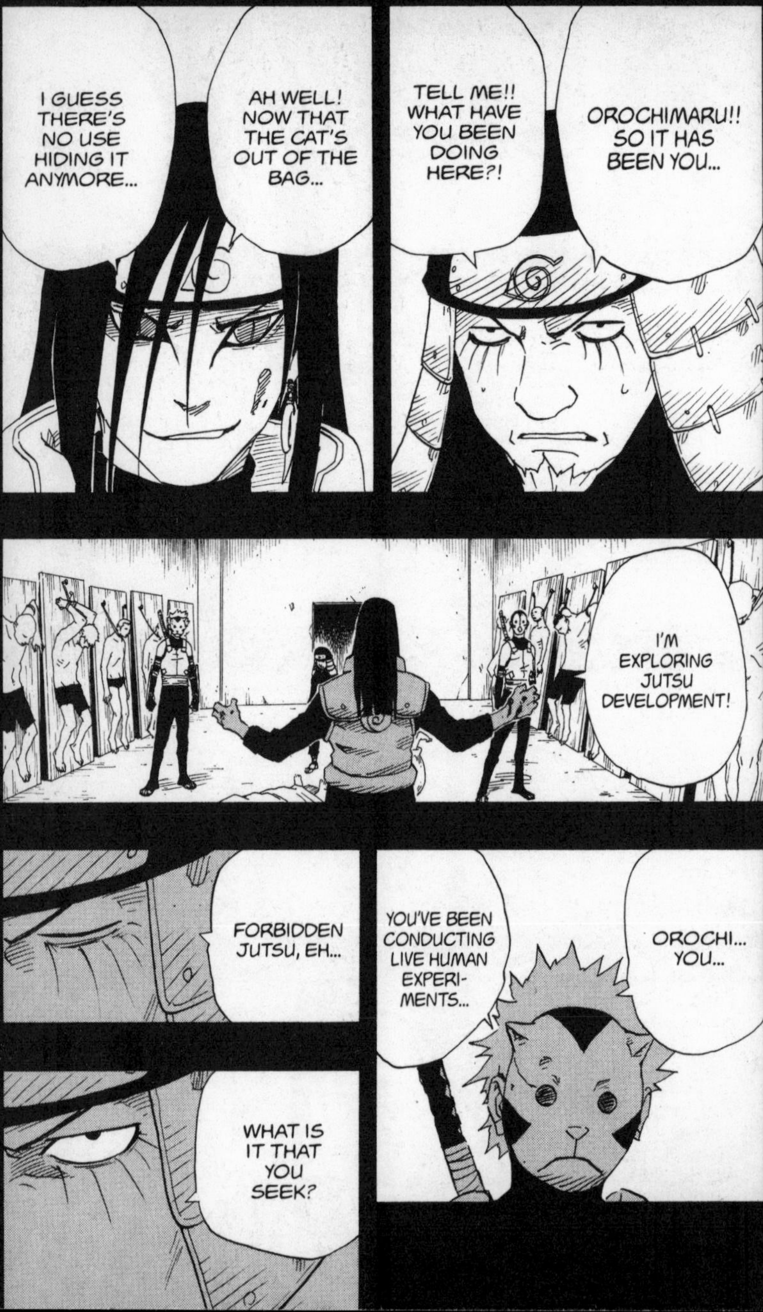
OROCHIMARU!! SO IT HAS BEEN YOU...
TELL ME!! WHAT HAVE YOU BEEN DOING HERE?!
AH WELL! NOW THAT THE CAT'S OUT OF THE BAG...
I GUESS THERE'S NO USE HIDING IT ANYMORE...
I'M EXPLORING JUTSU DEVELOPMENT!
OROCHI... YOU...
YOU'VE BEEN CONDUCTING LIVE HUMAN EXPERIMENTS...
FORBIDDEN JUTSU, EH...
WHAT IS IT THAT YOU SEEK?

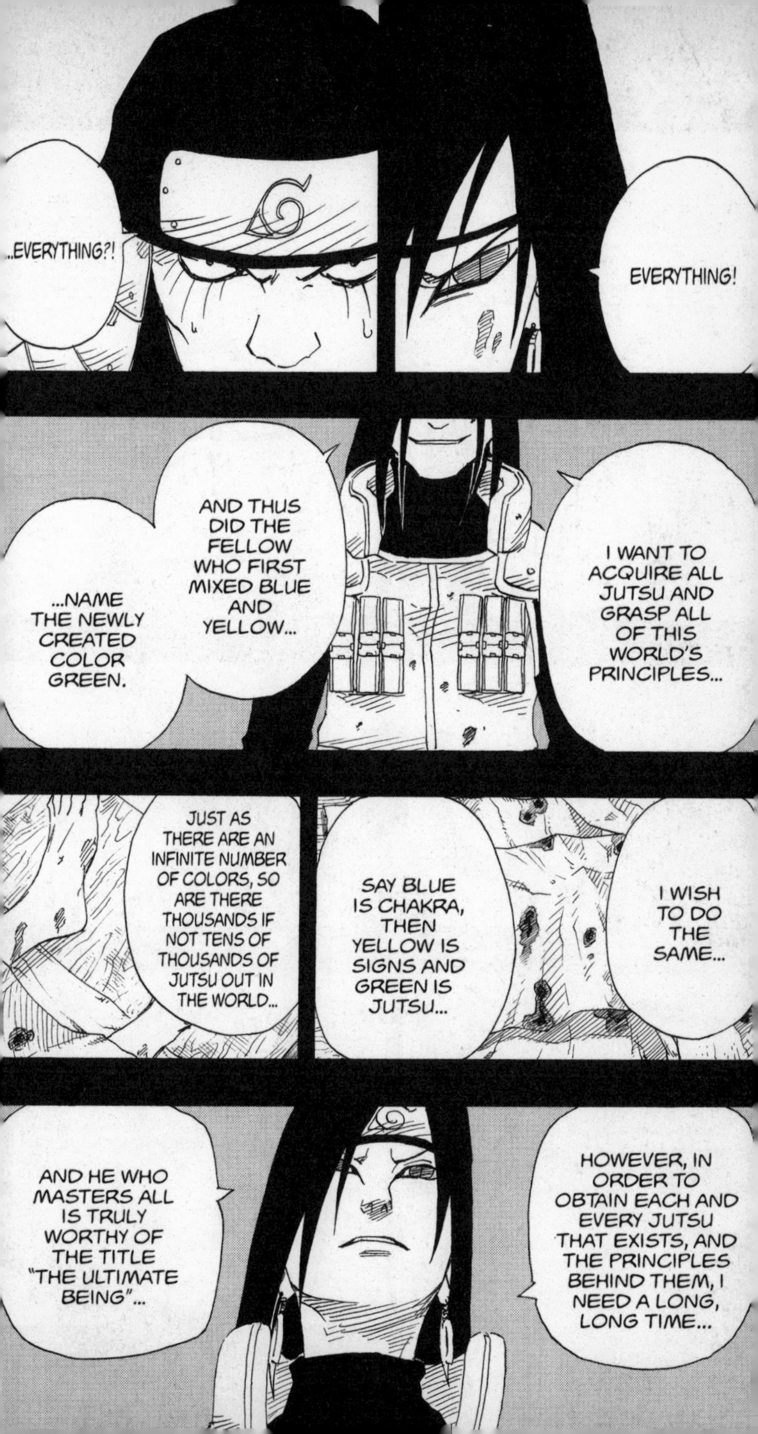
EVERYTHING!
...EVERYTHING?!
I WANT TO ACQUIRE ALL JUTSU AND GRASP ALL OF THIS WORLD'S PRINCIPLES...
AND THUS DID THE FELLOW WHO FIRST MIXED BLUE AND YELLOW...
...NAME THE NEWLY CREATED COLOR GREEN.
I WISH TO DO THE SAME...
SAY BLUE IS CHAKRA, THEN YELLOW IS SIGNS AND GREEN IS JUTSU...
JUST AS THERE ARE AN INFINITE NUMBER OF COLORS, SO ARE THERE THOUSANDS IF NOT TENS OF THOUSANDS OF JUTSU OUT IN THE WORLD...
HOWEVER, IN ORDER TO OBTAIN EACH AND EVERY JUTSU THAT EXISTS, AND THE PRINCIPLES BEHIND THEM, I NEED A LONG, LONG TIME...
AND HE WHO MASTERS ALL IS TRULY WORTHY OF THE TITLE "THE ULTIMATE BEING"...

READ THIS WAY

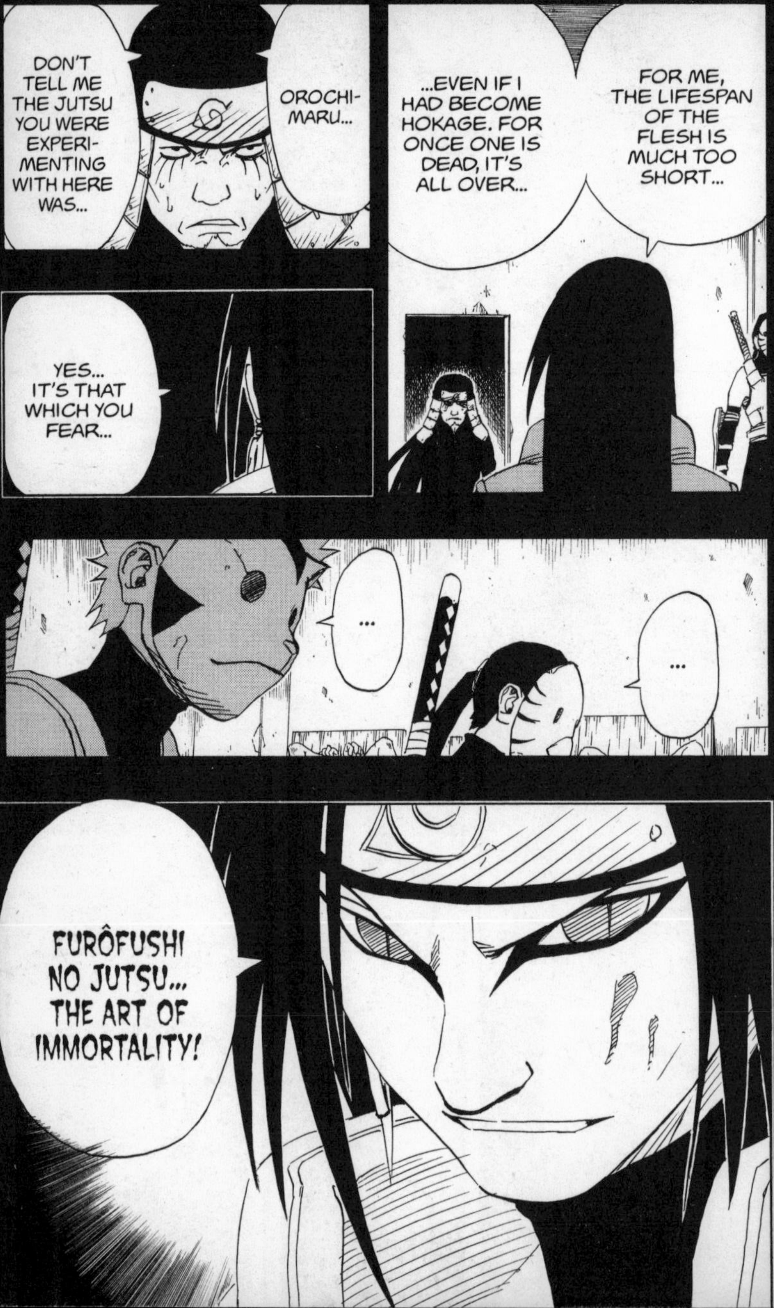

FOR ME, THE LIFESPAN OF THE FLESH IS MUCH TOO SHORT...
...EVEN IF I HAD BECOME HOKAGE. FOR ONCE ONE IS DEAD, IT'S ALL OVER...
OROCHIMARU...
DON'T TELL ME THE JUTSU YOU WERE EXPERIMENTING WITH HERE WAS...
YES... IT'S THAT WHICH YOU FEAR...
...
...
FURÔFUSHI NO JUTSU... THE ART OF IMMORTALITY!

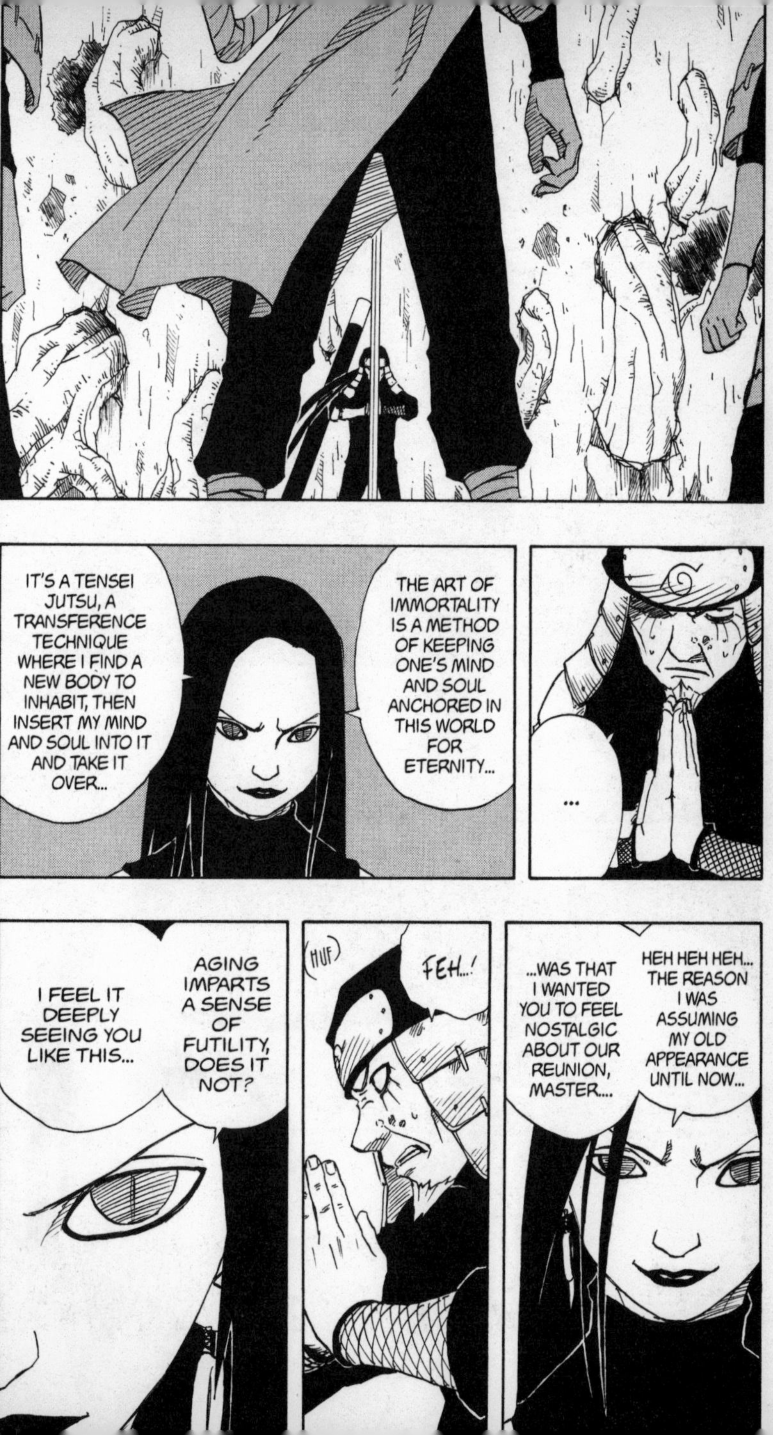
...
THE ART OF IMMORTALITY IS A METHOD OF KEEPING ONE'S MIND AND SOUL ANCHORED IN THIS WORLD FOR ETERNITY...
IT'S A TENSEI JUTSU, A TRANSFERENCE TECHNIQUE WHERE I FIND A NEW BODY TO INHABIT, THEN INSERT MY MIND AND SOUL INTO IT AND TAKE IT OVER...
HEH HEH HEH... THE REASON I WAS ASSUMING MY OLD APPEARANCE UNTIL NOW...
...WAS THAT I WANTED YOU TO FEEL NOSTALGIC ABOUT OUR REUNION, MASTER....
FEH...!
(HUF)
AGING IMPARTS A SENSE OF FUTILITY, DOES IT NOT?
I FEEL IT DEEPLY SEEING YOU LIKE THIS...

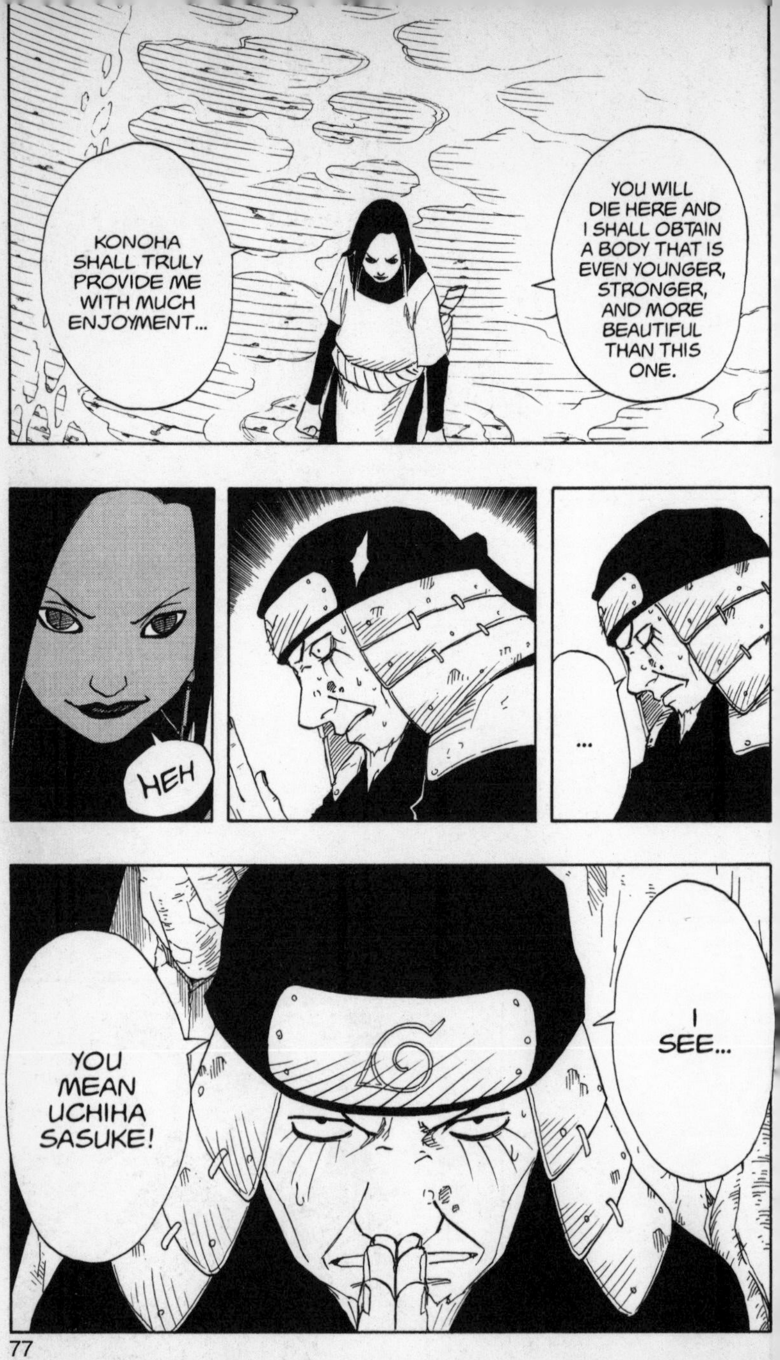
YOU WILL DIE HERE AND I SHALL OBTAIN A BODY THAT IS EVEN YOUNGER, STRONGER, AND MORE BEAUTIFUL THAN THIS ONE.
KONOHA SHALL TRULY PROVIDE ME WITH MUCH ENJOYMENT...
...
HEH
I SEE...
YOU MEAN UCHIHA SASUKE!

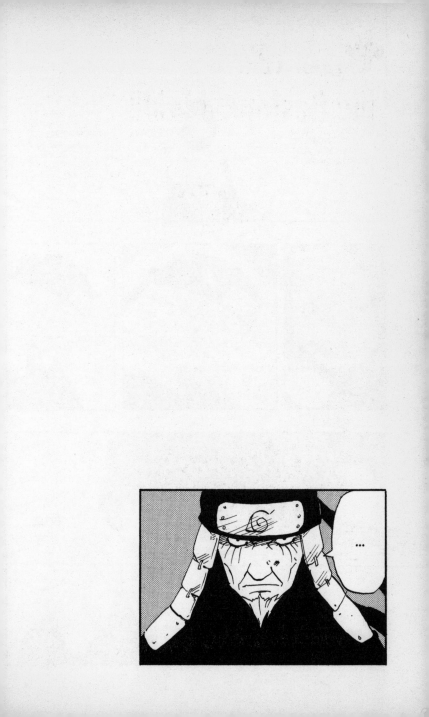

Number 122: The Bestowed Will!!

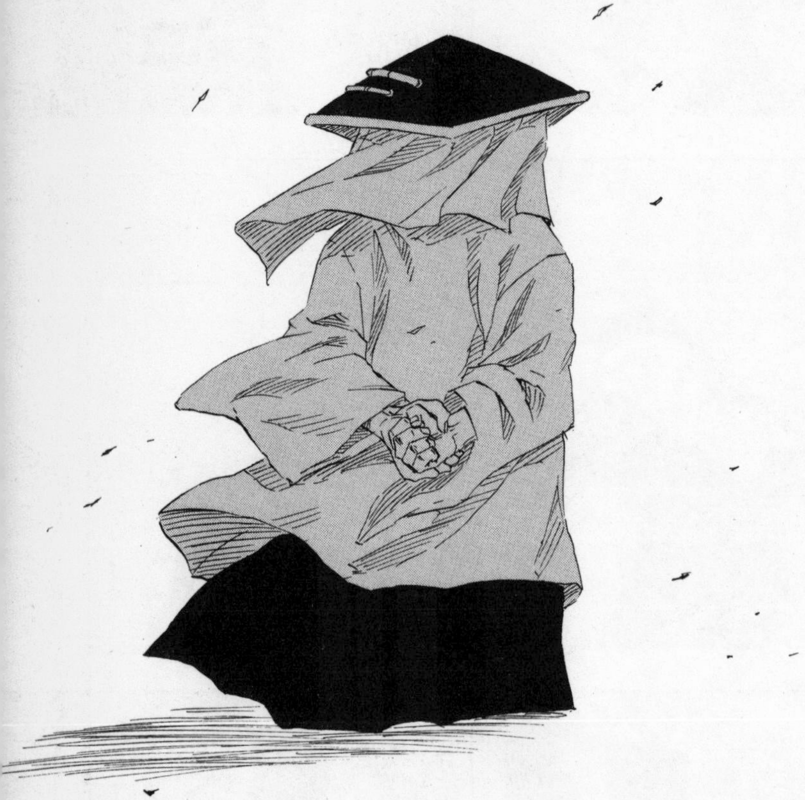

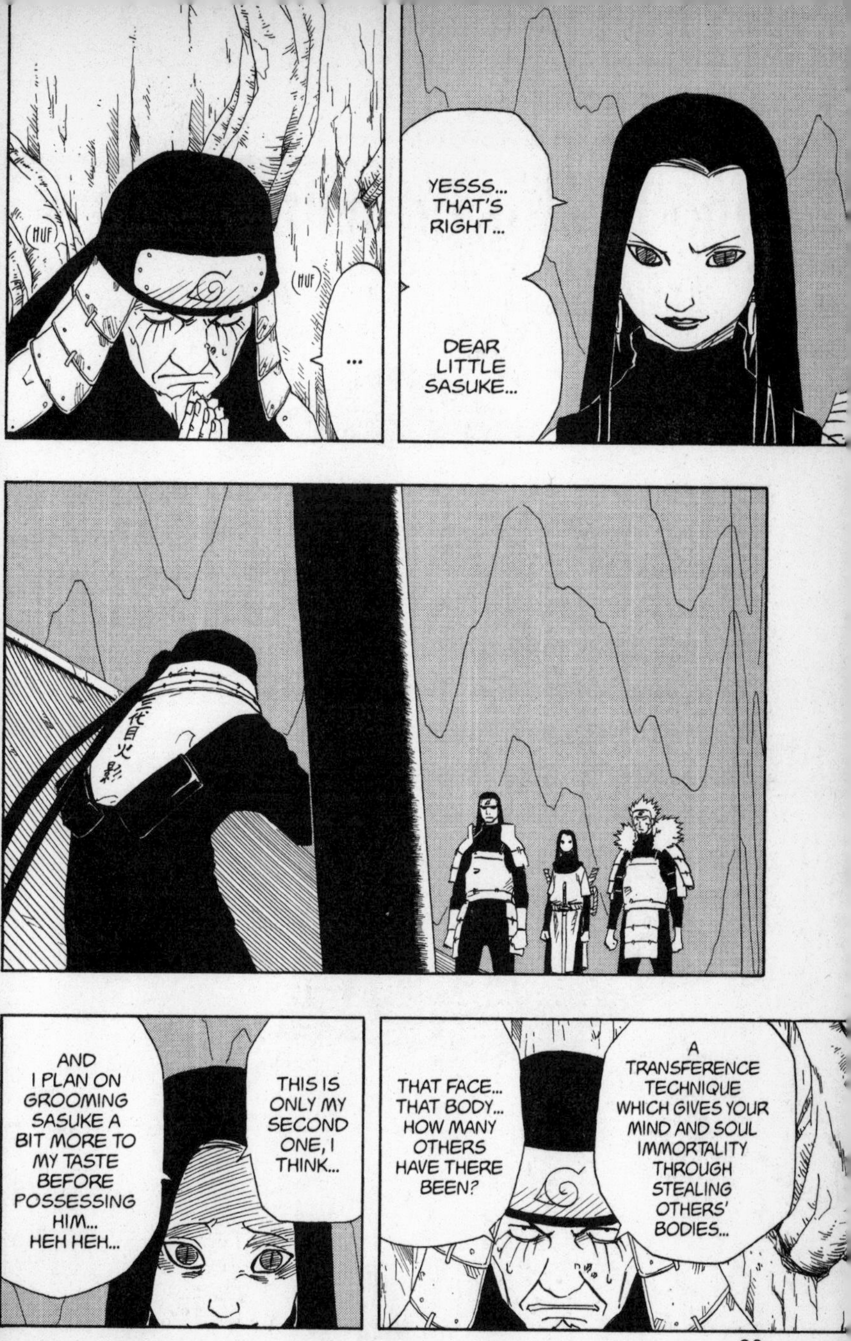
YESSS... THAT'S RIGHT...
DEAR LITTLE SASUKE...
(HUF)
(HUF)
...
三代目火影
A TRANSFERENCE TECHNIQUE WHICH GIVES YOUR MIND AND SOUL IMMORTALITY THROUGH STEALING OTHERS' BODIES...
THAT FACE... THAT BODY... HOW MANY OTHERS HAVE THERE BEEN?
THIS IS ONLY MY SECOND ONE, I THINK...
AND I PLAN ON GROOMING SASUKE A BIT MORE TO MY TASTE BEFORE POSSESSING HIM... HEH HEH...

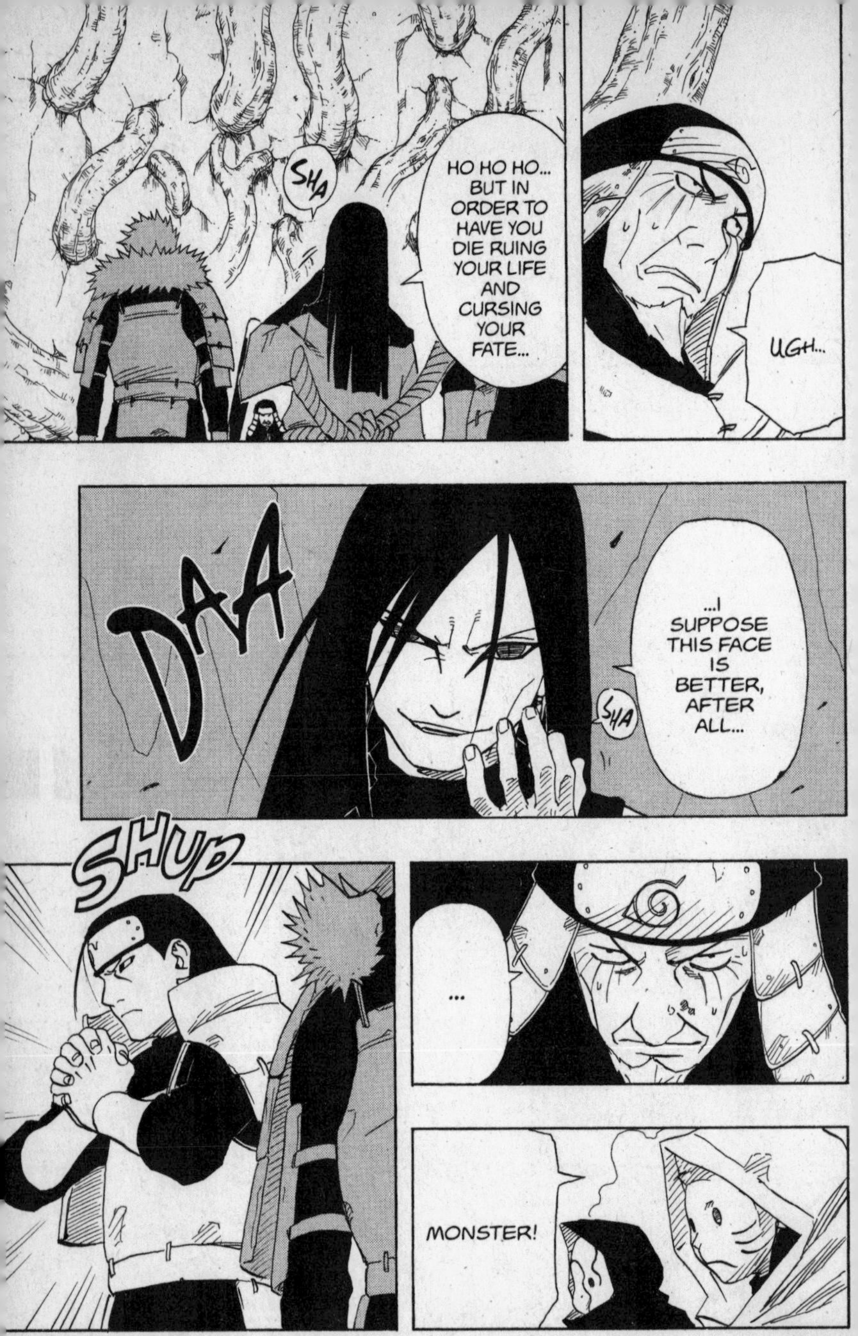
UGH...
HO HO HO... BUT IN ORDER TO HAVE YOU DIE RUING YOUR LIFE AND CURSING YOUR FATE...
SHA
...I SUPPOSE THIS FACE IS BETTER, AFTER ALL...
SHA
DAA
...
MONSTER!
SHUP

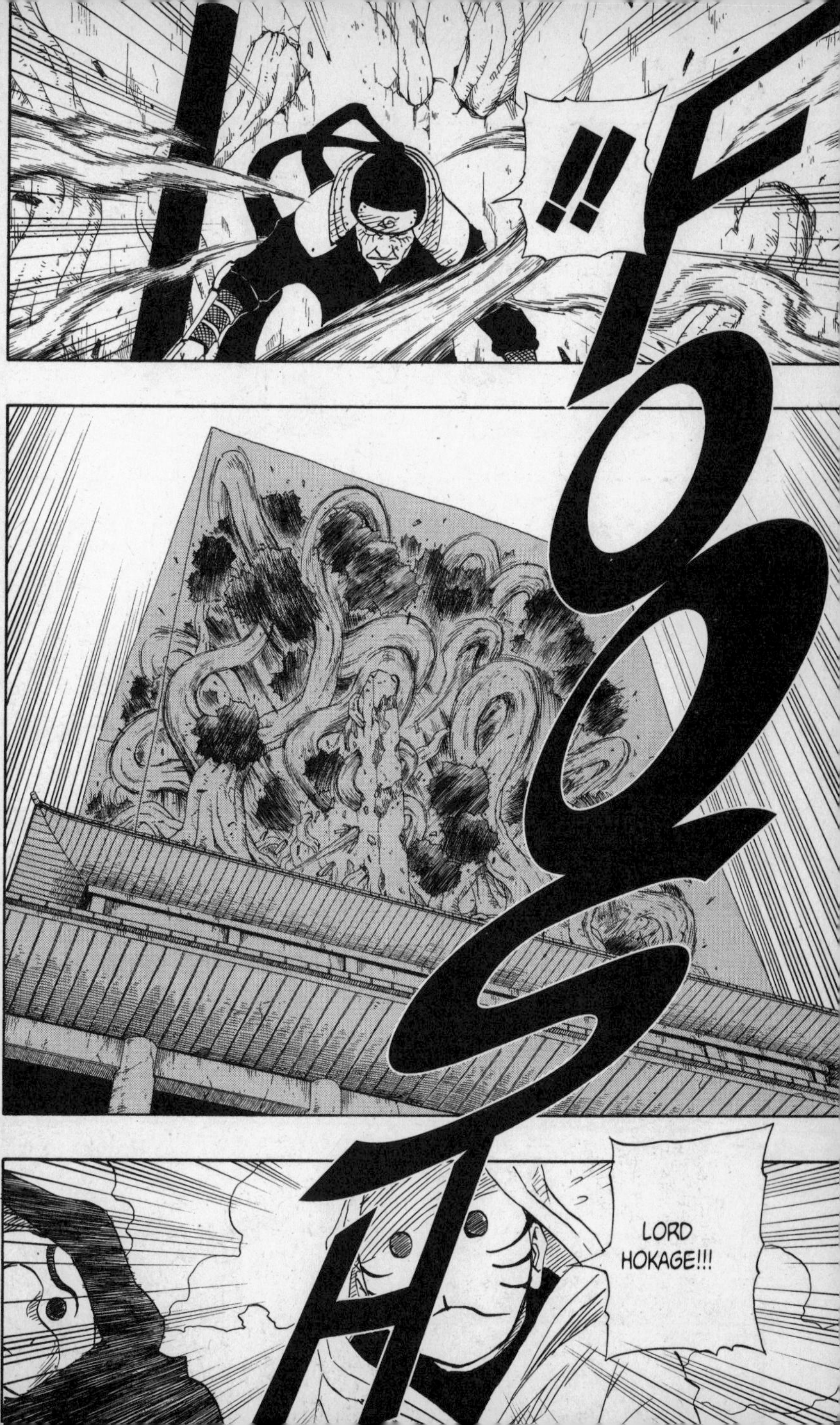
!!
FWOOSH
LORD
HOKAGE!!!

READ THIS WAY

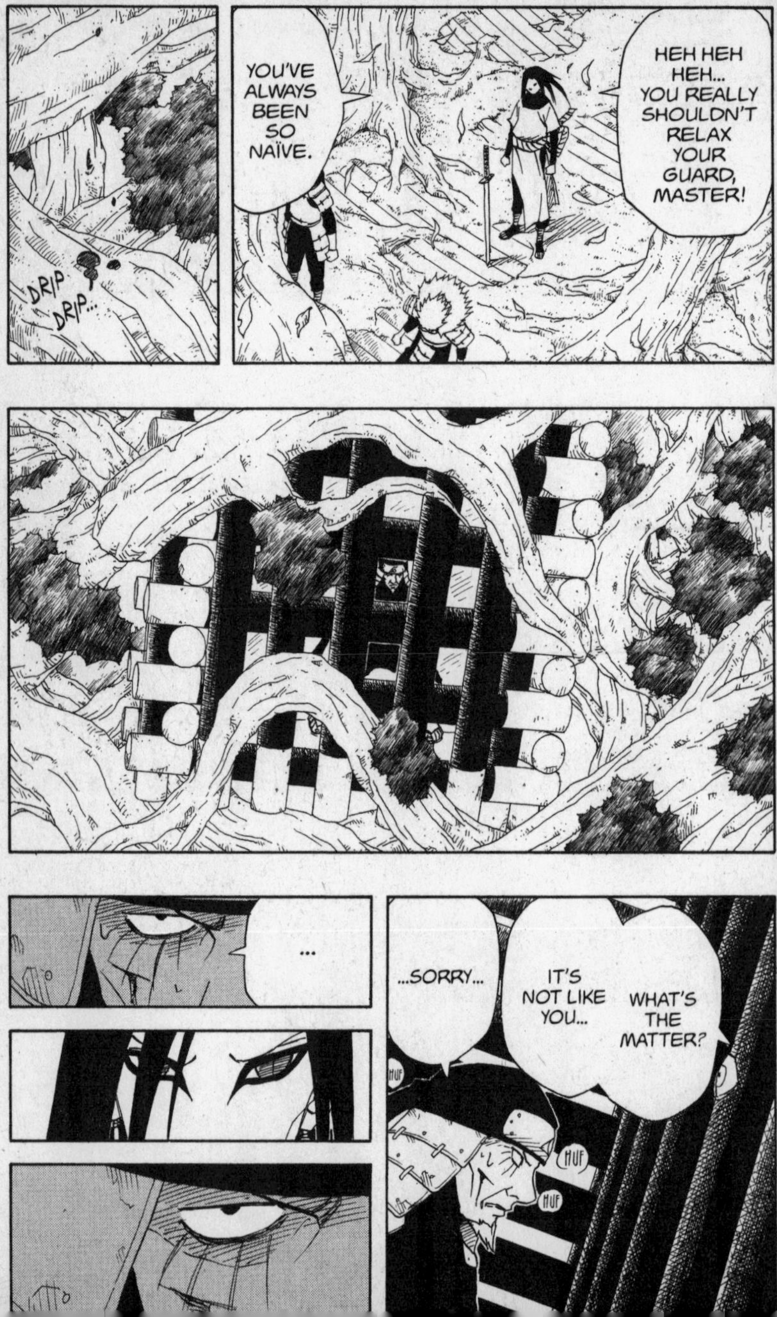
HEH HEH HEH... YOU REALLY SHOULDN'T RELAX YOUR GUARD, MASTER!
YOU'VE ALWAYS BEEN SO NAÏVE.
DRIP DRIP...
WHAT'S THE MATTER?
IT'S NOT LIKE YOU...
...SORRY...
HUF
HUF
HUF
...

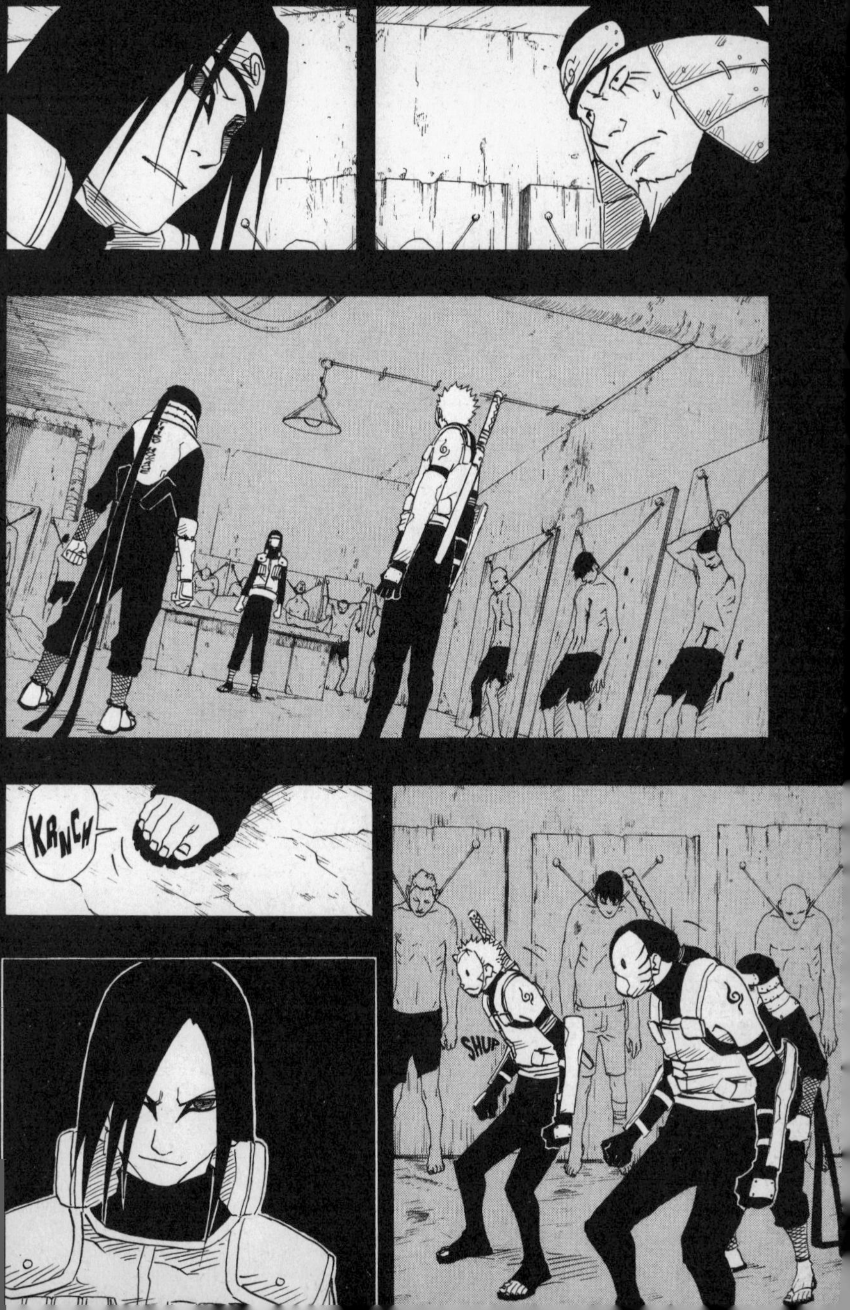
KRNCH
SHUP

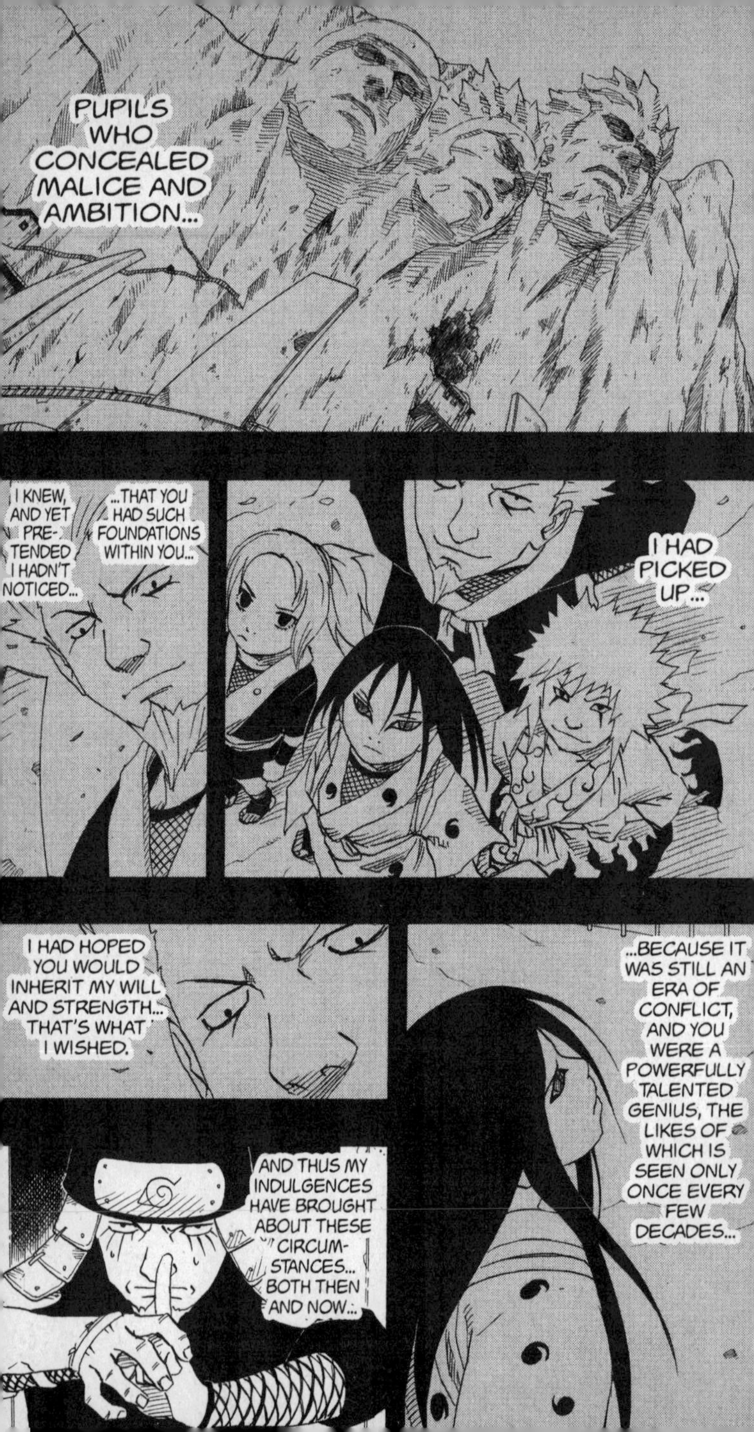
PUPILS WHO CONCEALED MALICE AND AMBITION...
I HAD PICKED UP...
I KNEW, AND YET PRE-TENDED I HADN'T NOTICED...
...THAT YOU HAD SUCH FOUNDATIONS WITHIN YOU...
...BECAUSE IT WAS STILL AN ERA OF CONFLICT, AND YOU WERE A POWERFULLY TALENTED GENIUS, THE LIKES OF WHICH IS SEEN ONLY ONCE EVERY FEW DECADES...
I HAD HOPED YOU WOULD INHERIT MY WILL AND STRENGTH... THAT'S WHAT I WISHED.
AND THUS MY INDULGENCES HAVE BROUGHT ABOUT THESE CIRCUM-STANCES... BOTH THEN AND NOW...

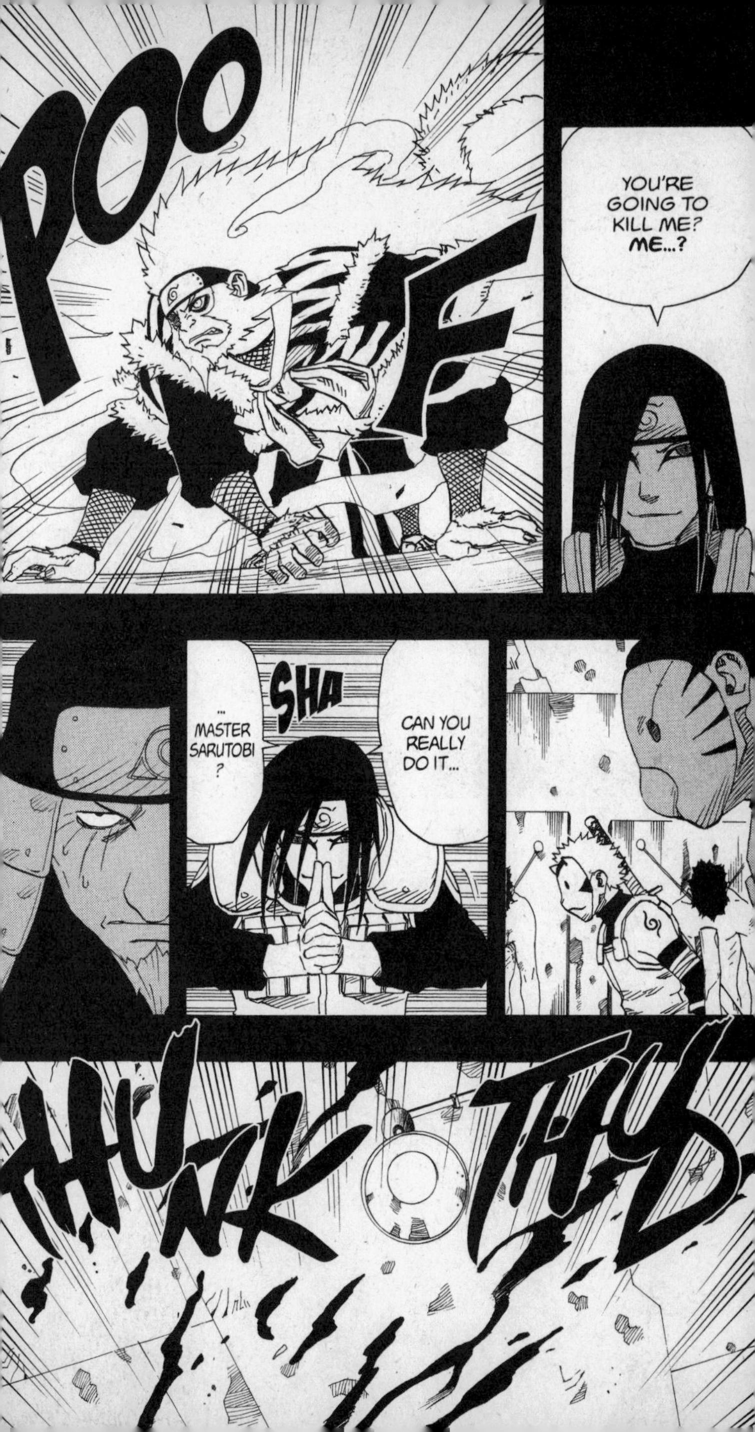
YOU'RE GOING TO KILL ME? ME...?
POOF
CAN YOU REALLY DO IT...
SHA
... MASTER SARUTOBI ?
THUD
THUNK

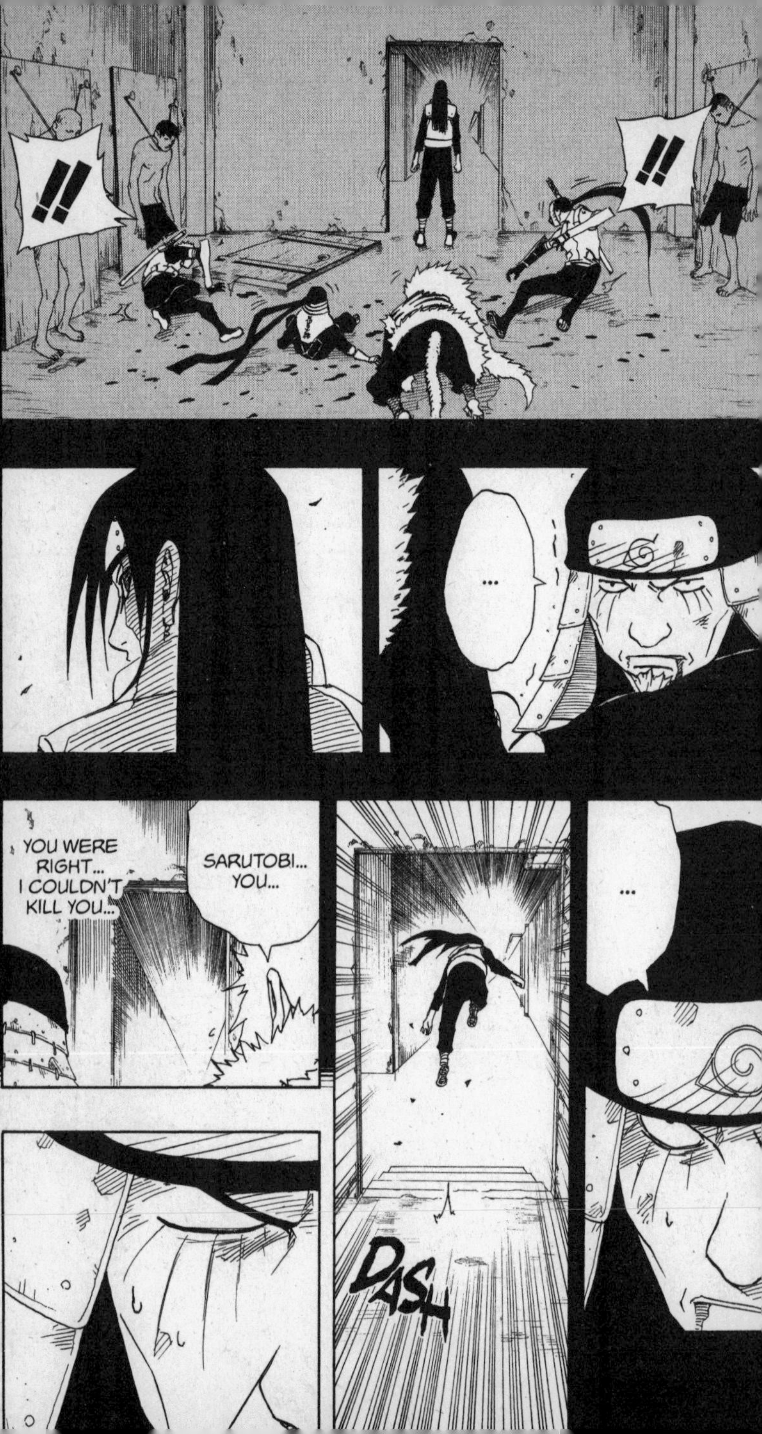
!!
!!
...
...
DASH
SARUTOBI... YOU...
YOU WERE RIGHT... I COULDN'T KILL YOU...

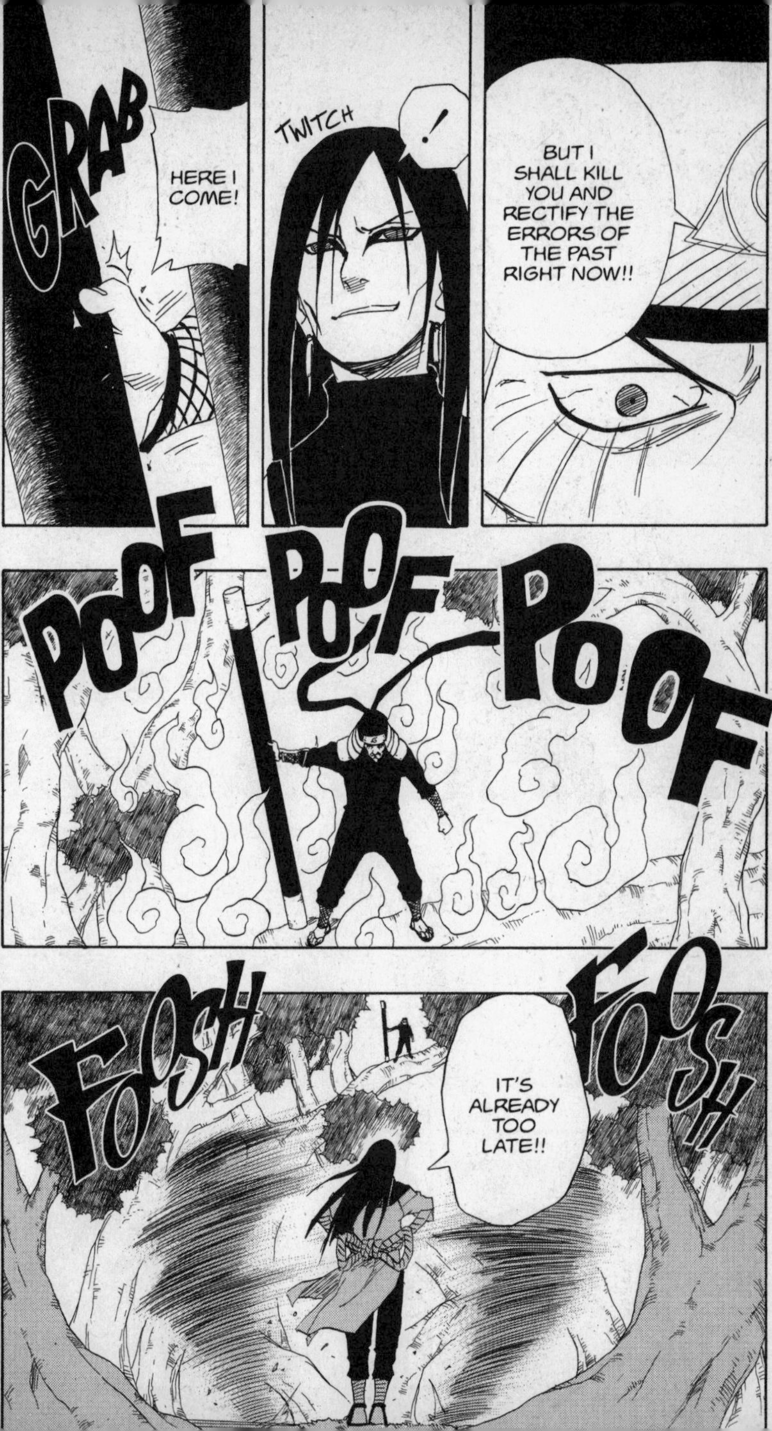

BUT I SHALL KILL YOU AND RECTIFY THE ERRORS OF THE PAST RIGHT NOW!!
!
TWITCH
GRAB
HERE I COME!
POOF
POOF
POOF
FOOSH
IT'S ALREADY TOO LATE!!
FOOSH

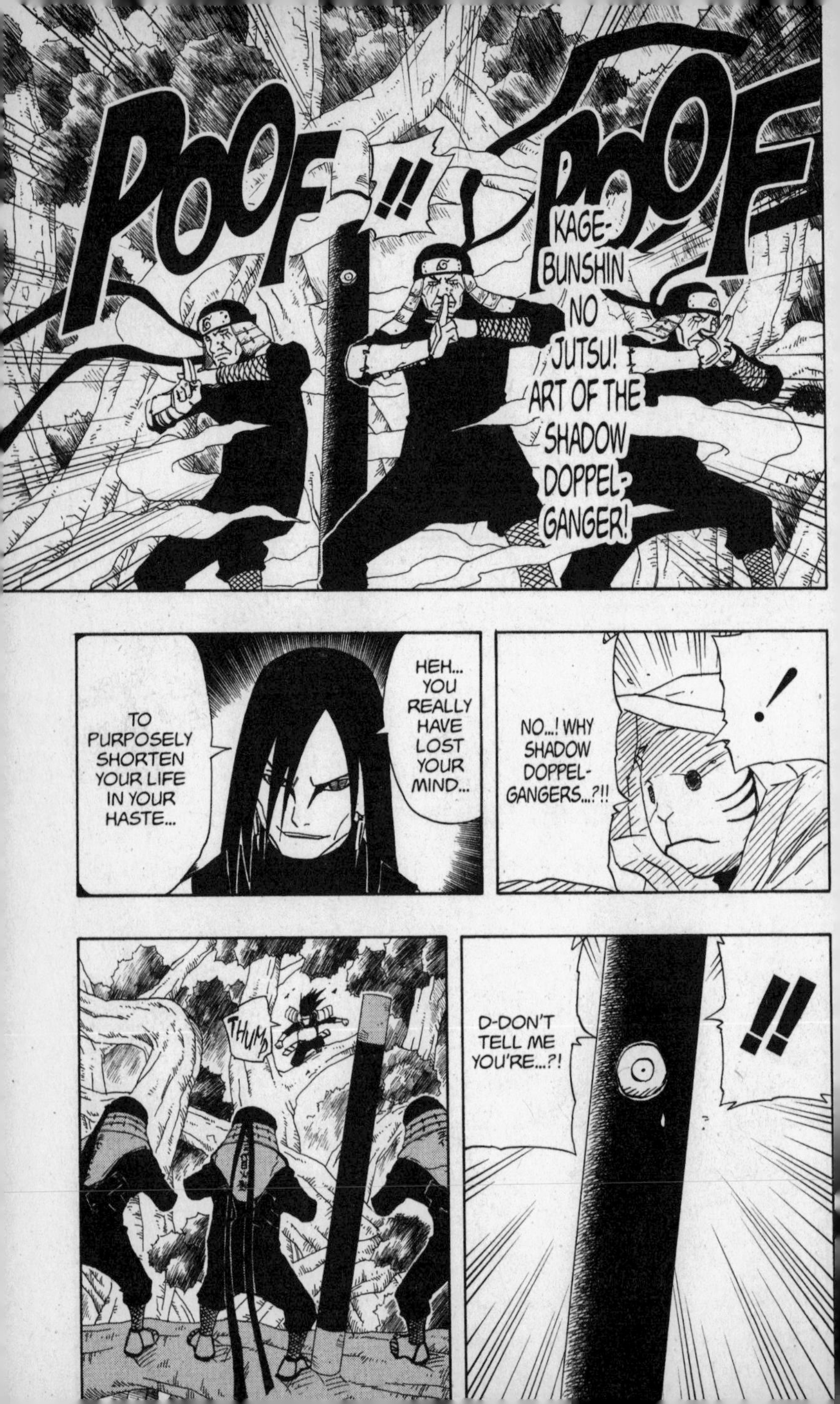
POOF
KAGE-BUNSHIN NO JUTSU! ART OF THE SHADOW DOPPEL-GANGER!
!!
POOF
!
NO...! WHY SHADOW DOPPEL-GANGERS...?!!
HEH... YOU REALLY HAVE LOST YOUR MIND...
TO PURPOSELY SHORTEN YOUR LIFE IN YOUR HASTE...
!!
D-DON'T TELL ME YOU'RE...?!
THUMP

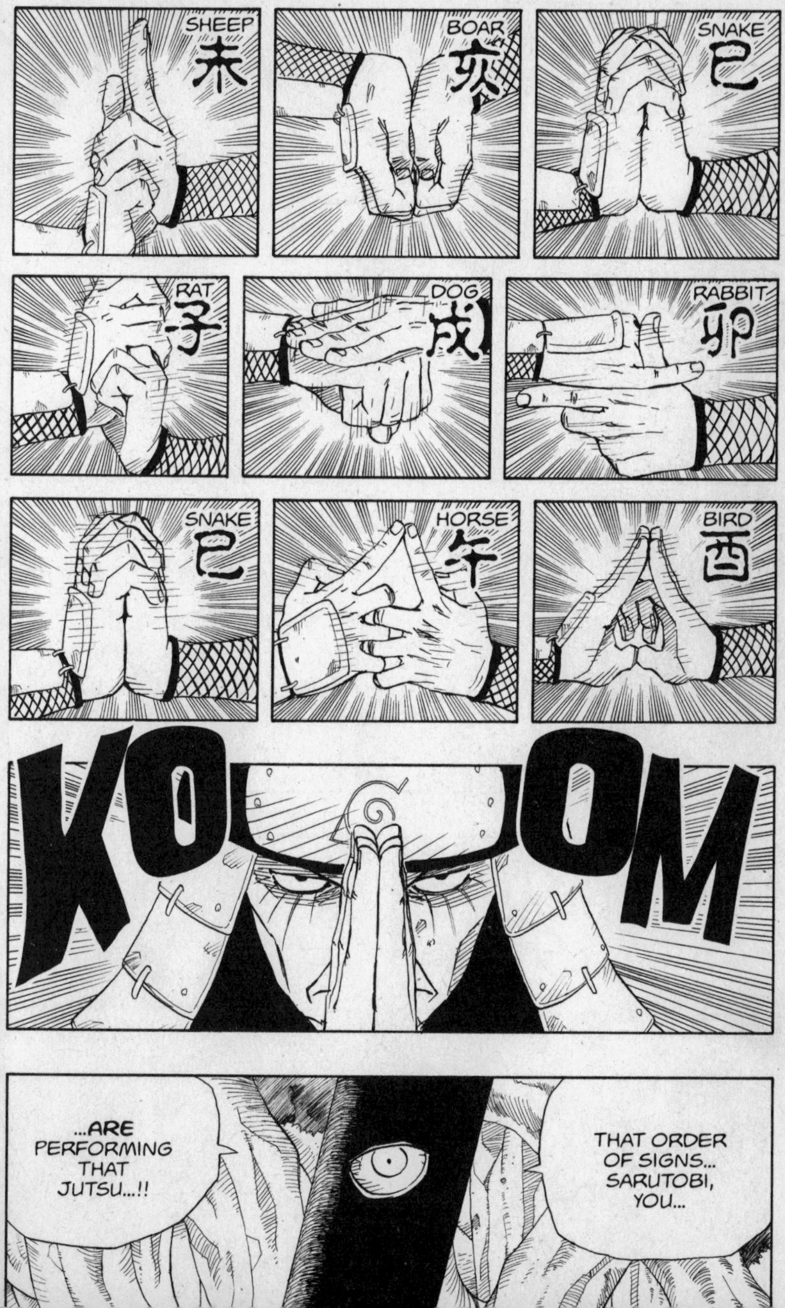

SNAKE
巳
BOAR
亥
SHEEP
未
RABBIT
卯
DOG
戌
RAT
子
BIRD
酉
HORSE
午
SNAKE
巳
KO OM
THAT ORDER OF SIGNS... SARUTOBI, YOU...
...ARE PERFORMING THAT JUTSU...!!

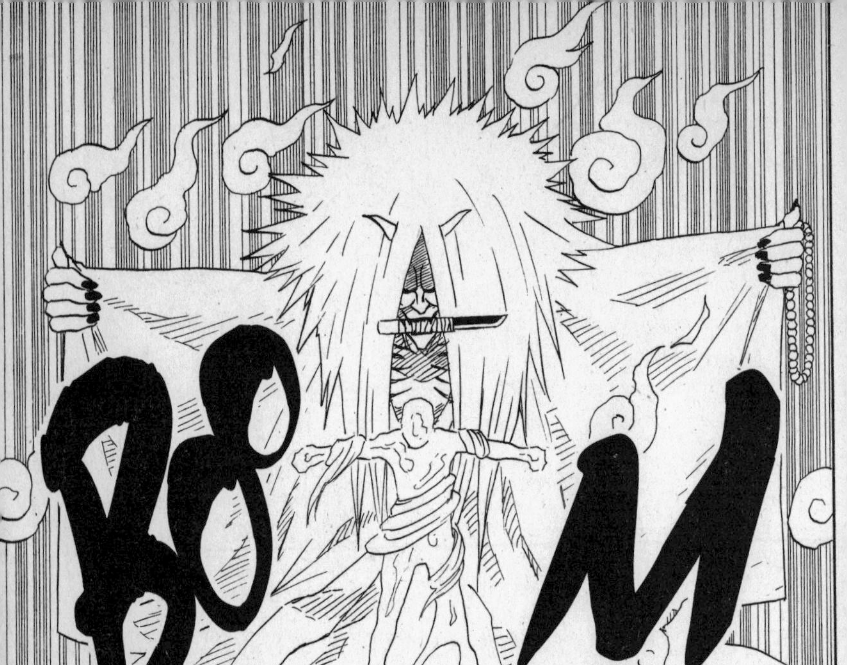
BOOM
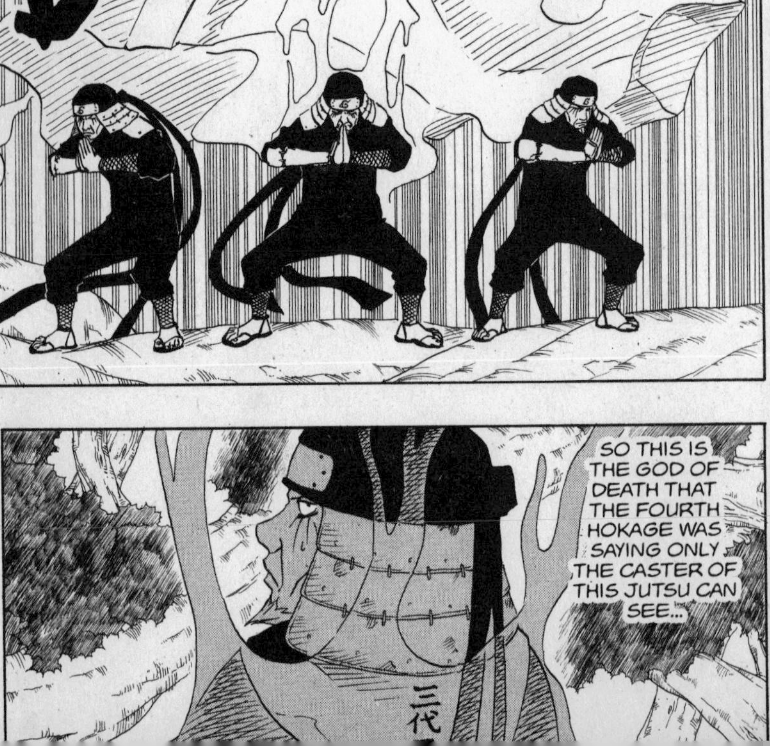
SO THIS IS THE GOD OF DEATH THAT THE FOURTH HOKAGE WAS SAYING ONLY THE CASTER OF THIS JUTSU CAN SEE...
三代

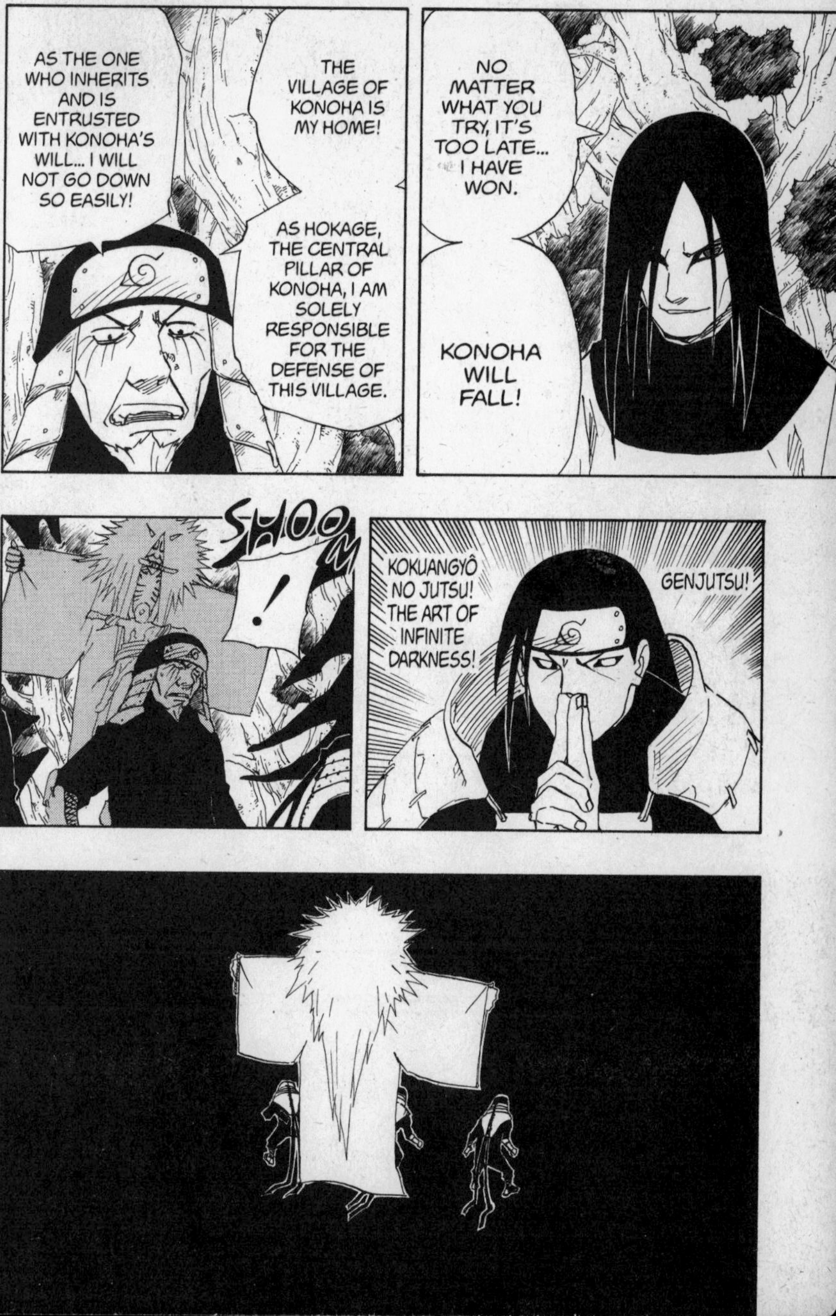

NO MATTER WHAT YOU TRY, IT'S TOO LATE... I HAVE WON.
KONOHA WILL FALL!
THE VILLAGE OF KONOHA IS MY HOME!
AS HOKAGE, THE CENTRAL PILLAR OF KONOHA, I AM SOLELY RESPONSIBLE FOR THE DEFENSE OF THIS VILLAGE.
AS THE ONE WHO INHERITS AND IS ENTRUSTED WITH KONOHA'S WILL... I WILL NOT GO DOWN SO EASILY!
GENJUTSU!
KOKUANGYÔ NO JUTSU! THE ART OF INFINITE DARKNESS!
SHOOM
!

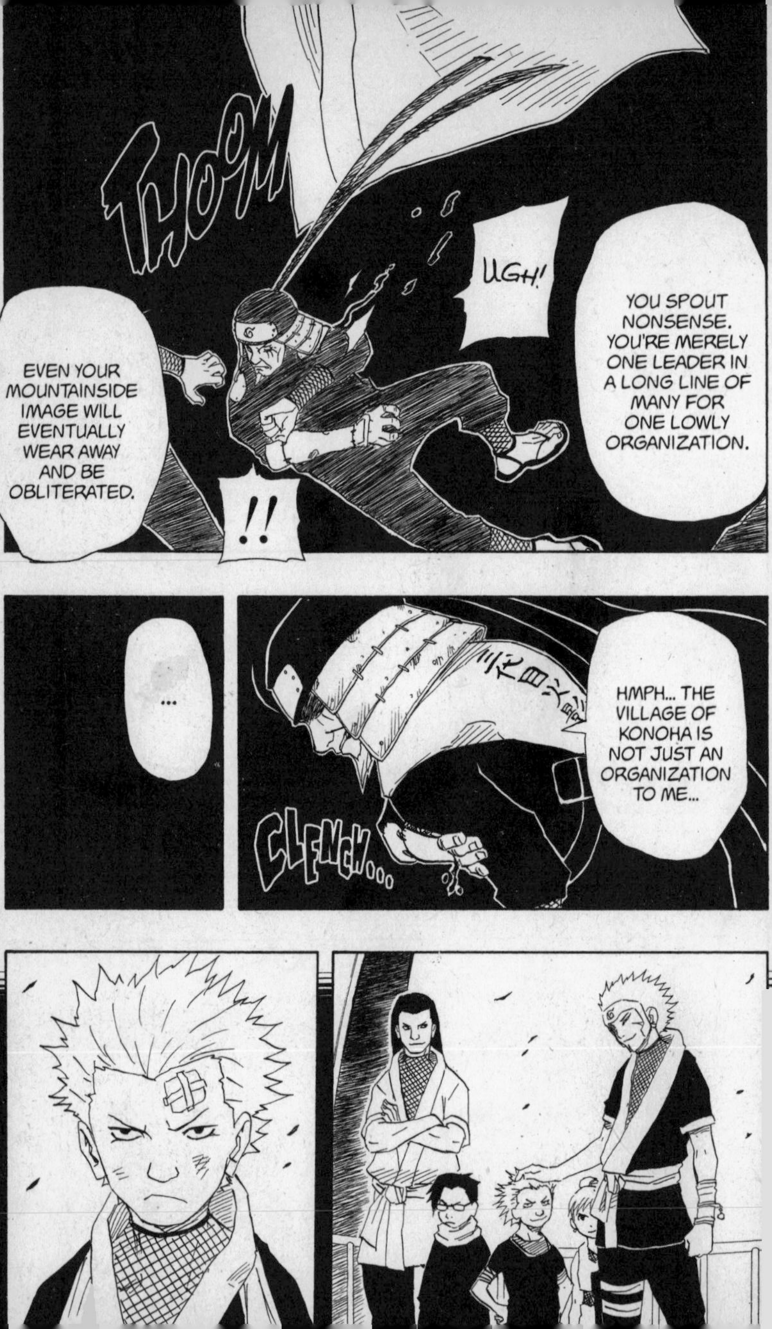
YOU SPOUT NONSENSE. YOU'RE MERELY ONE LEADER IN A LONG LINE OF MANY FOR ONE LOWLY ORGANIZATION.
UGH!
THOOM
EVEN YOUR MOUNTAINSIDE IMAGE WILL EVENTUALLY WEAR AWAY AND BE OBLITERATED.
!!
HMPH... THE VILLAGE OF KONOHA IS NOT JUST AN ORGANIZATION TO ME...
CLENCH...
...

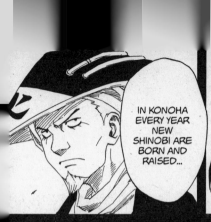

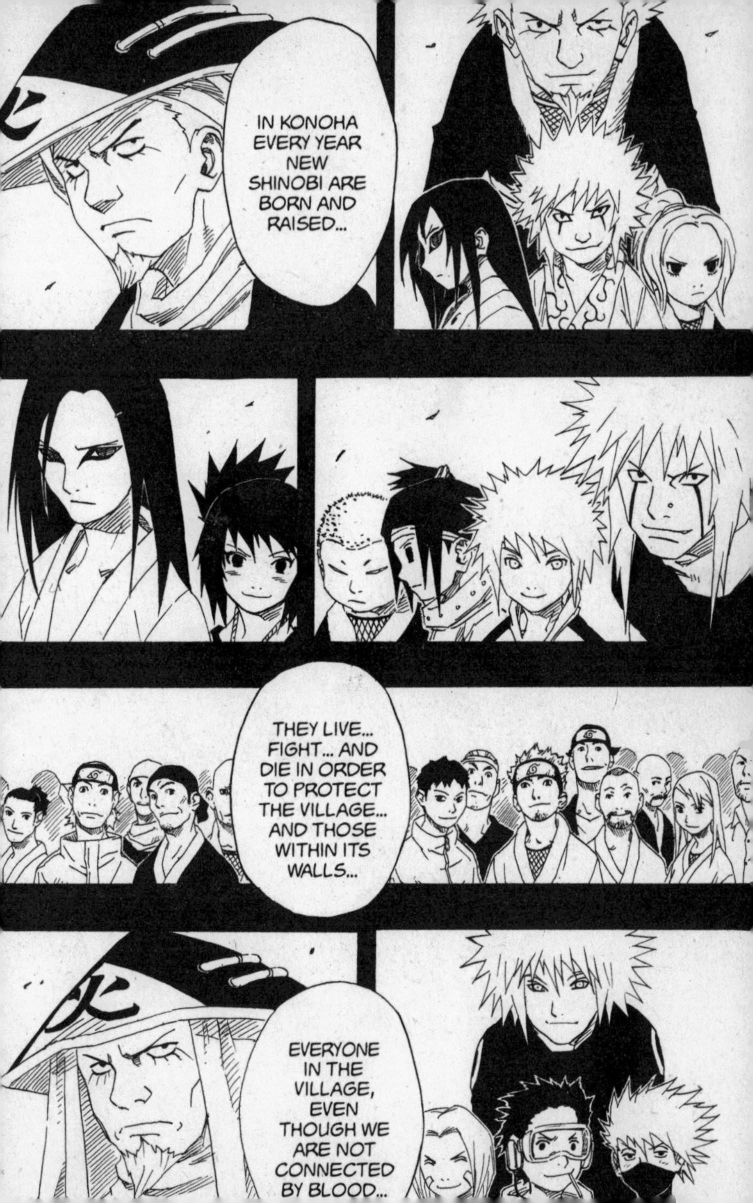
IN KONOHA EVERY YEAR NEW SHINOBI ARE BORN AND RAISED...
THEY LIVE... FIGHT... AND DIE IN ORDER TO PROTECT THE VILLAGE... AND THOSE WITHIN ITS WALLS...
EVERYONE IN THE VILLAGE, EVEN THOUGH WE ARE NOT CONNECTED BY BLOOD...

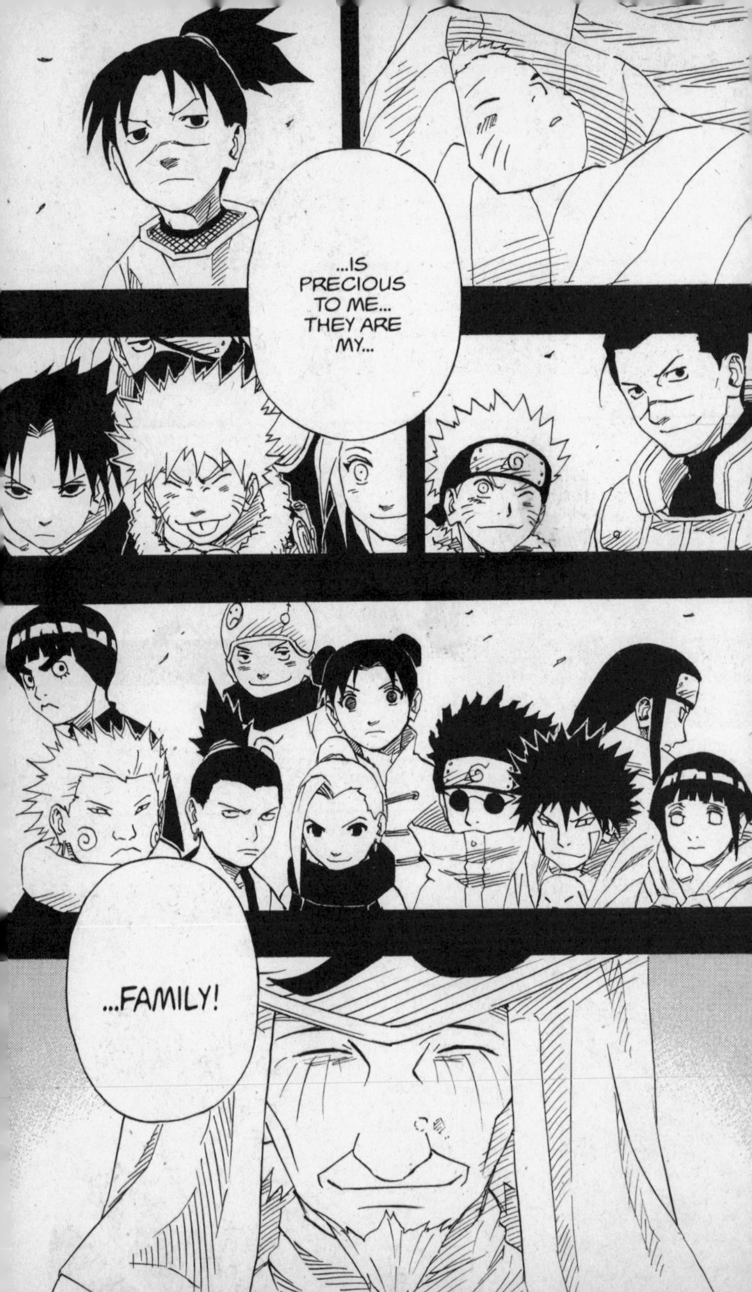
...IS PRECIOUS TO ME... THEY ARE MY...
...FAMILY!

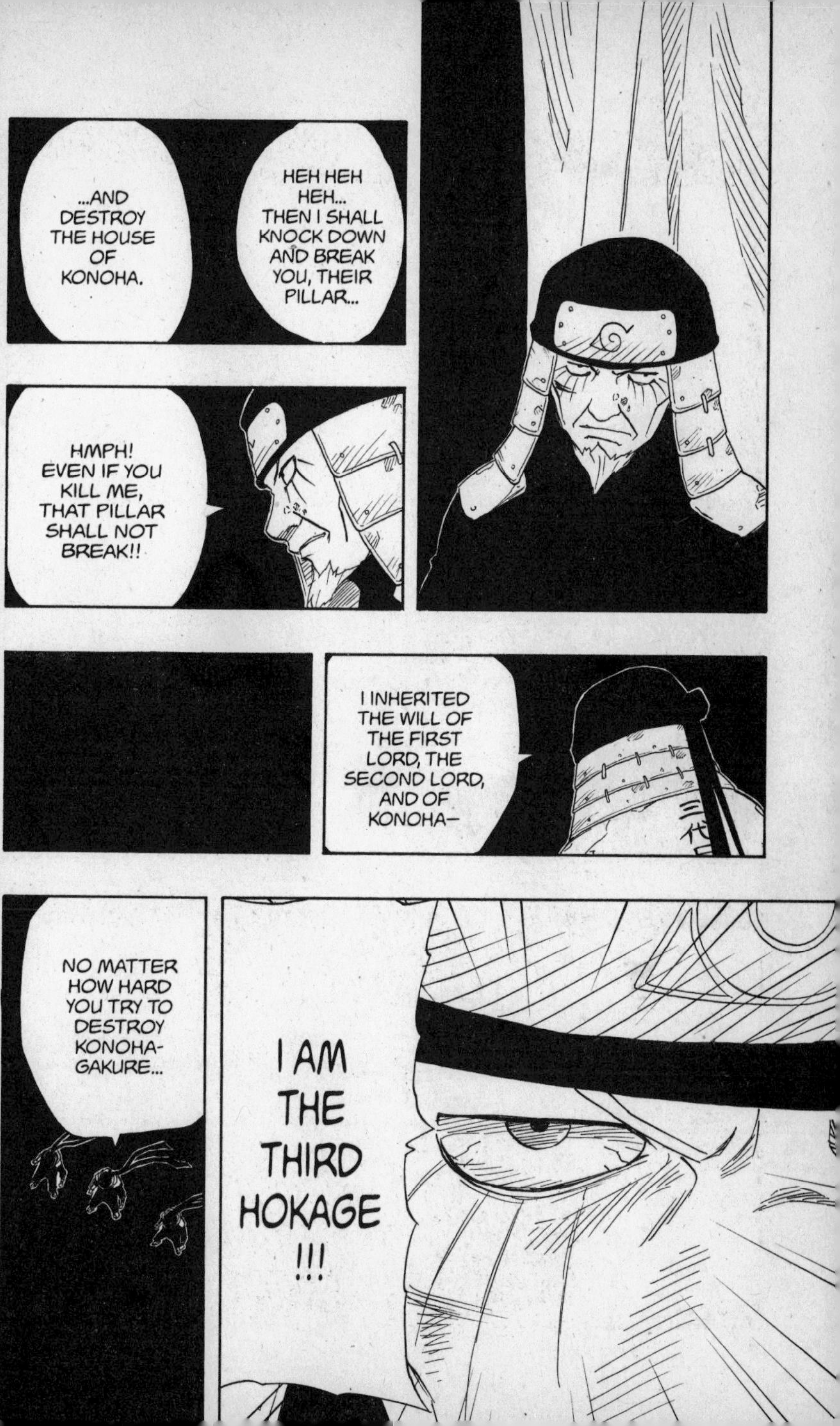
HEH HEH HEH... THEN I SHALL KNOCK DOWN AND BREAK YOU, THEIR PILLAR...
...AND DESTROY THE HOUSE OF KONOHA.
HMPH! EVEN IF YOU KILL ME, THAT PILLAR SHALL NOT BREAK!!
I INHERITED THE WILL OF THE FIRST LORD, THE SECOND LORD, AND OF KONOHA—
I AM THE THIRD HOKAGE!!!
NO MATTER HOW HARD YOU TRY TO DESTROY KONOHA-GAKURE...

READ THIS WAY

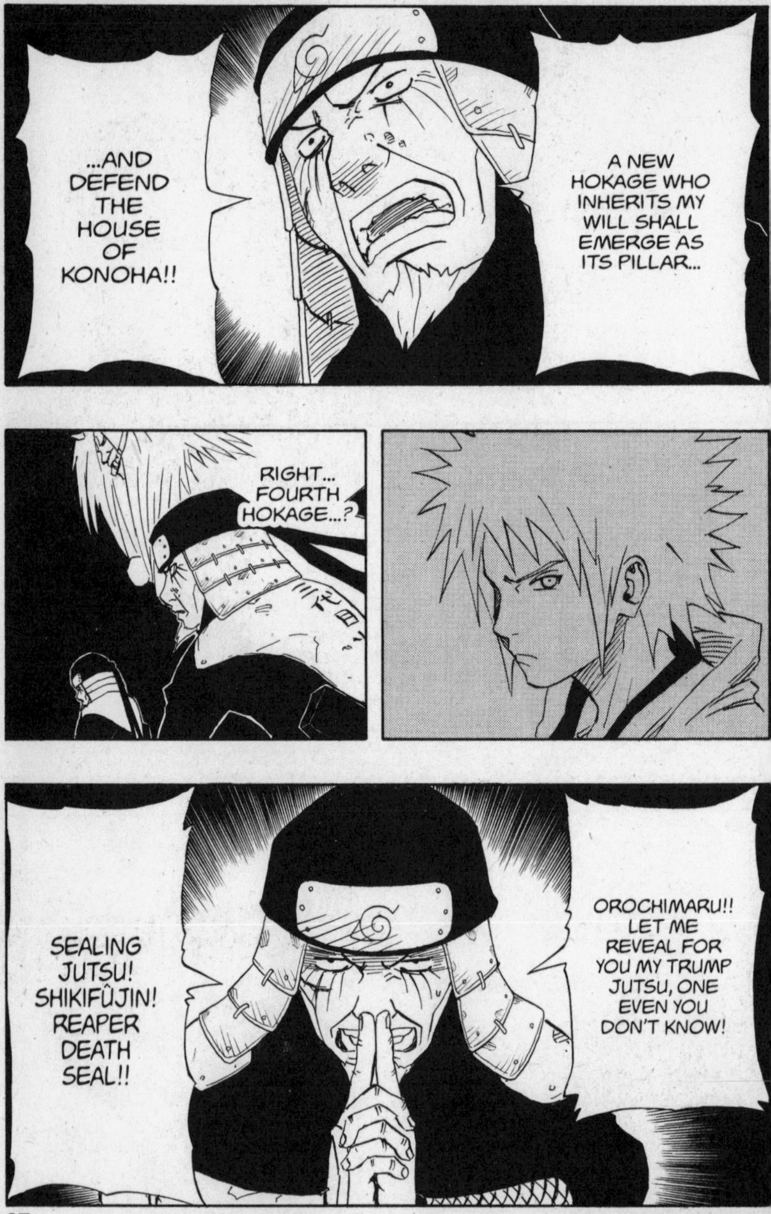

A NEW HOKAGE WHO INHERITS MY WILL SHALL EMERGE AS ITS PILLAR...
...AND DEFEND THE HOUSE OF KONOHA!!
RIGHT... FOURTH HOKAGE...?
OROCHIMARU!! LET ME REVEAL FOR YOU MY TRUMP JUTSU, ONE EVEN YOU DON'T KNOW!
SEALING JUTSU! SHIKIFÛJIN! REAPER DEATH SEAL!!

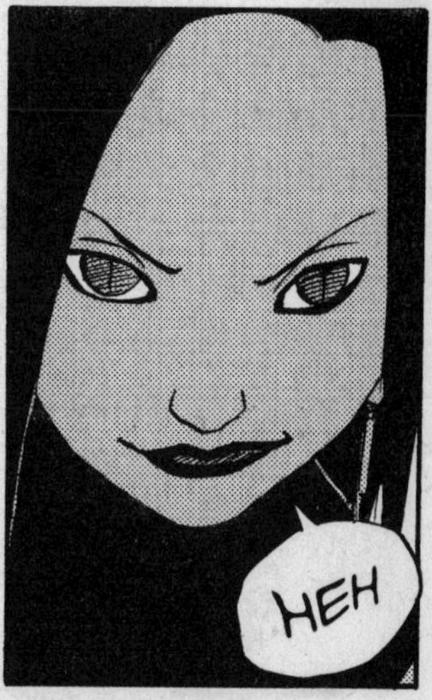
HEH

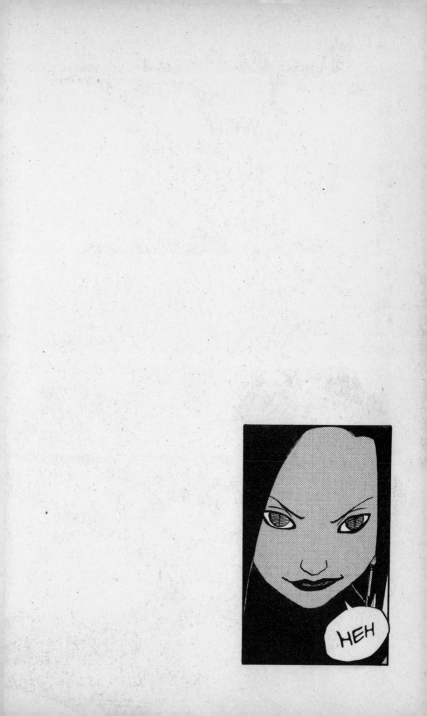

Number 123: The Final Seal

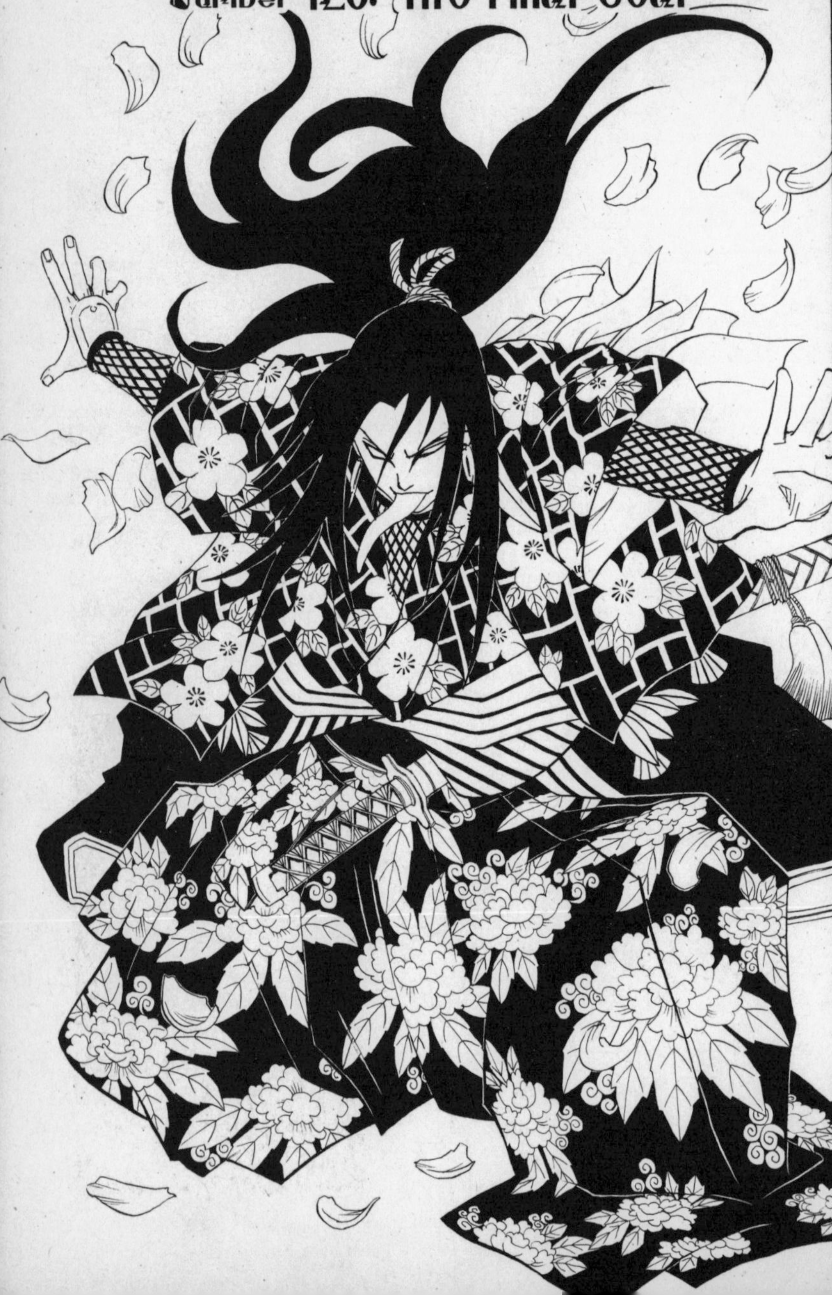

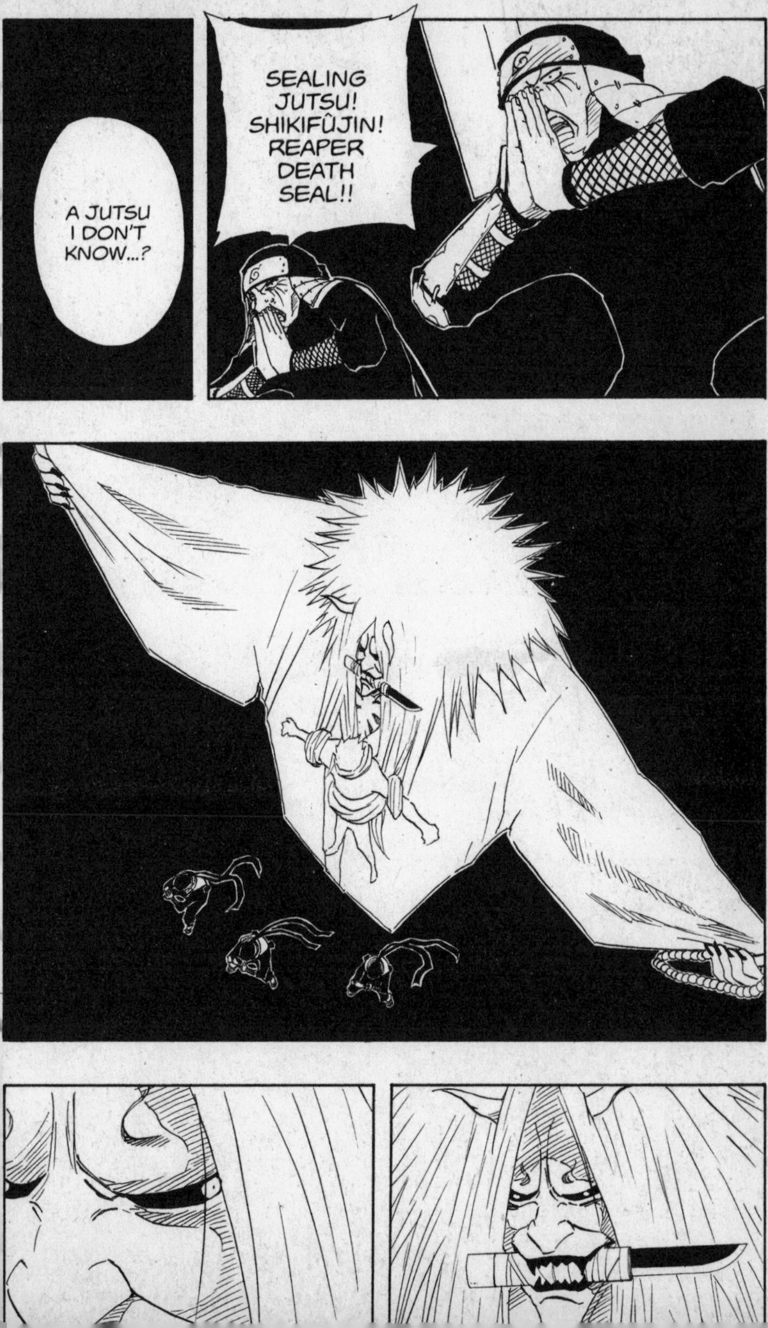
SEALING JUTSU! SHIKIFÛJIN! REAPER DEATH SEAL!!
A JUTSU I DON'T KNOW...?

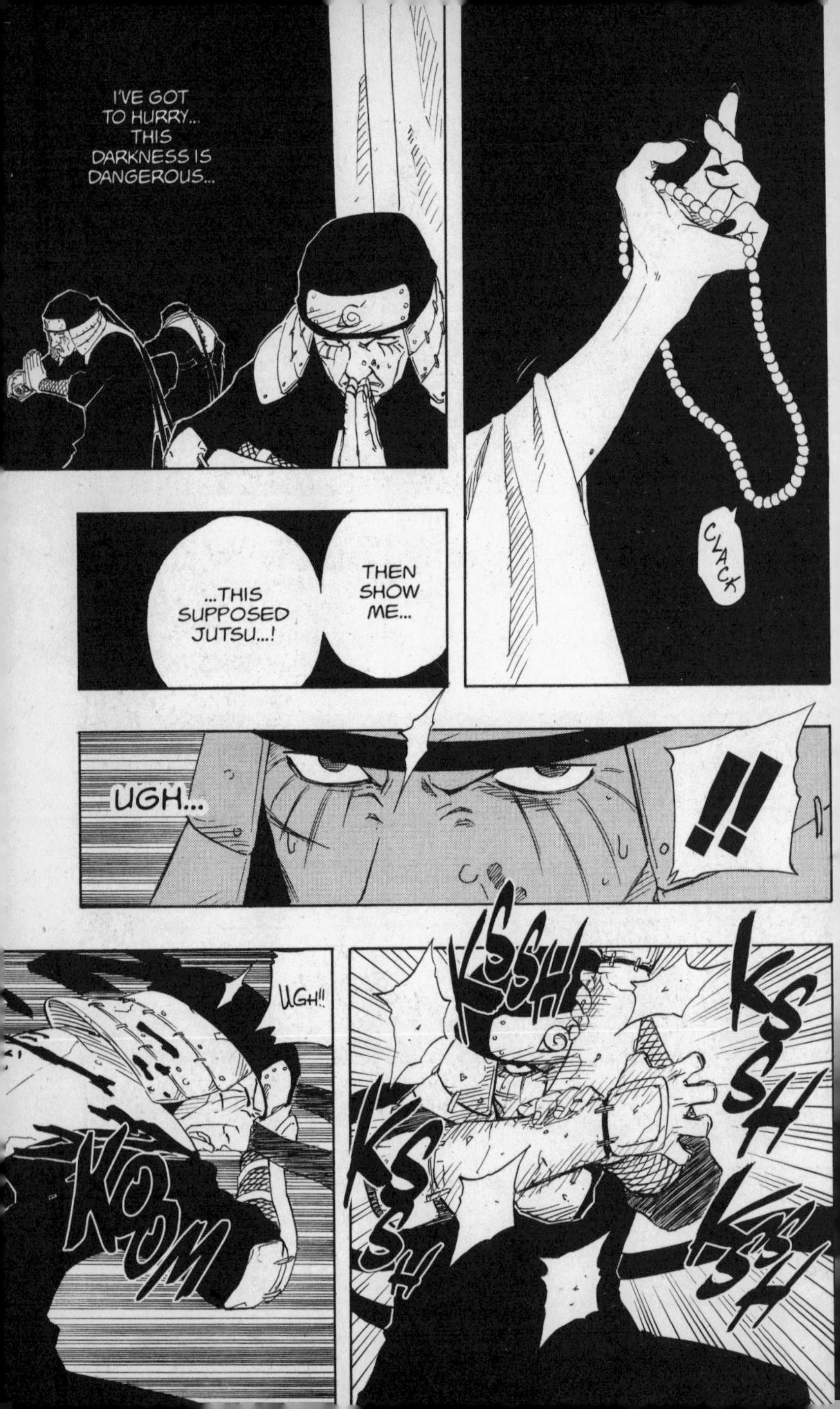
CLACK
I'VE GOT TO HURRY... THIS DARKNESS IS DANGEROUS...
THEN SHOW ME...
...THIS SUPPOSED JUTSU...!
!!
UGH...
KSSH
KSSH
KSH
KSSH
UGH!!
KOOM

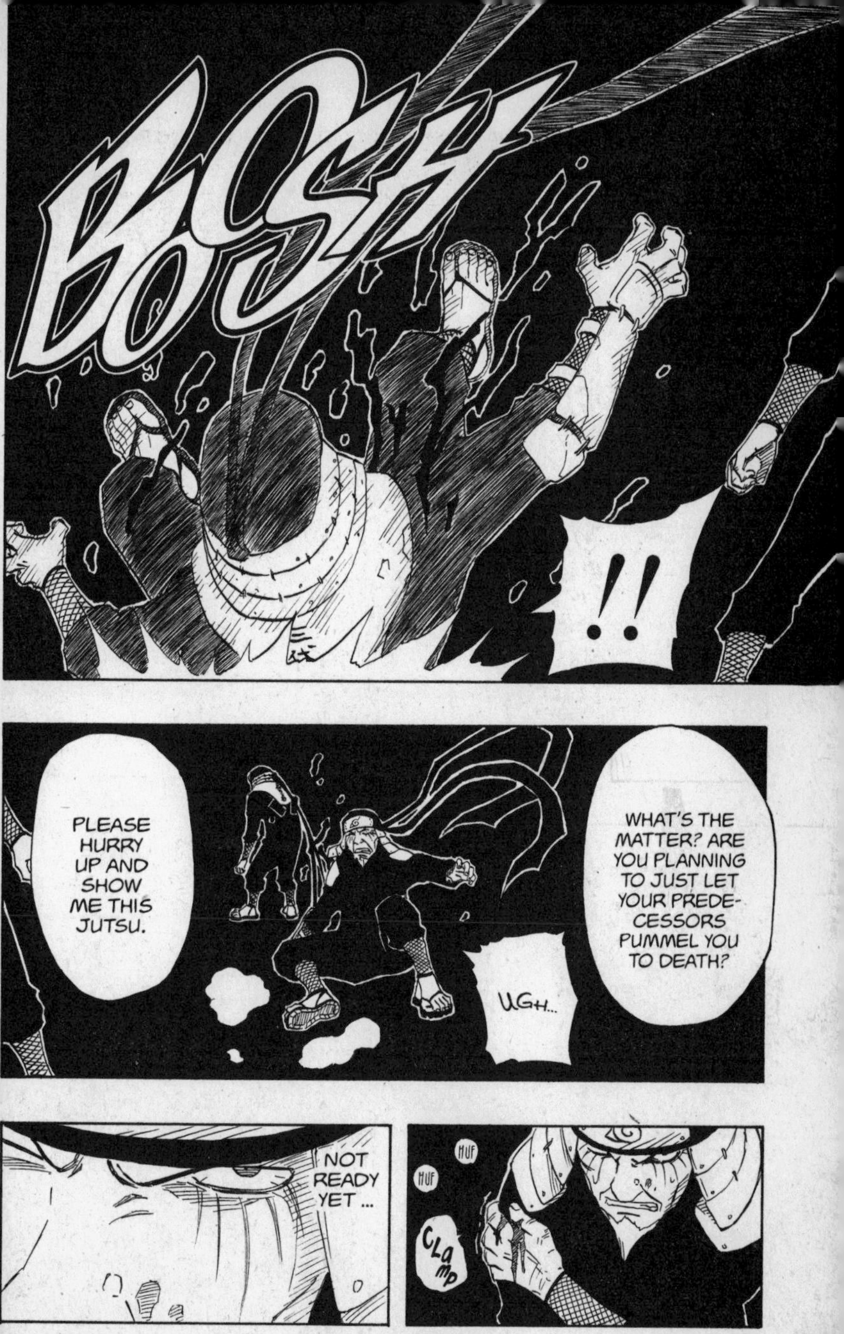
BOOSH
!!
WHAT'S THE MATTER? ARE YOU PLANNING TO JUST LET YOUR PREDECESSORS PUMMEL YOU TO DEATH?
UGH...
PLEASE HURRY UP AND SHOW ME THIS JUTSU.
HUF
HUF
CLAMP
NOT READY YET ...

READ THIS WAY

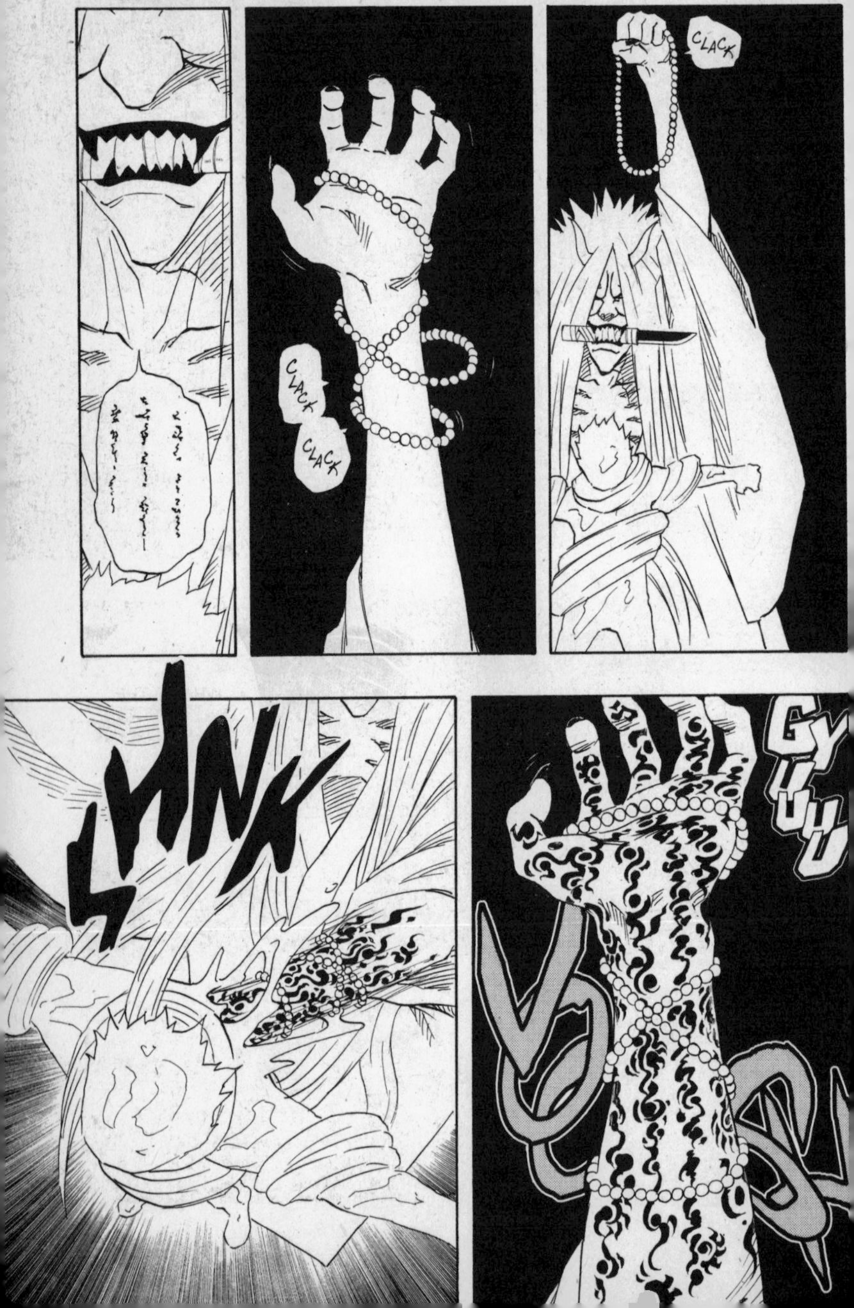
CLACK
CLACK
CLACK
GYUUU
SHINK

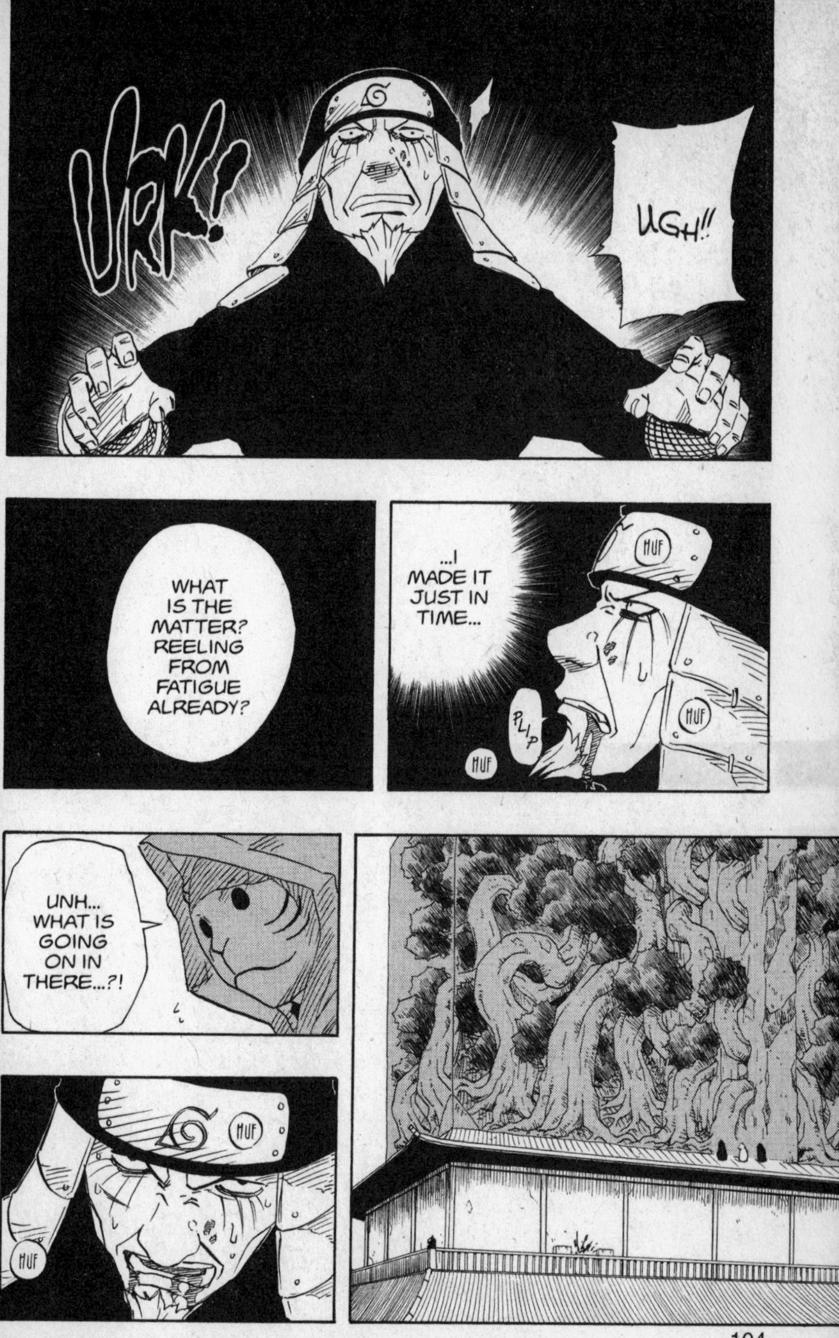
UGH!!
URK!
HUF
...I MADE IT JUST IN TIME...
HUF
PLIP
HUF
WHAT IS THE MATTER? REELING FROM FATIGUE ALREADY?
UNH... WHAT IS GOING ON IN THERE...?!
HUF
HUF

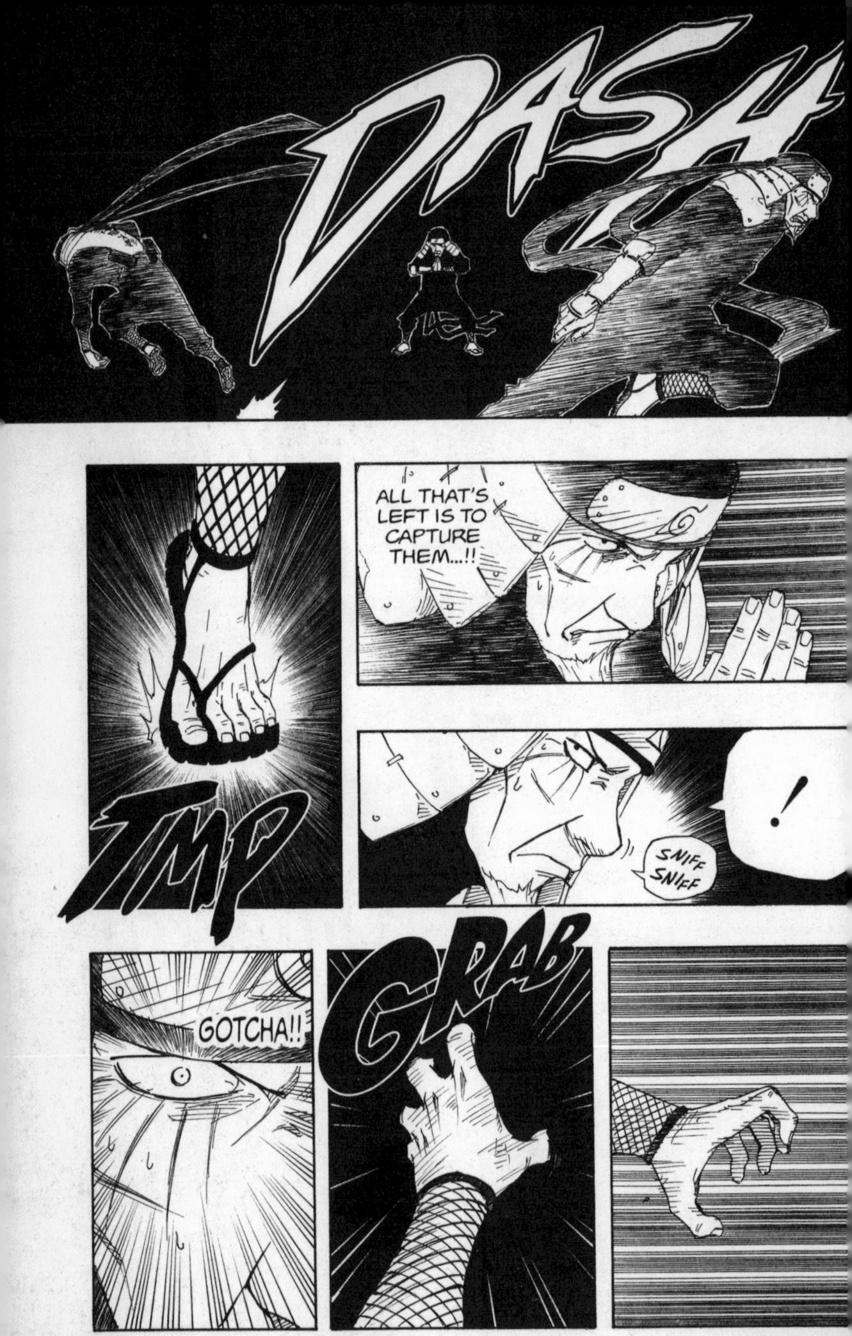
DASH
ALL THAT'S LEFT IS TO CAPTURE THEM...!!
!
SNIFF SNIFF
TMP
GRAB
GOTCHA!!

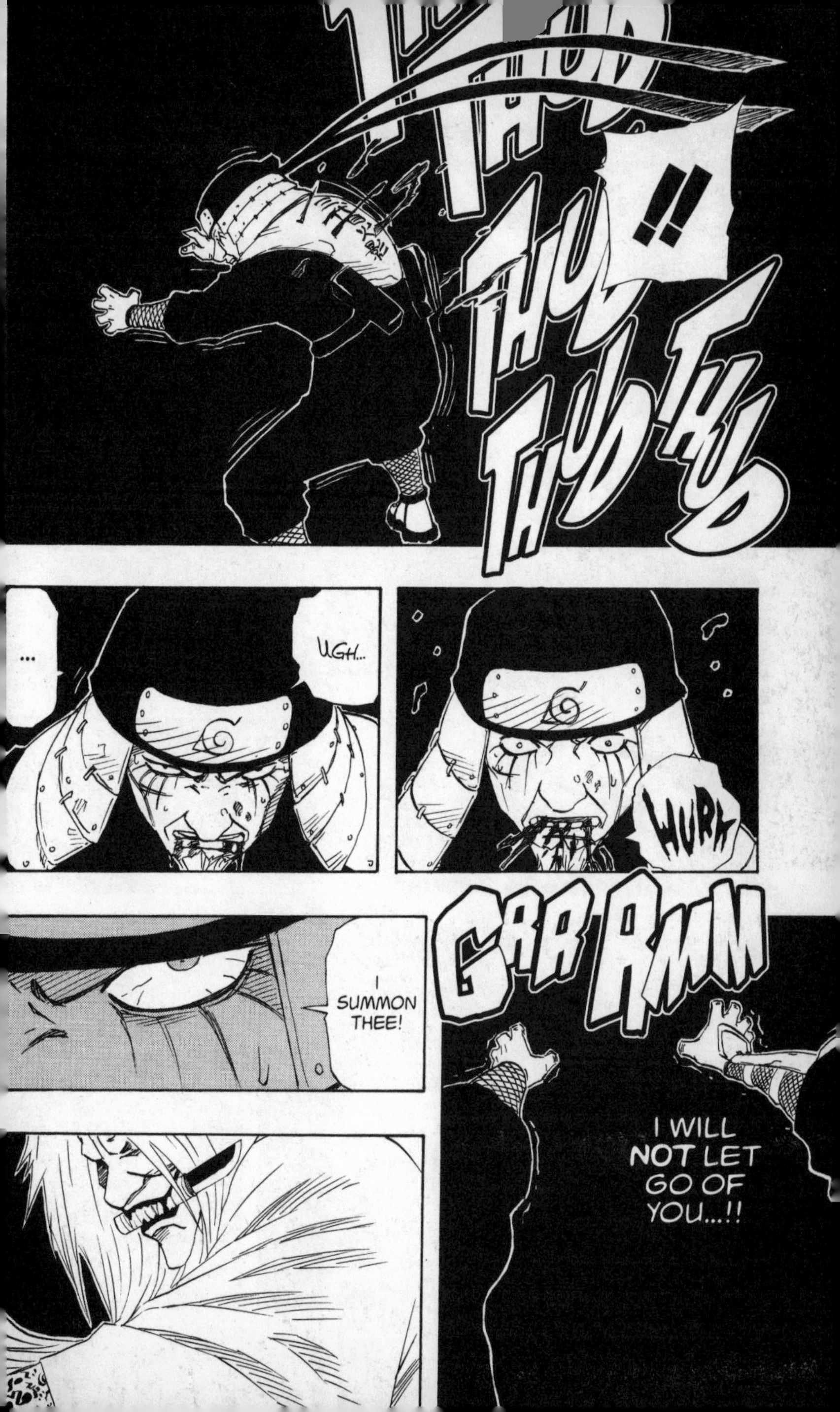
THUD
THUD!!
THUD THUD THUD
HURK
UGH...
...
GRRRMM
I SUMMON THEE!
I WILL NOT LET GO OF YOU...!!

READ THIS WAY

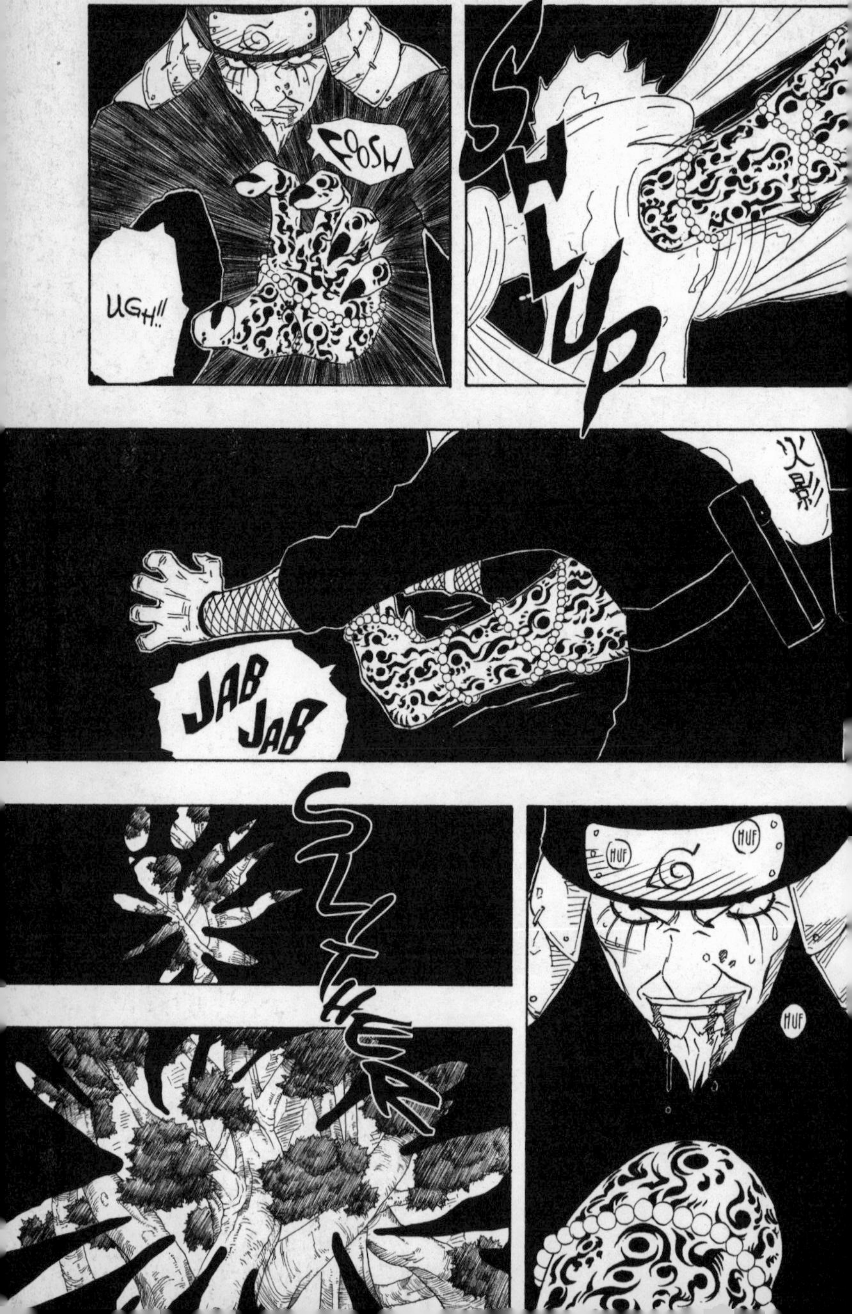
SHLLUP
FOOSH
UGH!!
火影
JAB JAB
HUF
HUF
HUF
SLITHER

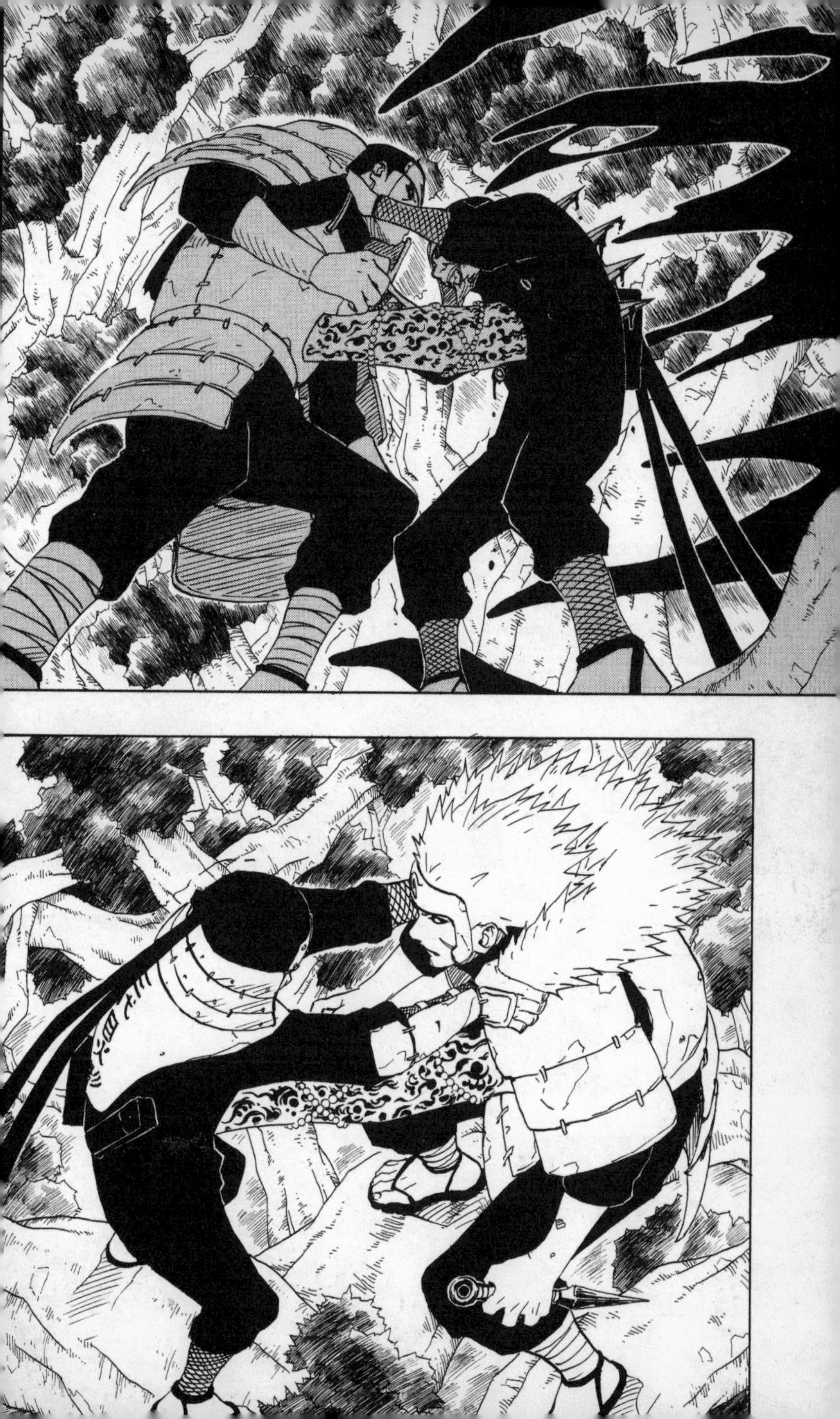

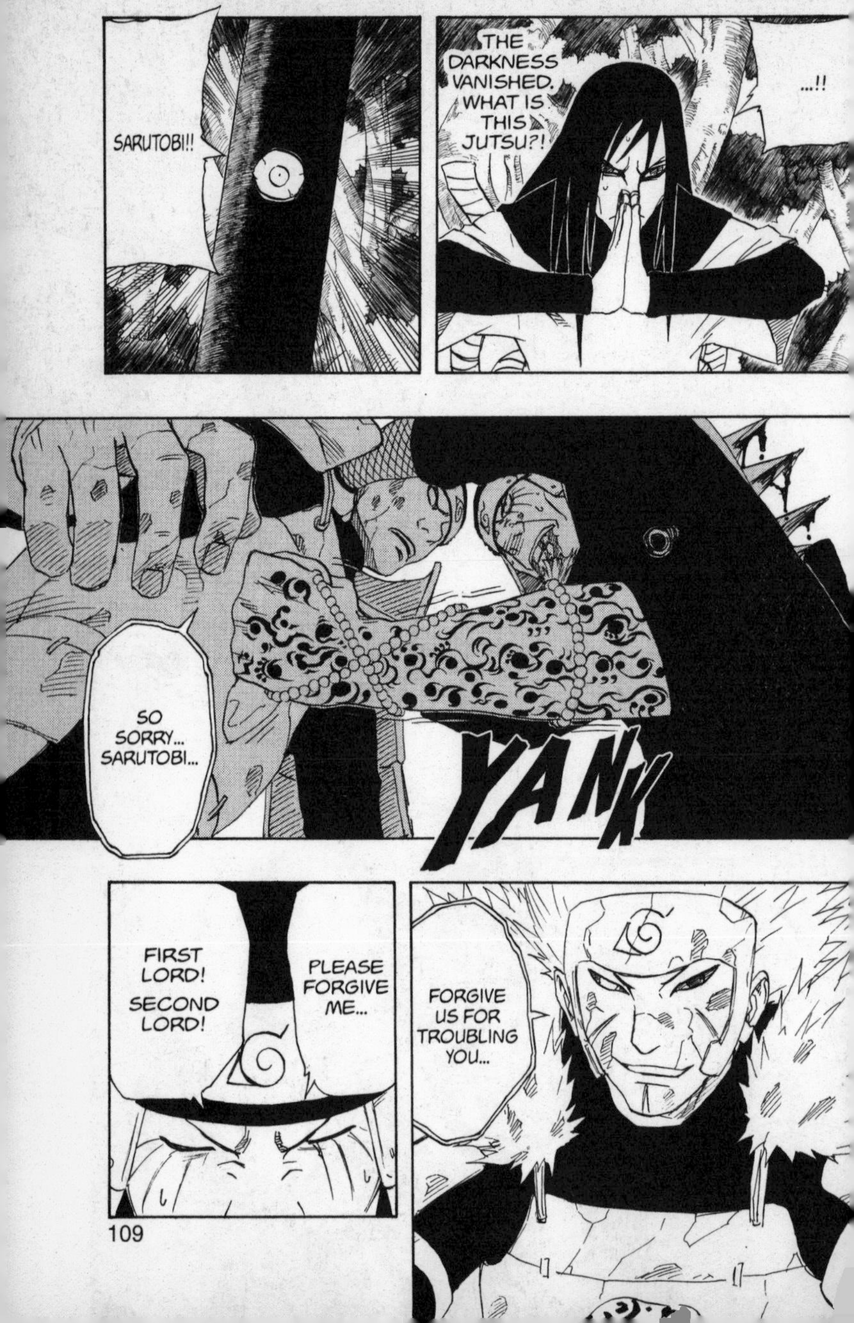
...!!
THE DARKNESS VANISHED. WHAT IS THIS JUTSU?!
SARUTOBI!!
YANK
SO SORRY... SARUTOBI...
FORGIVE US FOR TROUBLING YOU...
PLEASE FORGIVE ME...
FIRST LORD!
SECOND LORD!

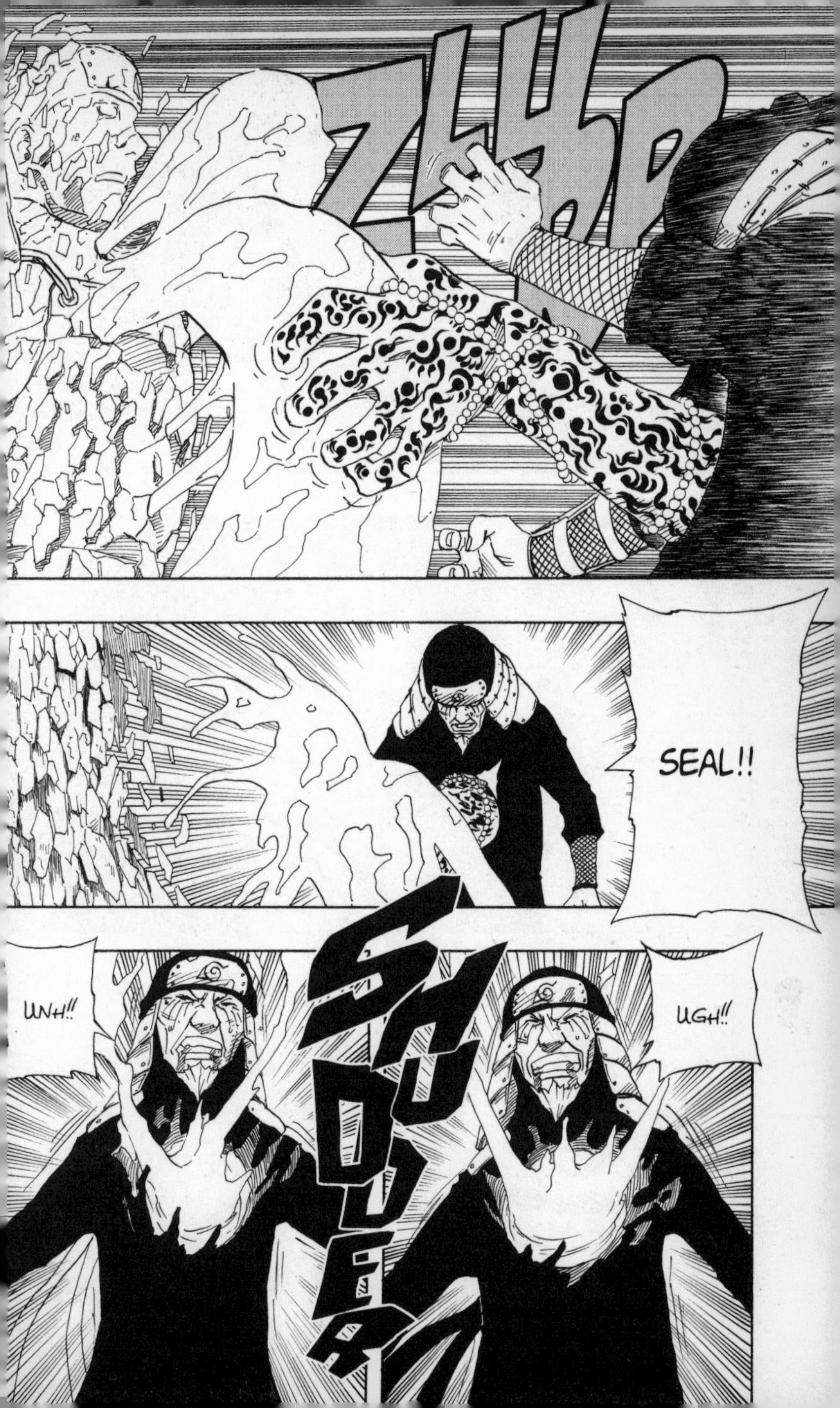
SEAL!!
UGH!!
SHUDDER
UNH!!

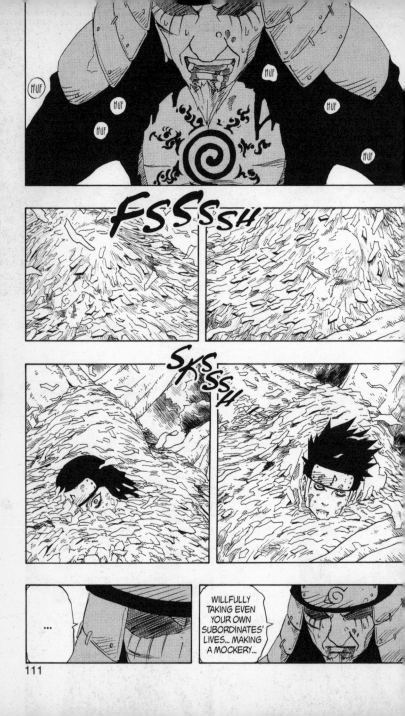

HUF HUF HUF HUF HUF HUF HUF

FSSSSH

SKSSSSH

...

WILLFULLY TAKING EVEN YOUR OWN SUBORDINATES' LIVES... MAKING A MOCKERY...

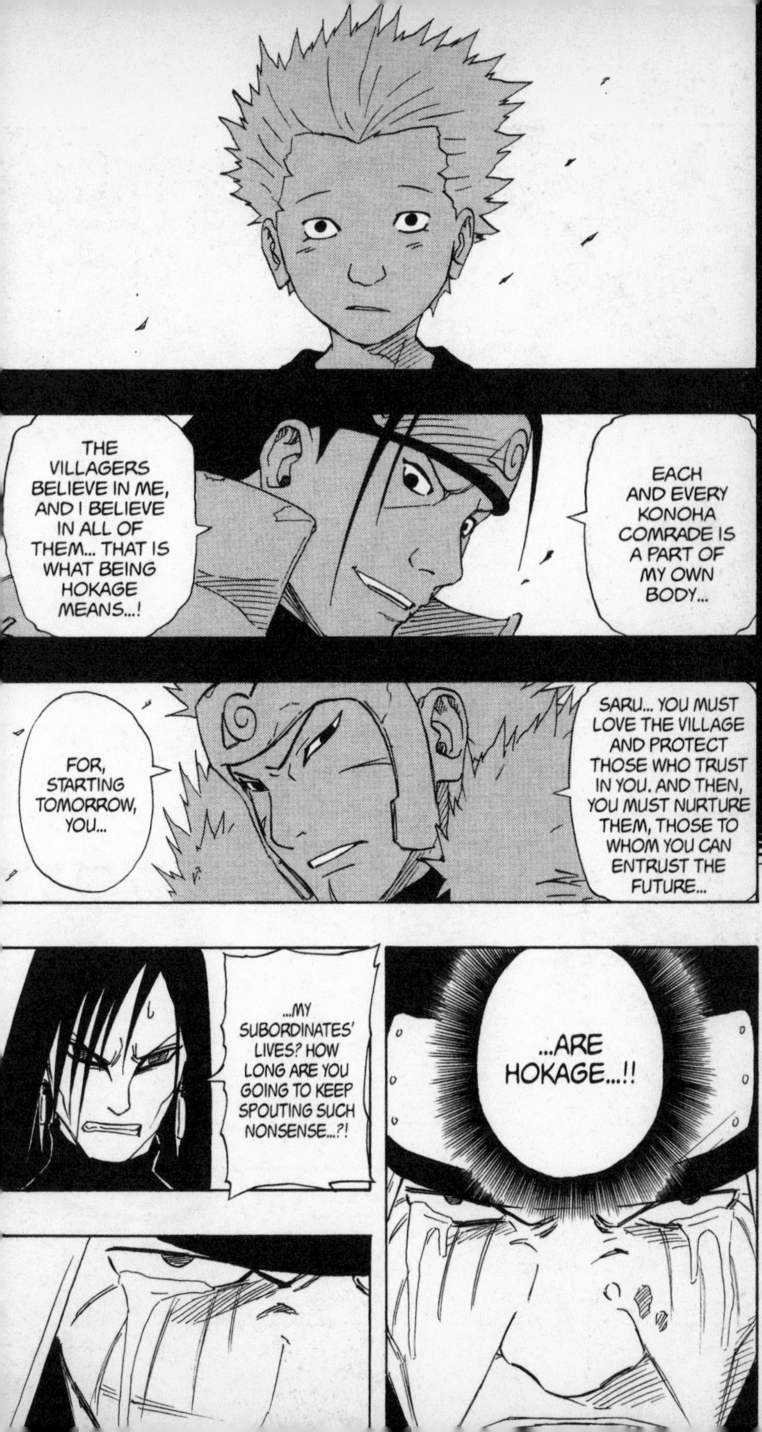
EACH AND EVERY KONOHA COMRADE IS A PART OF MY OWN BODY...
THE VILLAGERS BELIEVE IN ME, AND I BELIEVE IN ALL OF THEM... THAT IS WHAT BEING HOKAGE MEANS...!
SARU... YOU MUST LOVE THE VILLAGE AND PROTECT THOSE WHO TRUST IN YOU. AND THEN, YOU MUST NURTURE THEM, THOSE TO WHOM YOU CAN ENTRUST THE FUTURE...
FOR, STARTING TOMORROW, YOU...
...ARE HOKAGE...!!
...MY SUBORDINATES' LIVES? HOW LONG ARE YOU GOING TO KEEP SPOUTING SUCH NONSENSE...?!

READ THIS WAY

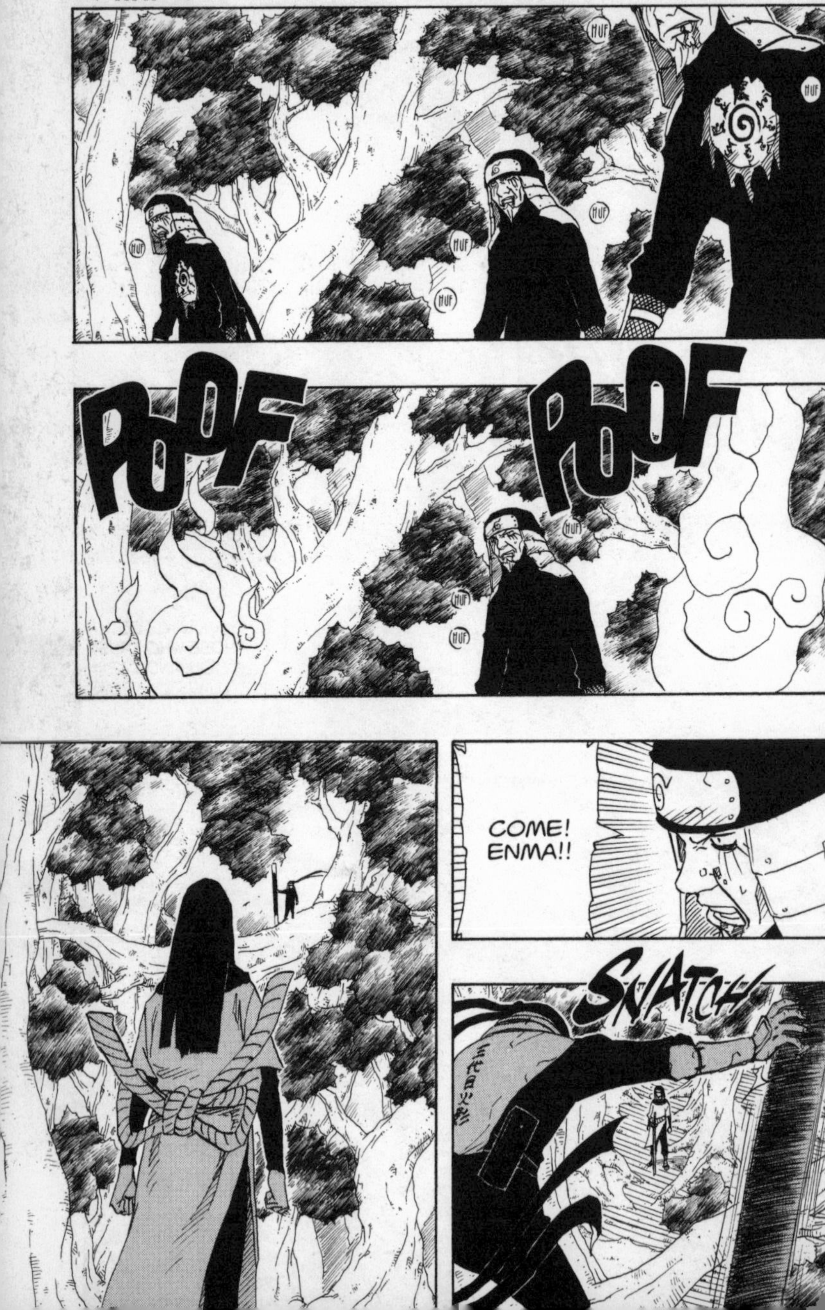
HUF
HUF
HUF
HUF
HUF
HUF
POOF
POOF
HUF
HUF
HUF
COME! ENMA!!
SNATCH

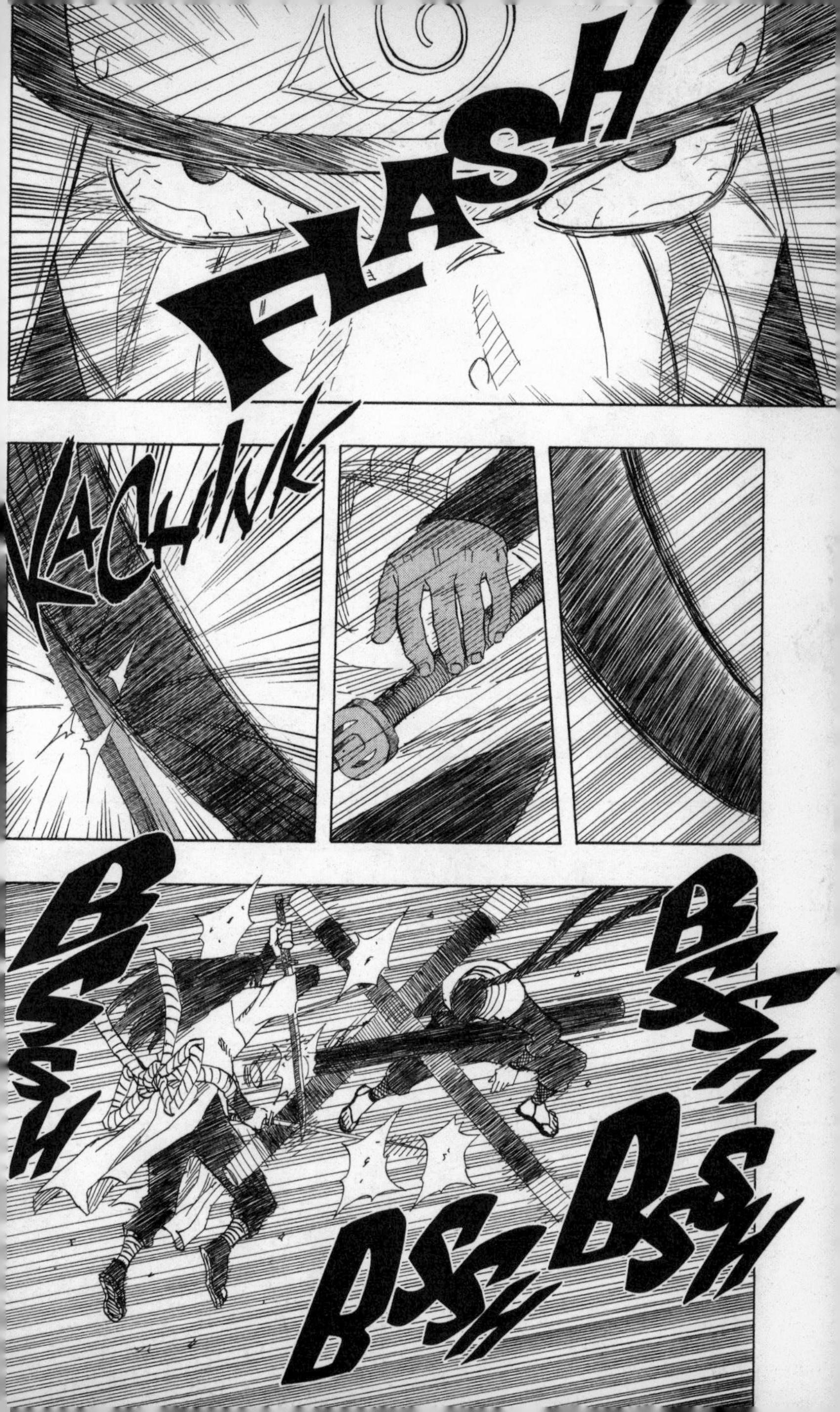
FLASH
KACHINK
BSSH
BSSH
BSH
BASHSH

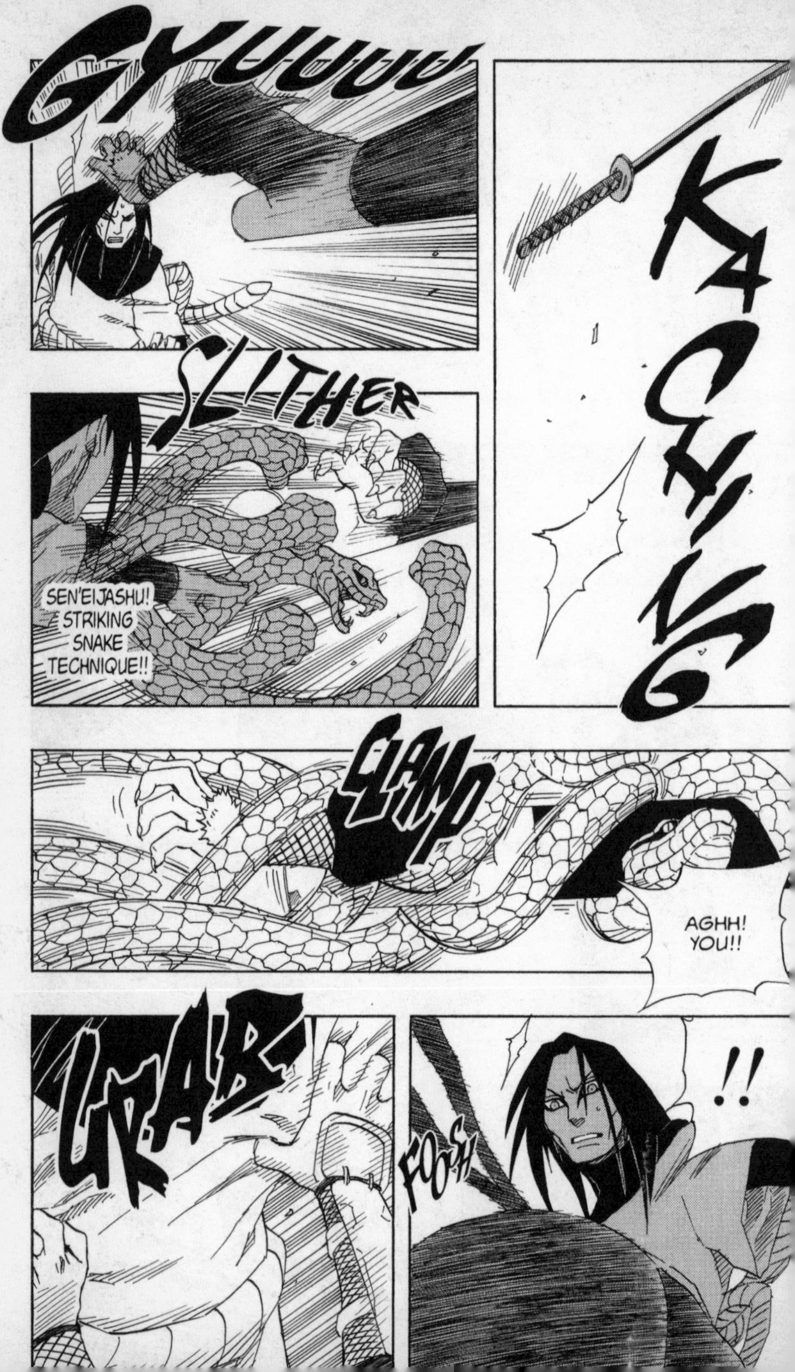
KACHING
GYUUUUU
SLITHER
SEN'EIJASHU! STRIKING SNAKE TECHNIQUE!!
CLAMP
AGHH! YOU!!
!!
FOOSH
GRAB

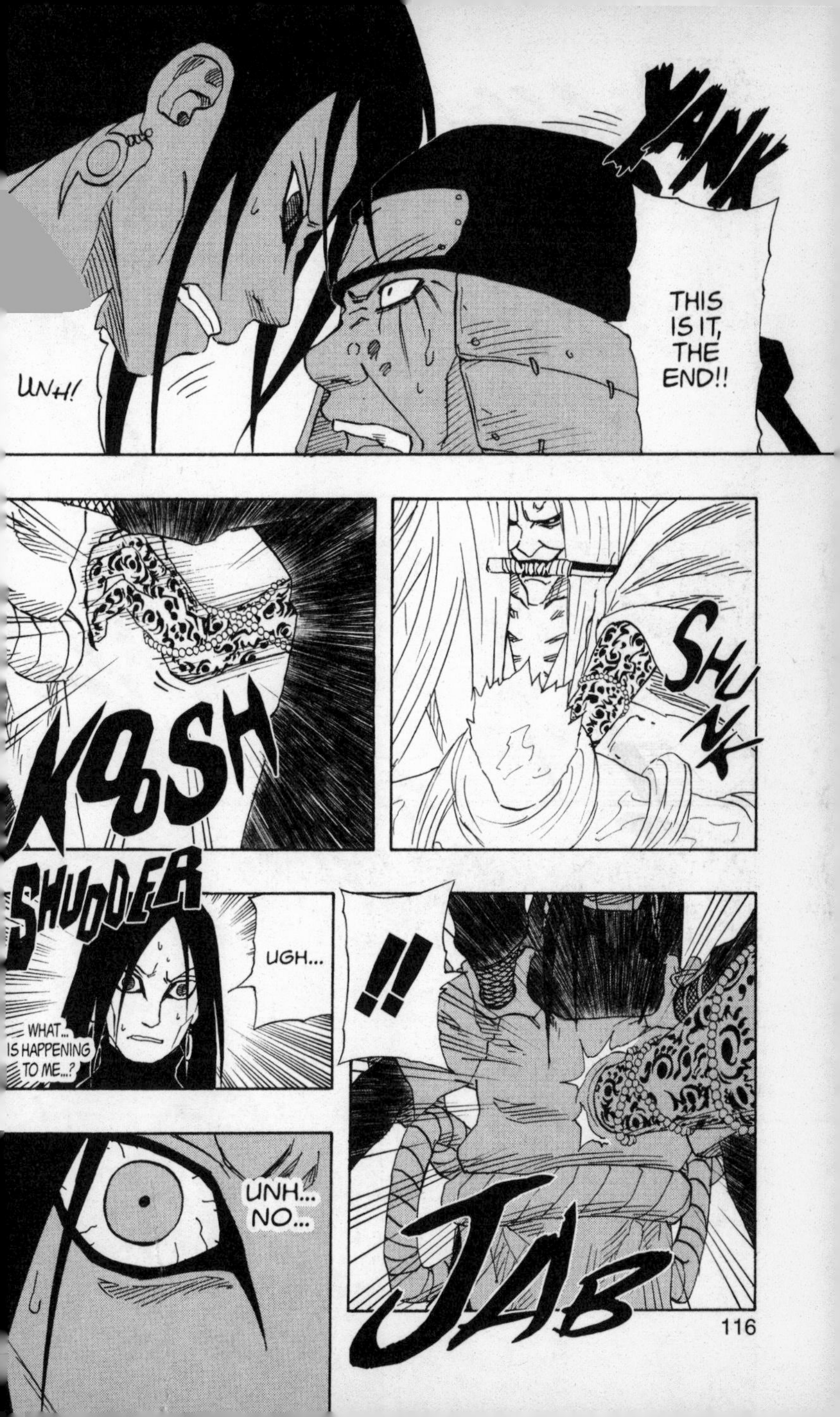
YANK
THIS IS IT, THE END!!
UNH!
SHUNK
KOOSH
!!
JAB
SHUDDER
UGH...
WHAT... IS HAPPENING TO ME...?
UNH... NO...

READ THIS WAY

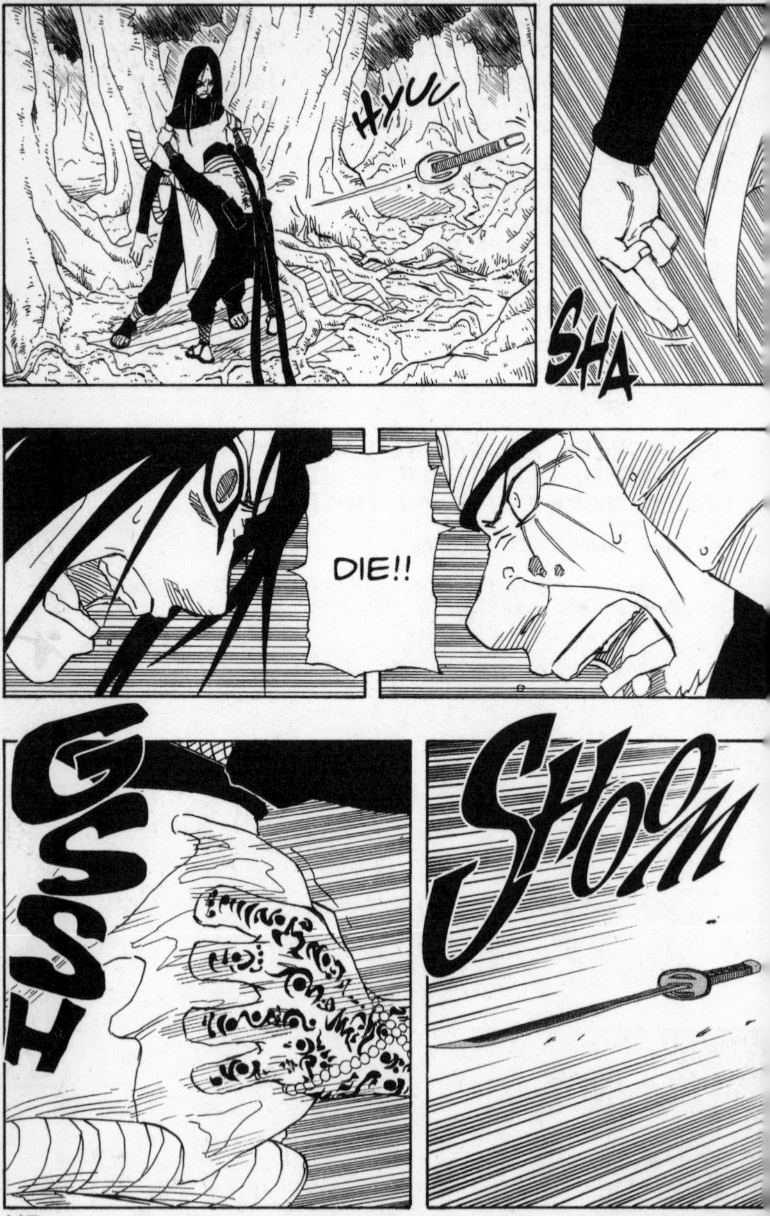
SHA
HYUU
DIE!!
SHOOM
GUSH

THE WORLD OF KISHIMOTO MASASHI
MY PERSONAL HISTORY, PART 20

AROUND THE TIME OF MY THIRD YEAR IN COLLEGE, I STARTED
WATCHING MOVIES A LOT. THERE ARE VARIOUS FILM CONCEPTS THAT
APPLY TO MANGA, SO THEY ARE GOOD REFERENCES.

PERHAPS BECAUSE OF THAT, I STARTED RENTING VIDEOS MORE AND
MORE, UNTIL I WAS WATCHING AT LEAST ONE MOVIE A DAY. EVENTU-
ALLY, EVEN RENTALS WEREN'T ENOUGH, SO I STARTED GOING TO THE
THEATER TO WATCH NEW RELEASES. ONE SUCH DAY, I STARTED
HEARING RUMORS ABOUT THE BRAD PITT/MORGAN FREEMAN
MOVIE "SEVEN." IT WAS A BLOCKBUSTER HIT THAT WAS SECOND IN
BOX OFFICE TICKET SALES IN 1996. A PSYCHOLOGICAL THRILLER
WHOSE TITULAR THEME REFERS TO THE SEVEN DEADLY SINS, IT
RAISED MY EXPECTATIONS QUITE A BIT. "THIS IS A MUST! I'VE GOT TO
GET TO THE THEATER!" MY DETERMINATION AND ZEAL KEPT ON
CLIMBING! I EVEN DECIDED TO GO TO THE SALON FOR A CUT
BECAUSE MY BANGS HAD GROWN SO LONG I WAS AFRAID IT WOULD
MAKE IT HARDER TO SEE THE MOVIE SCREEN.

...HOWEVER!! KISHIMOTO WAS NOT YET AWARE AT THIS TIME THAT A FRIGHTFUL INCIDENT WOULD TAKE PLACE AT THAT SALON!!

DUN-DA-DUN-DUN~~~DUN!!!

(I'M GOING TO STRETCH THIS OUT IN TYPICAL MYSTERY/SUSPENSE
GENRE FASHION... HURRY ON TO PAGE 138!)

Number 124: The Eternal Battle...!!

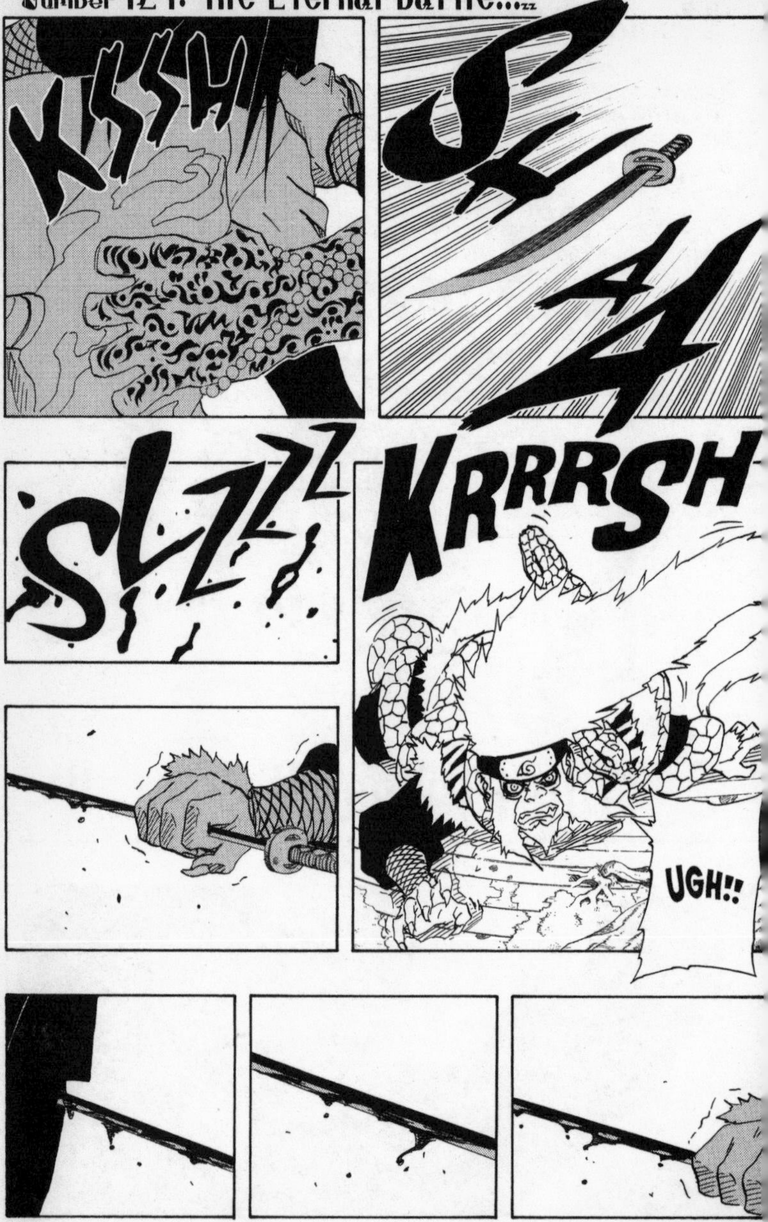

SHAAA
KSSSH
KRRRSH
UGH!!
SLZZZ

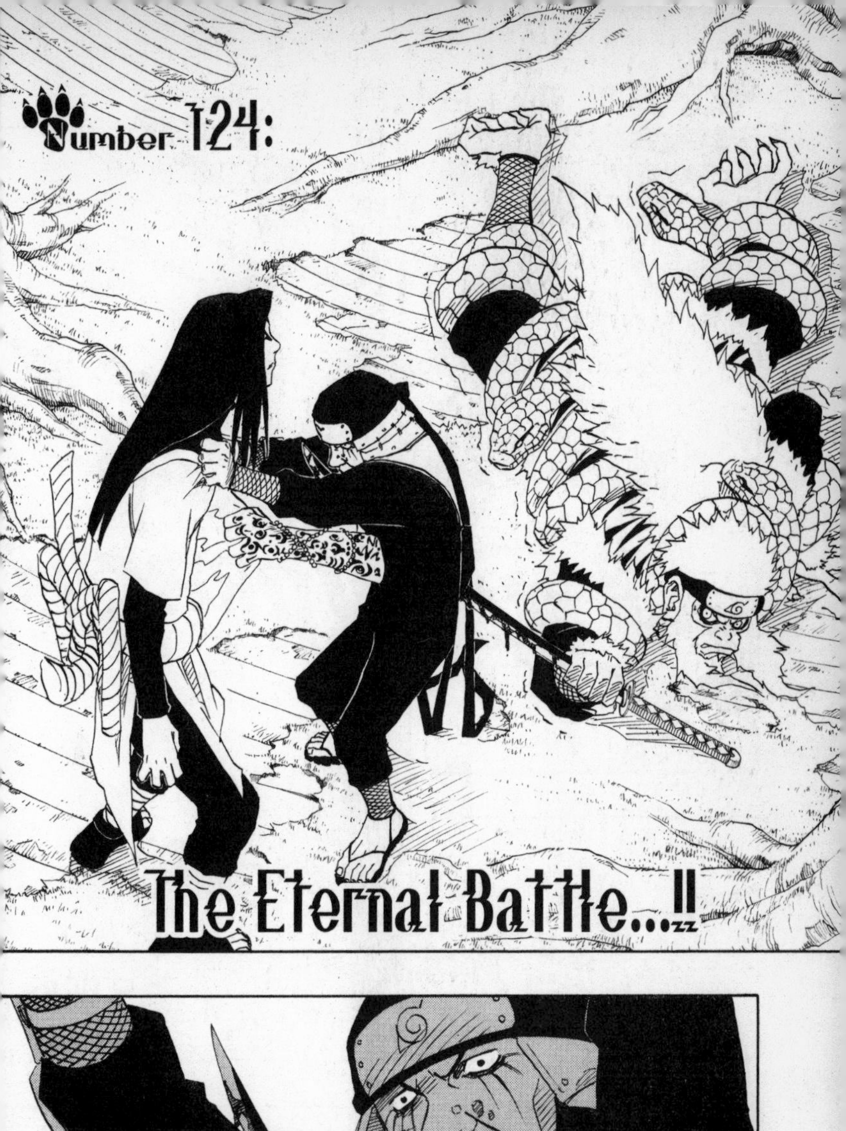
Number 124:
The Eternal Battle...!!

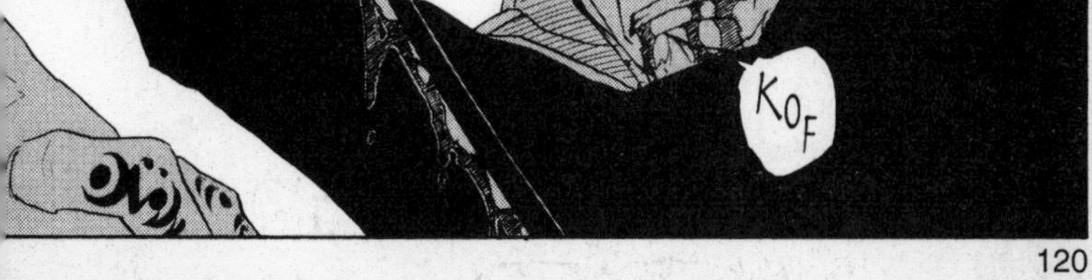
KOF

READ THIS WAY

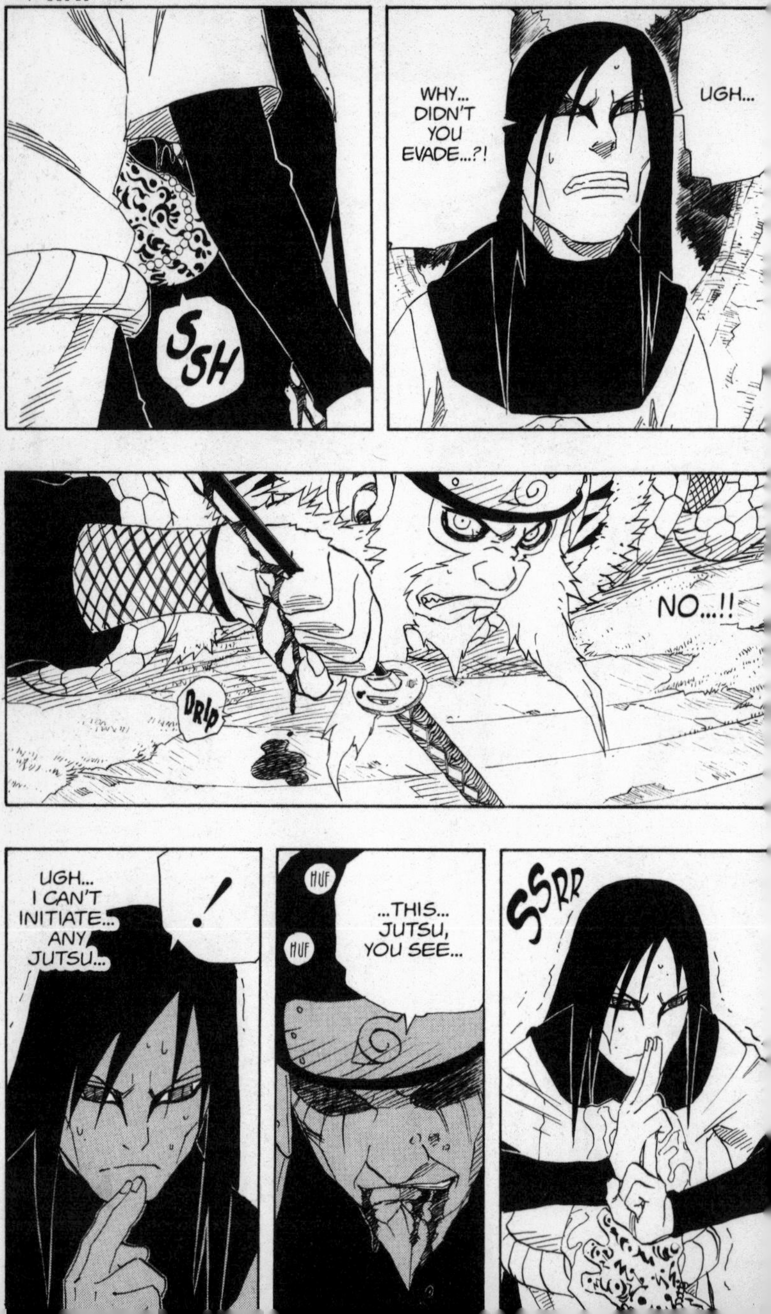
UGH...
WHY... DIDN'T YOU EVADE...?!
SSH
NO...!!
DRIP
SSRR
...THIS... JUTSU, YOU SEE...
HUF
HUF
!
UGH... I CAN'T INITIATE... ANY JUTSU...

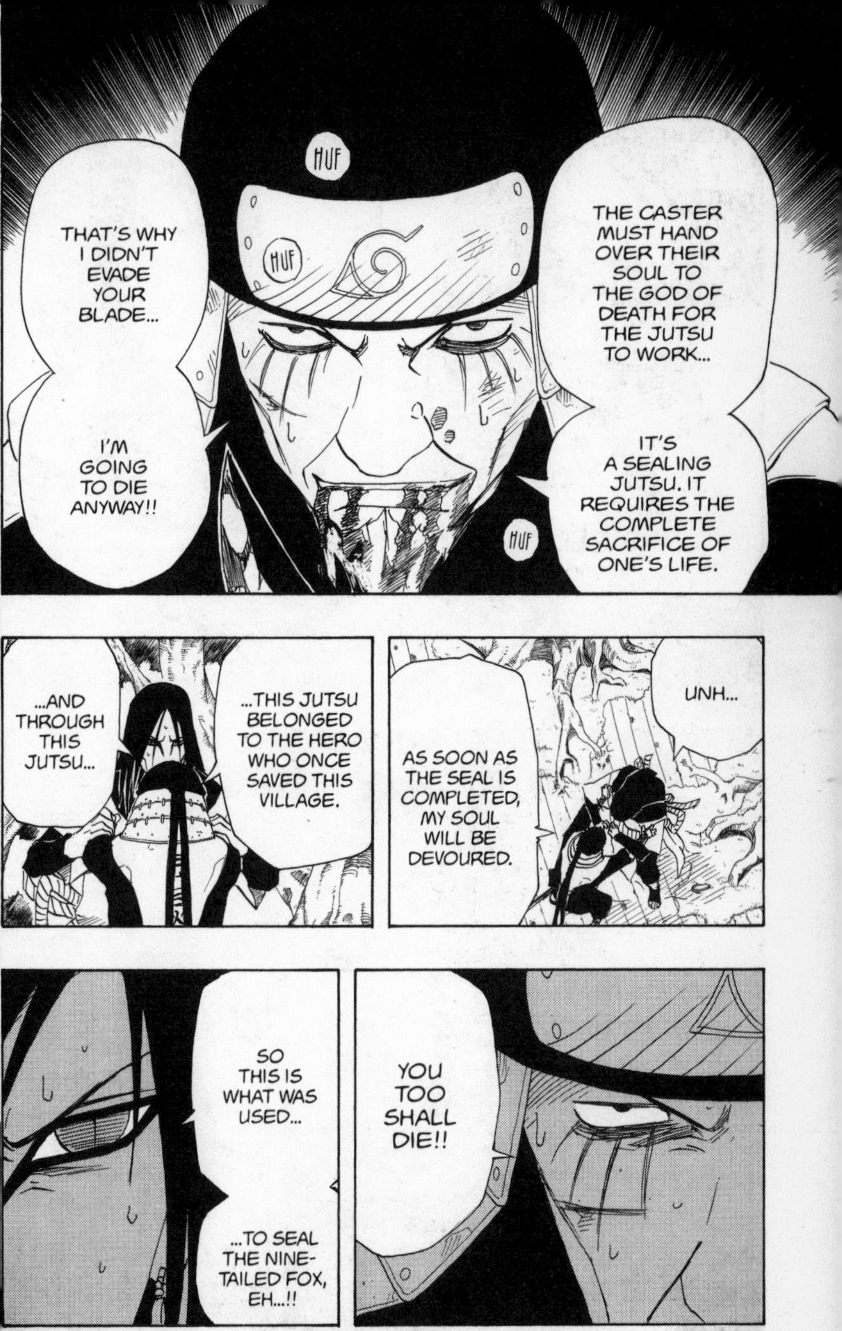
HUF
THE CASTER MUST HAND OVER THEIR SOUL TO THE GOD OF DEATH FOR THE JUTSU TO WORK...
IT'S A SEALING JUTSU. IT REQUIRES THE COMPLETE SACRIFICE OF ONE'S LIFE.
HUF
THAT'S WHY I DIDN'T EVADE YOUR BLADE...
HUF
I'M GOING TO DIE ANYWAY!!
UNH...
AS SOON AS THE SEAL IS COMPLETED, MY SOUL WILL BE DEVOURED.
...THIS JUTSU BELONGED TO THE HERO WHO ONCE SAVED THIS VILLAGE.
...AND THROUGH THIS JUTSU...
YOU TOO SHALL DIE!!
SO THIS IS WHAT WAS USED...
...TO SEAL THE NINE-TAILED FOX, EH...!!

READ THIS WAY

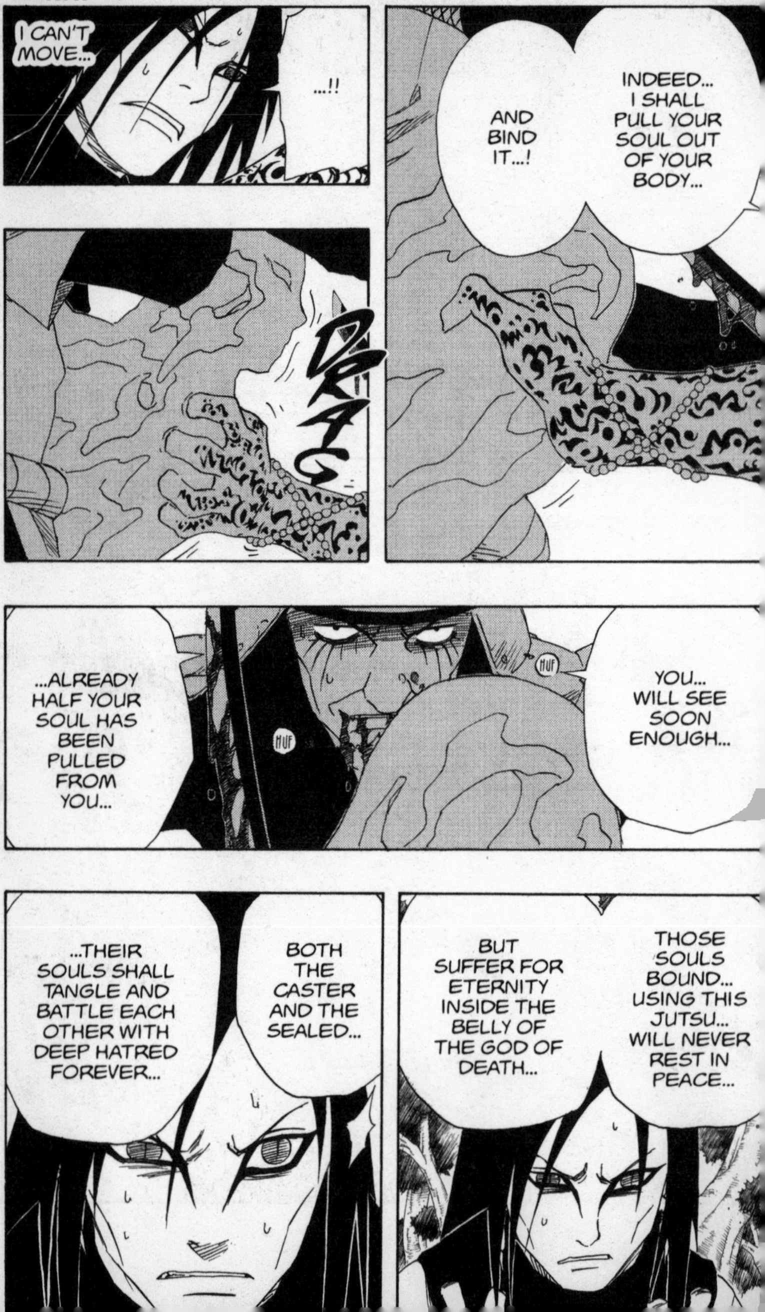
INDEED... I SHALL PULL YOUR SOUL OUT OF YOUR BODY...
AND BIND IT...!
...!!
I CAN'T MOVE...
DRAG
YOU... WILL SEE SOON ENOUGH...
HUF
...ALREADY HALF YOUR SOUL HAS BEEN PULLED FROM YOU...
HUF
THOSE SOULS BOUND... USING THIS JUTSU... WILL NEVER REST IN PEACE...
BUT SUFFER FOR ETERNITY INSIDE THE BELLY OF THE GOD OF DEATH...
BOTH THE CASTER AND THE SEALED...
...THEIR SOULS SHALL TANGLE AND BATTLE EACH OTHER WITH DEEP HATRED FOREVER...

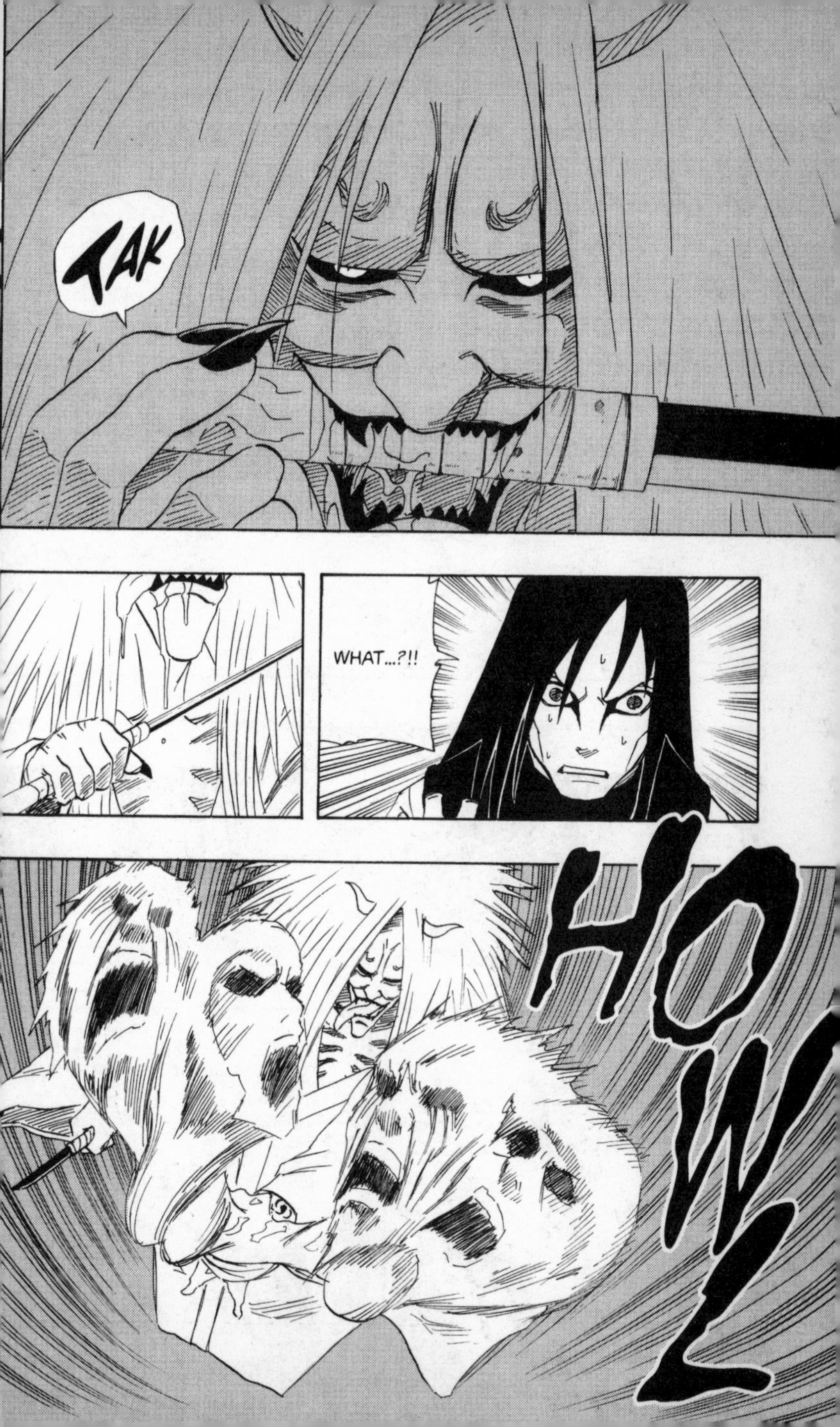
TAK
WHAT...?!!
HOWL

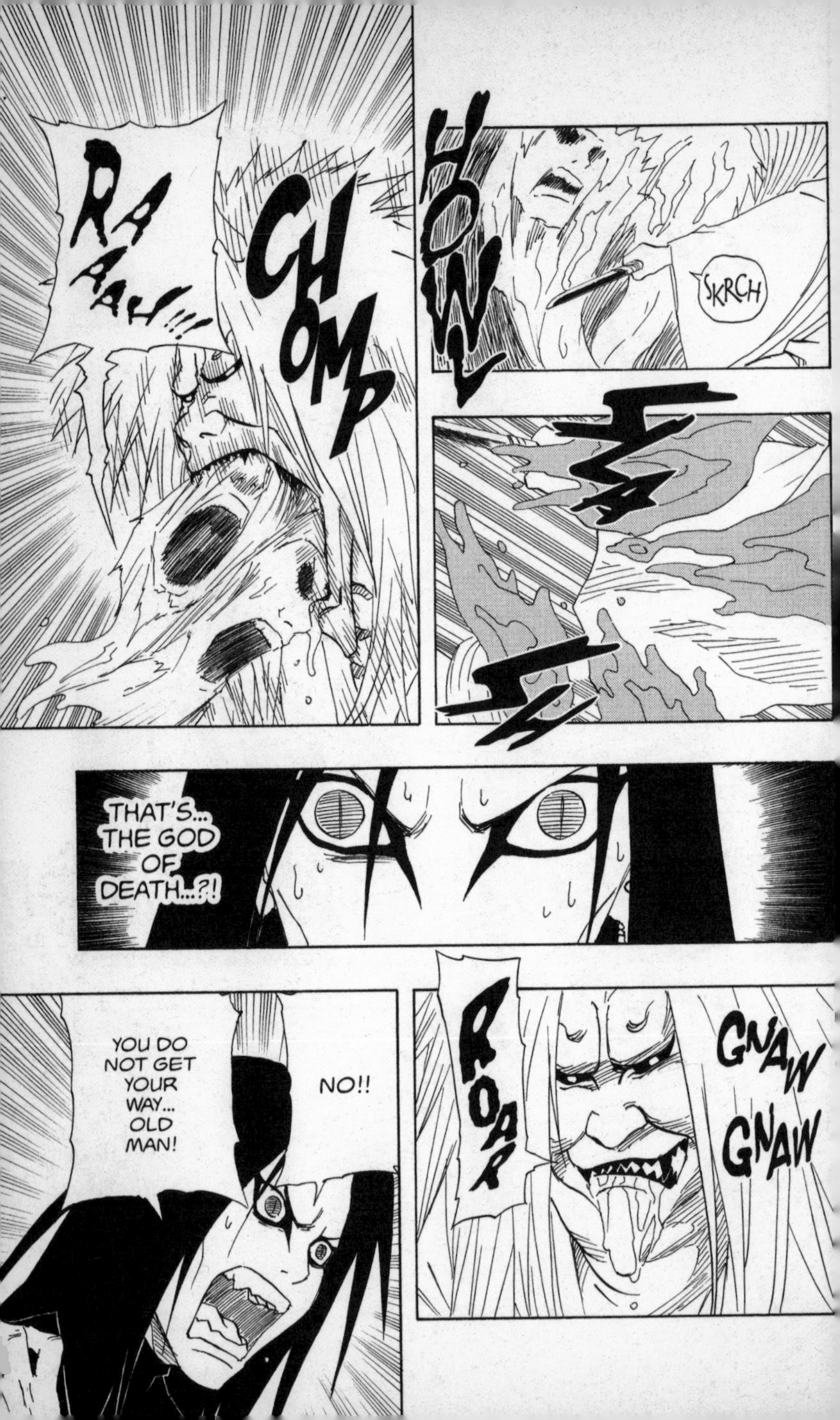
HOWL
SKRCH
RAAAH!!!
CHOMP
THAT'S... THE GOD OF DEATH...?!
GNAW GNAW
ROAR
NO!!
YOU DO NOT GET YOUR WAY... OLD MAN!

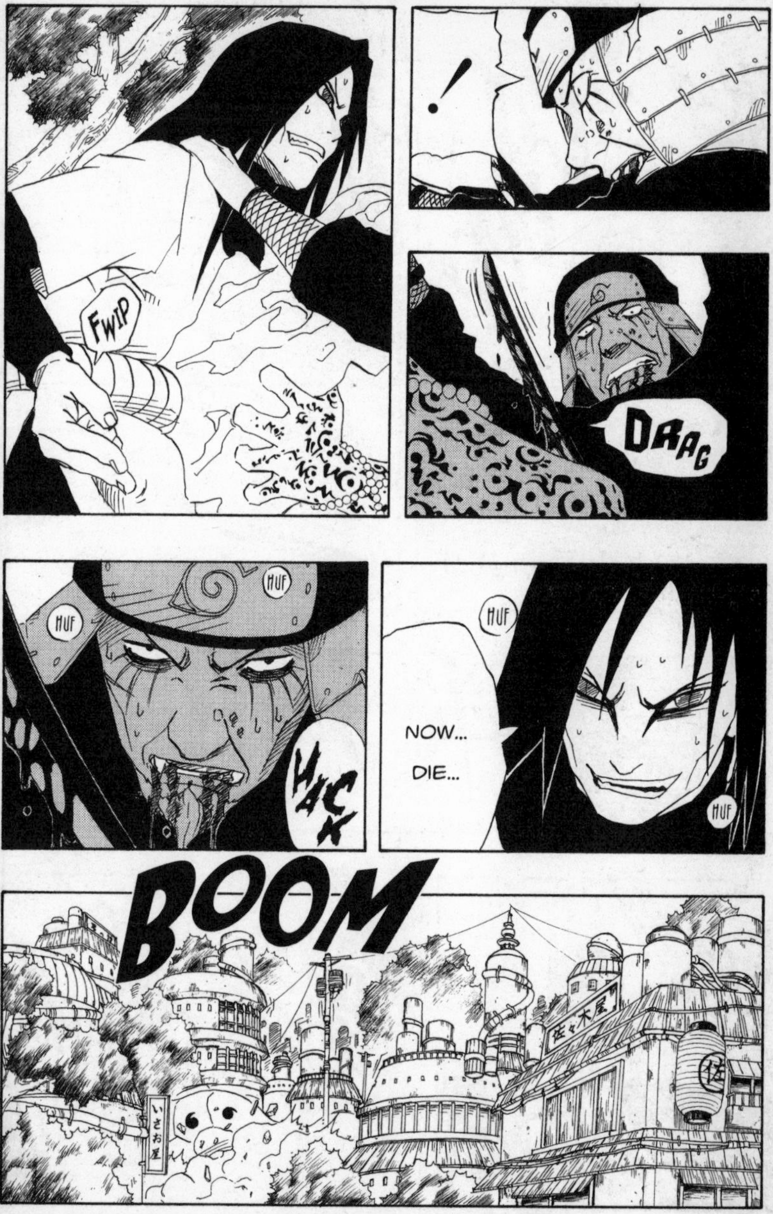
!
DRAG
FWIP
HUF
NOW...
DIE...
HUF
HUF
HUF
HACK
BOOM
佐々木屋
佐
いさお屋

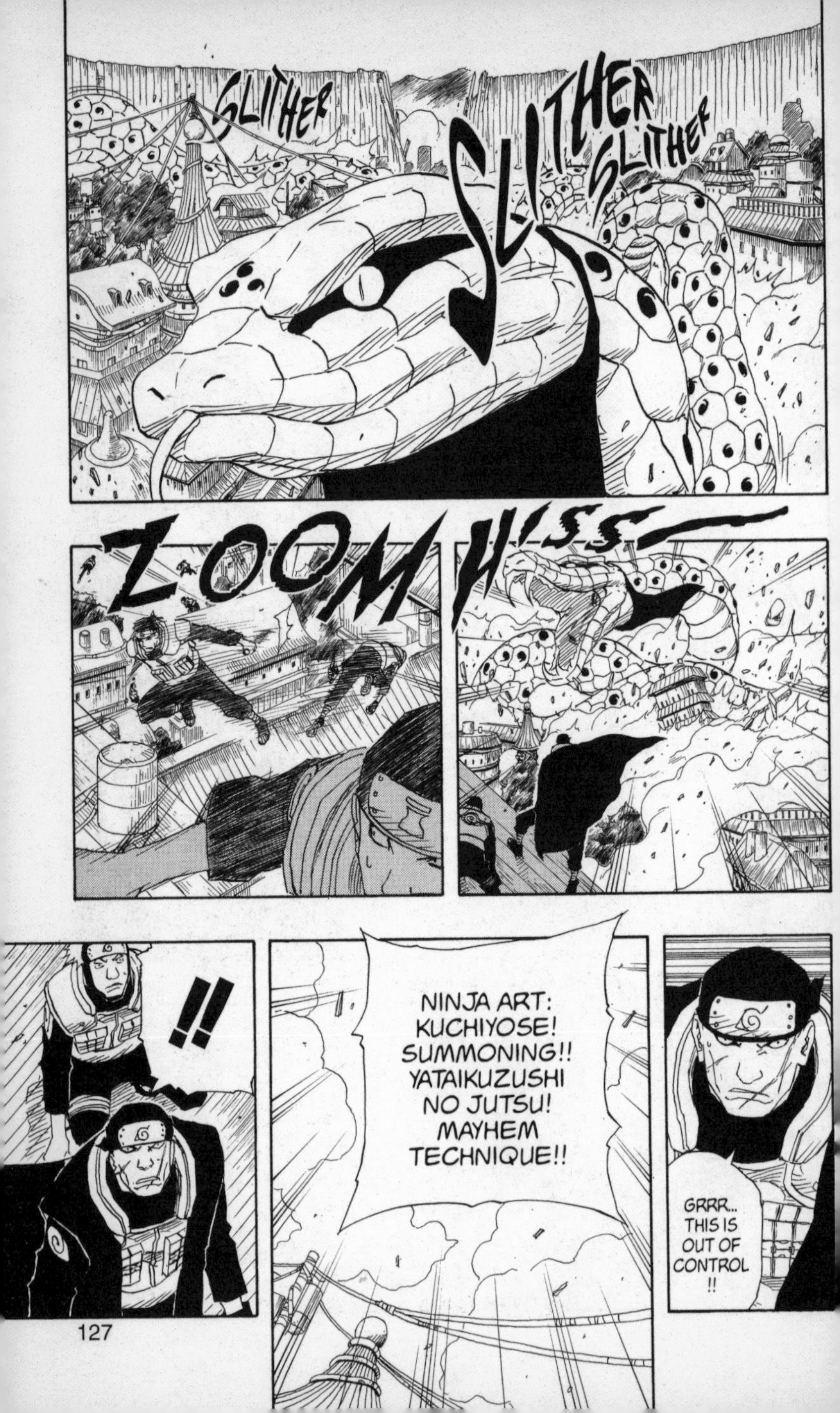
SLITHER
SLITHER
SLITHER
HISS—
ZOOM
GRRR... THIS IS OUT OF CONTROL !!
NINJA ART: KUCHIYOSE! SUMMONING!! YATAIKUZUSHI NO JUTSU! MAYHEM TECHNIQUE!!
!!

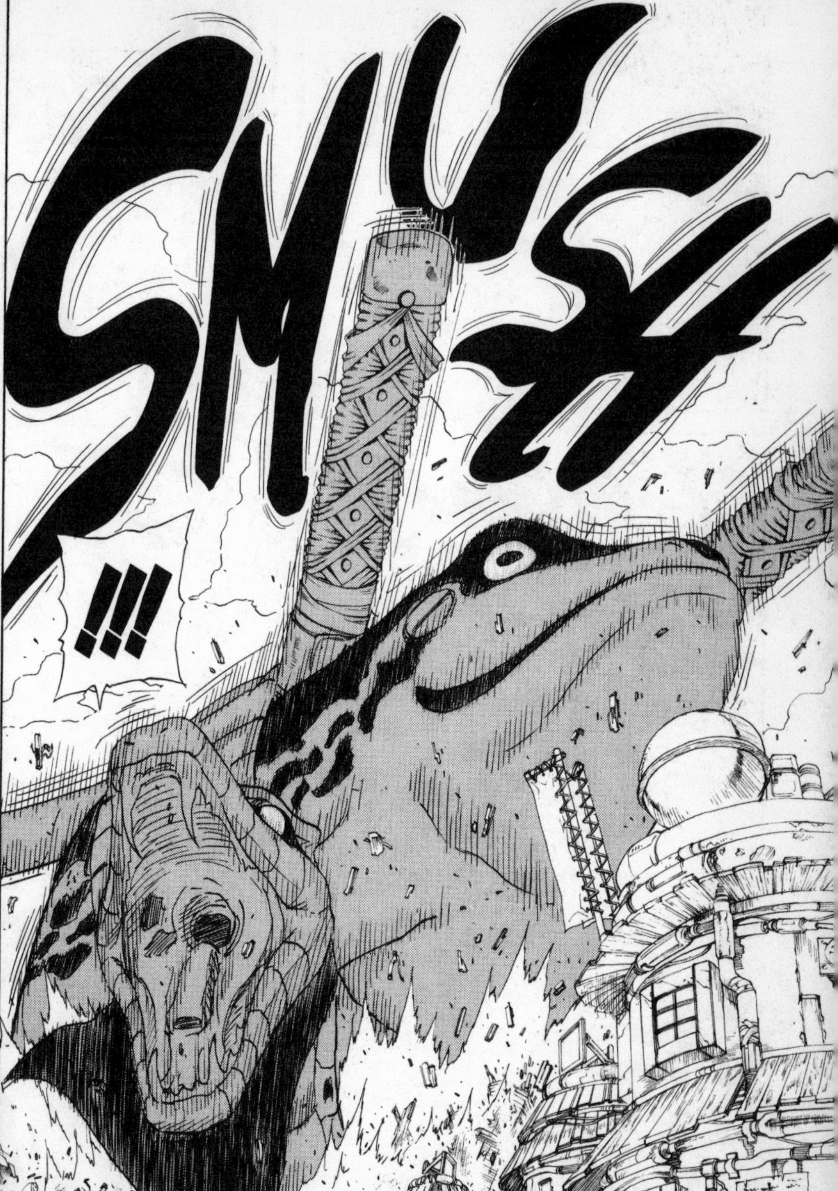
SMUSH
!!!

READ THIS WAY

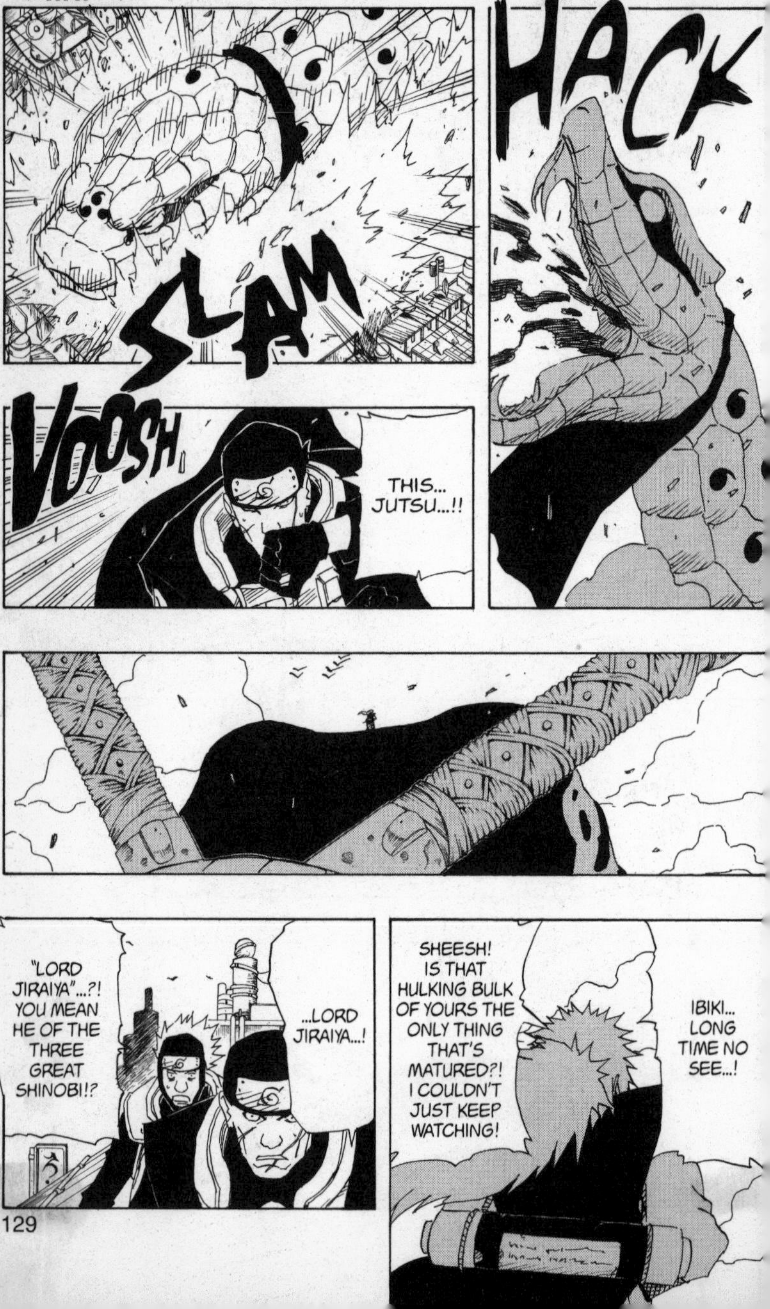
HACK
SLAM
VOOSH
THIS... JUTSU...!!
IBIKI... LONG TIME NO SEE...!
SHEESH! IS THAT HULKING BULK OF YOURS THE ONLY THING THAT'S MATURED?! I COULDN'T JUST KEEP WATCHING!
...LORD JIRAIYA...!
"LORD JIRAIYA"...?! YOU MEAN HE OF THE THREE GREAT SHINOBI!?

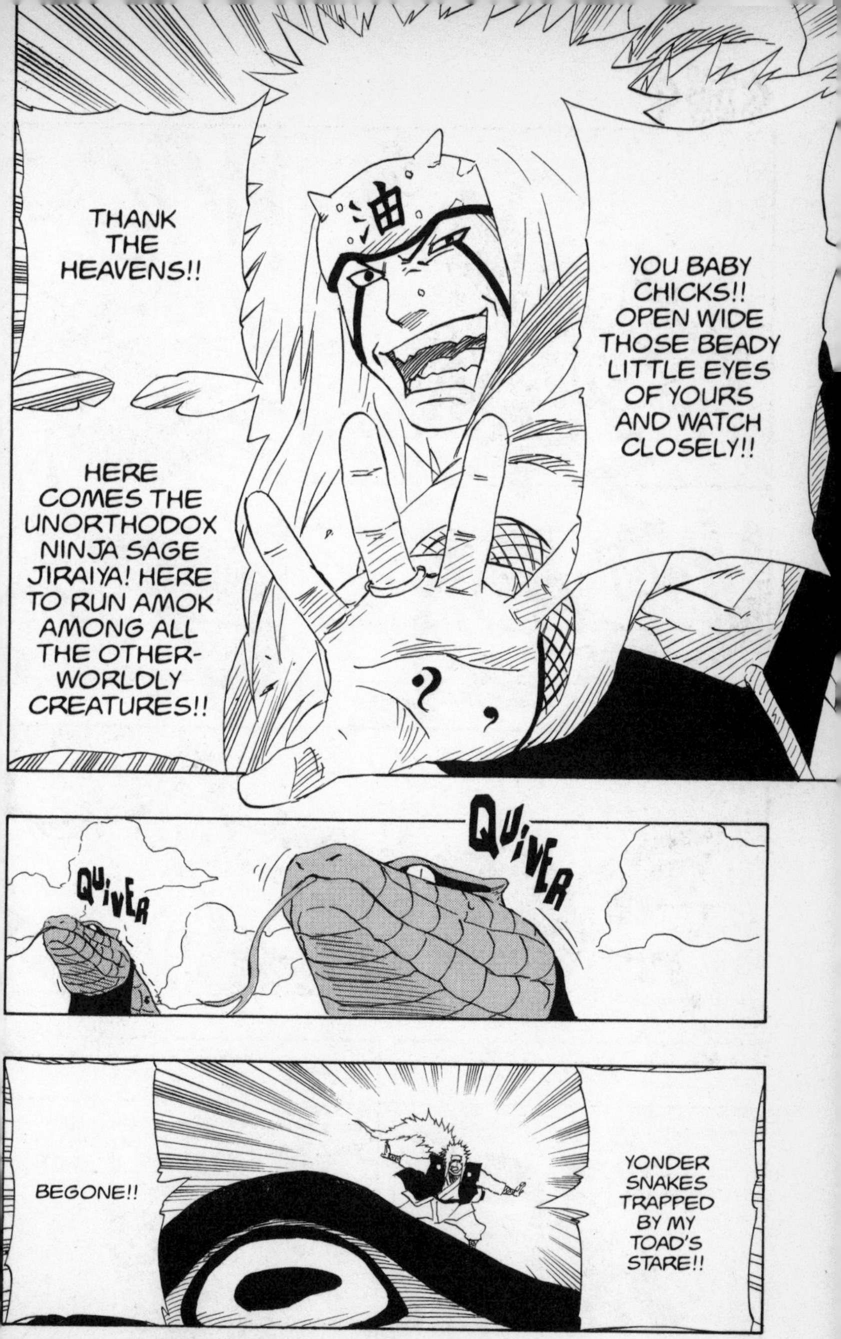
YOU BABY CHICKS!! OPEN WIDE THOSE BEADY LITTLE EYES OF YOURS AND WATCH CLOSELY!!
THANK THE HEAVENS!!
HERE COMES THE UNORTHODOX NINJA SAGE JIRAIYA! HERE TO RUN AMOK AMONG ALL THE OTHER-WORLDLY CREATURES!!
QUIVER
QUIVER
YONDER SNAKES TRAPPED BY MY TOAD'S STARE!!
BEGONE!!

READ THIS WAY

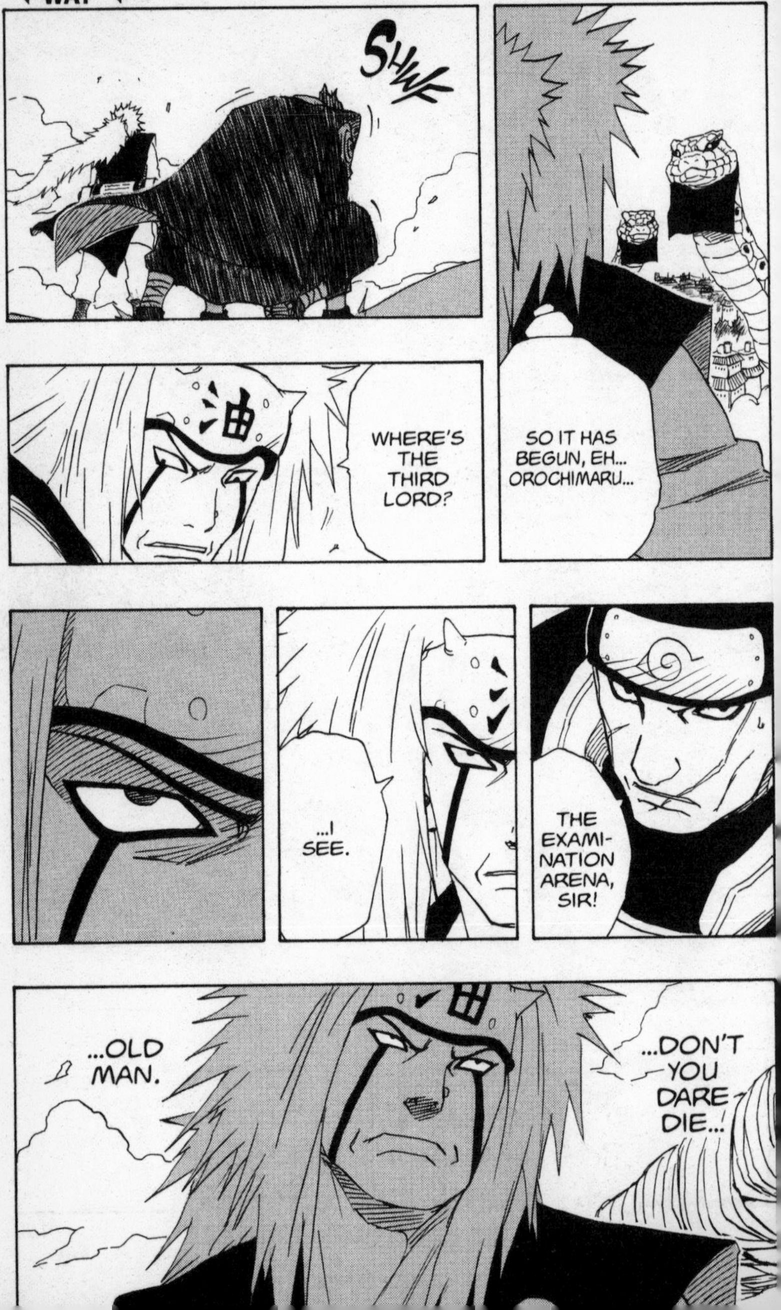
SO IT HAS BEGUN, EH... OROCHIMARU...
SHWF
WHERE'S THE THIRD LORD?
THE EXAMINATION ARENA, SIR!
...I SEE.
...DON'T YOU DARE DIE...
...OLD MAN.

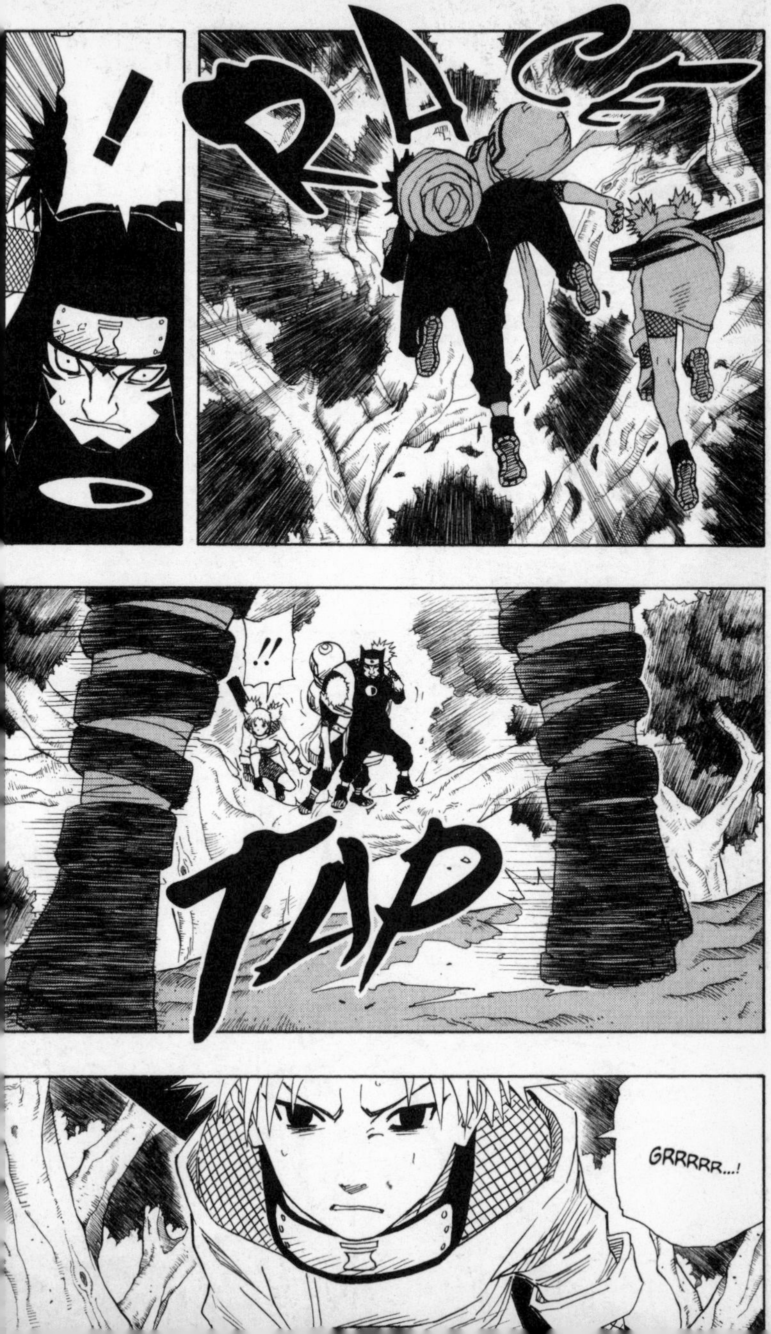

!
!!
TAP
GRRRRR...!

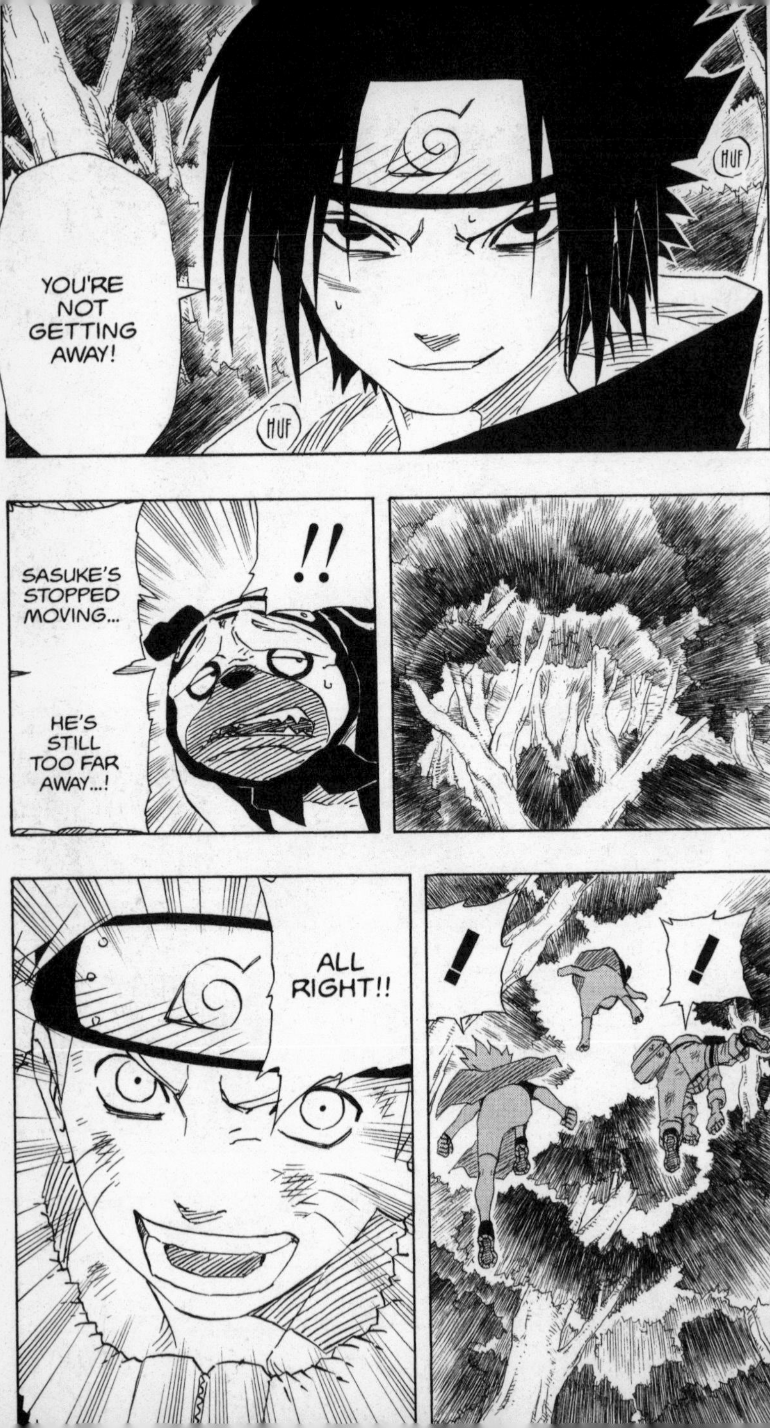
HUF
YOU'RE NOT GETTING AWAY!
HUF
!!
SASUKE'S STOPPED MOVING...
HE'S STILL TOO FAR AWAY...!
!
!
ALL RIGHT!!

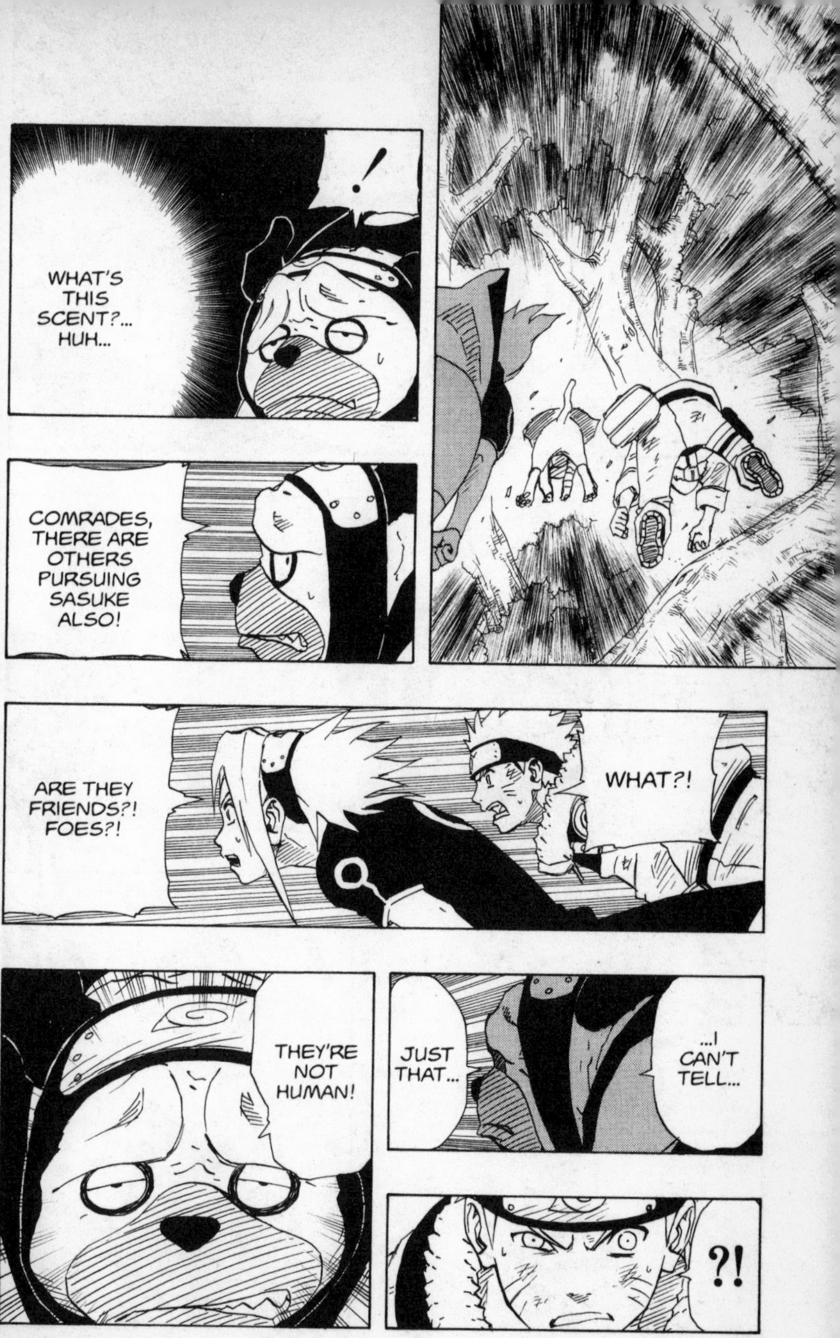
!
WHAT'S THIS SCENT?... HUH...
COMRADES, THERE ARE OTHERS PURSUING SASUKE ALSO!
WHAT?!
ARE THEY FRIENDS?! FOES?!
...I CAN'T TELL...
JUST THAT...
?!
THEY'RE NOT HUMAN!

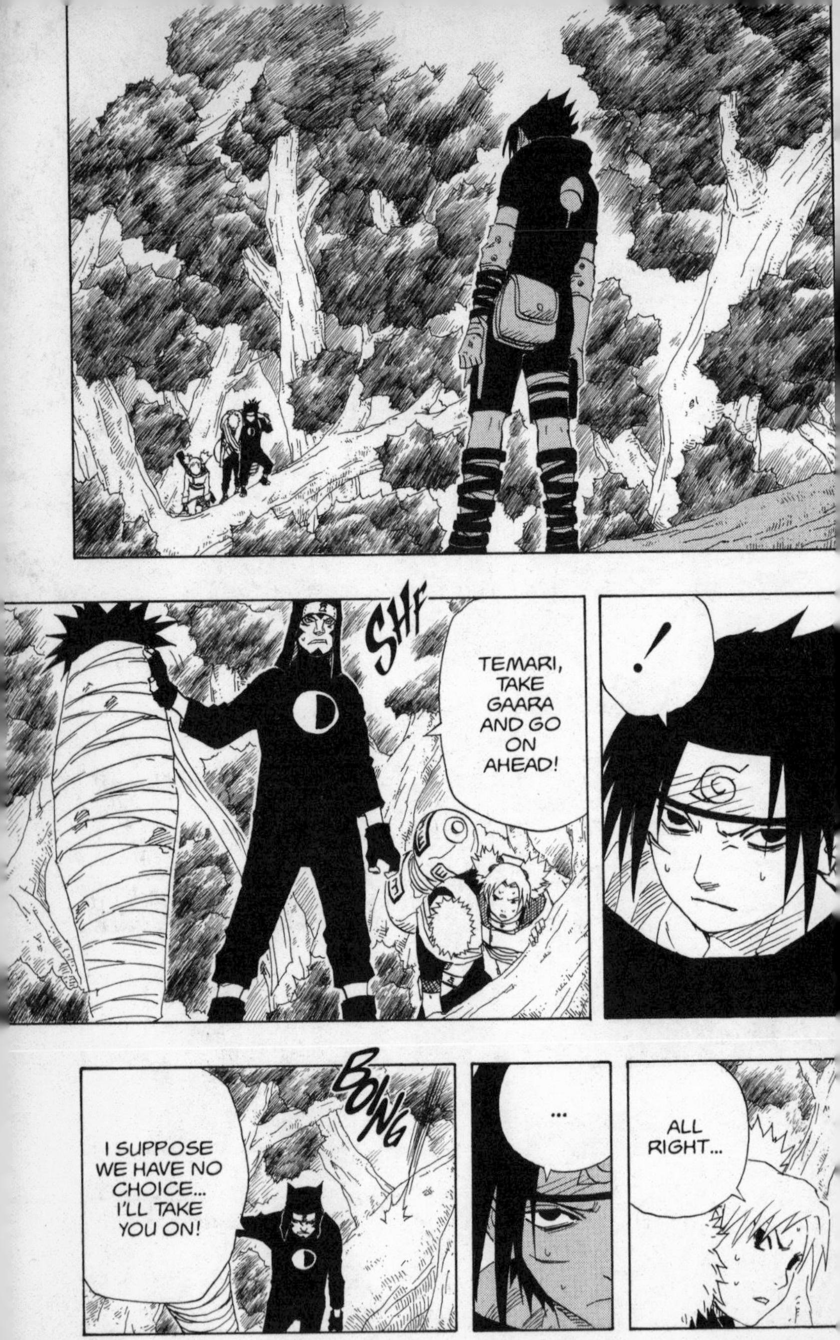
!
TEMARI, TAKE GAARA AND GO ON AHEAD!
SHF
ALL RIGHT...
...
BOING
I SUPPOSE WE HAVE NO CHOICE... I'LL TAKE YOU ON!

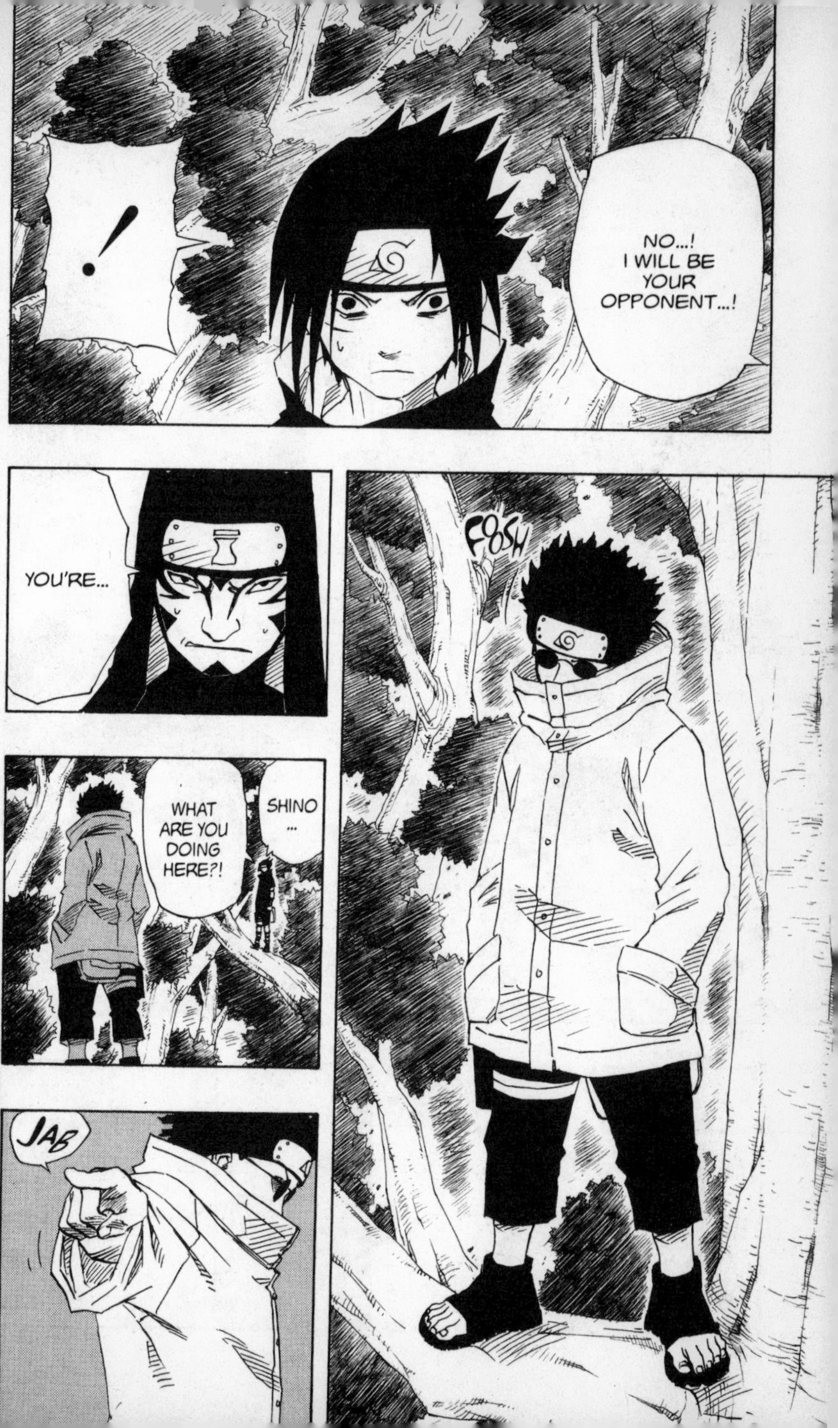
NO...! I WILL BE YOUR OPPONENT...!
!
FOSH
YOU'RE...
SHINO ...
WHAT ARE YOU DOING HERE?!
JAB

READ THIS WAY

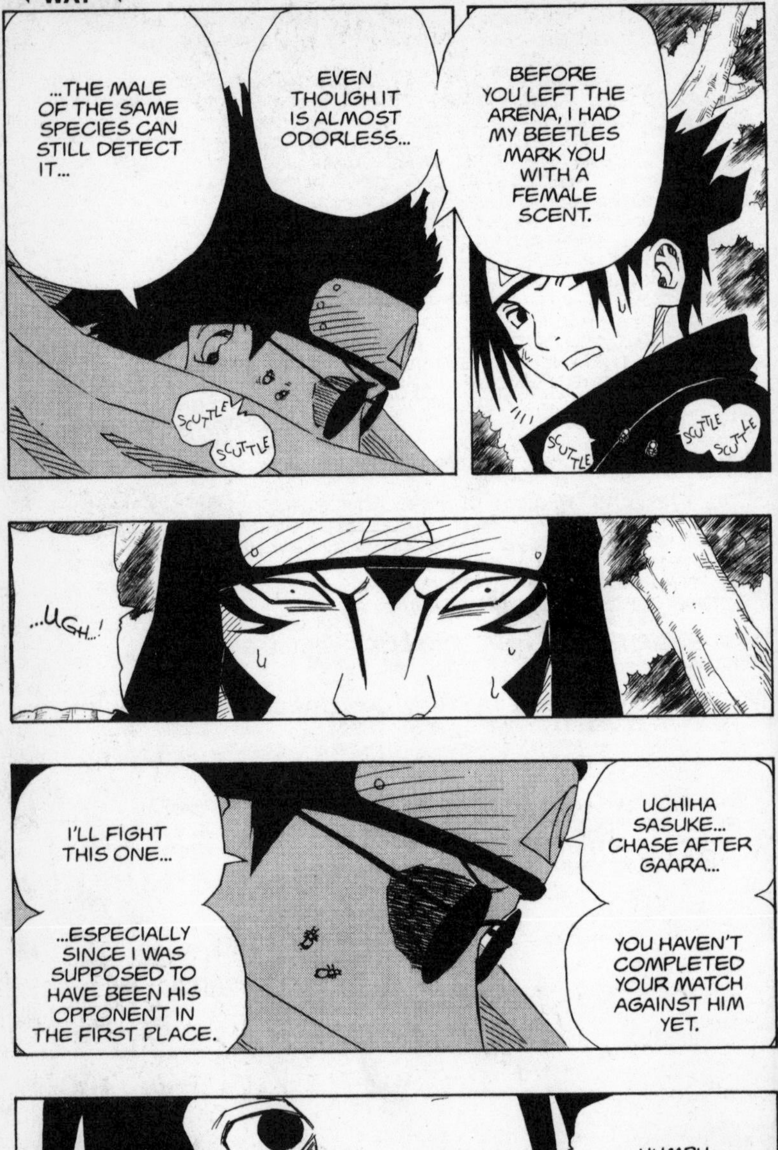
BEFORE YOU LEFT THE ARENA, I HAD MY BEETLES MARK YOU WITH A FEMALE SCENT.
SCUTTLE
SCUTTLE SCUTTLE
EVEN THOUGH IT IS ALMOST ODORLESS...
...THE MALE OF THE SAME SPECIES CAN STILL DETECT IT...
SCUTTLE
SCUTTLE
...UGH...!
UCHIHA SASUKE... CHASE AFTER GAARA...
YOU HAVEN'T COMPLETED YOUR MATCH AGAINST HIM YET.
I'LL FIGHT THIS ONE...
...ESPECIALLY SINCE I WAS SUPPOSED TO HAVE BEEN HIS OPPONENT IN THE FIRST PLACE.
HUMPH...

THE WORLD OF KISHIMOTO MASASHI
MY PERSONAL HISTORY, PART 20 (CONTINUED)

I WENT TO THE SALON TO GET MY BANGS TRIMMED, SO I SAT IN THE HAIRCUT SEAT. MY HEAD WAS FULL OF... "I'M GOING TO GO SEE *SEVEN* TOMORROW--! I WONDER WHAT THE SEVEN DEADLY SINS ARE--?! THE DIRECTOR IS DAVID FINCHER, SO I BET THE FRIGHT SCENES ARE GOING TO BE PRETTY AMAZING! WITH MORGAN FREEMAN AS THE VETERAN DETECTIVE AND BRAD PITT AS THE GREEN YOUNG DETECTIVE, WHAT A FANTASTIC TEAM! I HEARD IT HAS AN UNEXPECTED ENDING, A SUDDEN REVERSAL, BUT I WONDER WHAT IT IS..." I WAS ALL EXCITED. AND JUST AS THEY STARTED CUTTING MY HAIR, SOME WOMAN CAME IN FOR A HAIRCUT AND SAT DOWN IN THE NEXT CHAIR OVER. THIS WOMAN STARTED UP A FRIENDLY CHAT WITH HER STYLIST, BRAGGING, "I WENT ON A DATE YESTERDAY." I HAD NOTHING TO TALK ABOUT WITH MY STYLIST, SO I WAS SILENT AND PRETENDED TO BE ASLEEP. TO MY DISGUST, THE LOUDMOUTHED WOMAN NEXT TO ME STARTED GOING INTO DETAILS ABOUT HER DATE. "GRODY~" I THOUGHT TO MYSELF, BUT... BECAUSE HER VOICE WAS SO LOUD, I ENDED UP HEARING HER BRAGGING TALE WHETHER I WANTED TO OR NOT. SUDDENLY, SHE STARTED SAYING SHE HAD GONE TO THE MOVIES WITH THIS GUY, AND THAT THE FILM THEY HAD SEEN WAS THE CURRENTLY POPULAR *SEVEN*.

JUST AS I WAS THINKING TO MYSELF "I'M GOING TO GO SEE IT TOO, TOMORROW...", OH NO! THAT CHATTERBOX GIRL STARTED DESCRIBING THE PLOT OF *SEVEN*!! NEEDLESS TO SAY, SHE WAS LOUD!! I WANTED TO COVER MY EARS, BUT MY HANDS WERE UNDER THE CAPE BECAUSE I WAS GETTING MY HAIR CUT...!! AND SO, IN THAT MOMENT, I BEGGED THAT WOMAN...

"PLEASE! THE CLINCHER... JUST DON'T SPILL THE CLINCHER, PLEASE~~~~~!!!"

"AND WHAT WAS INSIDE THAT BOX. CAN YOU BELIEVE IT... IT WAS THE HEAD OF BRAD PITT'S WIFE--! AND THEN--!"

...SHE HAD SPILLED IT...

THE NEXT DAY, I DECIDED NOT TO GO SEE *SEVEN*... (I CAN JUST RENT THE VIDEO... ESPECIALLY NOW THAT I KNOW THE WHOLE STORY...) FURTHERMORE, THEY HAD CUT MY BANGS TOO MUCH AND I ENDED UP LOOKING LIKE A BUSINESSMAN.

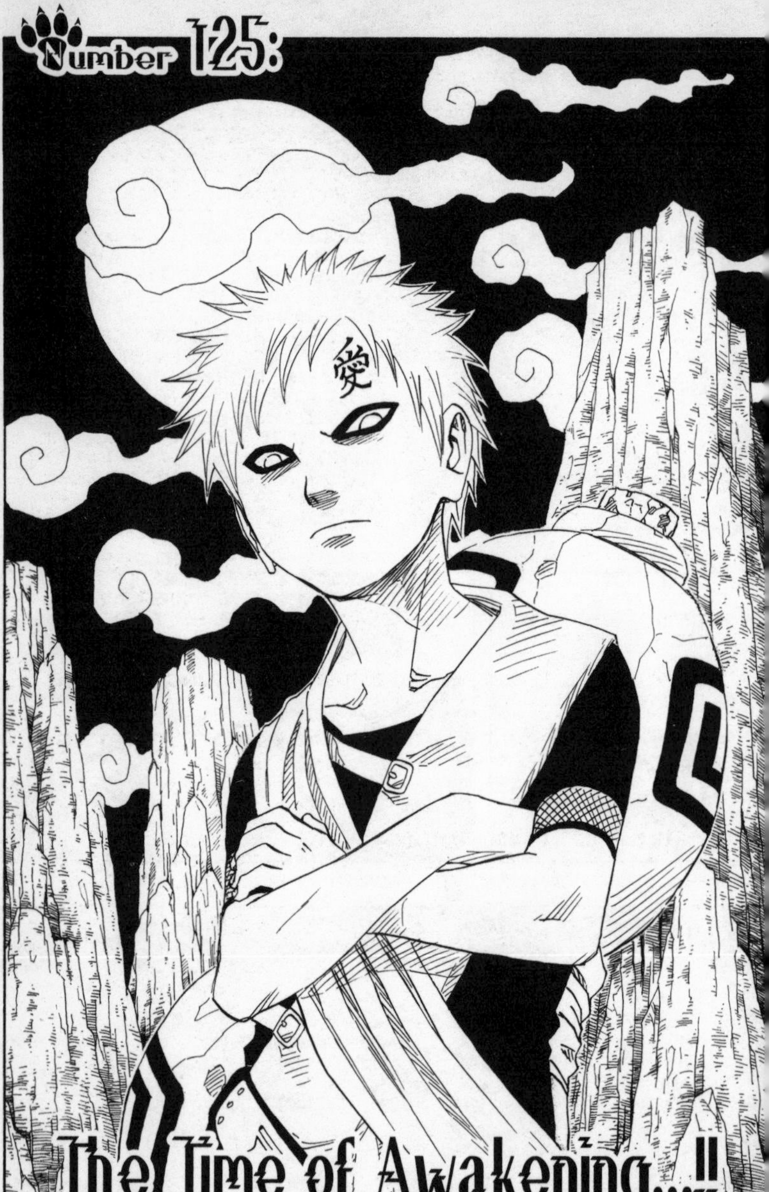
Number 125:
The Time of Awakening...!!

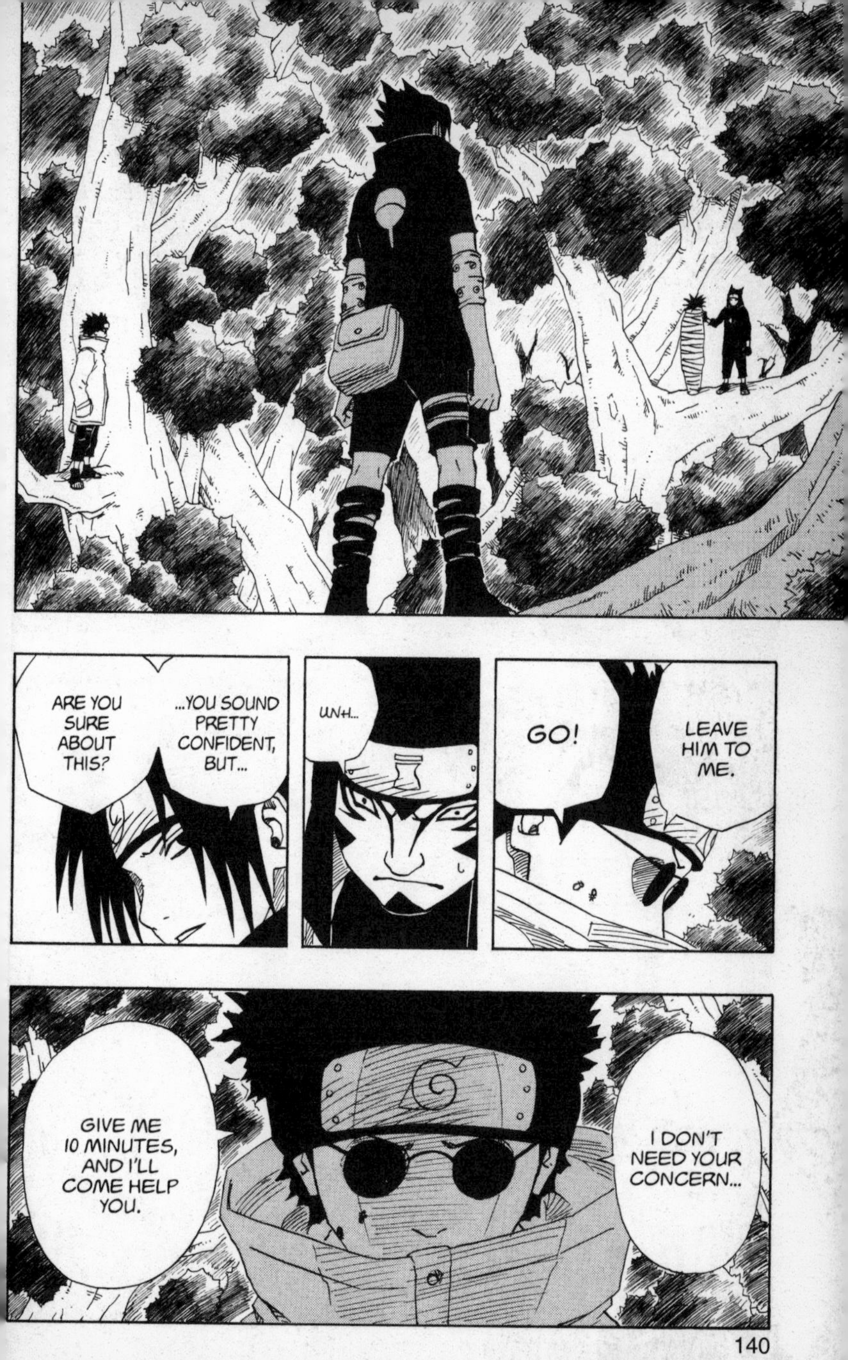
LEAVE HIM TO ME.
GO!
UNH...
...YOU SOUND PRETTY CONFIDENT, BUT...
ARE YOU SURE ABOUT THIS?
I DON'T NEED YOUR CONCERN...
GIVE ME 10 MINUTES, AND I'LL COME HELP YOU.

READ THIS WAY

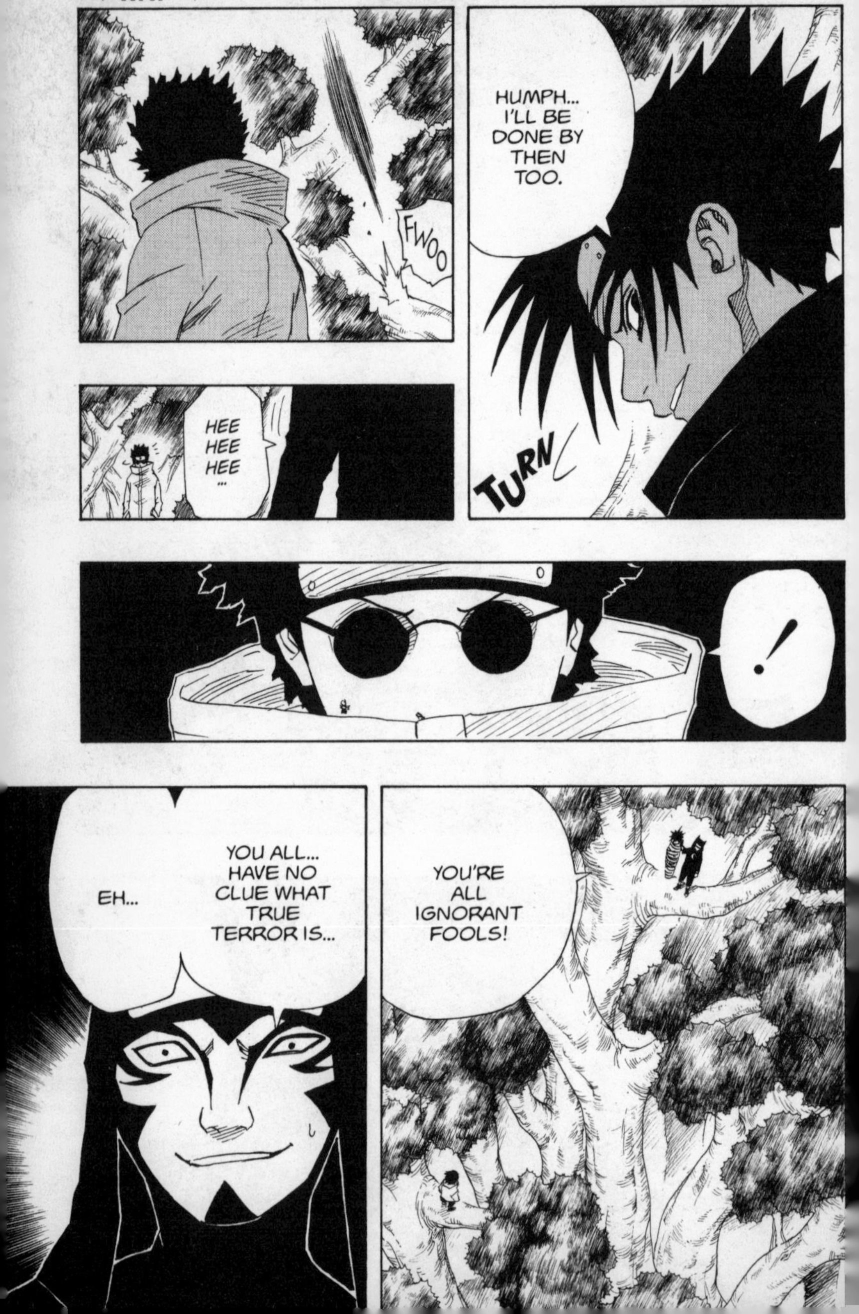

HUMPH... I'LL BE DONE BY THEN TOO.
TURN
FWOO
HEE HEE HEE ...
!
YOU'RE ALL IGNORANT FOOLS!
YOU ALL... HAVE NO CLUE WHAT TRUE TERROR IS...
EH...

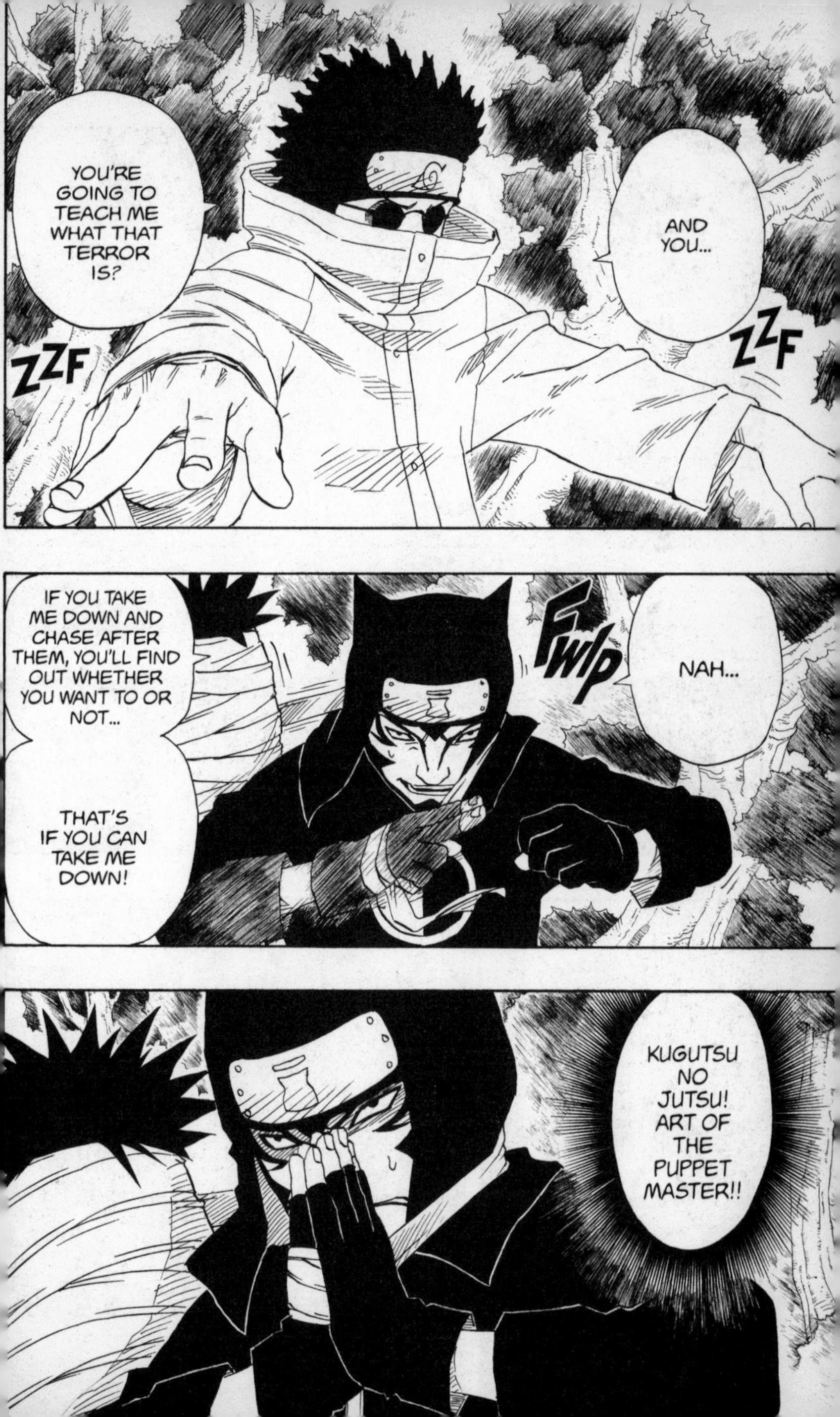
AND YOU...
ZZF
YOU'RE GOING TO TEACH ME WHAT THAT TERROR IS?
ZZF
NAH...
FWIP
IF YOU TAKE ME DOWN AND CHASE AFTER THEM, YOU'LL FIND OUT WHETHER YOU WANT TO OR NOT...
THAT'S IF YOU CAN TAKE ME DOWN!
KUGUTSU NO JUTSU! ART OF THE PUPPET MASTER!!

READ THIS WAY

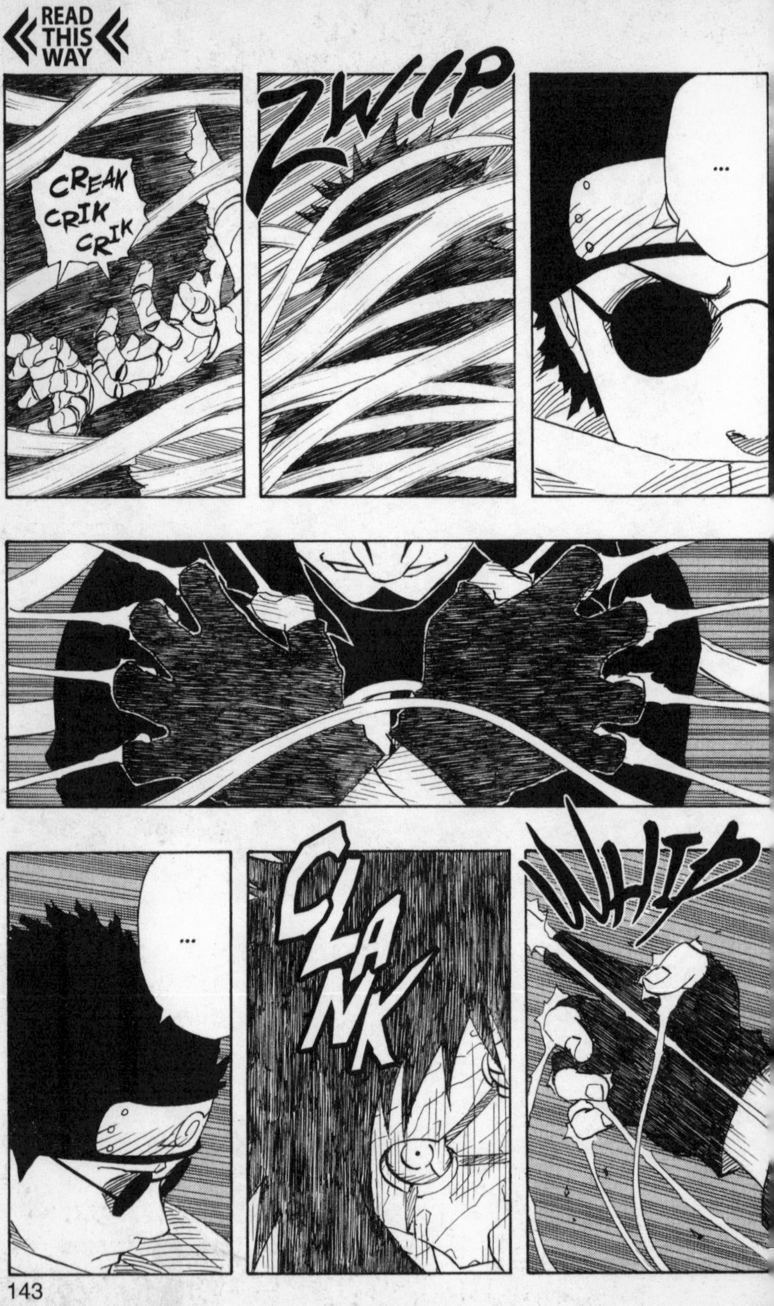
...
ZWIP
CREAK CRIK CRIK
WHIP
CLANK
...

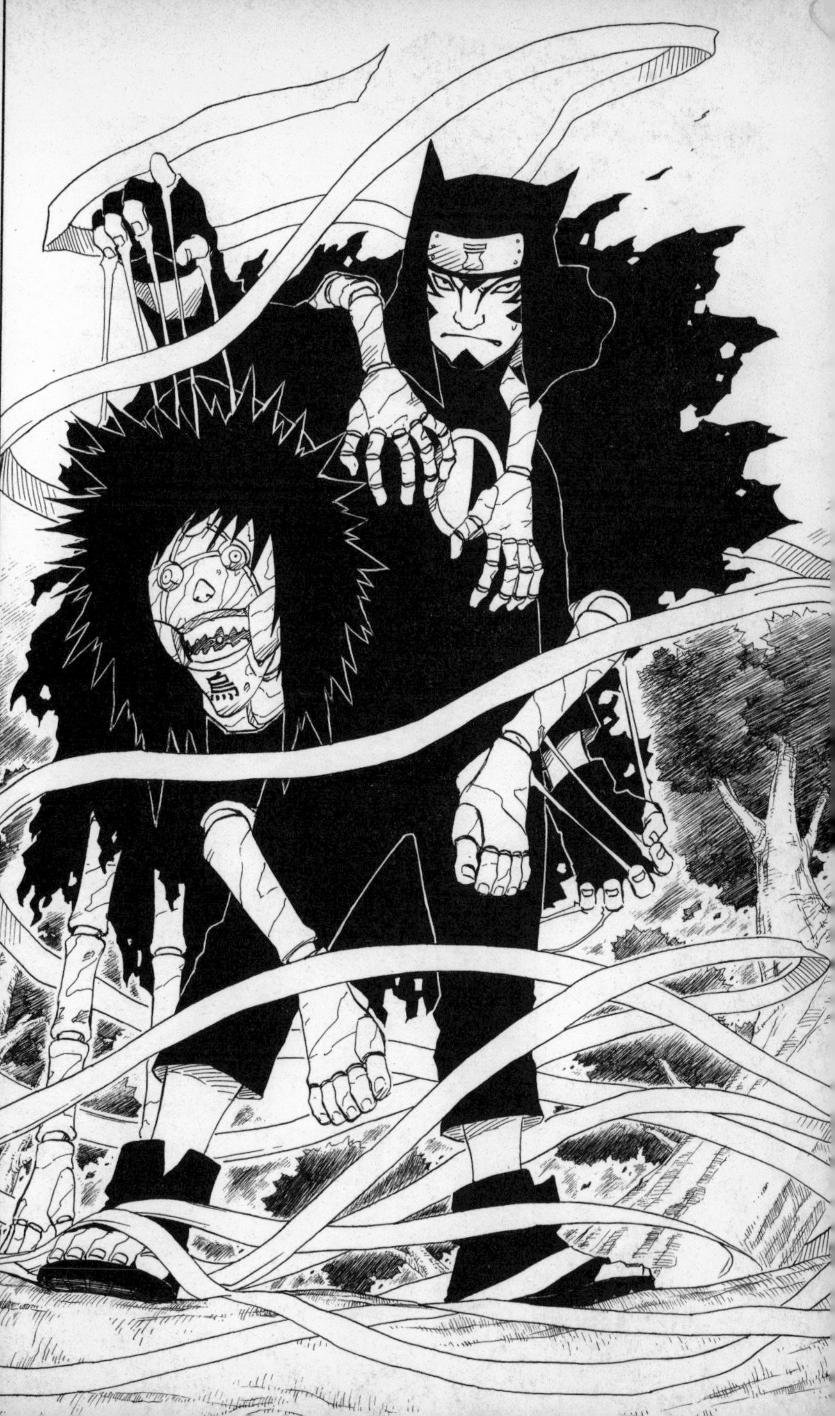
烏

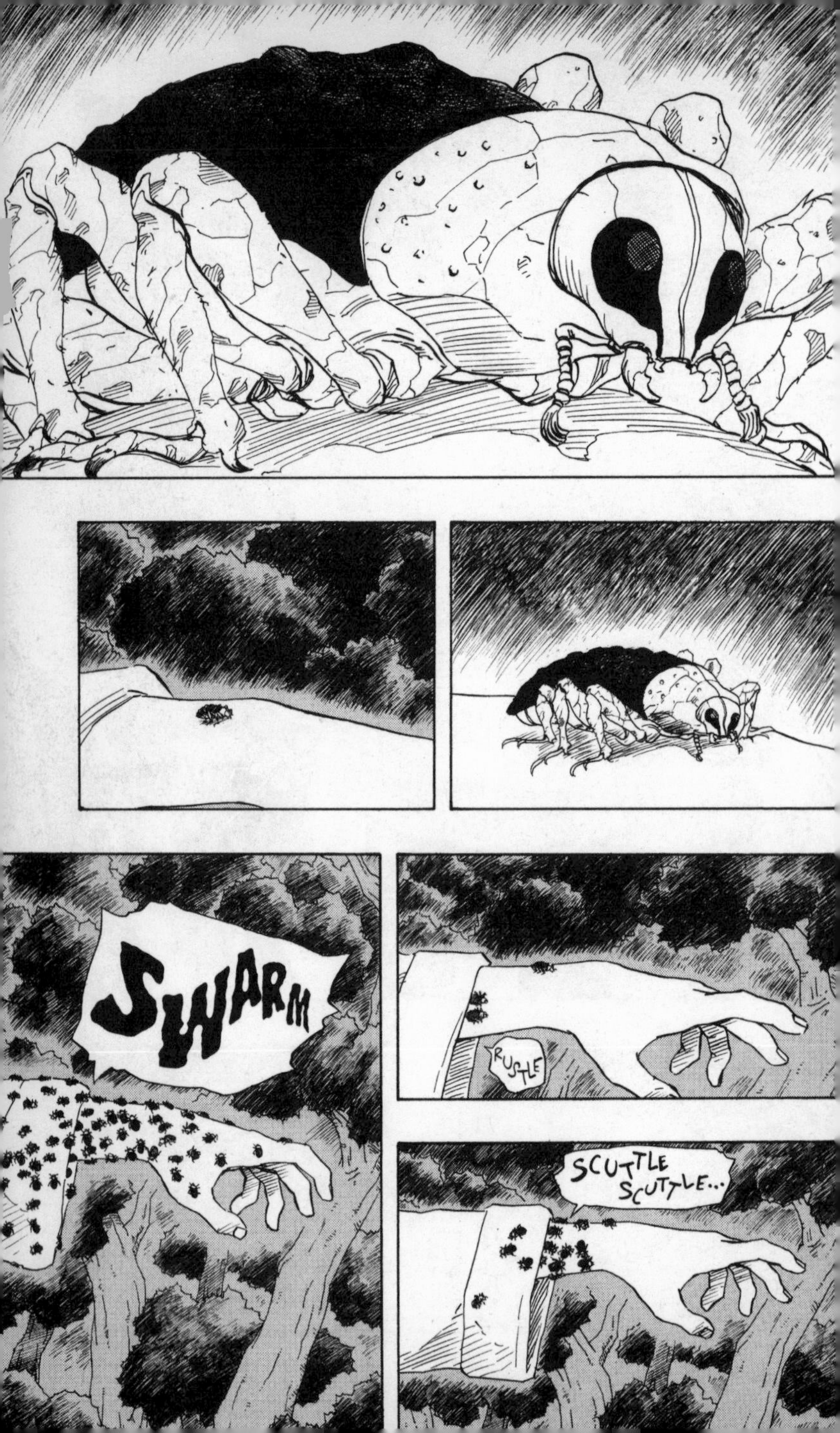
RUSTLE
SCUTTLE SCUTTLE...
SWARM

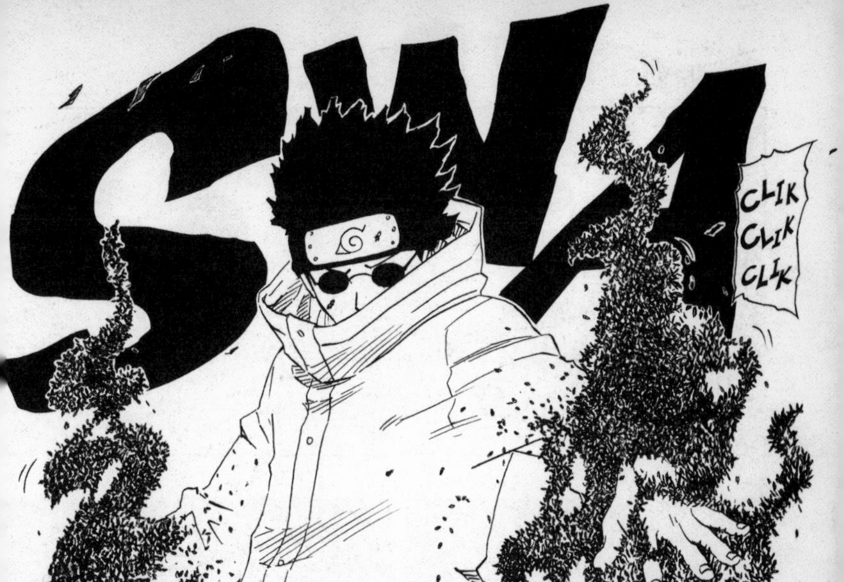
SWARM
CLIK CLIK CLIK
CREAK CRIK CRIK CRIK

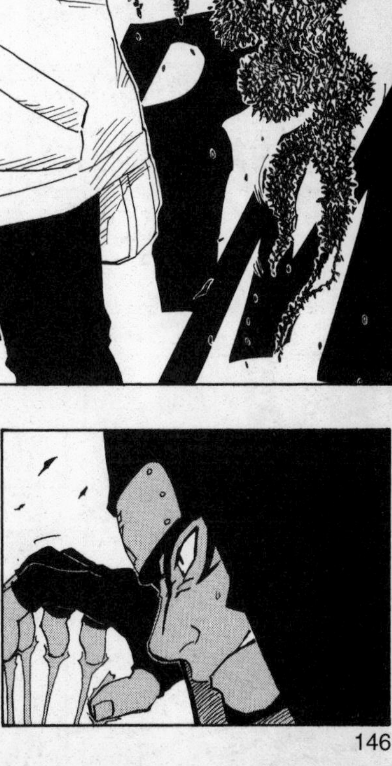

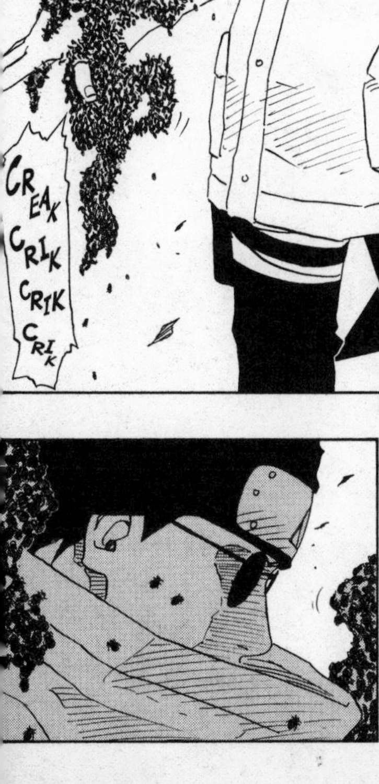

READ THIS WAY

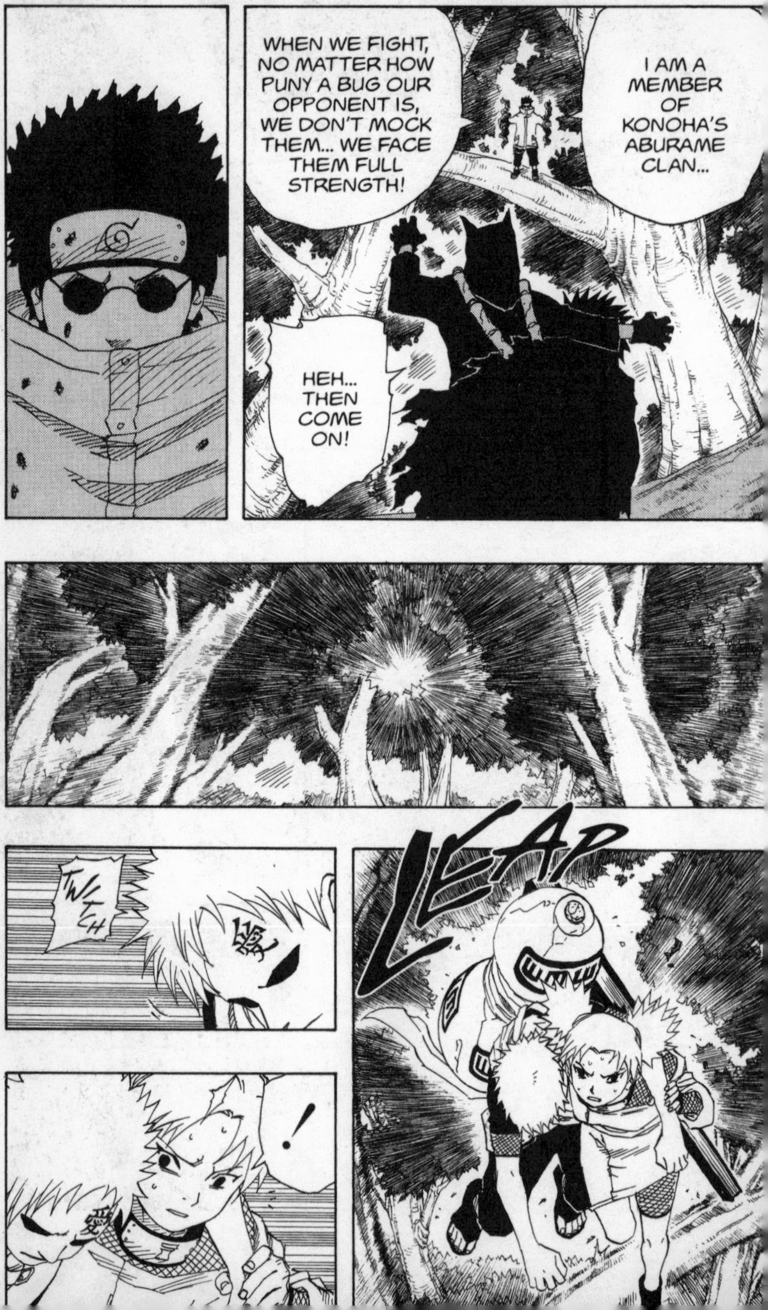
I AM A MEMBER OF KONOHA'S ABURAME CLAN...
WHEN WE FIGHT, NO MATTER HOW PUNY A BUG OUR OPPONENT IS, WE DON'T MOCK THEM... WE FACE THEM FULL STRENGTH!
HEH... THEN COME ON!
LEAP
TWITCH
!

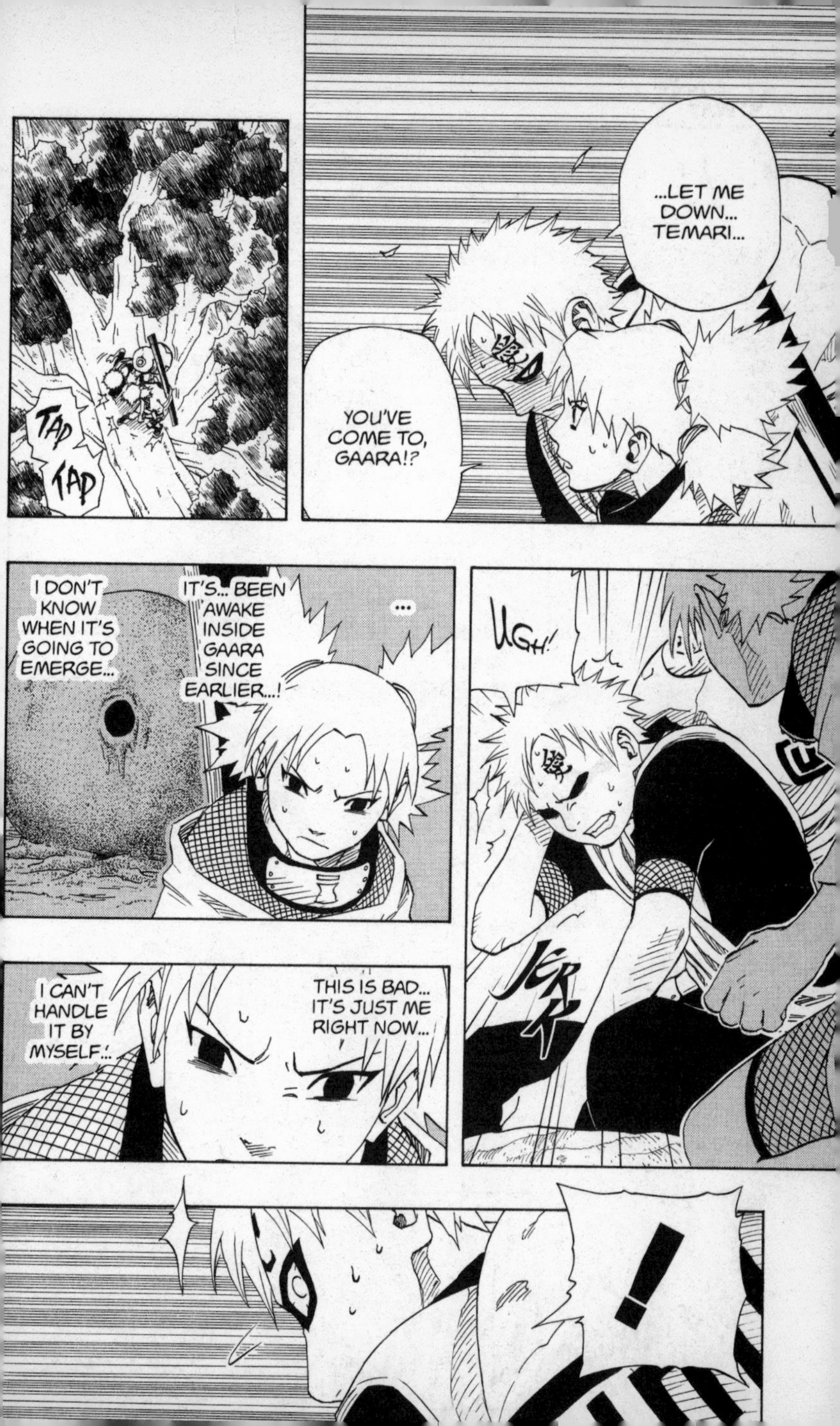
...LET ME DOWN... TEMARI...
YOU'VE COME TO, GAARA!?
TAP
TAP
UGH!
JERK
...
IT'S... BEEN AWAKE INSIDE GAARA SINCE EARLIER...!
I DON'T KNOW WHEN IT'S GOING TO EMERGE...
THIS IS BAD... IT'S JUST ME RIGHT NOW...
I CAN'T HANDLE IT BY MYSELF...!
!

READ THIS WAY

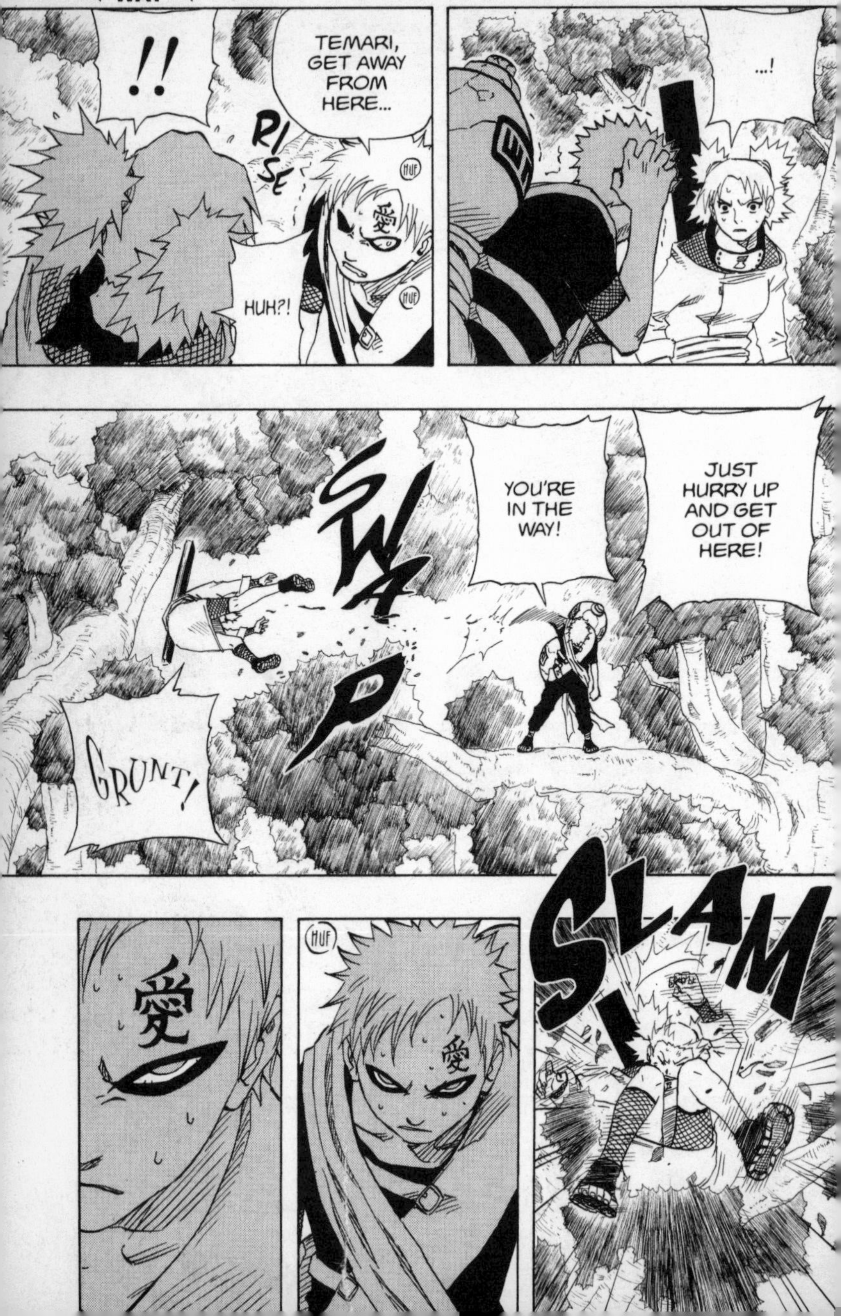
...!
TEMARI, GET AWAY FROM HERE...
!!
RISE
HUF
HUF
HUH?!
JUST HURRY UP AND GET OUT OF HERE!
YOU'RE IN THE WAY!
SWAP
GRUNT!
SLAM
HUF

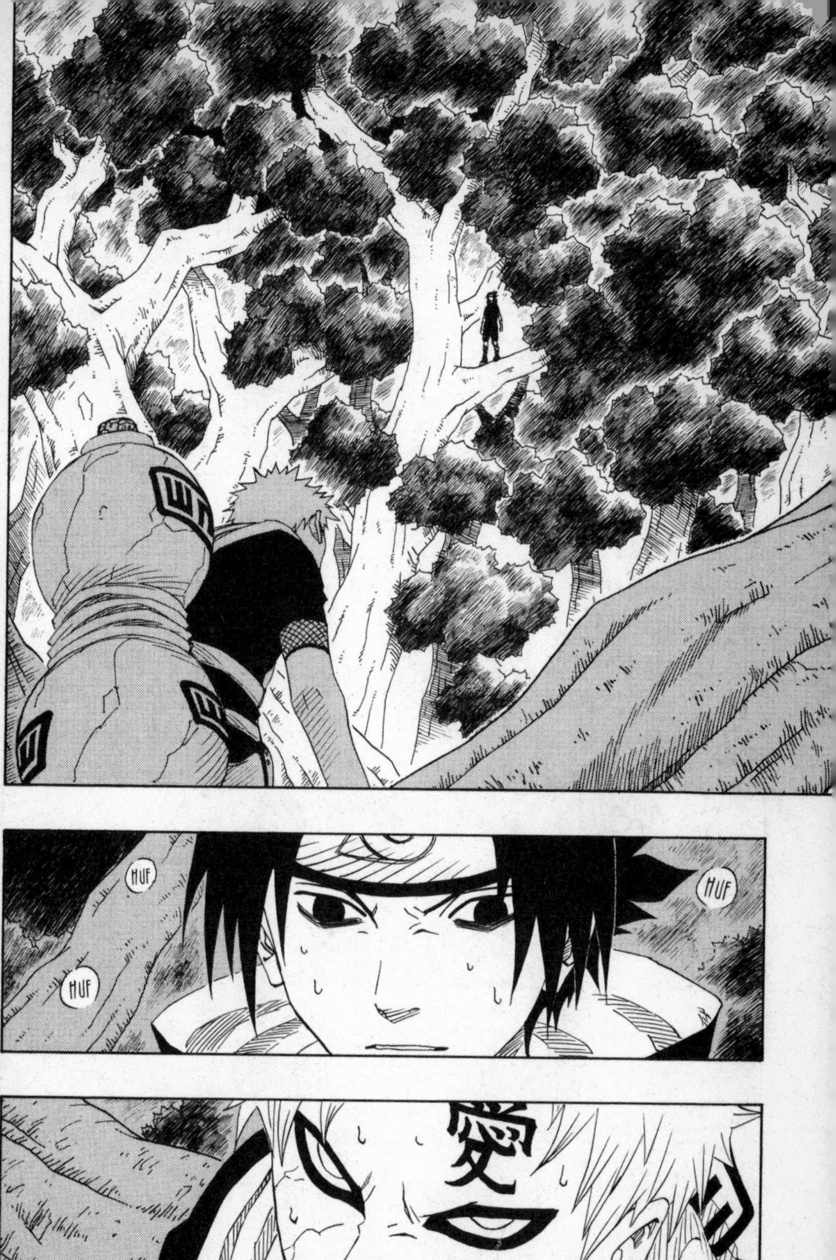
HUF
HUF
HUF

READ THIS WAY

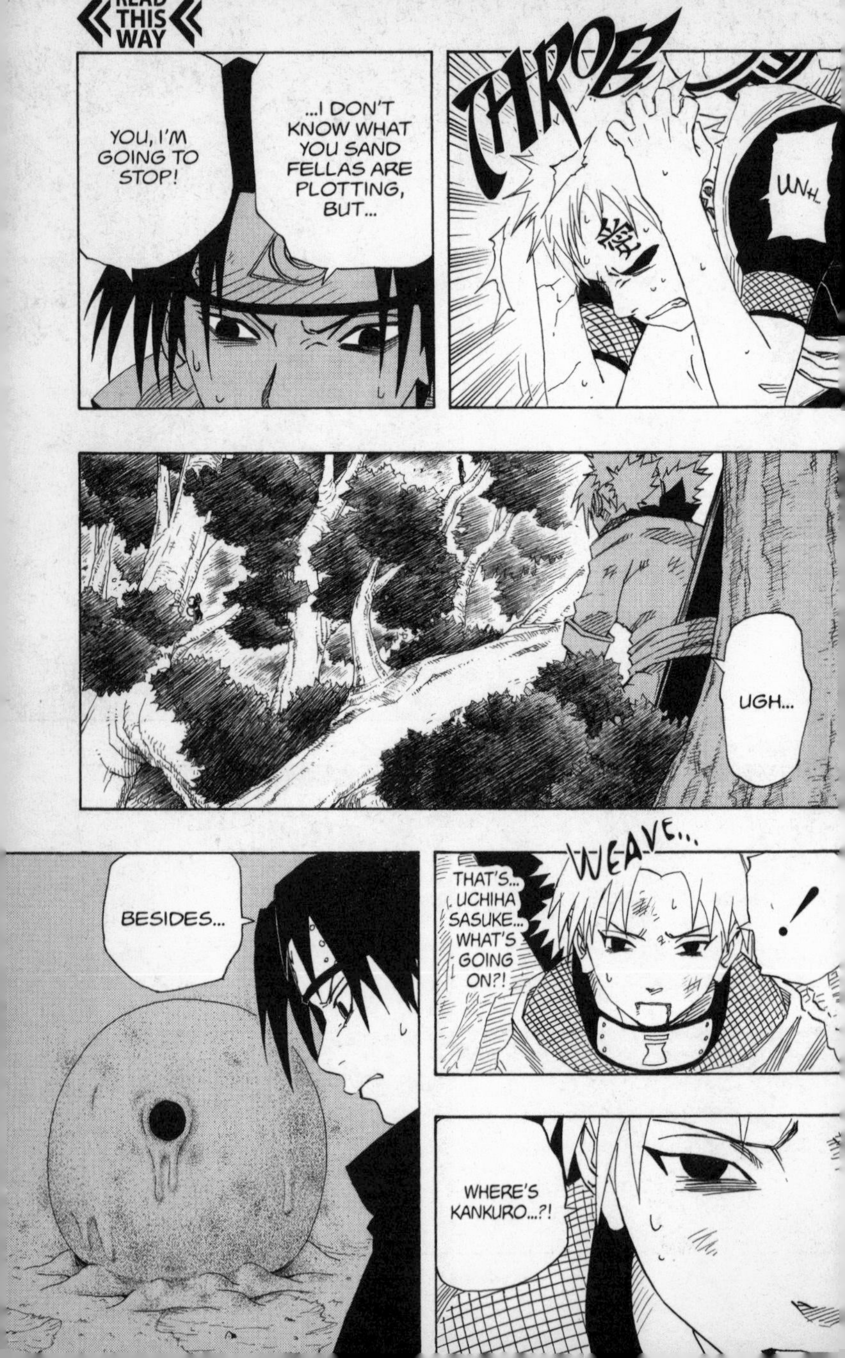
THROB
UNH...
...I DON'T KNOW WHAT YOU SAND FELLAS ARE PLOTTING, BUT...
YOU, I'M GOING TO STOP!
UGH...
WEAVE...
!
THAT'S... UCHIHA SASUKE... WHAT'S GOING ON?!
WHERE'S KANKURO...?!
BESIDES...

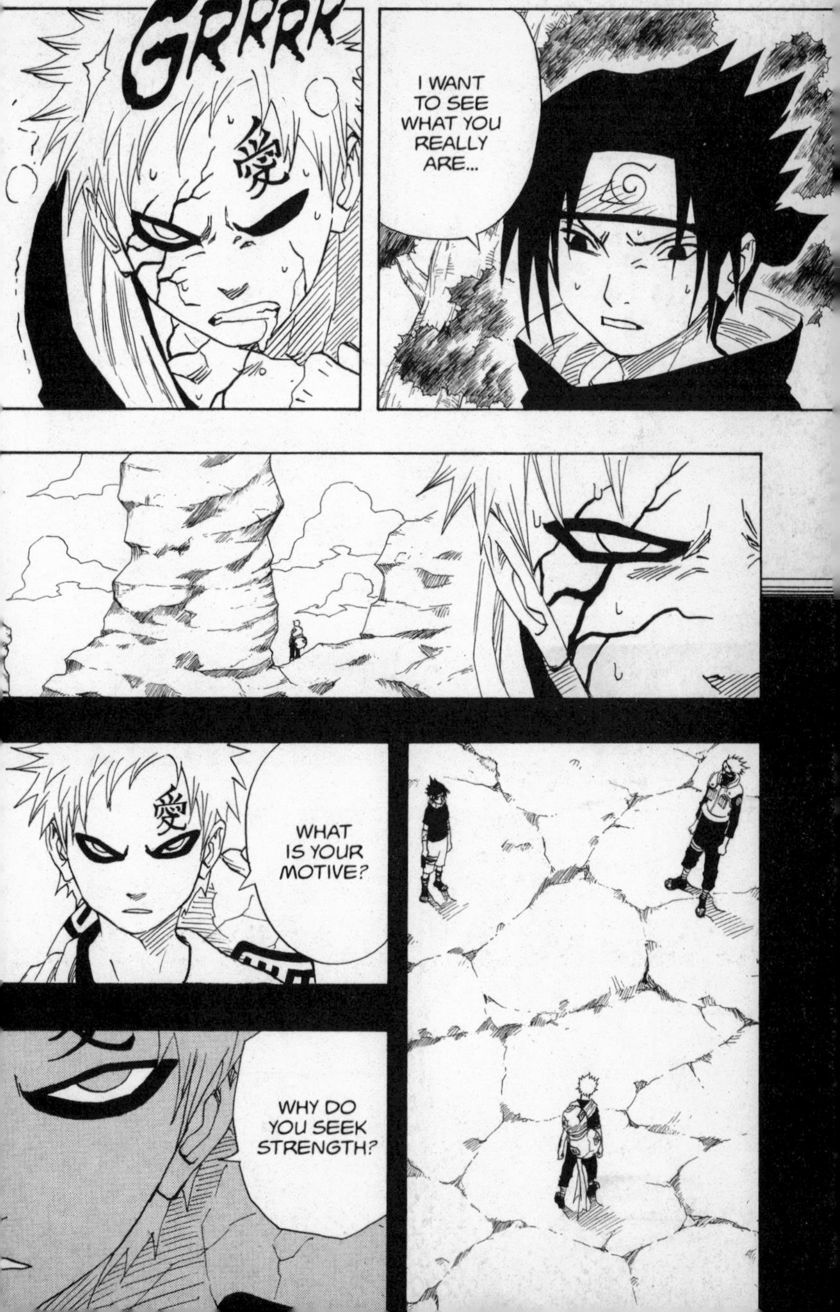
I WANT TO SEE WHAT YOU REALLY ARE...
GRRRR
WHAT IS YOUR MOTIVE?
WHY DO YOU SEEK STRENGTH?

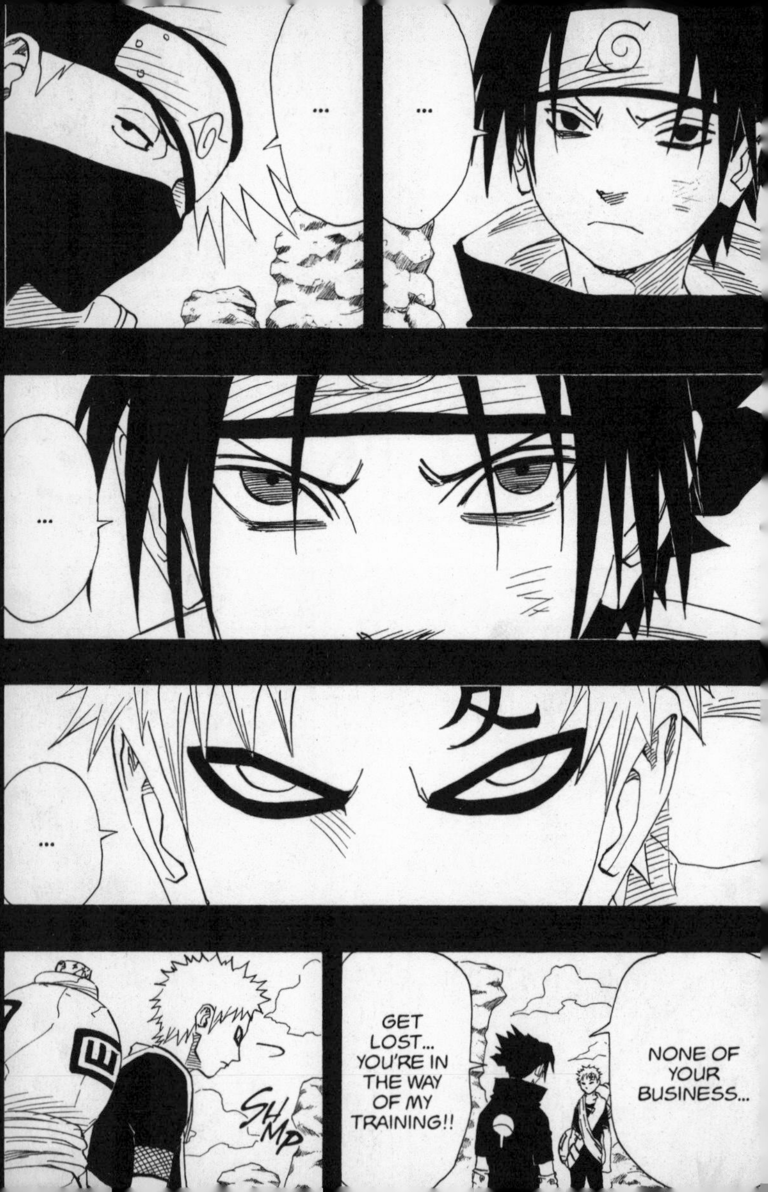

...
...
...
...
NONE OF YOUR BUSINESS...
GET LOST... YOU'RE IN THE WAY OF MY TRAINING!!
SHMP

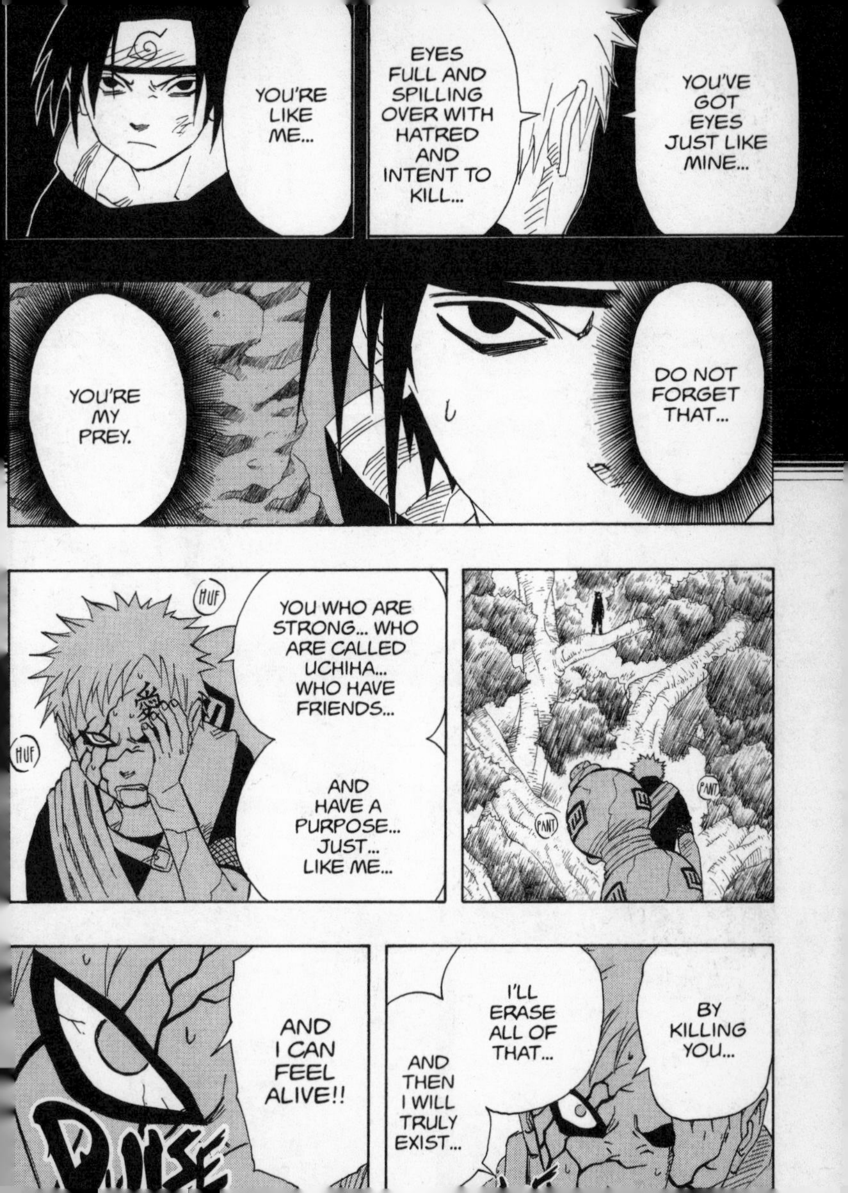
YOU'VE GOT EYES JUST LIKE MINE...
EYES FULL AND SPILLING OVER WITH HATRED AND INTENT TO KILL...
YOU'RE LIKE ME...
DO NOT FORGET THAT...
YOU'RE MY PREY.
PANT
PANT
HUF
YOU WHO ARE STRONG... WHO ARE CALLED UCHIHA... WHO HAVE FRIENDS...
AND HAVE A PURPOSE... JUST... LIKE ME...
HUF
BY KILLING YOU...
I'LL ERASE ALL OF THAT...
AND THEN I WILL TRULY EXIST...
AND I CAN FEEL ALIVE!!

READ THIS WAY

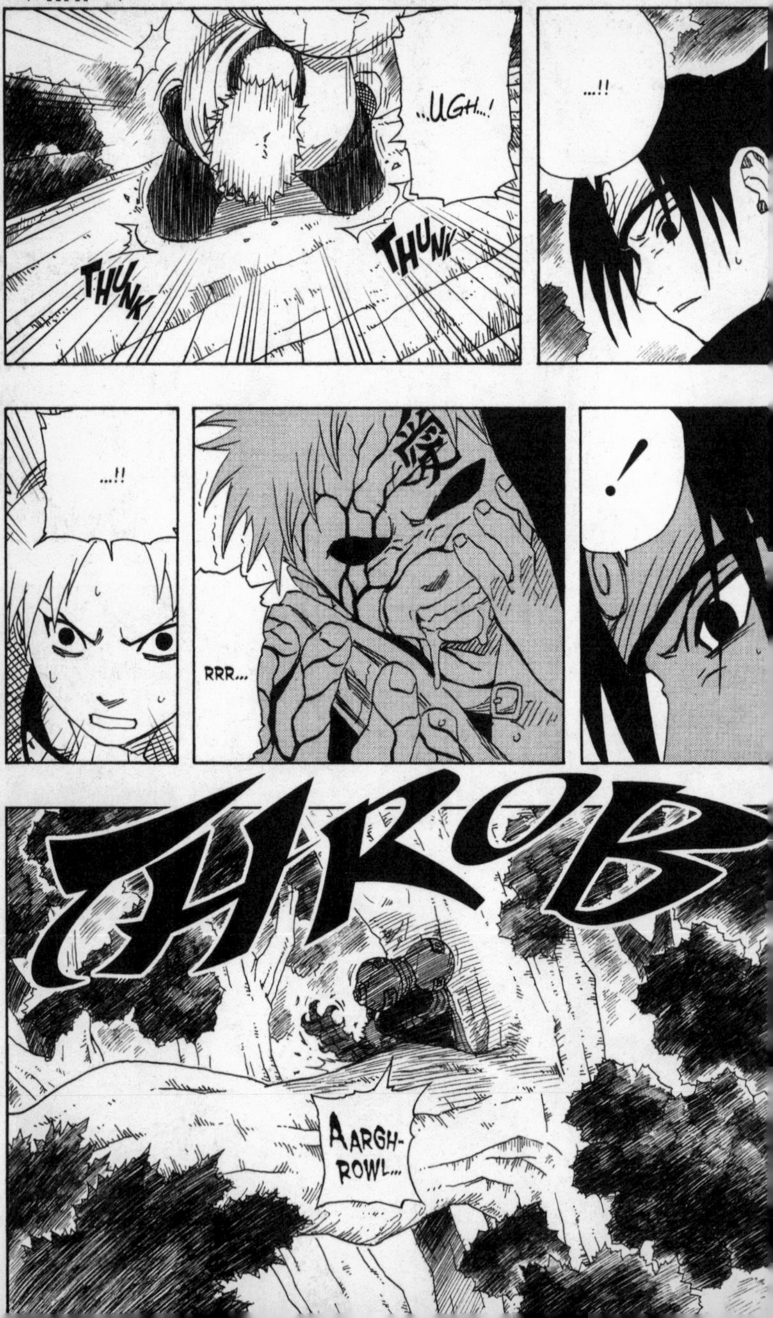
...!!
...UGH...!
THUNK
THUNK
!
RRR...
...!!
THROB
AARGH-ROWL...

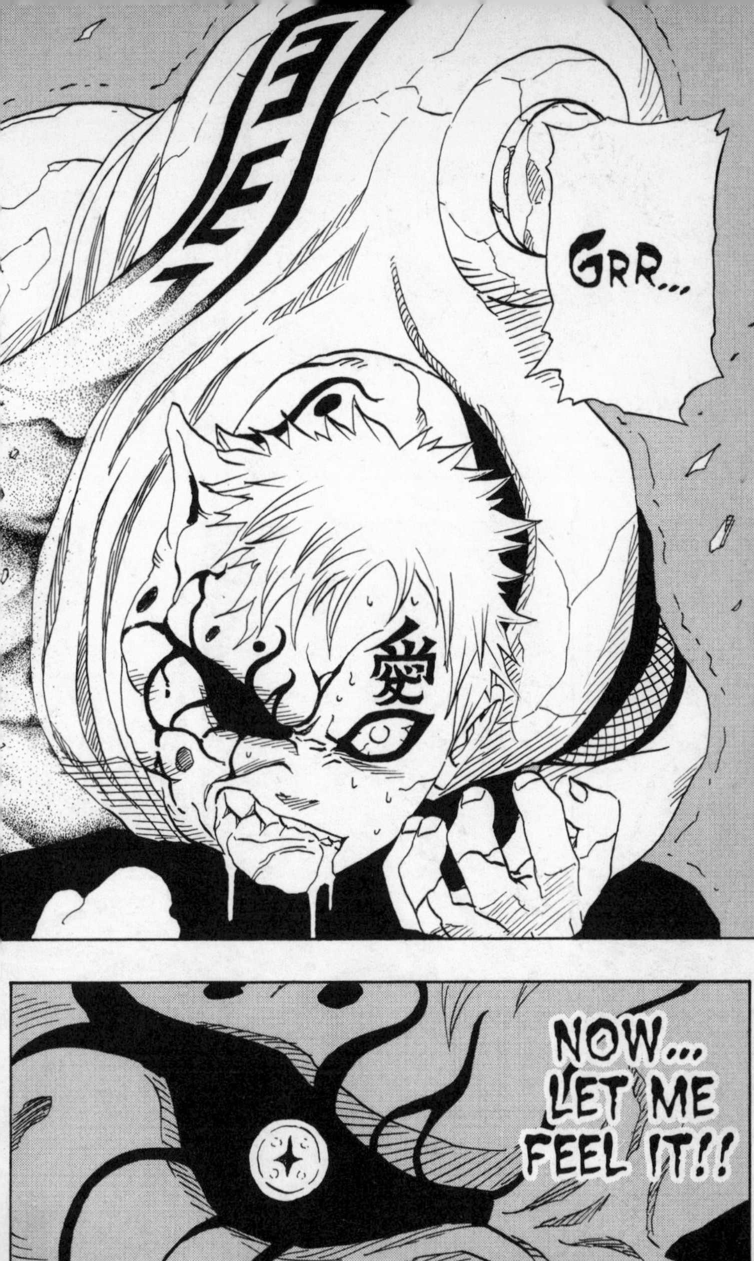
GRR...
NOW... LET ME FEEL IT!!

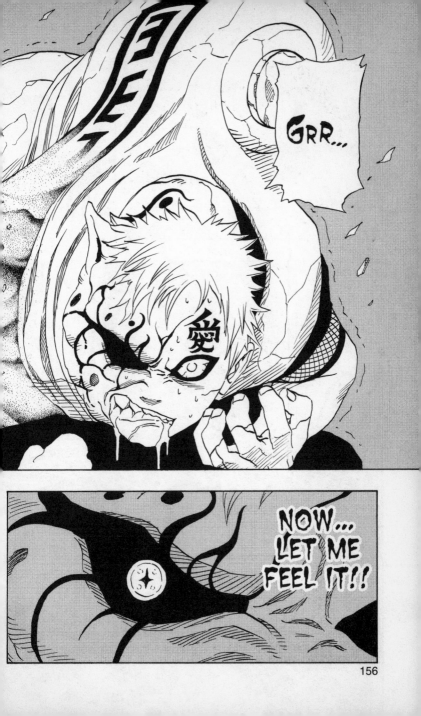

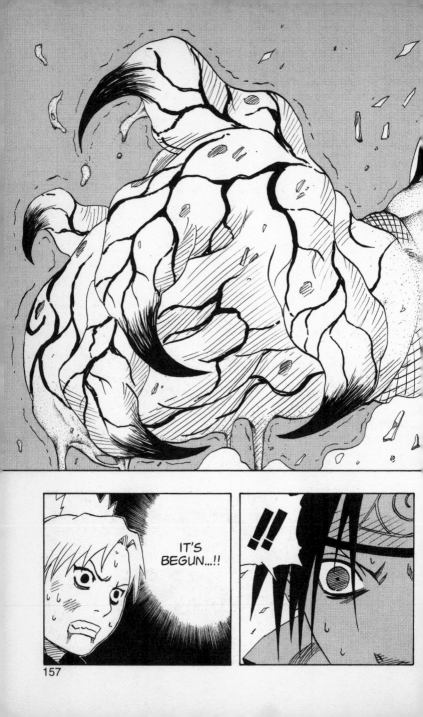

IT'S BEGUN...!!

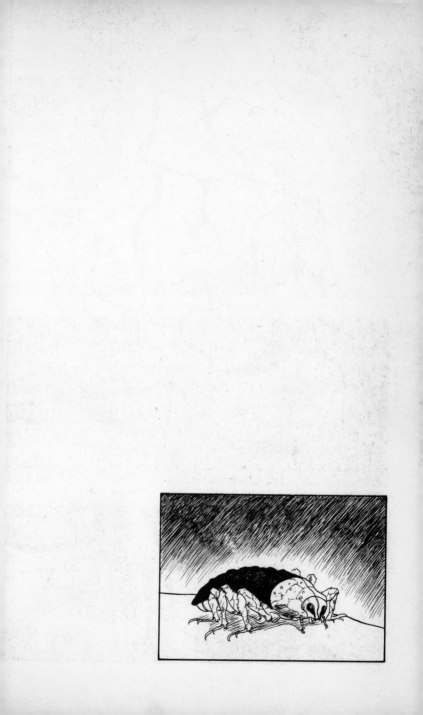

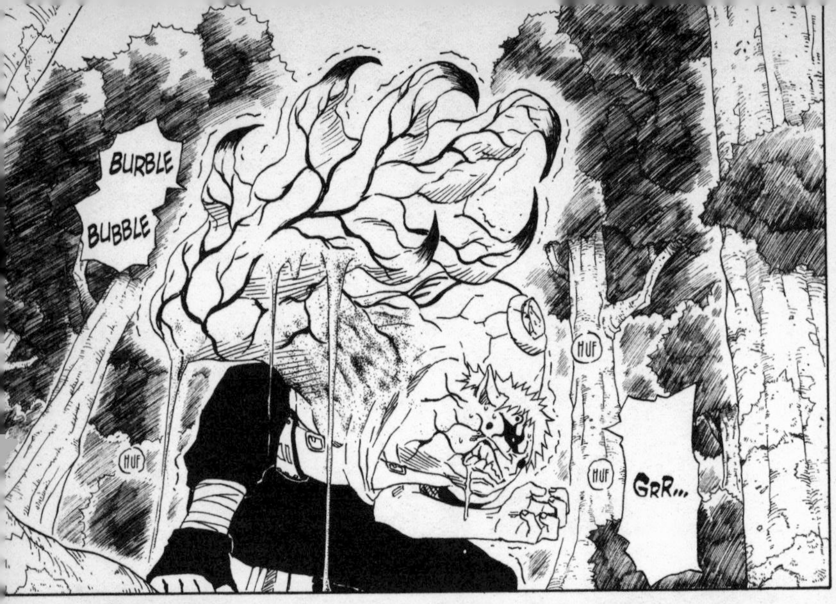
HUF
GRR...
HUF
BURBLE
BUBBLE
HUF

Number 126: Off Guard...!!

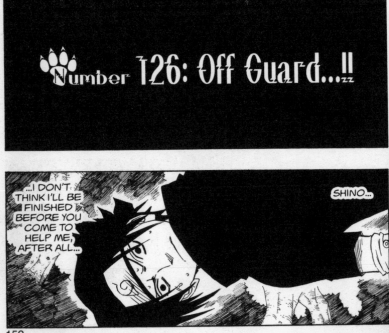

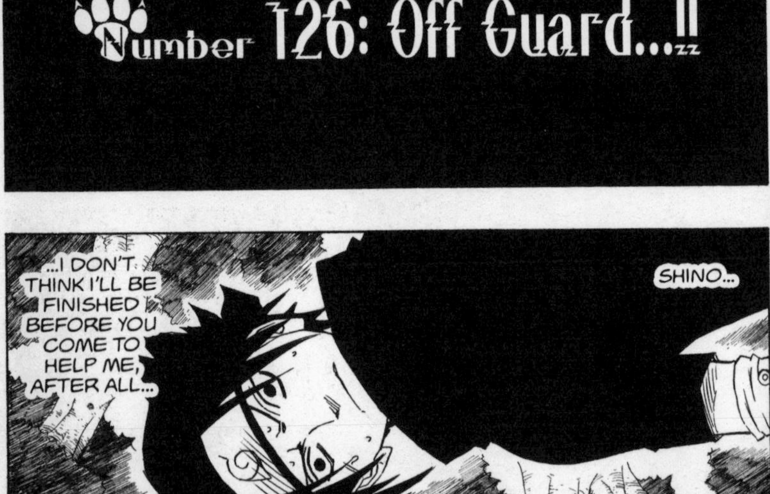
SHINO...
...I DON'T THINK I'LL BE FINISHED BEFORE YOU COME TO HELP ME, AFTER ALL...

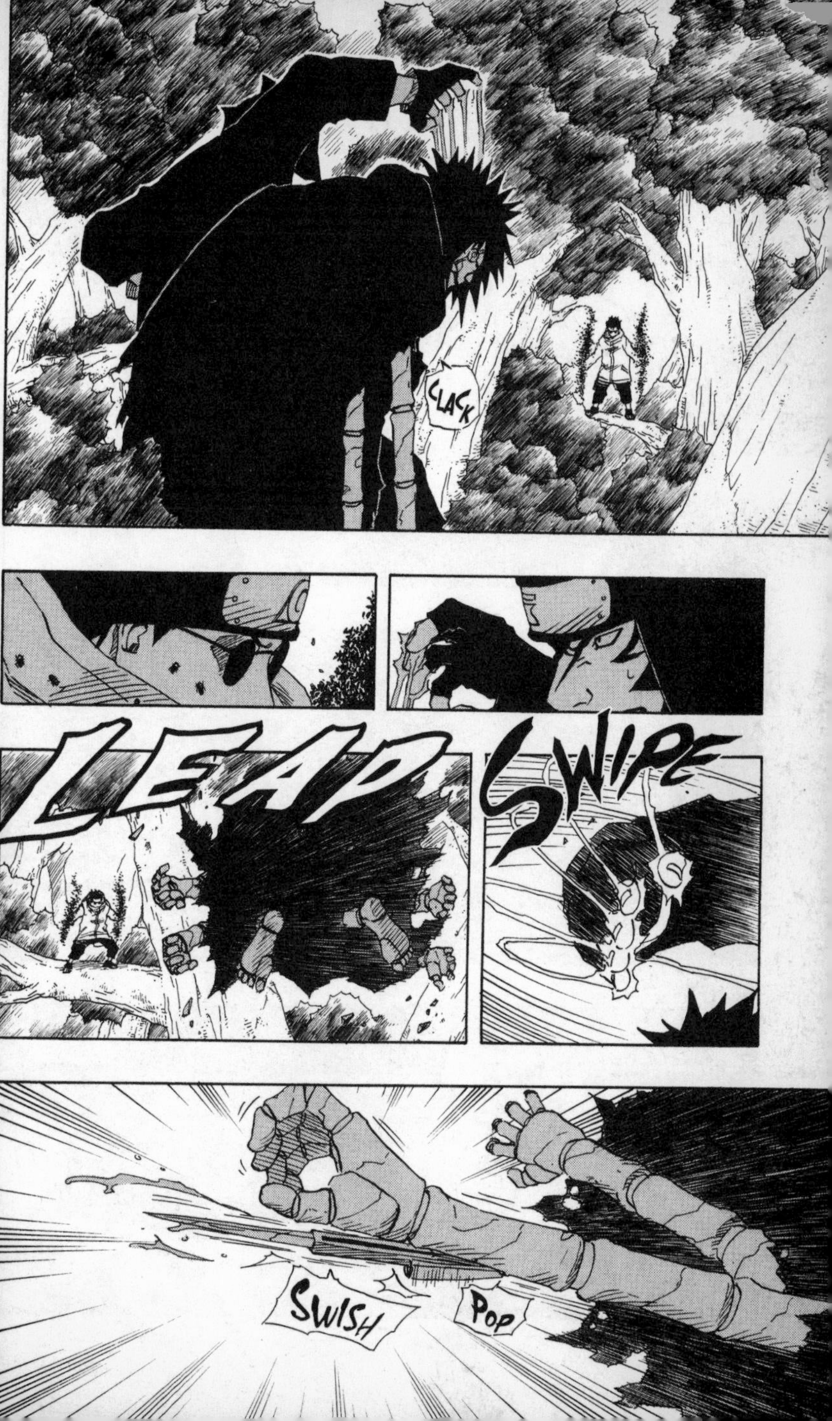
CLACK
SWIPE
LEAP
POP
SWISH

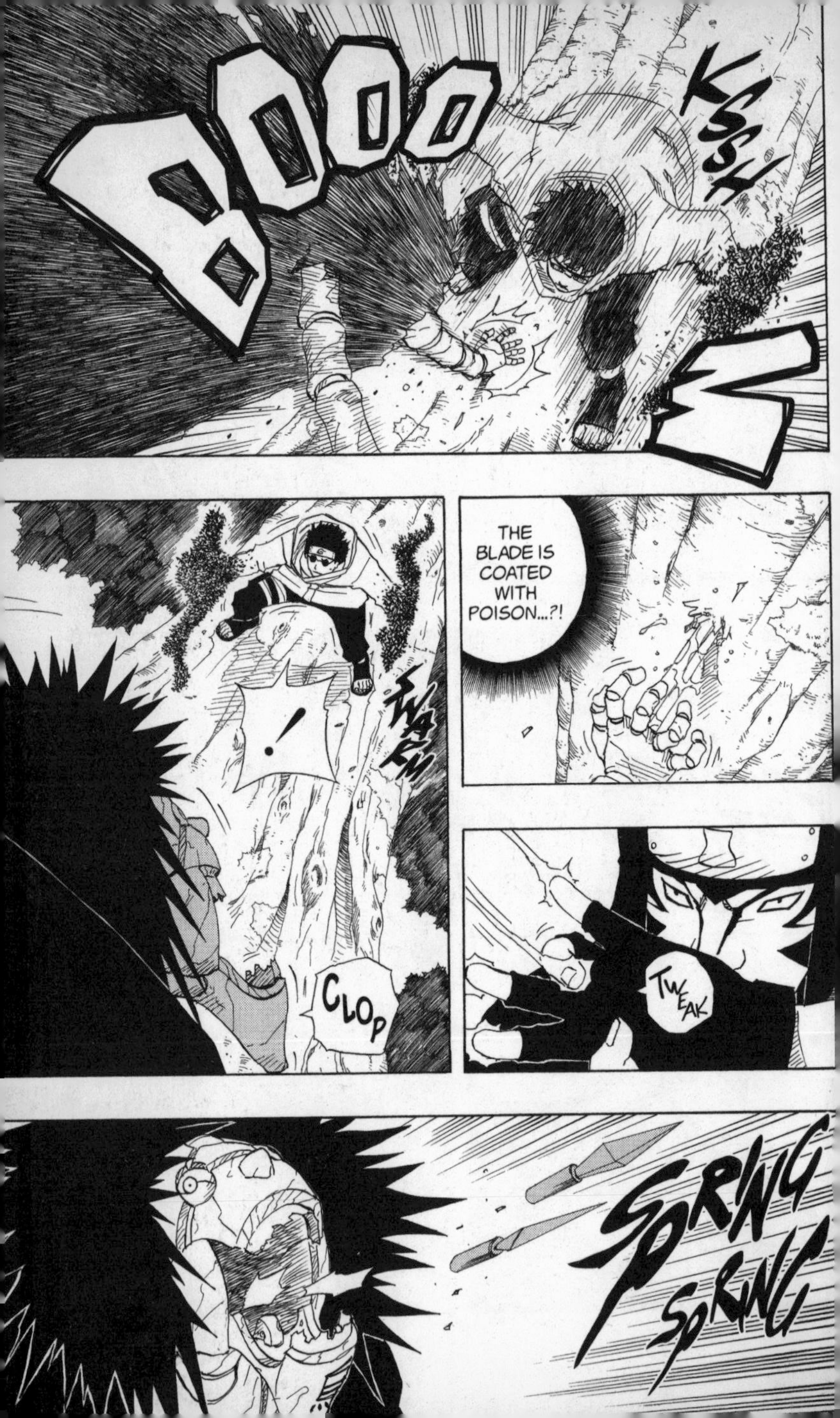
KSCH
BOOOOM
THE BLADE IS COATED WITH POISON...?!
!
TWARM
CLOP
TWEAK
SPRING
SPRING

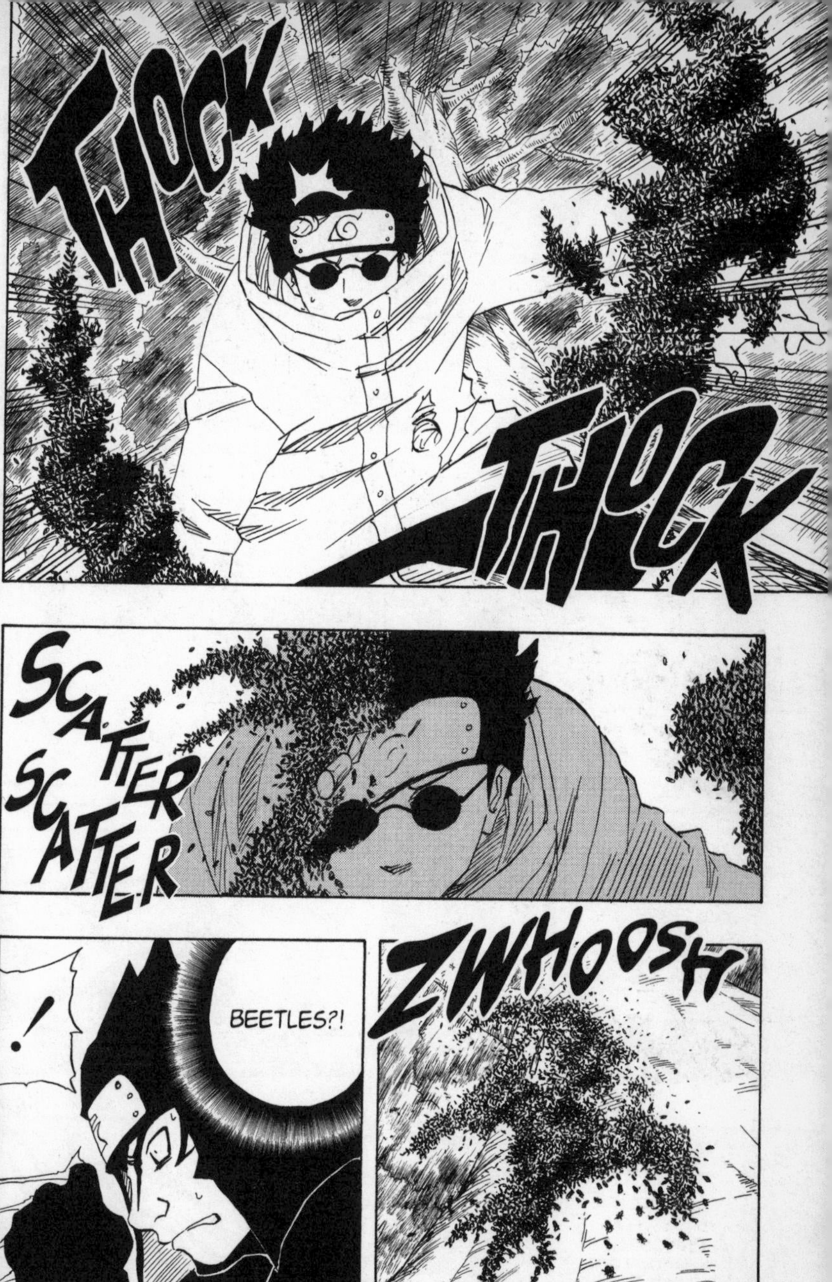
THOCK
THOCK
SCATTER SCATTER
ZWHOOSH
!
BEETLES?!

READ THIS WAY

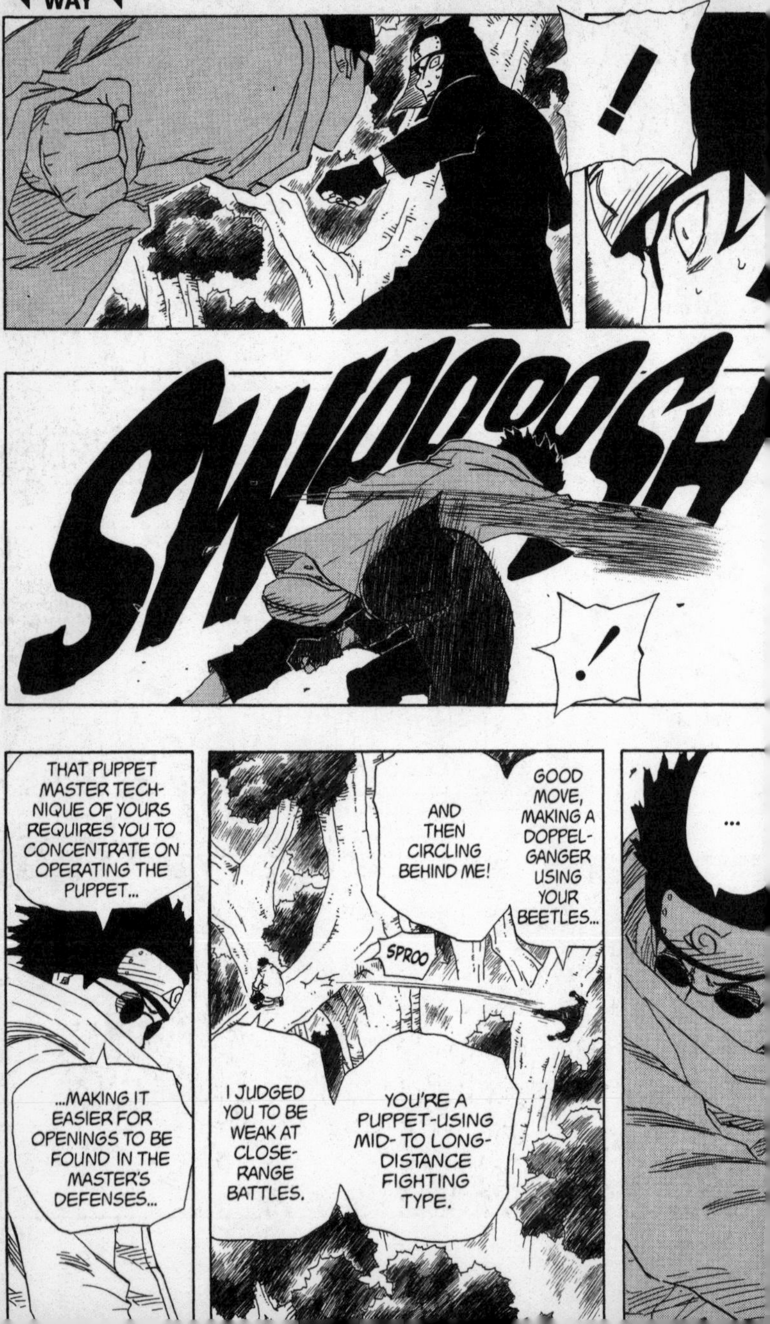
!
SWOOOOSH
!
...
GOOD MOVE, MAKING A DOPPEL-GANGER USING YOUR BEETLES...
AND THEN CIRCLING BEHIND ME!
SPROO
YOU'RE A PUPPET-USING MID- TO LONG-DISTANCE FIGHTING TYPE.
I JUDGED YOU TO BE WEAK AT CLOSE-RANGE BATTLES.
THAT PUPPET MASTER TECH-NIQUE OF YOURS REQUIRES YOU TO CONCENTRATE ON OPERATING THE PUPPET...
...MAKING IT EASIER FOR OPENINGS TO BE FOUND IN THE MASTER'S DEFENSES...

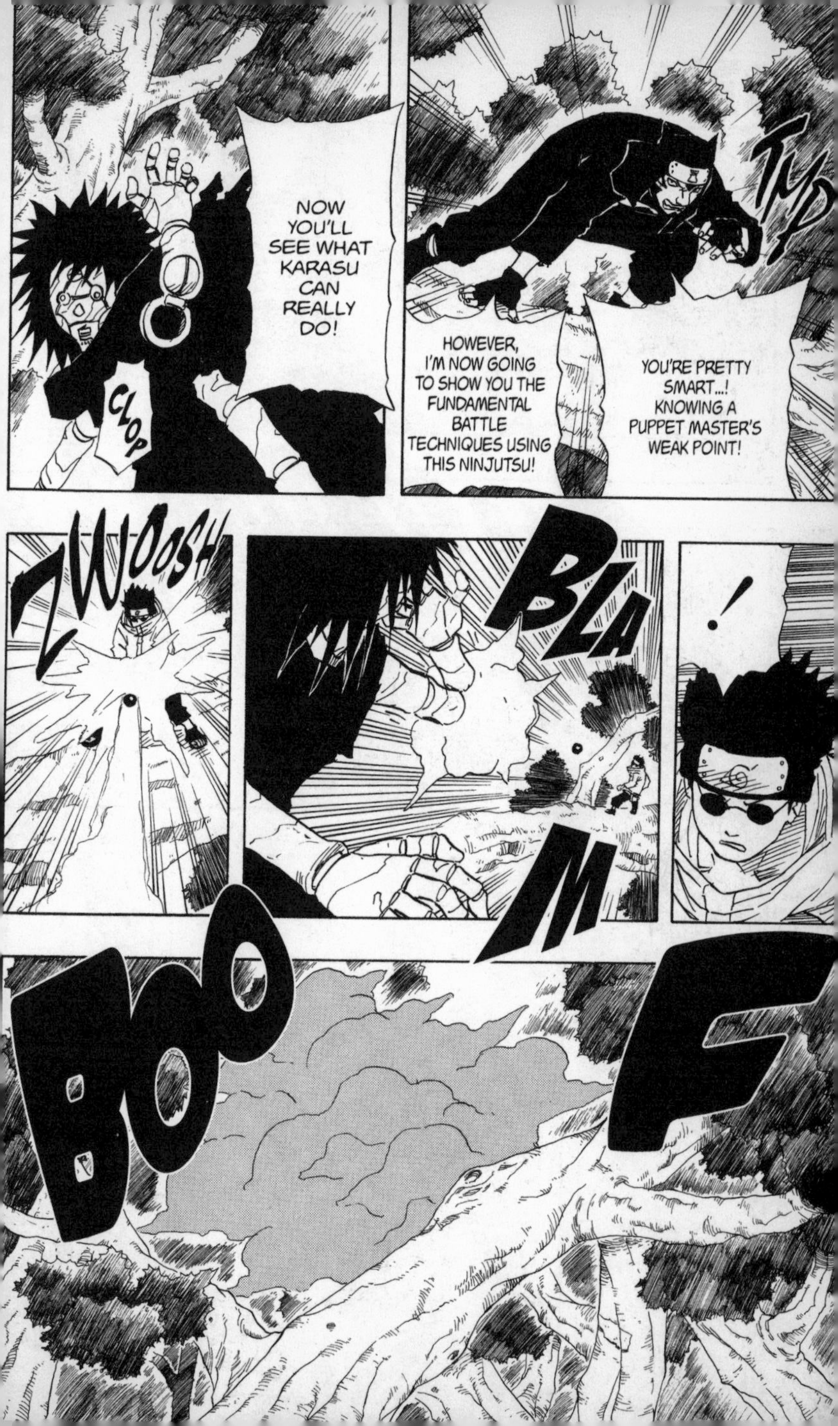
YOU'RE PRETTY SMART...! KNOWING A PUPPET MASTER'S WEAK POINT!
HOWEVER, I'M NOW GOING TO SHOW YOU THE FUNDAMENTAL BATTLE TECHNIQUES USING THIS NINJUTSU!
NOW YOU'LL SEE WHAT KARASU CAN REALLY DO!
CLOP
!
BLAM
ZWOOSH
BOOF

READ THIS WAY

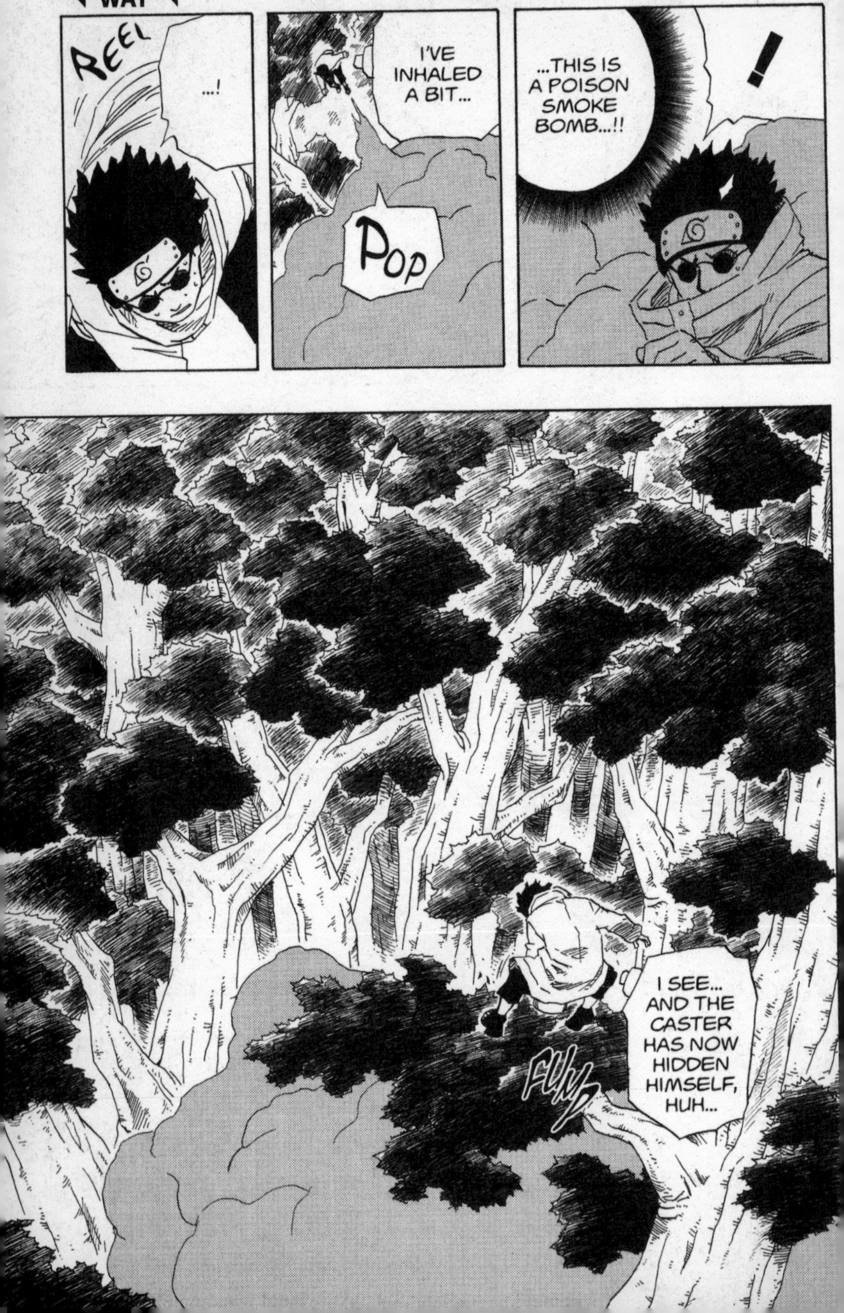
!
...THIS IS A POISON SMOKE BOMB...!!
I'VE INHALED A BIT...
POP
REEL
...!
I SEE... AND THE CASTER HAS NOW HIDDEN HIMSELF, HUH...

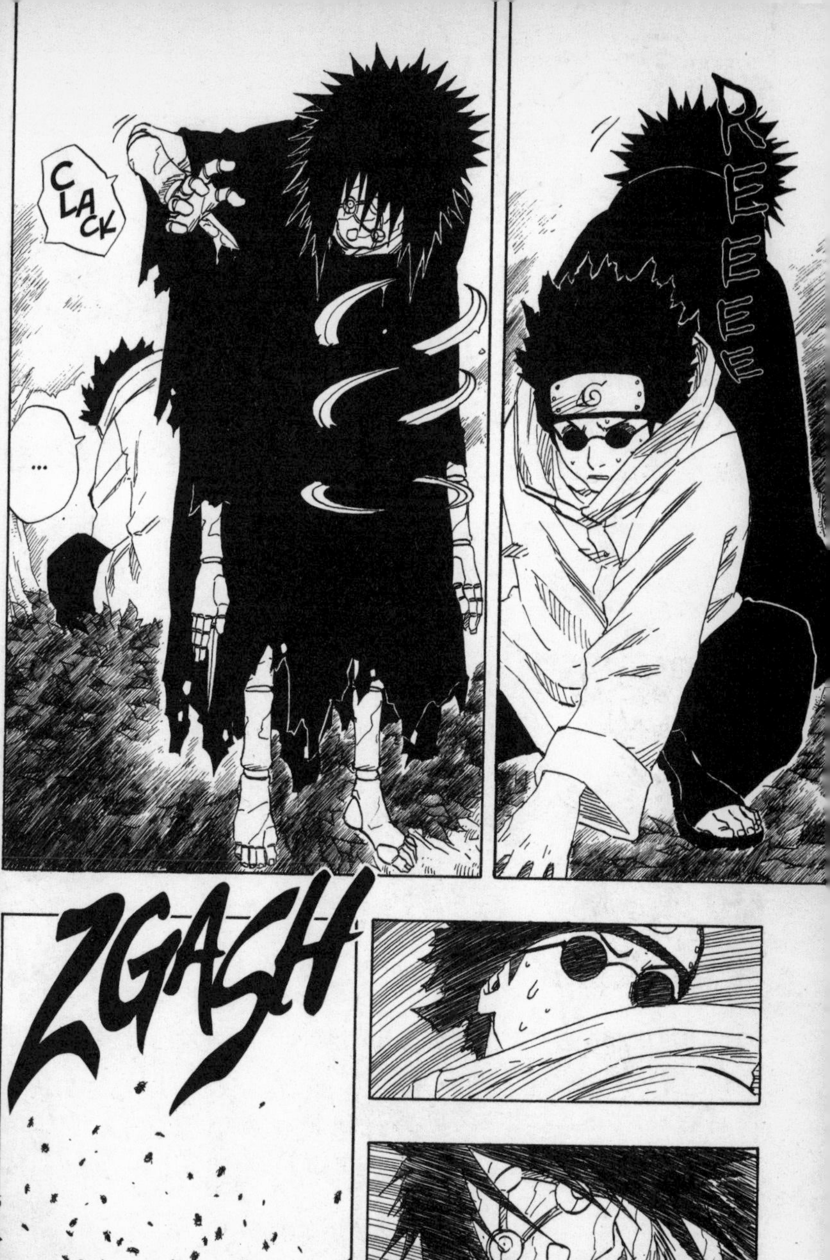
REEEEE
CLACK
...
ZGASH

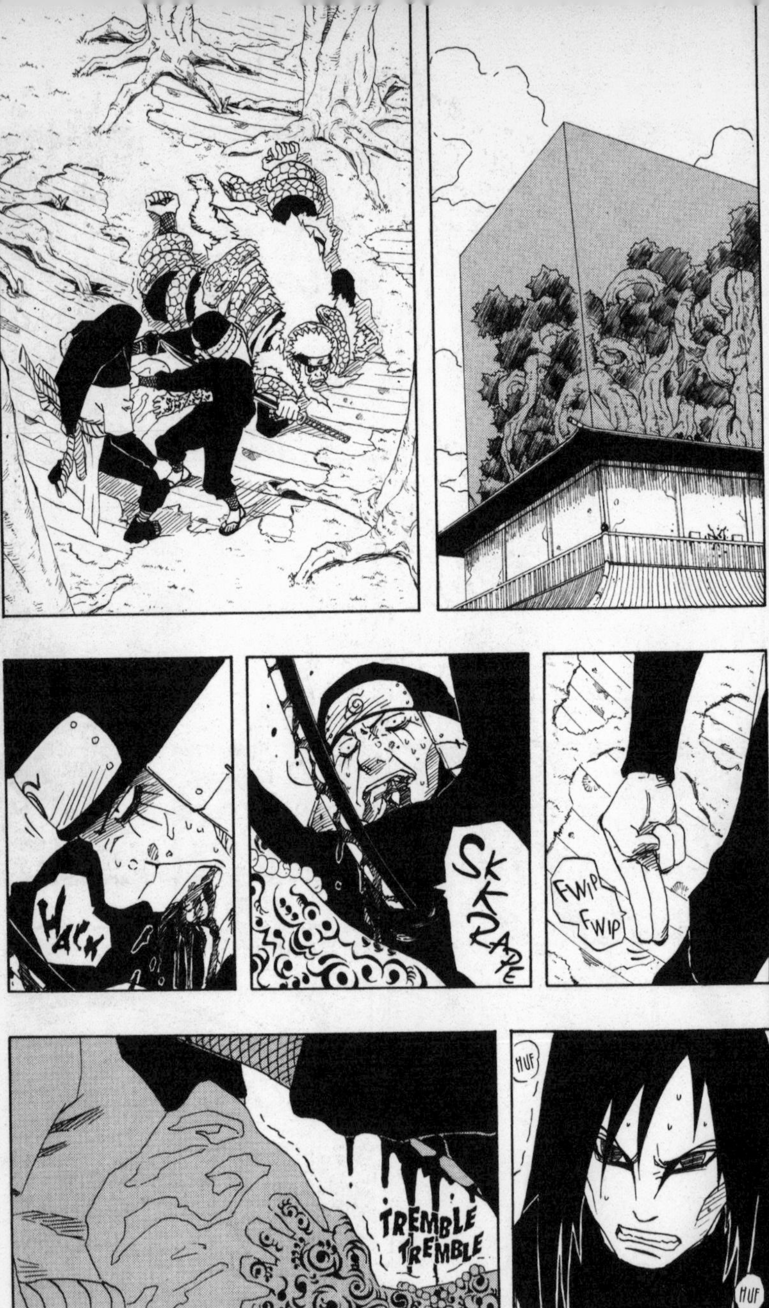
FWIP
FWIP
SKKRAPE
HACK
HUF
HUF
TREMBLE
TREMBLE

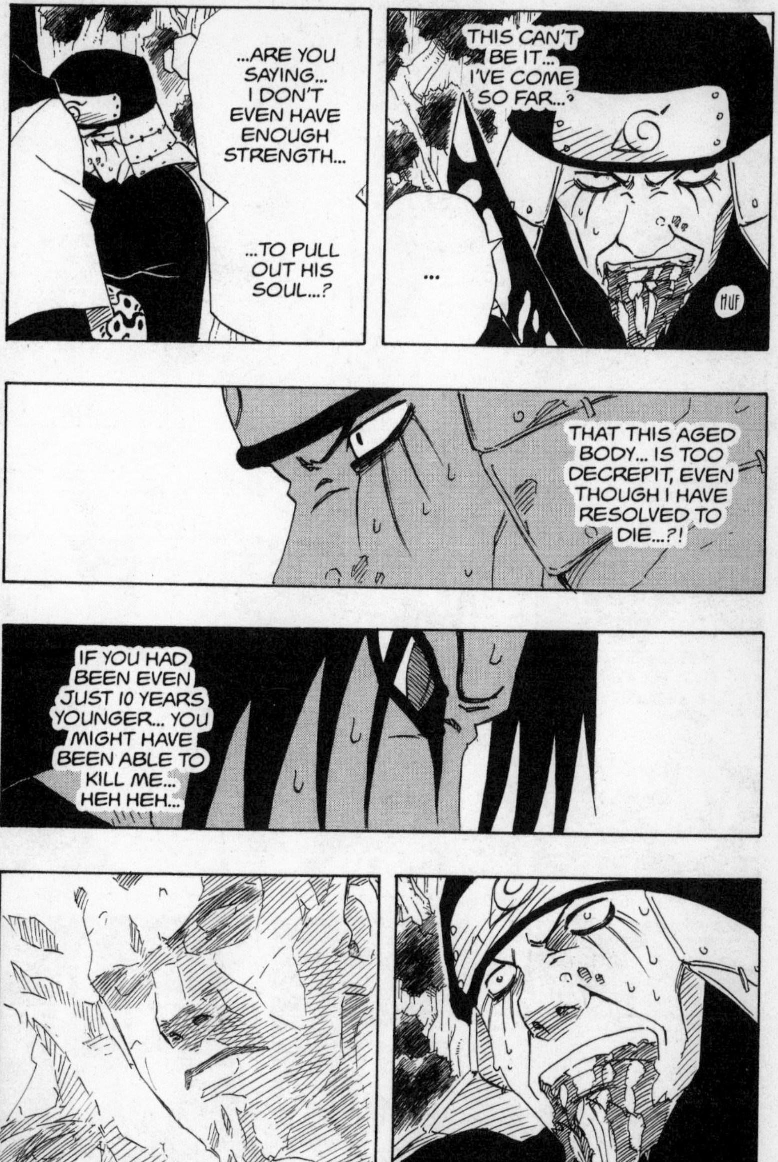
THIS CAN'T BE IT... I'VE COME SO FAR...
HUF
...
...ARE YOU SAYING... I DON'T EVEN HAVE ENOUGH STRENGTH...
...TO PULL OUT HIS SOUL...?
THAT THIS AGED BODY... IS TOO DECREPIT, EVEN THOUGH I HAVE RESOLVED TO DIE...?!
IF YOU HAD BEEN EVEN JUST 10 YEARS YOUNGER... YOU MIGHT HAVE BEEN ABLE TO KILL ME... HEH HEH...

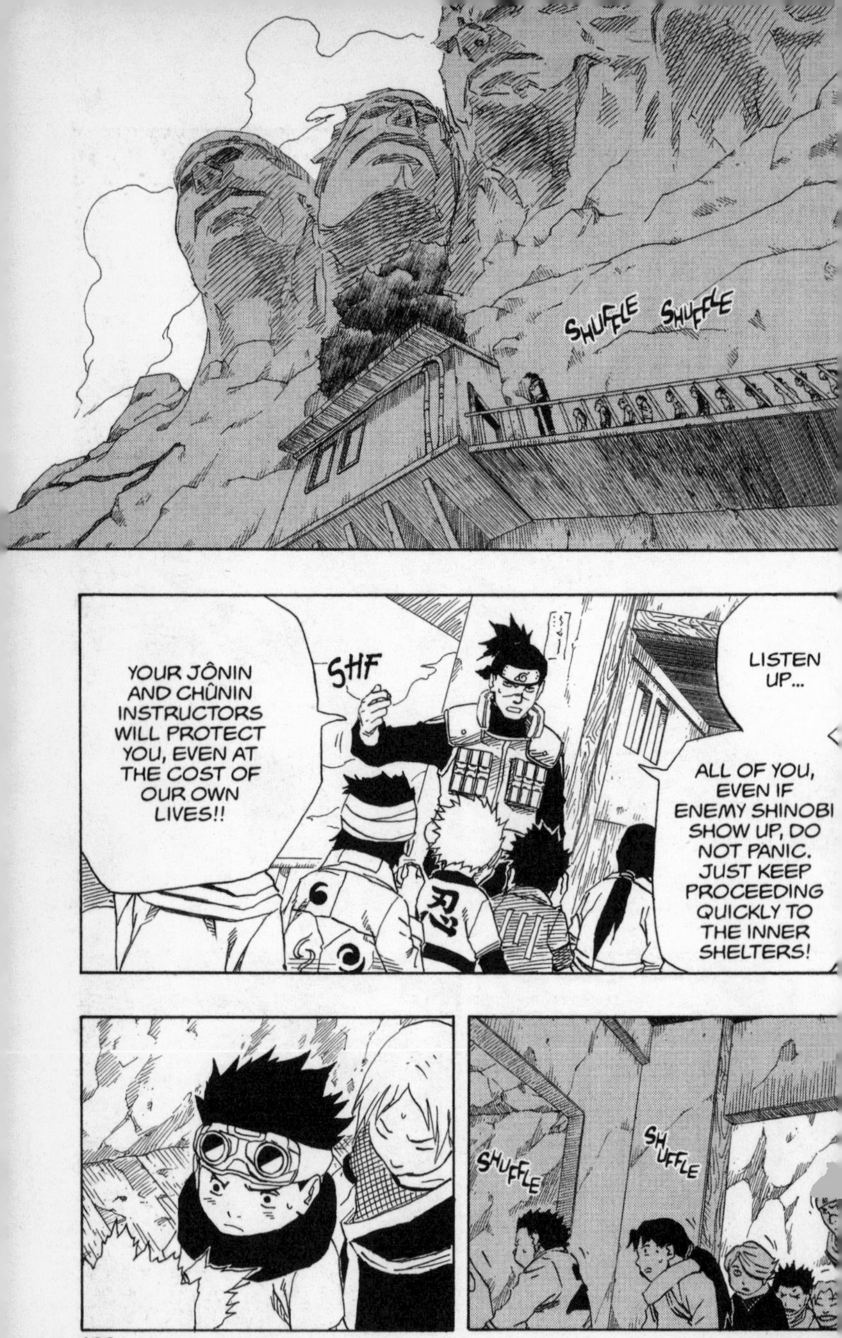
SHUFFLE SHUFFLE
LISTEN UP...
ALL OF YOU, EVEN IF ENEMY SHINOBI SHOW UP, DO NOT PANIC. JUST KEEP PROCEEDING QUICKLY TO THE INNER SHELTERS!
SHF
YOUR JÔNIN AND CHÛNIN INSTRUCTORS WILL PROTECT YOU, EVEN AT THE COST OF OUR OWN LIVES!!
SHUFFLE
SHUFFLE

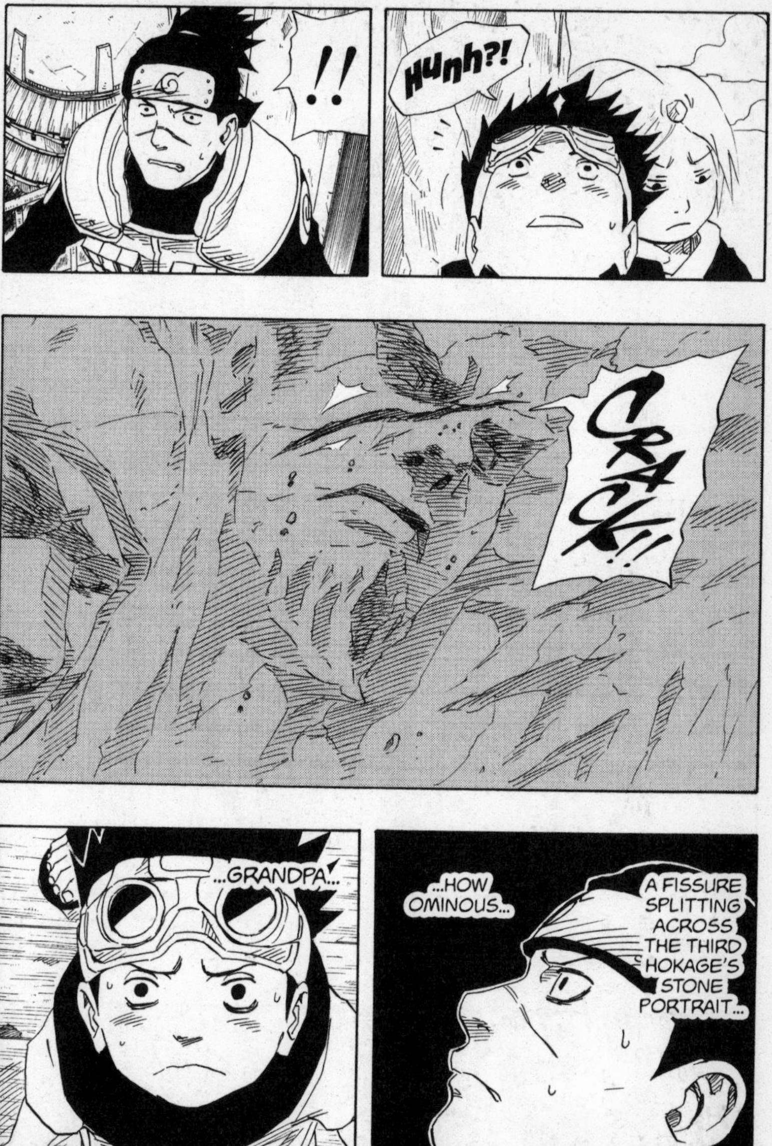
HUNH?!
!!
CRACK!!
A FISSURE SPLITTING ACROSS THE THIRD HOKAGE'S STONE PORTRAIT...
...HOW OMINOUS...
...GRANDPA...

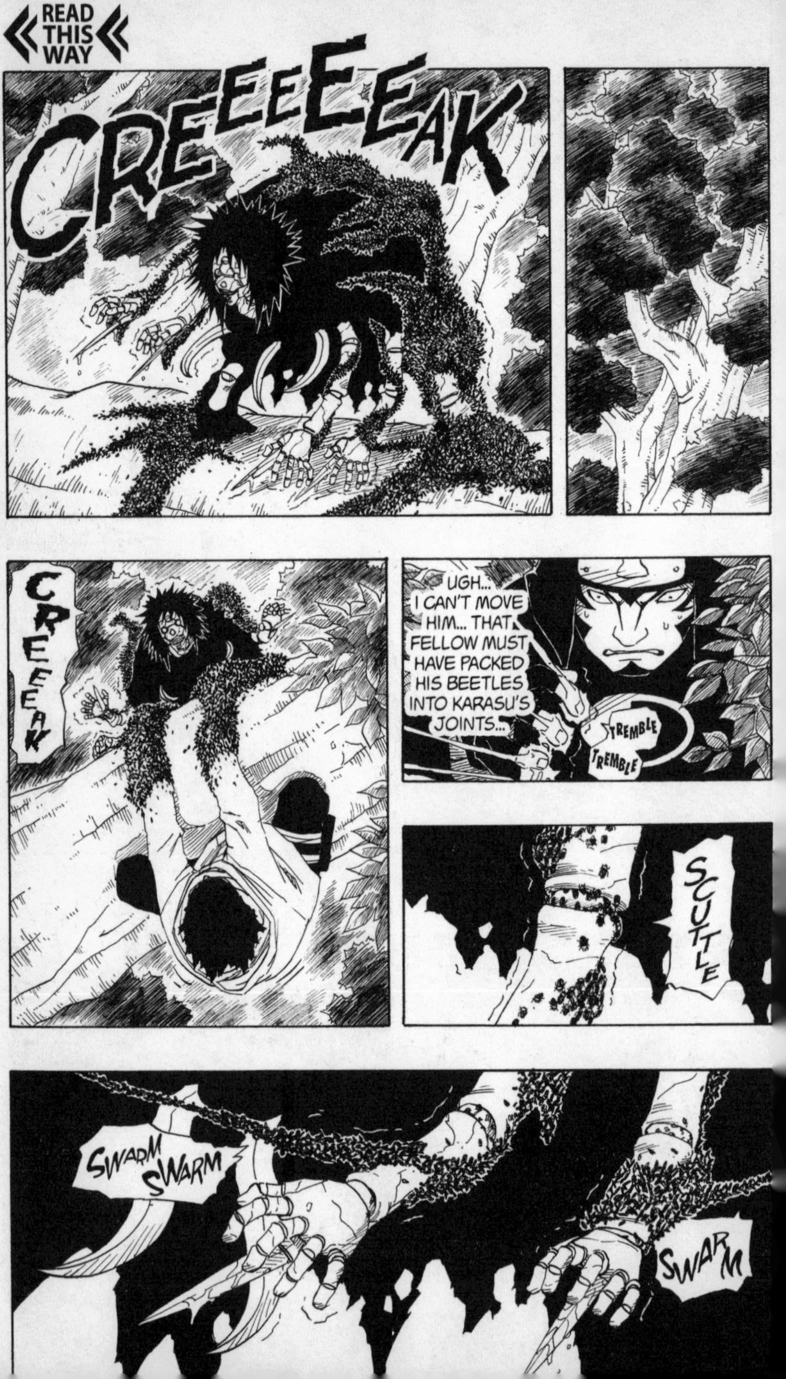
READ THIS WAY
CREEEEEEAK
UGH... I CAN'T MOVE HIM... THAT FELLOW MUST HAVE PACKED HIS BEETLES INTO KARASU'S JOINTS...
TREMBLE TREMBLE
SCUTTLE
CREEEEAK
SWARM SWARM
SWARM

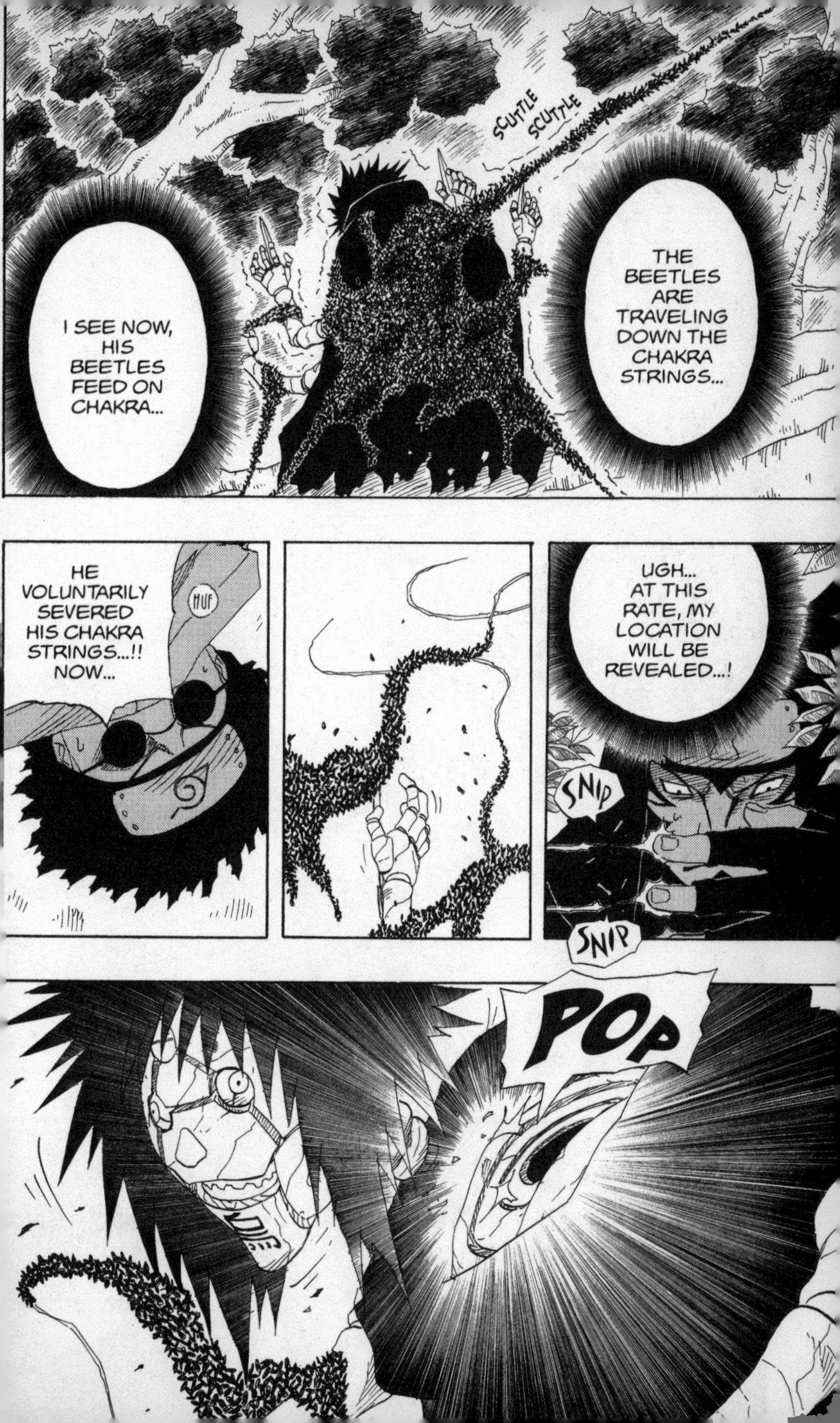
SCUTTLE SCUTTLE
THE BEETLES ARE TRAVELING DOWN THE CHAKRA STRINGS...
I SEE NOW, HIS BEETLES FEED ON CHAKRA...
UGH... AT THIS RATE, MY LOCATION WILL BE REVEALED...!
SNIP
SNIP
HE VOLUNTARILY SEVERED HIS CHAKRA STRINGS...!! NOW...
HUF
POP

READ THIS WAY

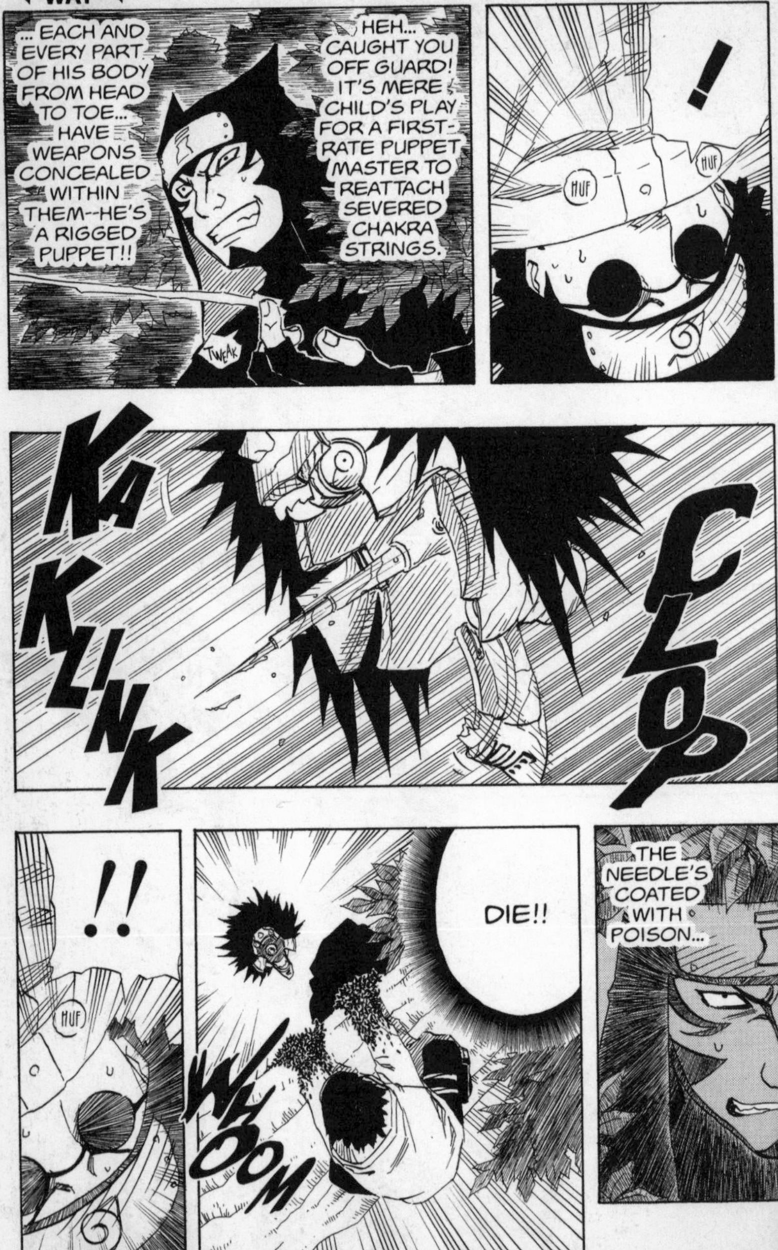
!
HUF
HUF
HEH... CAUGHT YOU OFF GUARD! IT'S MERE CHILD'S PLAY FOR A FIRST-RATE PUPPET MASTER TO REATTACH SEVERED CHAKRA STRINGS.
... EACH AND EVERY PART OF HIS BODY FROM HEAD TO TOE... HAVE WEAPONS CONCEALED WITHIN THEM--HE'S A RIGGED PUPPET!!
TWEAK
CLOP
KA KLINK
THE NEEDLE'S COATED WITH POISON...
DIE!!
WHOOM
!!
HUF

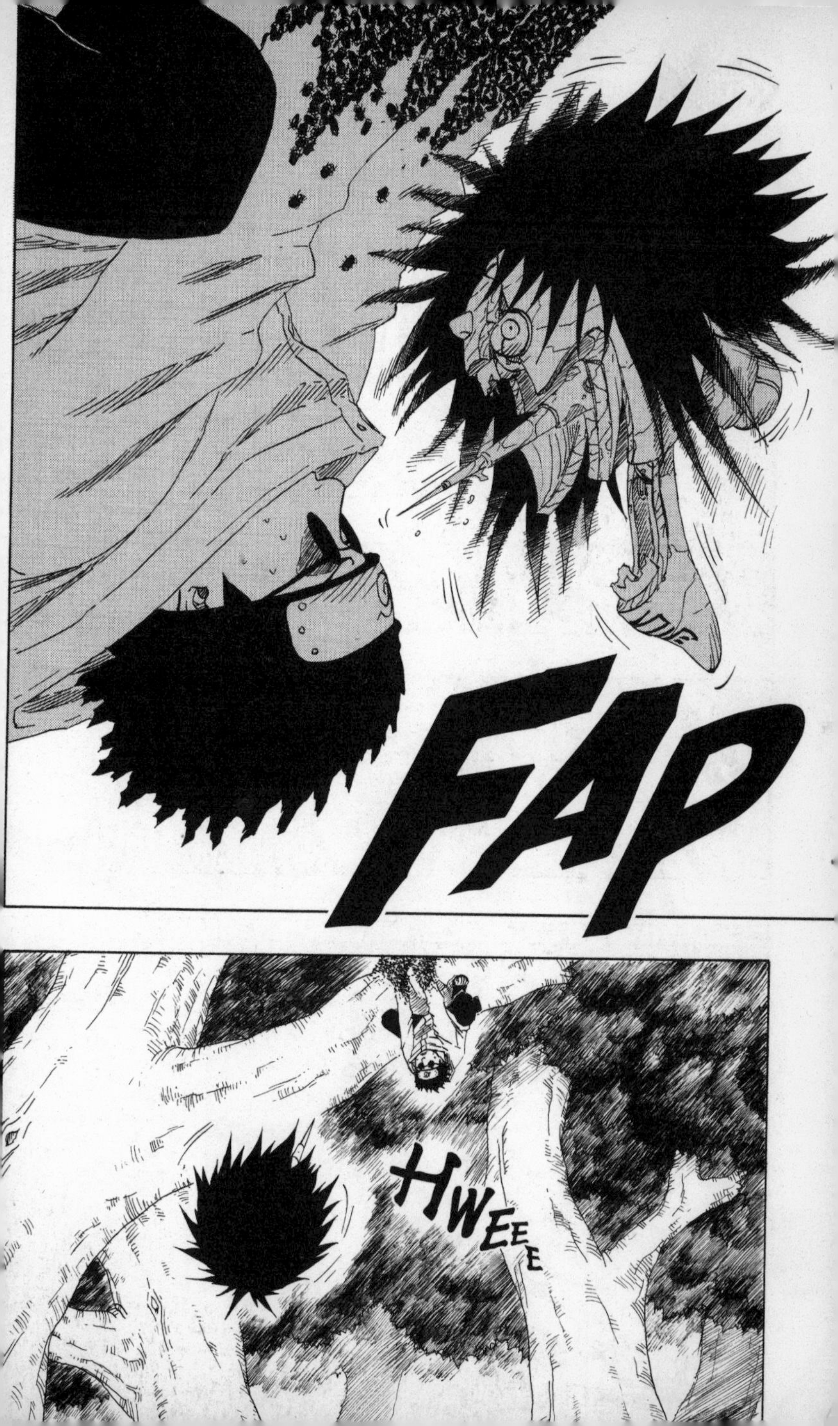
FAP
HWEEE

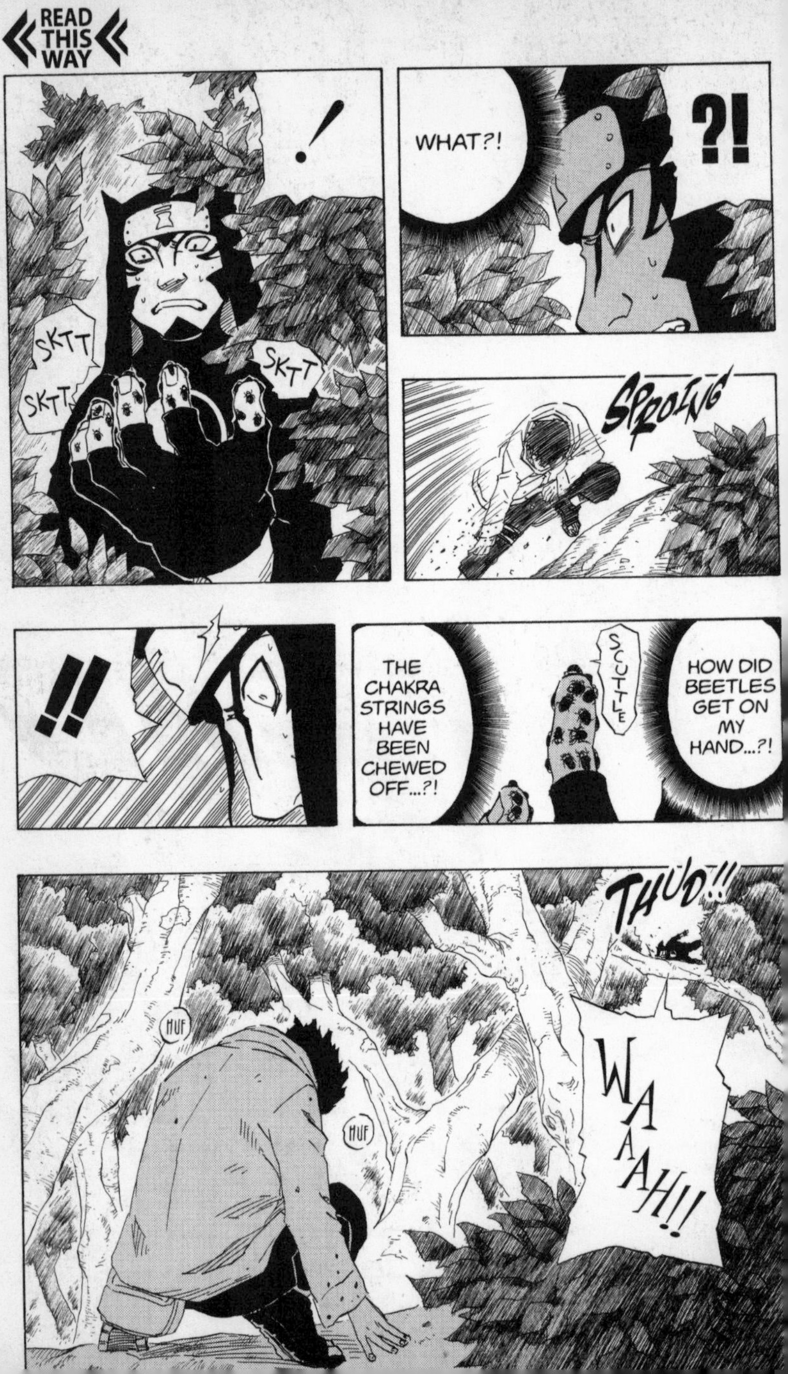
READ THIS WAY
?!
WHAT?!
!
SKTT
SKTT
SKTT
SPROING
HOW DID BEETLES GET ON MY HAND...?!
SCUTTLE
THE CHAKRA STRINGS HAVE BEEN CHEWED OFF...?!
!!
THUD!!
WAAAAH!!
HUF
HUF

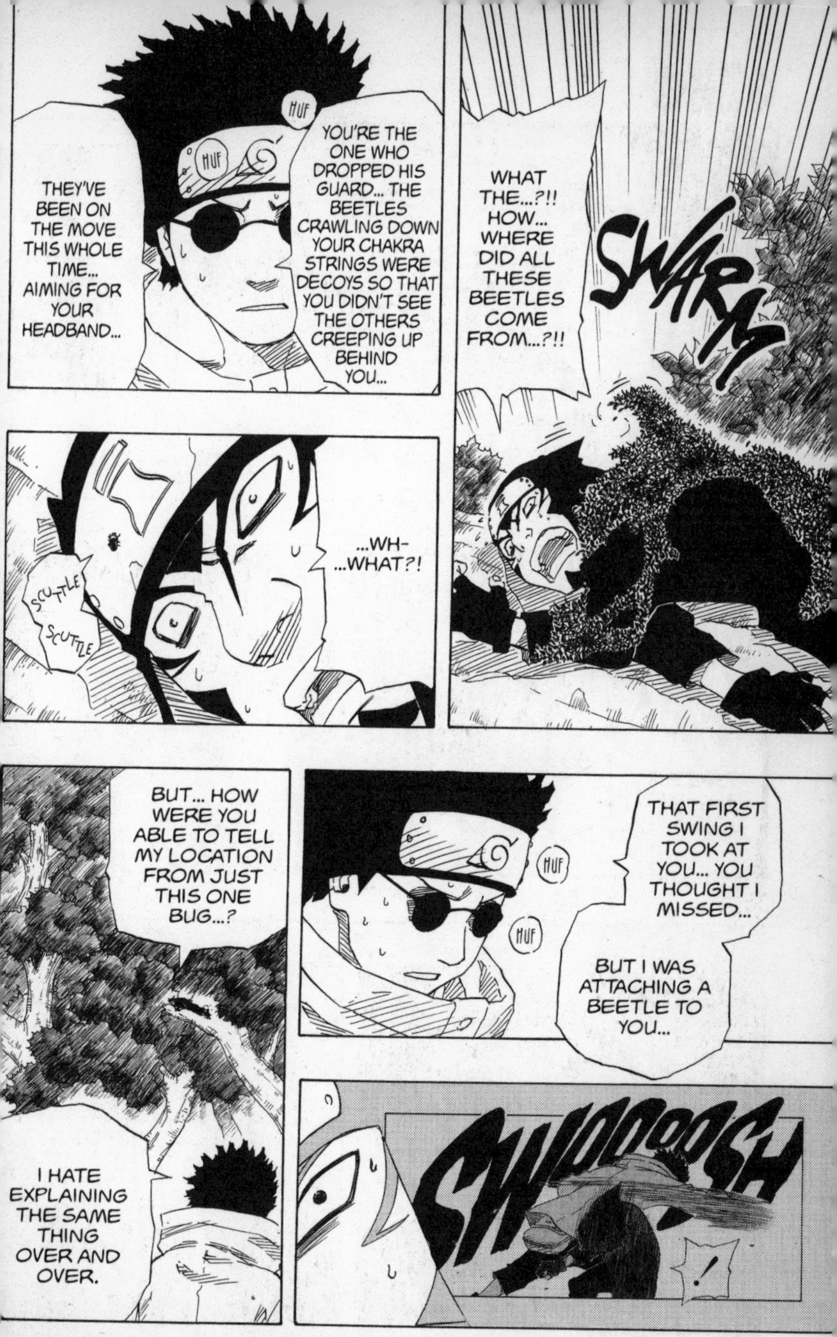
WHAT THE...?!! HOW... WHERE DID ALL THESE BEETLES COME FROM...?!!
SWARM
HUF
HUF
YOU'RE THE ONE WHO DROPPED HIS GUARD... THE BEETLES CRAWLING DOWN YOUR CHAKRA STRINGS WERE DECOYS SO THAT YOU DIDN'T SEE THE OTHERS CREEPING UP BEHIND YOU...
THEY'VE BEEN ON THE MOVE THIS WHOLE TIME... AIMING FOR YOUR HEADBAND...
...WH- ...WHAT?!
SCUTTLE
SCUTTLE
THAT FIRST SWING I TOOK AT YOU... YOU THOUGHT I MISSED...
HUF
HUF
BUT I WAS ATTACHING A BEETLE TO YOU...
SWOOOOSH
!
BUT... HOW WERE YOU ABLE TO TELL MY LOCATION FROM JUST THIS ONE BUG...?
I HATE EXPLAINING THE SAME THING OVER AND OVER.

READ THIS WAY

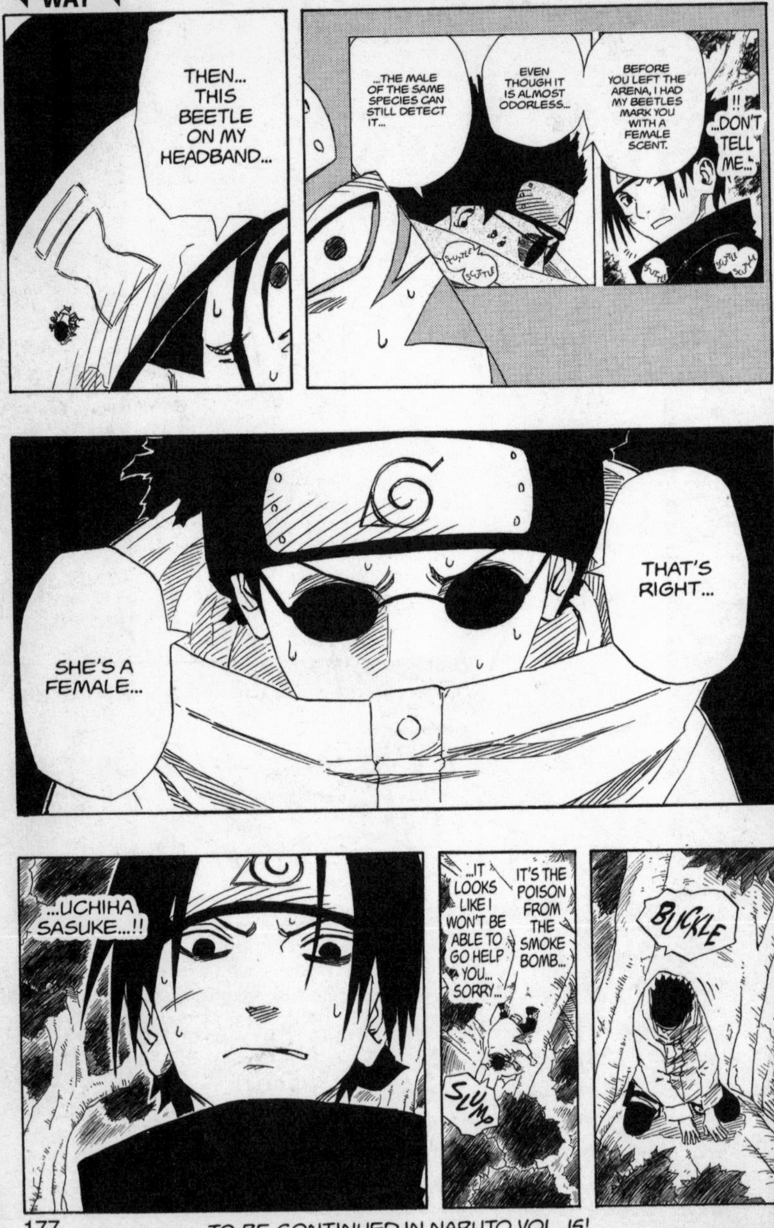

!! ...DON'T TELL ME...
BEFORE YOU LEFT THE ARENA, I HAD MY BEETLES MARK YOU WITH A FEMALE SCENT.
SCUTTLE SCUTTLE
EVEN THOUGH IT IS ALMOST ODORLESS...
...THE MALE OF THE SAME SPECIES CAN STILL DETECT IT...
SCUTTLE SCUTTLE
THEN... THIS BEETLE ON MY HEADBAND...
THAT'S RIGHT...
SHE'S A FEMALE...
BUCKLE
IT'S THE POISON FROM THE SMOKE BOMB...
...IT LOOKS LIKE I WON'T BE ABLE TO GO HELP YOU... SORRY...
SLUMP
...UCHIHA SASUKE...!!

TO BE CONTINUED IN NARUTO VOL. 15!

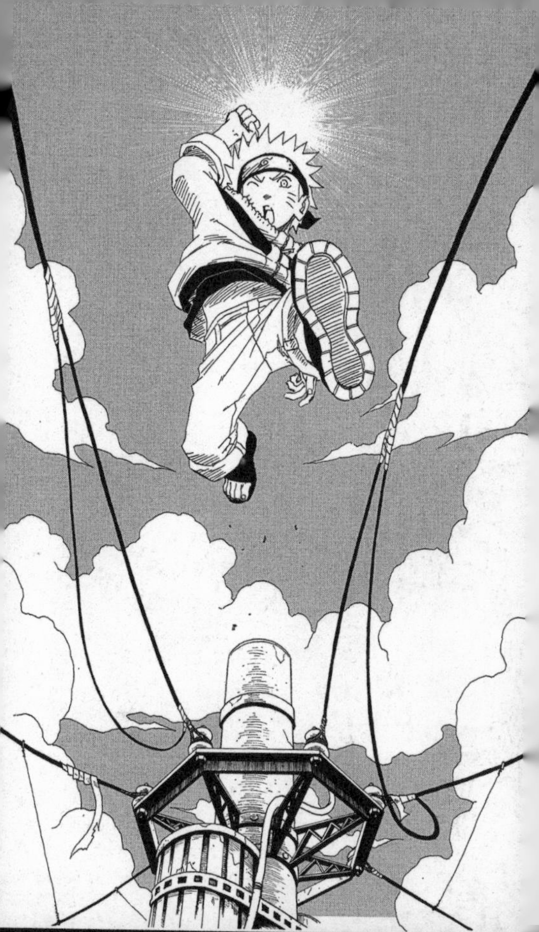

N THE NEXT VOLUME...

'he tension between Naruto and Gaara builds, and Naruto finds himself not only understanding his riva ut also sympathizing with him. But that doesn't me e's gone soft. As Gaara continues to mutate, Narut eaps toward the fight of his life!

VAILABLE JULY 2007!

ead it first in SHONEN JUMP magazine!

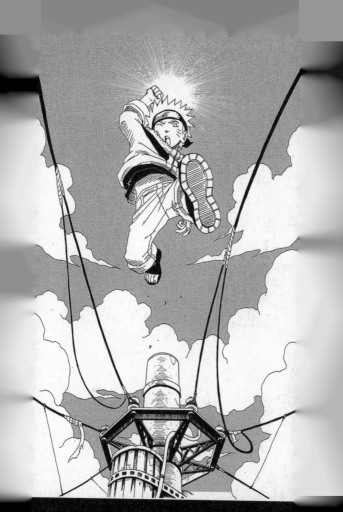

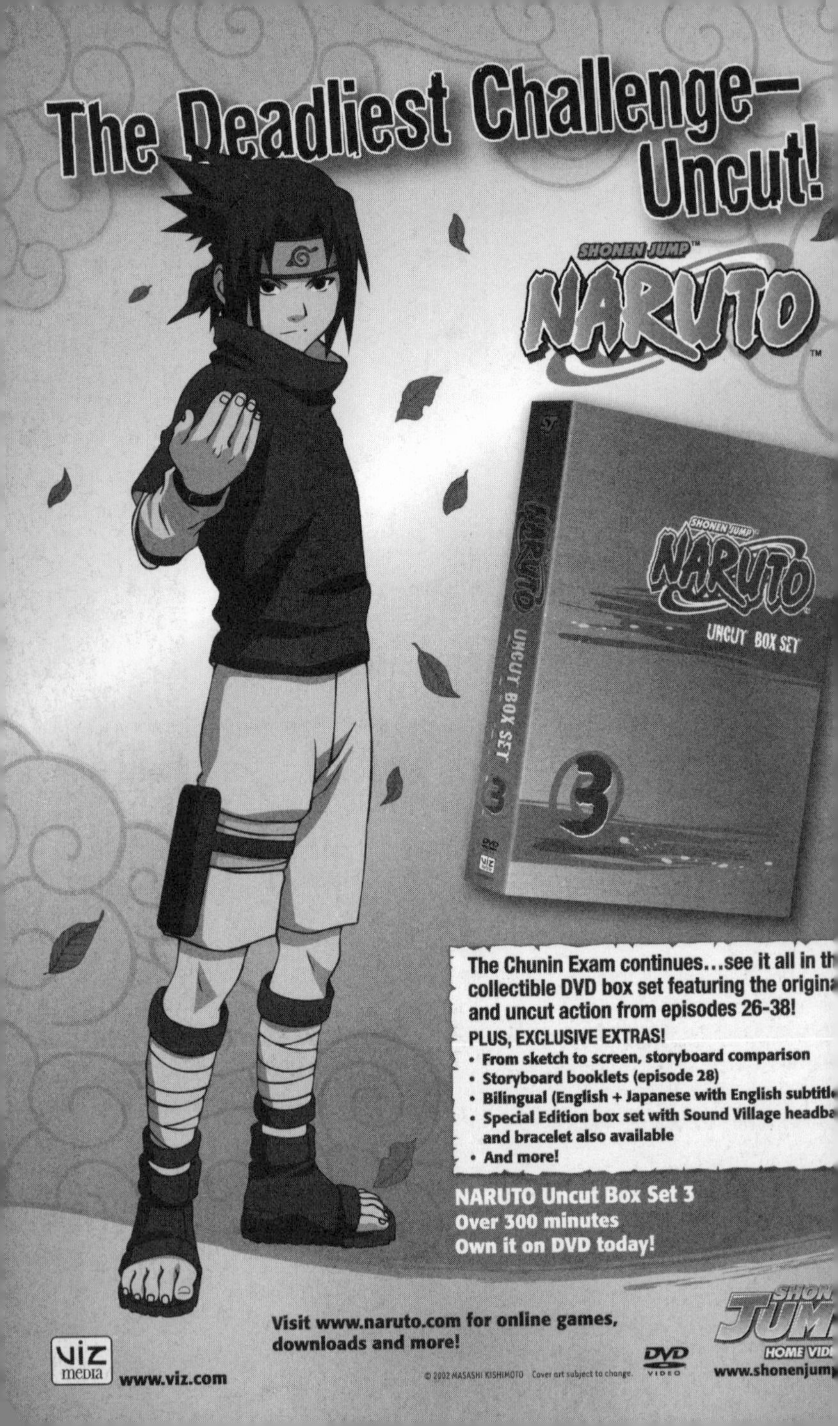

The Deadliest Challenge—Uncut!
SHONEN JUMP™
NARUTO™
SHONEN JUMP NARUTO UNCUT BOX SET 3
NARUTO UNCUT BOX SET 3
The Chunin Exam continues…see it all in th
collectible DVD box set featuring the origina
and uncut action from episodes 26-38!
PLUS, EXCLUSIVE EXTRAS!
• From sketch to screen, storyboard comparison
• Storyboard booklets (episode 28)
• Bilingual (English + Japanese with English subtitl
• Special Edition box set with Sound Village headba
and bracelet also available
• And more!
NARUTO Uncut Box Set 3
Over 300 minutes
Own it on DVD today!
Visit www.naruto.com for online games, downloads and more!
VIZ MEDIA
www.viz.com
© 2002 MASASHI KISHIMOTO Cover art subject to change.
DVD VIDEO
HOME VID
www.shonenjum

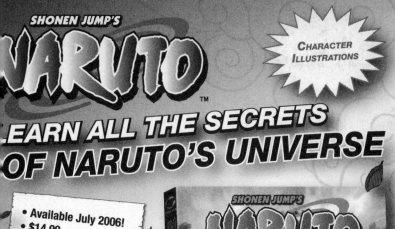
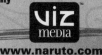

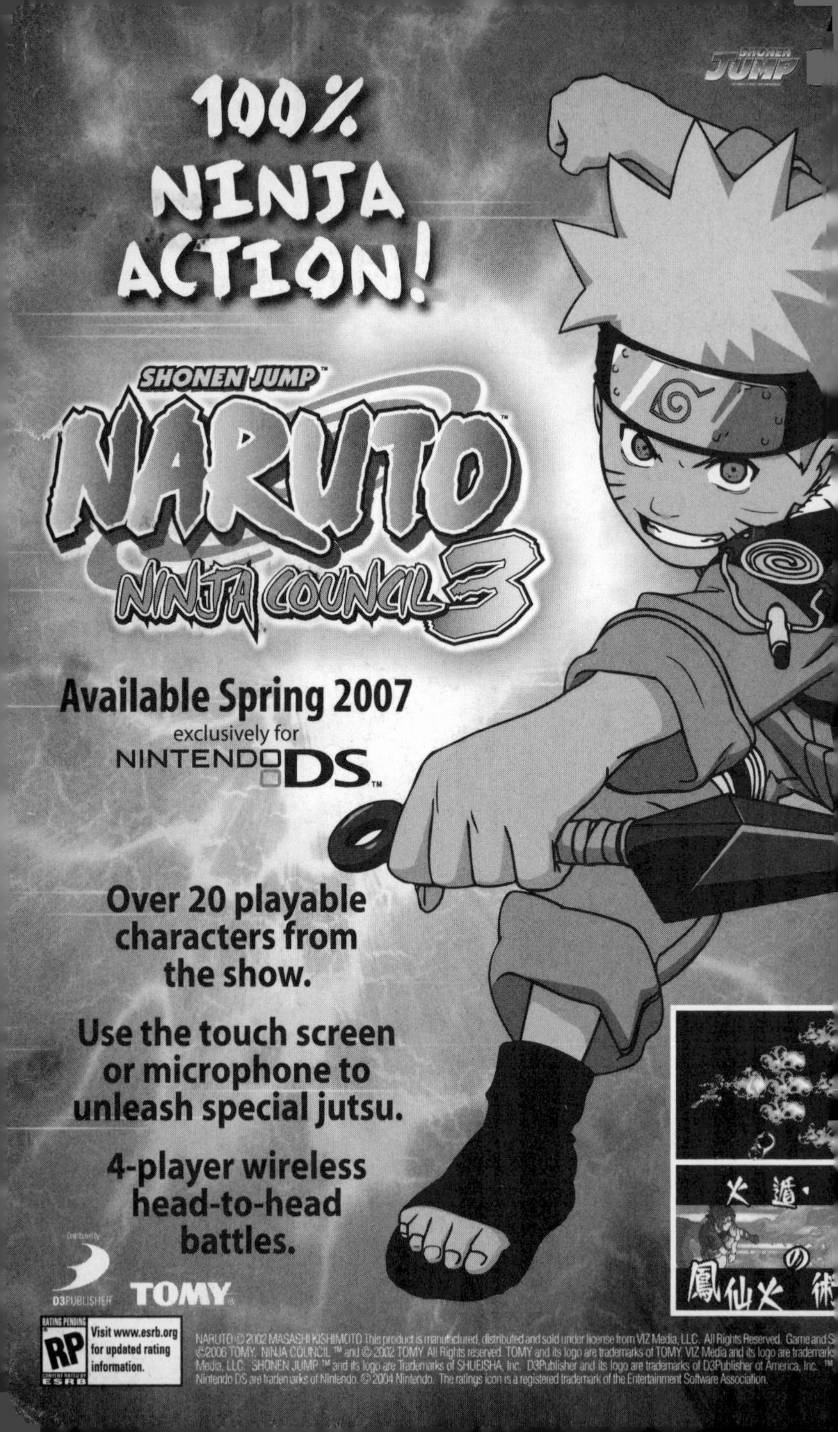
SHONEN JUMP
100% NINJA ACTION!
SHONEN JUMP™
NARUTO™
NINJA COUNCIL 3
Available Spring 2007
exclusively for
NINTENDO DS™
Over 20 playable characters from the show.
Use the touch screen or microphone to unleash special jutsu.
4-player wireless head-to-head battles.
火遁・鳳仙火の術
Distributed by
D3PUBLISHER
TOMY
RATING PENDING
RP
CONTENT RATED BY ESRB
Visit www.esrb.org for updated rating information.
NARUTO © 2002 MASASHI KISHIMOTO This product is manufactured, distributed and sold under license from VIZ Media, LLC. All Rights Reserved. Game and S
©2006 TOMY. NINJA COUNCIL ™ and © 2002 TOMY All Rights reserved. TOMY and its logo are trademarks of TOMY. VIZ Media and its logo are trademarks
Media, LLC. SHONEN JUMP ™ and its logo are Trademarks of SHUEISHA, Inc. D3Publisher and its logo are trademarks of D3Publisher of America, Inc. ™
Nintendo DS are trademarks of Nintendo. © 2004 Nintendo. The ratings icon is a registered trademark of the Entertainment Software Association.

Tell us what you

SHONEN JUMP manga!

Our survey is now available online.
o to: ***www.SHONENJUMP.com/mangasurvey***

Help us make our product offering better!

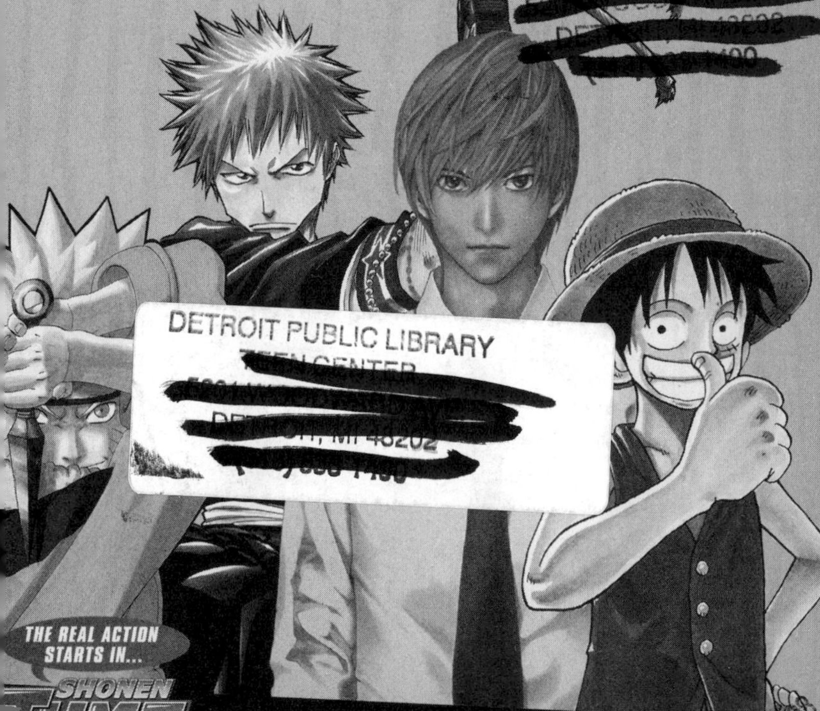

THE REAL ACTION STARTS IN...

SHONEN JUMP
WORLD'S MOST POPULAR MANGA
ww.shonenjump.com

SJ ADVANCED

SJ

VIZ media